ICSA
STUDY TEXT

Pre-Professional Paper 9

Managing Information Systems

New in this September 2000 edition

- Recent developments in hardware and software

- Revised and updated material on the Internet and data protection

- New Illustrations and case examples

FOR EXAMS IN DECEMBER 2000 AND SEPTEMBER 2001

BPP Publishing
September 2000

First edition 1993
Sixth edition September 2000

ISBN 0 7517 5133 2 (previous edition 0 7517 5023 9)

British Library Cataloguing-in-Publication Data
A catalogue record for this book
is available from the British Library

First published by

BPP Publishing Limited
Aldine House, Aldine Place
London W12 8AW

Reprinted in the UK under licence from BPP Publishing Limited by

ICSA Publishing Limited
16 Park Crescent
London W1B 1AH

Printed in Great Britain by The Basingstoke Press Limited

We are grateful to the Institute of Chartered Secretaries and Administrators for persmission to reproduce in this text the syllabus of which the Institute holds the copyright.

We are grateful to the Institute of Chartered Secretaries and Administrators , the Assoication of Accounting Technicians and the Chartered Institute of Management Accountants for permission to reproduce past examination questions. The suggested solutions have been prepared by BPP Publishing Limited.

BPP PUBLISHING

HOW TO USE THIS STUDY TEXT

Aims of this Study Text

To provide you with the knowledge and understanding, skills and application techniques that you need if you are to be successful in your exams

This Study Text has been written around the **Managing Information Systems** syllabus.

- It is **comprehensive**. We do not omit sections of the syllabus as the examiner is liable to examine any angle of any part of the syllabus - and you do not want to be left high and dry.

- It keeps you **up-to-date** in developments in Managing Information Systems and the way in which the examiner is designing questions.

- It is **on-target**. We do not include any material which is not examinable. You can therefore rely on the BPP Study Text as the stand-alone source of all your information for the exam, without worrying that any of the material is irrelevant.

To allow you to study in the way that best suits your learning style and the time you have available, by following your personal Study Plan

You may be studying at home on your own until the date of the exam, or you may be attending a full-time course. You may like to (and have time to) read every word, or you may prefer to (or only have time to) skim-read and devote the remainder of your time to question practice. Wherever you fall in the spectrum, you will find the BPP Study Text meets your needs in designing and following your personal Study Plan.

To tie in with the rest of the BPP Effective Study Package to ensure you have the best possible chance of passing the exam

Recommended period of use	Elements of the BPP Effective Study Package
3-12 months before exam	**Study Text** Use the Study Text to acquire knowledge, understanding, skills and the ability to use application techniques.
1-3 months before exam	**Practice & Revision Kit** Attempt the tutorial questions and read the helpful checklists which are provided for each topic area in the Kit. Then try the numerous examination questions, for which there are realistic suggested answers.

BPP
PUBLISHING

Settling down to study

By this stage in your career you are probably very experienced at learning and taking exams. But have you ever thought about *how* you learn? Let's have a quick look at the key elements required for effective learning.

Key element of learning	Using the BPP Study Text
Motivation	You can rely on the comprehensiveness and technical quality of BPP material. You've chosen the right Study Text - so you're in pole position to pass your exam!
Clear objectives and standards	Do you want to be a prizewinner or simply achieve a moderate pass? Only you can decide.
Feedback	Work through the examples in this text and do the Exercises and Test your knowledge quizzes. Evaluate your efforts critically - how are you doing?
Study Plan	You need to be honest with yourself about your progress - don't be over-confident, but don't be negative either. Make your Study Plan (see below) and try to stick to it. Focus on the short-term objectives – completing two chapters a week, say - but beware of losing sight of your study objectives.
Practice	Use the Test your knowledge quizzes and Chapter roundups to refresh your memory after you have completed your initial study of each chapter.

These introductory pages let you see exactly what you are up against. But however you study, you should:

- **Read through the syllabus and syllabus commentary:** these will help you to identify areas you have already covered, perhaps at a lower level of detail, and areas that are totally new to you.

- **Study the examination paper section,** where we show you the format of the exam and analyse the recent papers **including the one set in June 2000.**

Developing your personal Study Plan

Preparing a Study Plan (and sticking closely to it) is one of the key elements in learning success. First you need to be aware of your style of learning. There are four typical learning styles. Consider yourself in the light of the following descriptions and work out which you fit most closely. You can then plan to follow the key study steps in the sequence suggested on page (viii).

Learning styles	Characteristics
Motivation	Seeks to understand principles before applying them in practice
Reflector	Seeks to observe phenomena, thinks about them and then chooses to act
Activist	Prefers to deal with practical, active problems; does not have much patience with theory
Pragmatist	Prefers to study only if a direct link to practical problems can be seen; not interested in theory for its own sake

Key study steps

We have broken the learning process down into a series of key steps, which you can apply to each chapter in turn. We list them here in the order which seems to work best for **theorists** and **reflectors**. If you are an **activist** or a **pragmatist** you may prefer to use a different sequence. The various options are summarised after the table of steps. Tackle the chapters in the order you find them in the Study Text. Taking into account your individual learning style, follow these key study steps for each chapter.

Key study steps	Activity
Step 1 *Chapter topic list*	Study the list. Each numbered topic is a numbered section in the chapter.
Step 2 *Introduction*	Read through it. It is designed to show you *why* the topics in the chapter need to be studied - how they lead on from previous topics, and how they lead into subsequent ones.
Step 3 *Explanations*	Proceed methodically through the chapter, reading each section thoroughly and making sure your understand. Where a topic has been examined, we state the month and year of examination against the appropriate heading. You should pay particular attention to these topics.
Step 4 *Note taking*	Take brief notes if you wish, avoiding the temptation to copy out too much.
Step 5 *Examples*	Follow each through to its solution very carefully.
Step 6 *Case examples*	Study each one, and try to add flesh to them from your own experience - they are designed to show how the topics you are studying come alive (and often come unstuck) in the real world.
Step 7 *Exercises*	Make a very good attempt at each one in the chapter. These are designed to put your knowledge into practice.
Step 8 *Solutions*	Check yours against ours, and make sure you understand the reasons why they may differ.
Step 9 *Chapter roundup*	Work through it very carefully, to make sure you have grasped the major points it is highlighting.
Step 10 *Test your knowledge quiz*	When you are happy that you have covered the chapter, use the Test your knowledge quiz to check how much you have remembered of the topics covered. The answers are in the paragraphs in the chapter that we refer you to.
Step 11 *Illustrative questions*	Either at this point, or later when you are thinking about revising, make a full attempt at the question(s) suggested at the very end of the chapter. You can find these at the end of the Study Text, along with the answers so you can see how you did.

BPP
PUBLISHING

Learning style approaches

Learning style	Sequence of key study steps in the BPP Study Text
Theorist	1, 2, 3, 5, 6, 7, 8, 9, 10, 11, (4 continuous)
Reflector	
Activist	1, 2, 7/8 (read through), 5, 6, 9, 3, 7/8 (full attempt), 10, 11 (4 continuous)
Pragmatist	7/8 (read through), 2, 5, 6, 9, 1, 3, 7/8 (full attempt), 10, 11 (4 continuous)

Planning your studies

Next you should complete the following checklist.

Am I motivated? (a) [ ]

Do I have an objective and a standard that I want to achieve? (b) [ ]

Am I a theorist, a reflector, an activist or a pragmatist? (c) [ ]

How much time do I have available per week, given: (d) [ ]

- the standard I have set myself
- the time I need to set aside later for work on the Practice and Revision Kit
- the other exam(s) I am sitting, and (of course)
- practical matters such as work, travel, exercise, sleep and social life?

Now:

- take the time you have available per week for this Study Text (d), and multiply it by the number of weeks available to give (e). (e) [ ]
- divide (e) by the number of chapters to give (f) (f) [ ]
- set about studying each chapter in the time represented by (f), following the key study steps in the order suggested by your particular learning style.

This is your personal Study Plan.

Moving on...

However you study, when you are ready to embark on the practice and revision phase of the BPP Effective Study Package, you should still refer back to this Study Text, both as a source of reference (you should find the index particularly helpful for this) and as a refresher (the Chapter roundups and Test your knowledge quizzes help you here).

And remember to keep careful hold of this Study Text - you will find it invaluable in your work.

SYLLABUS

Objective

To enhance the understanding of and develop practical skills in the identification and definition of user problems and needs; together with the analysis, design, implementation and maintenance of systems, using appropriate methodologies, tools and techniques.

The emphasis will be on the selection, evaluation and practical value of the methodologies, tools and techniques; an in-depth knowledge of the technical aspects will not be required.

	Covered in Chapter
A: Systems development	
Management Information Systems concepts.	1, 2
Relationship to planning and setting of objectives, place in planning and control cycle.	2
Influence of organisation style and culture, communication structures and behavioural aspects.	3
Influences on design, external influences, information technology environment.	3, 4, 5
Management by exception reporting, environmental scanning, influence of artificial intelligence, multi-media applications.	2, 3, 4, 5
B: Problem definition	
Information needs relative to management levels and functions: identifying and defining user needs.	2, 3, 4, 5
Contrast soft and hard systems approach: features of soft systems methodologies, use of soft systems tools for formulating problem definitions and scope, building abstracts and models, evaluating solution strategies: the socio-technical environment.	2, 3, 7
C: Analysis	
Systems investigation.	6
Gathering reliable data, problem analysis, feasibility study report.	6
Selecting and using structured systems methodologies.	7
Basic features of Structured Systems Analysis and Design Method.	7
User involvement, structured walkthroughs, joint applications development.	7
CASE tools, prototyping, evolutionary prototyping, object orientated methods, information centre concepts.	7 - 9
Data and entity modelling.	8, 9
Usability and human-computer interaction.	2
D: Database approach	
Database approach to Management Information Systems.	10
Decision support.	2, 10
Data structure design, physical data design, storage and access procedures, concurrency, maintenance and recovery.	8 - 10
Database Management Systems and facilities, data dictionary, using structured query languages.	10

THE EXAMINATION PAPER

Paper format

The examination paper contains two sections. Each section contains a short case study followed by five questions. Students are required to answer two or three questions from each section, but no more than five questions overall. All questions carry 20 marks.

Students are specifically asked to 'utilise fully the context of the case studies and to enhance their answers with examples from their own work experience as appropriate'.

Analysis of past papers

June 2000

Section A – Sarak Property Services
1   Feasibility study team
2   Systems development
3   CASE tools
4   Structured walkthroughs
5   MIS and decision making

Section B – Mail delivery service
6   Environmental influences on MIS design
7   Environmental scanning
8   Encouraging acceptance of change
9   Outsourcing advantages and disadvantages
10   Using current technologies to improve the MIS

December 1999

Section A – Kwon Lee Leisure plc
1   Purpose and benefits of new MIS
2   MIS user and business needs
3   Soft Systems Methodology (SSM) versus Structured Systems Analysis
    and Design Methodology (SSAD)
4   Decision support systems and unstructured data
5   Role of an Information Centre

Section B – Feyi Footwear Limited
6   Project manager job specification
7   Relational database approach
8   Prevention of fraud
9   New system – staff training and development needs
10   System performance measurement

June 1999

Section A – Vegos plc
1   Planning the Management Information System (MIS)
2   Graphical user interfaces
3   Customer needs of the new information system
4   Effects of new system on training and planning
5   Contingency plan for system failure

Section B – Educational Programme
6   Organisation culture and new system development
7   Conceptual approach to information gathering
8   Project personnel use of systems development tools
9   Use of soft systems methodology (SSM)
10   The Internet

BPP
PUBLISHING

Part A
Systems development

Chapter 1

BASIC CONCEPTS

This chapter covers the following topics.

1   Information management

2   Good information

3   Systems theory

4   Types of system

5   Systems concepts

Introduction

This chapter covers the basics of information and systems. This is material that you should have studied at Foundation level for the *Information Systems* exam. You won't be asked simply to regurgitate this material in the *Managing Information Systems* exam, but these concepts provide useful background for the chapters that follow and useful frameworks for virtually any exam question. In particular make sure you know what the qualities of good information are, and understand the input-process-output nature of all systems. Throughout we try to point out business and organisational examples of the concepts described.

---

1   INFORMATION MANAGEMENT

Information management

1.1   Information must be managed just like any other organisational resource. Information management entails the following tasks.

(a)   Identifying current and future information needs.

(b)   Identifying information sources.

(c)   Collecting the information.

(d)   Storing the information.

(e)   Facilitating existing methods of using information and identifying new ways of using it.

(f)   Ensuring that information is communicated to those who need it.

(g)   Ensuring information is secure.

1.2   Technology has provided new sources of information, new ways of collecting it, storing it and processing it, and new methods of communicating it. This in turn has meant that information needs have changed and will continue to change as new technologies become available.

1.3   However, the *Managing Information Systems* paper is *not* primarily about technology. Your personal experience of using information in organisations will have taught you that:

(a)   Much of the information used in organisations is still conveyed on paper or by oral means.

(b) Some aspects of meaning cannot be conveyed effectively electronically.

(c) Although computing and telecommunications technology provide fabulous tools for carrying out the information management tasks listed above, they are not *always* the best tools; nor are they always even available.

Data and information

1.4 In normal everyday speech the terms data and information are used interchangeably. However, strictly speaking the terms have distinct meanings.

(a) *Data* is the raw material for data processing. Data consists of numbers, letters and symbols and relates to facts, events, and transactions.

(b) *Information* is data that has been processed in such a way as to be meaningful to the person who receives it.

Exercise 1

This distinction should be very familiar from your earlier studies. Can you provide a business example?

Solution

A pile of weekly timesheets is an example of *data*. These may be processed in the wages office to produce a payroll analysis. To the wages clerk, the payroll analysis is *information*. It shows, among other things, how much money needs to be included in each pay packet when these are made up.

However, one person's information is another person's data. The personnel director may wish to assess how likely the company is to fall foul of potential legislation restricting the number of hours an employee may work. She wants to know about staff who have worked more than ten hours' overtime in the period. She does not have time to leaf through the payroll analysis looking to see who has worked overtime, and even less will she wish to flick through the pile of timesheets, which have in any case already been authorised by departmental managers. Both of these are data to her. She receives information in the form of an *exception report* showing all staff who have recorded over ten hours' overtime.

1.5 Processing data involves the following steps, whether the processing is carried out manually or electronically.

(a) Data is *collected*. There must be data to process and this may arise in the course of operations. There has to be a system or procedure for ensuring that all the data needed for processing is collected and made available for processing. The quality, accuracy and completeness of the data will affect the quality of information produced.

(b) Data is *processed* into information, perhaps by summarising it or classifying it and/or producing total figures. For example, a sales ledger system might be required to process data about goods despatched to satisfy customer orders so as to:

    (i) Produce and send out invoices.

    (ii) Record the invoices sent out in the customers' personal ledgers.

    (iii) Produce a report of the total value of invoices sent out in the day/week etc.

    (iv) Record the total value of invoices sent out in the debtors' control account in the nominal ledger.

(c) Information is *communicated*. Continuing the example of the sales ledger system, the output consists of invoices and figures for sales totals (ie management information). Updating the personal ledgers and the debtors control account are file updating activities to keep the sales ledger records up to date. Communication might involve the *routine* dissemination of information to users. This includes routine management control information - for example comparing actual and budgeted results for the month. Communication also involving the provision of *non-routine* information to users on request.

(d) Files are *updated* to incorporate the processed data. The example of sales ledger work has already been mentioned. Updating files means bringing them up to date to record current transactions.

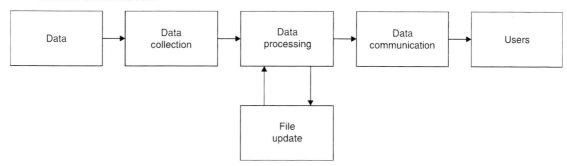

Storage and retrieval of data and information

1.6 Often, when data is processed, the information is communicated immediately to the person who wishes to use it. However, there is no reason why processed information should be used straightaway. It might be kept for later use. If it is, it must be stored, or filed away, and then retrieved when it is eventually needed, although presumably there will be a limit to its useful life.

(a) Some information might have been gathered several years previously and filed away for future use. Eventually, it will be associated with more current information so as to analyse past trends in order to predict the future. In other words, forecasting the future is often based on an analysis of historical information.

(b) Information which is several years old might also be used to compare past and current performance - for example to compare today's return on capital employed and profit/sales ratio with what was being achieved a few years before. Comparisons of this sort are useful for control purposes because they help to identify possible weaknesses in current performance.

1.7 Storage and retrieval of data are two interrelated aspects of holding data for a later use because data must be stored in such a way that it can be found again when it is eventually wanted.

1.8 In business, vast quantities of data are stored. In accounting systems, there are many such examples, including the data recorded in the sales ledger, purchase ledger and payroll systems.

1.9 Possibly the major issue in modern information management is finding ways in which this vast resource can safely and efficiently be *shared* by the staff who need it.

2 GOOD INFORMATION   *12/95*

2.1 The qualities of good information can be summarised in the mnemonic **ACCURATE**.

A Ccurate

C Omplete

C ost-beneficial

U ser-targeted

R Elevant

A Uthoritative

T Imely

E asy to use

Accurate

2.2 Information should obviously be accurate because using incorrect information could have serious and damaging consequences. However, information should only be accurate enough for its purpose and there is no need to go into unnecessary detail for pointless accuracy.

(a) Supervisors and office workers might need information that is accurate to the nearest penny, second or kilogram. For example, a cashier will do a bank reconciliation to the exact penny and purchase ledger staff will pay creditors exactly what they are owed. Much financial accounting information for day-to-day transactions must indicate amounts to the exact penny.

(b) Middle managers might be satisfied with revenues and costs rounded to the nearest £100 or £1,000, since greater detail would serve no purpose. For example, in budgeting, revenue and cost figures are often rounded to the nearest £1,000 because trying to be more exact would usually only give a spurious accuracy.

(c) Senior managers in a medium-sized to large organisation might be satisfied with figures to the nearest ten thousand pounds, or even hundred thousand or million pounds. Estimates to the nearest pound at this level of decision-making would be so inappropriate that they would seem ridiculous and so, oddly enough, perhaps undermine the user's confidence in the accuracy of estimates.

2.3 Do not forget that not all information is certain. Information relating to the future or to the external environment is uncertain and can never (except by fluke) be expected to be totally accurate. The assumptions underlying future information should therefore be clearly stated.

Complete

2.4 An information user should have all the information he needs to do his job properly. If he does not have a complete picture of the situation, he might well make bad decisions.

2.5 There are many examples. Should past data be included? What about budget figures and comparatives? What about competitor information?

Cost -beneficial

2.6 Information should have some value, otherwise it would not be worth the cost of collecting and storing it. For information to have value, it must lead to a decision to take action which results in reducing costs, eliminating losses, increasing sales, better utilisation of resources, prevention of fraud (audit requirements) or providing management with information about the consequences of alternative courses of action.

2.7 In particular the benefits obtainable from the information must exceed the costs of acquiring it.

User-targeted

2.8 Within any organisation, individuals are given the authority to do certain tasks, and they must be given the information they need to do them. An office manager might be made responsible for controlling expenditures in his office, and given a budget expenditure limit for the year. As the year progresses, he might try to keep expenditure in check but unless he is told throughout the year what is his current total expenditure to date, he will find it difficult to judge whether he is keeping within budget or not.

2.9 Information that is needed might be communicated to the wrong person. In other words, it might be communicated to a person who does not have the authority to act on it, or who is not responsible for the matter and so does not see any need to act on it.

2.10 Later in this text we shall be discussing the information needs of different levels of management (strategic, tactical and operational levels).

Relevant

2.11 Information must be relevant to the purpose for which a manager wants to use it. If managers ask for a breakdown of last month's sales by customer they should not also (or instead) be given a breakdown of sales by product (unless they later request this information too).

The issue of relevance also includes matters dealt with again under other headings, such as whether information is user-targeted and whether it includes too much detail.

The consequences of irrelevant data are that managers will waste time reading it and might be confused by it.

Authoritative

2.12 Information must be trusted by the managers who are expected to use it. This means that it must come from an authoritative source, or one that they have confidence in.

   (a) Information sources will not be used if they have proved unreliable in the past.

   (b) The accessibility of information sources such as the Internet and the proliferation of media such as television and radio means that much more information is available, but that certainly does not mean that all of it is reliable.

   (c) A report prepared by an experienced member of staff is intrinsically likely to be more authoritative than one prepared by a new recruit.

Timely

2.13 Information which is not available until after a decision is made will be useful only for comparisons and longer-term control, and may serve no purpose even then. Information prepared too frequently can be a serious disadvantage. If, for example, a decision is taken at a monthly meeting about a certain aspect of a company's operations, information to make the decision is only required once a month, and weekly reports would be a time-consuming waste of effort. In a well designed management information system, the frequency with which information is provided will depend on the needs of:

   (a) The differing levels or status of persons to whom it is provided.
   (b) The differing functional groups.

Easy-to-use

2.14 Ease of use is dictated by how easy it is to take in the key points at a glance and how easy it is to find the details if they are required.

That completes the ACCURATE mnemonic. There are three further qualities of good information to discuss – three C's.

Concise

2.15 There are physical and mental limitations to what a person can read, absorb and understand properly before taking action. An enormous mountain of information, even if it is all relevant, cannot be handled. The user suffers information overload. Reports to management must therefore be clear and concise.

If a great deal of detail has to be given a summary should always precede it. If there is no need for the detail, the summary is enough. A summary gives totals, covers longer periods, expresses figures as ratios or percentages and highlights key conclusions and recommendations.

Clarity

2.16 Well-presented information will have features such as a one-paragraph executive summary, a contents page, an accurate and comprehensive index, and use of visual aids such as graphs, charts and diagrams if these are useful. Information presented as narrative may sometimes also be usefully presented as a table of figures, or *vice versa*. If information is transferred via electronic media, hyperlinks, sound-bites and video can be very helpful.

Channel of communication

2.17 One method of communication will usually be better than others. For example, job vacancies should be announced in a medium where they will be brought to the attention of the people most likely to be interested. The channel of communication might be the company's in-house journal, a national or local newspaper, a professional magazine, a job centre or school careers office.

Some information may be best sent by e-mail. Some information is best communicated informally by telephone or word-of-mouth, whereas other information is better formally communicated in a letter with enclosures.

3 SYSTEMS THEORY
6/94, 12/95

3.1 The term system is very hard to define because it is so widely used - the 'respiratory system', the 'political system', the 'long ball system', and so on.

3.2 Possibly the most useful and illuminating definition says simply that 'system' means connections.

Exercise 2

Apply the idea of connections to any 'systems' you can think of - the London Underground system, a computer system, the idea of working 'systematically', or anything else that comes to mind.

3.3 More formally, a system is set of interacting components that operate together to accomplish a purpose. A business system is a collection of people, machines and methods organised to accomplish a set of specific functions.

Why study systems theory?

3.4 An understanding of the concepts of systems theory is relevant to the design of business systems and it presents a particularly useful way of describing and analysing computer systems. The application of systems theory may achieve the following.

(a) It helps to define what the system is, by identifying its properties as a system as a whole, as distinct from the parts of which it is made up.

(b) In terms of problem solving, it provides a broad look at the system before the overly detailed scrutiny of the particular problem. This greatly reduces the danger of wasteful investment in tackling the wrong problem.

(c) It helps to identify and review the *purpose* of the system as a whole, its rationale and objectives.

(d) It creates an awareness of subsystems (the different parts of an organisation), each with potentially conflicting goals which must be brought into line with each other.

(e) It helps to identify the effect of the environment on systems. The external factors that affect an organisation may be wide ranging. For example, the government (in all its forms), competitors, trade unions, creditors and shareholders all have an interactive link with an organisation.

(f) It clarifies the sources and sinks of external information. Some of the information received from a particular source may not be returned to that same source, ie it may have a different destination.

(g) It facilitates a strategic review of the effectiveness of the system by comparing the desired and actual outputs. It highlights the dynamic aspects of the business organisation, and the factors which influence the growth and development of all its subsystems.

(h) It helps in the design and development of information systems to help decision makers ensure that decisions are made for the benefit of the organisation as a whole.

The component parts of a system

3.5 A system has three component parts: inputs, processes and outputs.

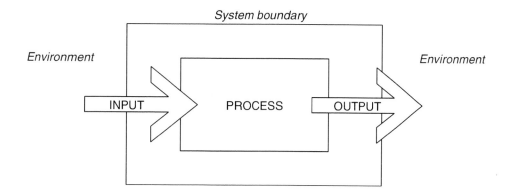

Inputs

3.6 Inputs provide the system with what it needs to be able to operate. Input may vary from matter, energy or human actions to information.

- Matter might include, in a manufacturing operation, adhesives or rivets

- Human input might consist of typing an instruction booklet or starting up a piece of machinery.

3.7 Inputs may be outputs from other systems. As we have seen, the output from a transactions processing system is part of the input for a management information system.

Processes

3.8 A process transforms an input into an output. Processes may involve tasks performed by humans, plant, computers, chemicals and a wide range of other actions.

3.9 Processes may consist of assembly, for example where electronic consumer goods are being manufactured, or disassembly, for example where oil is refined.

3.10 There is not necessarily a clear relationship between the number of inputs to a process and the number of outputs.

Outputs

3.11 Outputs are the results of the processing. They could be said to represent the purpose for which the system exists.

3.12 Many outputs are used as inputs to other systems.

3.13 Alternatively outputs may be discarded as waste (an input to the ecological system) or re-input to the system which has produced them, for example, in certain circumstances, defective products.

The system boundary

3.14 Every system has a boundary that separates it from its environment. For example, a cost accounting department's boundary can be expressed in terms of who works in it and what work it does. This boundary will separate it from other departments, such as the financial accounts department.

3.15 System boundaries may be natural or artificially created (an organisation's departmental structures are artificially created).

3.16 There may be interfaces between various systems, both internal and external to an organisation, to allow the exchange of resources. In a commercial context, this is most likely to be a reciprocal exchange, for example money for raw materials.

The environment
6/00

3.17 Anything which is outside the system boundary belongs to the system's environment and not to the system itself. A system accepts inputs from the environment and provides outputs into the environment. The parts of the environment from which the system receives inputs may not be the same as those to which it delivers outputs.

3.18 The environment exerts a considerable influence on the behaviour of a system; at the same time the system can do little to control the behaviour of the environment.

Exercise 3

The environment affects the performance of a system. Using a business organisation as an example of a system, give examples of environmental factors which might affect it.

Solution

(a) Policies adopted by the government or ruling political body.
(b) The strength of the domestic currency of the organisation's country of operation.
(c) Social attitudes: concern for the natural environment.
(d) The regulatory and legislative framework within which the company operates.
(e) The number of competitors in the marketplace and the strategies they adopt.
(f) The products of competitors; their price and quality.

Subsystems

3.19 Every system can be broken down into subsystems In turn, each subsystem can be broken down into sub-subsystems. Separate subsystems interact with each other, and respond to each other by means of communication or observation.

3.20 Subsystems may be differentiated from each other by, for example:

(a) function;
(b) space;
(c) time;
(d) people;
(e) formality; or
(f) automation.

Exercise 4

Using each of the above six factors by which subsystems may be differentiated, give examples of how an organisation may be structured. (For example, an organisation structured by function might have a production department, a sales department, an accounts department and a personnel department.)

Solution

(a)   Functional departments might include production, sales, accounts and personnel.

(b)   Differentiation by space might include the geographical division of a sales function (subsystem) into sales regions (sub-subsystems).

(c)   A production system might be subdivided into three eight-hour shifts.

(d)   The hierarchy may consist of senior management, middle management, junior (operational) management and the workforce.

(e)   There may be a formal management information system and a 'grapevine'.

(f)   Some systems might be automated (sales order processing, production planning), while others may be 'manual' (public relations, staff appraisal).

3.21   Often, whether something is a system or a subsystem is a matter of definition, and depends on the context of the observer. For example, an organisation is a social system, and its 'environment' may be seen as society as a whole. Another way of looking at an organisation would be to regard it as a *subsystem* of the entire social system.

3.22   As we have hinted at several points, what links up the different subsystems in an organisation is information.

4   TYPES OF SYSTEM

Open systems and closed systems   *12/94*

4.1   In systems theory a distinction is made between an open system and a closed system.

Closed system

4.2   A closed system is a system which is isolated from its environment and independent of it, so that no environmental influences affect the behaviour of the system, nor does the system exert any influence on its environment.

4.3   Some scientific systems might be described as closed systems. An example of a closed system is a chemical reaction in a sealed, insulated container. Another is the operation of a thermostat.

4.4   However, all social systems, including business organisations, have some interaction with their environment, and so cannot be closed systems.

Open system

4.5   An open system is a system connected to and interacting with its environment. It takes in influences (or 'energy') from its environment and also influences this environment by its behaviour (it exports energy).

4.6   Open and closed systems can be described by diagram as follows.

Closed system

Open system

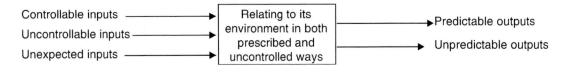

4.7   For example, a business is an open system where management decisions are influenced by or have an influence on suppliers, customers, competitors, society as a whole and the government.

4.8   Employees are obviously influenced by what they do in their job, but as members of society at large, they are also a part of the environment, just as their views and opinions expressed within the business are often a reflection of their opinions as members of society at large.

4.9   As noted earlier, every system has a boundary. An open system will have considerable cross-influences with its environment across its boundary, whereas a closed system's boundary would shut it off from its environment.

Deterministic systems

4.10   A deterministic system is one in which various states or activities follow on from each other in a completely predictable way, ie A will happen, then B, then C. A fully-automated production process is a typical example. A computer program is another.

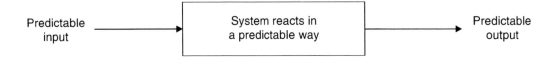

Probabilistic systems

4.11   A probabilistic system is one in which, although some states or activities can be predicted with certainty, others will occur with varying degrees of probability. In business, many systems can be regarded as probabilistic systems.

(a)   A company's credit control department can analyse customers' payment schedules as 10% cash with order, 50% within 1 month of invoice and 40% within 2 months of invoice.

(b)   A purchasing department might assess a supplier's delivery times as 0.75 on schedule, 0.20 one week late and 0.05 two weeks late.

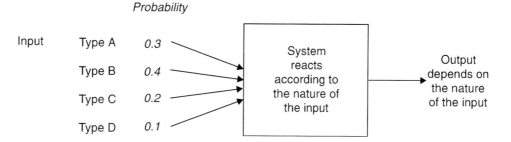

Self-organising systems

4.12 A self-organising system is one which adapts and reacts to a stimulus. The way in which it adapts is uncertain and the same input (stimulus) to the system will not always produce the same output (response). Social and psychological systems come within this category. Examples might be as follows.

(a) A bank which pays a rate of interest to depositors depending on the amount of money in the deposit account. Interest calculations (the output of the system is the calculated interest) will vary as the money in each depositor's account goes up or down.

(b) A stock re-ordering system where the quantity of a stock item that is ordered from a supplier varies according to changes in the usage of the item. For example, if consumption of stock item 12345 goes up by 20% per week, the reorder quantity of the item will be increased.

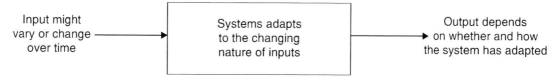

4.13 The three classifications are not mutually exclusive, and a system may contain elements of all three types.

5 SYSTEMS CONCEPTS

Control systems

5.1 A system must be controlled to keep it steady or enable it to change safely, in other words each system must have its control system. Control is required because unpredictable disturbances arise and enter the system, so that actual results (outputs of the system) deviate from the expected results or goals.

5.2 Examples of disturbances in a business system would be the entry of a powerful new competitor into the market, an unexpected rise in labour costs, the failure of a supplier to deliver promised raw materials, or the tendency of employees to stop working in order to chatter or gossip.

5.3 A control system must ensure that the business is capable of surviving these disturbances by dealing with them in an appropriate manner.

5.4 To have a control system, there has to be a plan, standard - budget, rule book or some other sort of target or guideline towards which the system as a whole should be aiming. The standard is defined by the objectives of the system.

5.5 A control system can be represented in a model, as shown below.

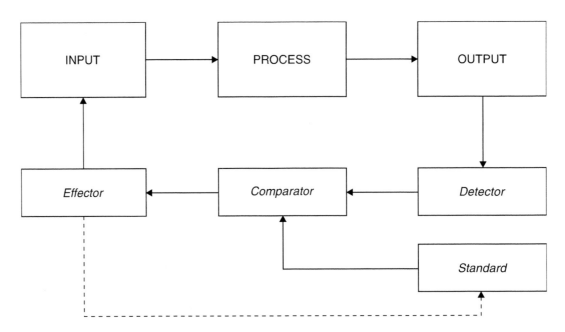

Sensor

5.6 A sensor is the device by which information (or data) is collected and measured.

5.7 Although an automatic meter is commonly cited as an example of a sensor, it is more appropriate for managers to think of a sensor as the means by which information is recorded on paper or computer file, or transmitted by telephone or computer screen.

5.8 A sensor may be inefficient because it does not record information as completely or accurately as required, or because it is too complete or unnecessarily accurate. It may not record information at the most appropriate time, or it may break down and fail to record anything (for example, a night-watchman might fall asleep, or a TV camera or computer might break down).

5.9 Some sensors are more efficient than others. A document that can be read by a scanner, for example, is better than a manually prepared computer input document because it saves data collection time, and reduces errors.

Comparator

5.10 A comparator is the means by which the actual results of the system are measured against the pre-determined plans or system objectives.

5.11 In a business organisation, the arithmetic of comparison (for example the calculation of variances, or productivity ratios) might be done by computer. Managers, however, will be the comparators who are expected to make some judgement on the results of the comparison, to decide whether investigation of the variances is advisable, and then (after investigation) whether control action is required.

Effector

5.12 An effector is the device or means by which control action is initiated.

5.13 In a production department, an effector may be a component in some automatic equipment which regulates the functioning of the equipment (for example a thermostat). An effector may also be a manager's instruction and a subordinate's action.

5.14 Just as any sensor may be inefficient, so too might a comparator or an effector do its job imperfectly. In designing a control system, it should be a requirement to optimise the efficiency of these control items.

Feedback

5.15 Feedback is the return of part of the output of a system to the input as a means towards improved quality or correction of errors. In a business organisation, feedback is information produced from within the organisation (for example management control reports) with the purpose of helping management and other employees and triggering control decisions.

5.16 Feedback may be defined as modification or control of a process or system by its results or effects, by measuring differences between desired and actual results.

5.17 In the control model described above part of the output is fed back, so that the output can initiate control action to change either the activities of the system or the system's input. A feedback system or a feedback loop carries output back to be compared with the input. This is also called a closed loop system.

5.18 You might like to think of a budgetary control system in a company, by which results are monitored, deviations from plan are identified and control (corrective) action taken as appropriate.

Negative feedback

5.19 Negative feedback is information which indicates that the system is deviating from its planned or prescribed course, and that some re-adjustment is necessary to bring it back on to course. This feedback is called 'negative' because control action would seek to reverse the direction or movement of the system back towards its planned course.

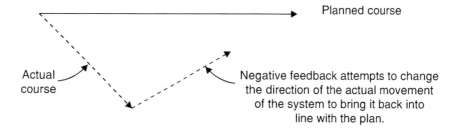

5.20 Thus, if the budgeted sales for a department for June and July were £100,000 in each month, whereas the report of actual sales in June showed that only £90,000 had been reached, this negative feedback would indicate that control action was necessary to raise sales in July to £110,000 in order to get back on to the planned course. Negative feedback in this case would necessitate July sales exceeding the budget by £10,000 because June sales fell short of budget.

Positive feedback

5.21 Positive feedback results in control action which causes actual results to maintain (or increase) their path of deviation from planned results.

5.22 Much positive feedback would be considered harmful, because deviations from the plan are usually adverse and undesirable.

5.23 Positive feedback occurs when there is some kind of problem in the feedback loop.

(a) The sensor may measure the total volume of units produced instead of the number of good units (as opposed to faulty ones). Positive feedback that indicated that total volume had fallen might result in control action to stretch resources and make the system produce more units, but in reality this might mean an increase in the number of faulty units and a fall in the overall number of good units.

(b) The standard may be set at the wrong level. For example a sales person might be set a sales target of £20,000 per month. If sales people find they can achieve £20,000 of sales in three weeks they may decide to reduce their inputs (the number of hours they work).

Exercise 5

See if you can think of examples of similar problems with the comparator and the effector.

5.24 There are occasions however when positive feedback is beneficial. Suppose, for example, that a company budgets to produce and sell 100 units of product each month, maintaining an average stock level of 40 units. Now if actual sales exceed the budget, and show signs of sustained growth, it will obviously be in the company's interests to produce and sell as much as possible (provided additional output earns extra contribution to profit).

(a) Positive feedback in the first month might show that sales are above budget, selling costs are a little higher than budget and that stocks have been run down to meet demand.

(b) Action should attempt to increase sales (ie promote the deviation of actual results from the plan) even if this requires extra selling costs for advertising or sales promotion (ie maintaining the adverse deviation of actual costs from budget).

5.25 Additional production volumes would be required, although initially, some extra sales might be made out of remaining stocks (resulting in further deviations from the production and finished goods stocks budgets.) Positive feedback is indeed fundamental to the growth of any system.

Filtering

5.26 Filtering means removing 'impurities' such as excessive detail from data as it is passed up the organisation hierarchy.

5.27 We met this concept in the context of good information. Operational staff may need all the detail to do their jobs, but when they report to higher and higher subsystems the data can be progressively summarised. Extraneous detail is filtered out leaving only the important points.

5.28 The problem with this is that sometimes the 'filter' may let through unimportant information and/or remove important information, with the result that the message is distorted at the next level.

Coupling and decoupling

5.29 If systems or subsystems are very closely connected or coupled this may cause difficulties.

5.30   For example, in order to sell goods, a manufacturing company must first of all make them. If the sales and production subsystems are closely coupled the company will produce in any week exactly the amounts required for sales. However the system would be prone to inefficiency through 'mishap', such as a late delivery of raw materials, a machine breakdown, or a strike, so that goods would not be available to meet sales demand.

5.31   From a traditional point of view greater efficiency is achieved between the production and sales systems by decoupling them. This means reducing the immediacy of the interaction between them by creating a finished goods stock for meeting sales orders.

5.32   From a modern point of view holding finished goods stock is expensive, and greater efficiency is achieved by adopting quality management philosophies to try to ensure that mishaps do not occur. If this is successful this means that a just-in-time (JIT) approach to production and purchasing can be adopted. JIT closely couples the sales and production subsystems and closely couples one organisation's purchasing function with another's supplying function.

Requisite variety

5.33   The so-called 'law' of requisite variety states that the variety *within a system* must be at least as great as the *environmental variety* against which it is attempting to regulate itself.

5.34   In other words, if there is variety in the environmental influences in the system, then the system itself must be suitably varied and variable to adapt itself successfully to its environment.

5.35   If a system does not have the requisite amount of variety, it will be unable to adapt to change and will eventually die or be replaced. History is full of examples of political systems that could not adapt to social, economic or political changes, and so were overthrown.

5.36   The law of requisite variety applies to self-regulating systems in general, but one application of the law relates to control systems. A control system (which is a sub-system of a larger system) must be sufficiently flexible to be able to deal with the variety that occurs naturally in the system that it is attempting to control.

Case example

A company making heavy equipment suddenly found its raw materials and in-process inventory climbing, but, at the same time, it was experiencing reduced sales and reduced production. The system was out of control.

The cause was traced to the materials analysts who made the detailed inventory decisions. They had been furnished with decision rules for ordering, cancelling, etc, under normal conditions, but they had no rules governing how to handle the inventory when production was decreasing and production lots were being cancelled.

In other words, the system did not provide the requisite variety of control responses. In this case, the urgency of remedy did not allow new rules to be formulated and validated. Instead, each materials analyst was treated as a self-organising system, given a target inventory, and told to achieve it. With the analysts given the freedom to generate control responses, the inventory was reduced in a few months.'

PUBLISHING

5.37 Way of introducing the requisite variety into a control system include the following.

    (a) Allowing a controller some discretion, to judge what control action is needed

        In a business system, managers should not be instructed that a problem must be handled in a particular way, especially when the problem involves labour relations, disciplinary procedures, motivating the workforce or any other such 'behavioural' matters. The response of individuals to control action by managers will be variable because people are different, and even one person's moods change from day to day. The control system must be flexible enough to use different methods to achieve the same ends.

    (b) Introducing tolerance limits

        When actual results differ from planned results, control action should not be instigated automatically in every instance. Control action should only be applied when the variance becomes excessive and exceeds allowable tolerance limits. Tolerance limits recognise that plans are based on an 'average' or 'norm' of what is expected to happen, and some variation around this average will be due to 'natural' causes which there should be no reason to get alarmed about.

Entropy

5.38 A final important term in information and systems theory is entropy.

5.39 Entropy is the amount of disorder or randomness present in any system.

5.40 Entropy arises because of the natural tendency of objects, and systems, to fall into a state of disorder. All inanimate systems display this tendency to move towards a state of disorder. If they remain unattended they will gradually lose all motion and degenerate into an inert state. When this state is reached and no observable systems activity can be discerned, the system has reached maximum entropy.

5.41 The term entropy is therefore used as a measure of *disorganisation*. A system will increase its entropy unless it receives negative entropy in the form of information or inputs from the environment.

5.42 For instance if a business does not listen to its customers' complaints about its products it will eventually fail because it will not be able to sell what it produces. The system will fall into a state of disorder, in the sense that it is ignoring its purpose, which is to sell things not just to produce them. Negative entropy is needed in the form of new or improved products or perhaps new, more open-minded management.

Chapter roundup

- Information management entails identifying information needs and sources, collecting and storing information, facilitating methods of using and communicating information and ensuring that it is protected.

- Data is the complete range of raw facts and measurements which exist within and outside an organisation. Information is data which has been processed in some way so as to make it meaningful to the person who receives it.

- Good information has a number of specific qualities: including relevance, completeness, accuracy, clarity, timeliness and cost.

- Systems theory is relevant to the study of information analysis because general system principles apply to any type of system, including an information system such as a computer system and a sound system such as a business organisation.

- A system receives inputs which it processes and generates into outputs. Any system can be thought of in terms of inputs, processing and outputs.

- A system exists in an environment. An environment surrounds the system but is not part of it, and a systems boundary separates the system from its environment. Systems are affected to different degrees and in various ways by their environments, and systems can therefore be classified according to how they are influenced by or respond to (communicate with) their environments.

- An open system has a relationship with its environment which has both prescribed and uncontrolled elements. A closed system is shut off from its environment and has no relationship with it.

- In a deterministic system, the value of certain variables and/or the relationship between them is known. Probabilistic systems use probability distribution to predict an expected outcome, or a range of possible outcomes. Self-organising systems adapt in an uncertain way to a stimulus.

- Control in a system is needed to ensure that the system's operations go according to plan. Control cannot be applied unless there is information about the operations of the system.

- In a control system sensors collect data, comparators measure data against system objectives or plans, and effectors implement any control action that needs to be taken.

- Feedback is control information generated by the system itself, and involves a comparison of actual results against the target or plan. Feedback may be negative or positive depending upon what control action it initiates.

- The terms coupling and decoupling relate to how closely one system depends on another.

- The law of requisite variety states that the variety within a system must be at least as great as the environmental variety against which it is attempting to regulate itself.

- Entropy is the amount of disorder or randomness there is in a system. Systems tend to fall into disorder unless they receive negative entropy in the form of information or inputs from the environment.

BPP PUBLISHING

Test your knowledge

1 What does information management entail? (see para 1.1)

2 How accurate should information be? (2.2)

3 Why study systems theory? (3.4)

4 What are the component parts of a system? (3.5 – 3.13)

5 Define the terms open system and closed system. (4.2 - 4.9)

6 What is a probabilistic system? (4.11)

7 Draw a diagram of a control system. (5.5)

8 What is negative feedback? (5.19)

9 Give an example of coupling. (5.29 - 5.32)

10 How can requisite variety be introduced into a control system? (5.37)

11 Give an example of entropy. (5.42)

Now try illustrative questions 1 and 2 at the end of the Study Text

Chapter 2

MANAGEMENT INFORMATION SYSTEMS

This chapter covers the following topics.

1   Information requirements

2   Planning and control

3   Decision making

4   Information for decision making

5   Management by exception

6   Types of information system

7   Decision support systems and models

8   Executive information systems

9   Artificial intelligence and expert systems

Introduction

Once again, much of the material in this chapter is likely to be familiar from your earlier studies, and yet much of it is fundamental to good exam answers. In this chapter we take a fairly *conventional* view of the way in which information is used in organisations and, in the opening sections in particular, we are not necessarily talking about *computerised* information systems.

The enabling power of *information technology* and newer ideas, such as Business Process Re-engineering and Computer Supported Co-operative Working, will be introduced in the chapters that follow.

1   INFORMATION REQUIREMENTS
6/99, 6/00

1.1   The *information requirements* of an organisation can be categorised as follows.

(a)   Information for planning.
(b)   Information for controlling.
(c)   Information for recording transactions.
(d)   Information for performance measurement.
(e)   Information for decision making.

1.2   Information is also used in co-ordination, that is, the process of integrating the work of individuals and workgroups towards the effective achievement of organisational objectives.

Planning

1.3   Once any decision has been made, it is necessary to plan how to implement the steps necessary to make it effective. Planning requires a knowledge of, among other things, available resources, possible timescales for implementation and the likely outcome under alternative scenarios.

BPP PUBLISHING

Controlling

1.4 Once a plan is implemented, its actual performance must be controlled. Information is required to assess whether it is proceeding as planned or whether there is some unexpected deviation from plan. It may consequently be necessary to take some form of corrective action.

Recording transactions

1.5 Information about each transaction or event is required for a number of reasons.

(a) Documentation of transactions can be used as evidence in a case of dispute.

(b) There may be a legal requirement to record transactions, for example for accounting and audit purposes.

(c) Detailed information on production costs can be built up, allowing a better assessment of profitability. Similarly, labour utilised in providing a particular service can be measured.

Performance measurement

1.6 Just as individual operations need to be controlled, so overall performance must be measured in order to enable comparisons against budget or plan to be carried out. This may involve the collection of information on, for example the following.

(a) Costs.
(b) Revenues.
(c) Volumes.
(d) Timescale.
(e) Profitability.

Decision making

1.7 Information is also required for decision making. This completes the full circle of organisational activity.

2 PLANNING AND CONTROL
6/96

2.1 Writers commonly refer to three levels of planning and control.

(a) Strategic planning.
(b) Management control.
(c) Operational control.

(This is sometimes referred to as the 'Anthony' hierarchy after the writer Robert Anthony, whose 1965 book, *Planning and Control Systems,* is a management classic. Note that these terms used to be used to refer to top, middle and junior *management* level, but this is no longer a valid distinction in many organisations.)

Strategic planning decisions

2.2 Strategic planning is a process of deciding on objectives of the organisation, on changes in these objectives, on the resources used to attain these objectives and on the policies that are to govern the acquisition, use and disposition of these resources.

2.3 Strategic decision-making therefore:

(a) is medium to long term;
(b) involves high levels of uncertainty and risk (the future is unpredictable);
(c) involves situations that do not necessarily recur;
(d) deals with complex issues.

Management control decisions

2.4 Management control (or 'tactical' control) means ensuring that *resources* are obtained and used effectively and efficiently in the accomplishment of the organisation's objectives.

(a) *Efficiency* means that resources input to a process produce the optimum (maximum) amount of outputs.

(b) *Effectiveness* means that the resources are used to achieve the desired ends.

2.5 Management control decisions are taken within the framework of strategic plans and objectives which have previously been made, or set.

Operational control

2.6 Operational control decisions ensure that specific operations are carried out effectively and efficiently. Operational control is carried out within the strictly defined guidelines issued by strategic planning and management control decisions.

2.7 Many operational control decisions can be automated or programmed. 'Programmed control' exists where the relationship between inputs and outputs is clearly defined, so that an optimal relationship can be specified for every activity. Mathematical models can be designed to provide optimal solutions to problems, and many physical procedures can be controlled by automatic devices. Programmed control will always be a form of operational control.

Exercise 1

Consider management decisions as they affect work in a bought ledger department. Classify each of the following three decisions according to the three types of decision identified by Anthony.

(a) The payment cycle will be extended by five days to improve cash flow.

(b) On receipt of an invoice, the purchase order form and goods received note relating to the order must be checked to the invoice. Specified details must be checked, and the invoice stamped to show that the checks have been carried out fully and satisfactorily.

(c) Core suppliers will be asked to join the company's EDI network.

Solution

The first is a management control decision, the second is an operational control decision and the third is a strategic planning decision.

---

3 DECISION MAKING

6/94, 12/97, 6/99, 6/00

Stages in decision making

3.1 The stages in making a decision are as follows.

(a) Problem recognition.
(b) Problem definition and structuring.
(c) Identifying alternative courses of action.
(d) Making and communicating the decision.
(e) Implementation of the decision.
(f) Monitoring the effects of the decision.

Problem recognition

3.2 Decisions are not made without information. The decision maker needs to be informed of a problem in the first place. This is sometimes referred to as the *decision trigger*. Normally further information is required.

Problem definition and structuring

3.3 This further information can be analysed so that the problem can be defined precisely. Consider, for example, a company with falling sales. The fall in revenue would be the trigger. Further information would be needed to identify where the revenue deficiencies were occurring. The problem can therefore be defined. If our company discovers that sales of product X in area Y are falling, the problem can be defined as 'decline of sales of product X in area Y due to new competitor: how can the decline be reversed?' Some 'problems' may be more vague, however. There are a number of ways of defining and structuring a problem, for example:

(a) as a mathematical model; or
(b) as a scenario in 'what-if?' analysis (perhaps using a spreadsheet).

3.4 One of the purposes of *defining* the problem is to identify the relationships between the various factors in it, especially if the problem is complex.

Identifying alternative courses of action

3.5 Where alternative courses of action are identified, information is needed about them so they can be assessed. So, in a situation where there are a number of alternatives, the decision maker will glean information as to their likely effect. As a simple example, if our company wishes to review the price of product X in area Y, information will be needed as to the effect of particular price levels on demand for the product. Such information can include external information such as market research (demand at a particular price) and the cost of the product, which can be provided internally. In this kind of decision, the company may use modelling techniques.

Making and communicating the decision

3.6 The decision is made after review of the information relating to alternatives. However, the decision is useless if it is not communicated. So, in our example, if the sales director decides to lower the price of product X and institute an intensive advertising campaign, nothing will happen unless the advertising department is informed, and even the manufacturing department, who will prepare new packaging to lower the price.

Implementation of the decision

3.7 The decision is then implemented. For large-scale decisions (for example to relocate factory 100 miles away from current site), implementation may need substantial planning and review. Information is needed to ensure that implementation is going according to plan.

Monitoring the effects of the decision

3.8 Once a decision has been made, information is needed so that its effects can be reviewed. For example, if a manufacturing organisation has installed new equipment in anticipation of savings in costs, then information will need to be obtained as to whether these are going to be met in practice.

Information and decision-making

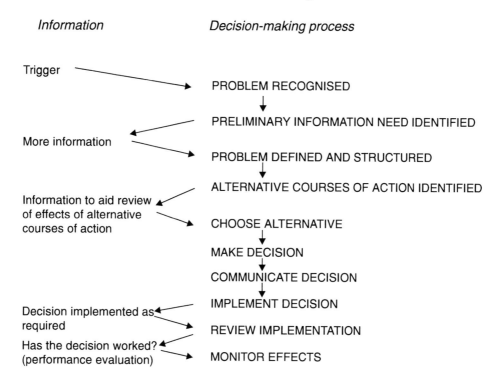

3.9 A further dimension to the decision-making process is the question of how well structured the problem situation is. A distinction can be drawn between structured, semi-structured and unstructured problems and decisions. What is meant by these terms? Arguably, a structured problem is one in which there is a defined number of elements, and it is possible to go about solving the problem in a systematic way. An unstructured problem, on the other hand, is less easy to analyse as it appears to lack any obvious logic, underlying procedures or rules for solving it.

3.10 A *structured* decision can also be described as a programmable decision, in that unambiguous decision rules can be specified in advance. Many structured decisions are automated, although they do not have to be. Structured decisions can often be characterised as routine and frequently repeated. Little or no human judgement is required. An organisation can prepare a decision procedure for a structured decision. This consists of a series of steps to be followed, and may be expressed in the form of, for example, a flowchart or a decision table. Examples of structured decisions include stock re-order formulae and rules for granting credit to customers.

3.11 An *unstructured* decision is said to be non-programmable. It cannot be pre-planned in the same way that a structured decision can be. It will usually occur less frequently and will be non-routine. There is no pre-prepared decision procedure for an unstructured decision, either because it does not occur frequently enough to warrant one or because it is too complex. Data requirements cannot be fully known in advance and so data retrieval may include ad hoc requests. Unstructured decisions usually involve a high degree of human judgement.

3.12 A *semi-structured* decision falls somewhere between the two categories described. It is likely to involve an element of human judgement and to have characteristics of standard procedures with some programmed elements.

3.13 Many operational control problems and decisions are structured ones. An example is a decision to out letters to customers who are late payers. Examples of unstructured and structured decisions at the different levels of management are given below.

Decision level	Structured	Semi-structured	Unstructured
Operational	Credit control or stock control procedures	Selection of new supplier	Hiring supervisor
Tactical	Selection of products to discount	Allocation of budget	Expanding into a new design
Strategic	Major investment decisions	Entry to new market; new product line	Reorganisation of whole company

4   INFORMATION FOR DECISION MAKING

Operational information

4.1   Operational information is used to ensure that specific operations are planned and carried out properly within a factory or office.

4.2   In the payroll office, for example, operational information might include the hours worked each week by each employee, his rate of pay per hour, details of his deductions, and for the purpose of wages analysis, details of the time each person spent on individual jobs during the week.

4.3   More urgent operational information, such as the amount of raw materials being input to a production process, may be required daily, hourly, or in the case of automated production, second by second.

4.4   Operational information:

- Is derived almost entirely from internal sources
- Is highly detailed, being the processing of raw data
- Relates to the immediate term
- Is task-specific
- Is prepared constantly, or very frequently
- Is largely quantitative

Tactical information

4.5   Tactical information is used to decide how the resources of the business should be employed, and to monitor how they are being, and have been, employed.

4.6   Such information includes productivity measurements (output per man hour or per machine hour) budgetary control or variance analysis reports, and cashflow forecasts, manning levels and profit results within a particular department of the organisation, labour turnover statistics within a department and short-term purchasing requirements.

4.7   Tactical information therefore:

- Is primarily generated from internal sources
- Is summarised although a report might include raw data as backup
- Is relevant to the short and medium term
- Describes or analyses activities or departments
- Is prepared routinely and regularly
- Is based on quantitative measures

4.8   A variety of systems can be used at this level, and there may be a greater reliance than at operational level on exception reporting, informal systems and some external sources.

4.9   Tactical information may be generated in the same processing operation as operational level information. For example, tactical level information comparing actual costs incurred to budget can be produced by a system in which those costs are recorded.

Strategic information

4.10   Strategic information is used to plan the objectives of their organisation, and to assess whether the objectives are being met in practice.

4.11   Such information includes overall profitability, the profitability of different segments of the business, future market prospects, the availability and cost of raising new funds, total cash needs, total manning levels and capital equipment needs.

4.12   Strategic information is therefore:

- Derived from both internal and external sources
- Summarised at a high level
- Relevant to the long term
- Deals with the whole organisation (although it might go into some detail)
- Often prepared on an 'ad hoc' basis
- Both quantitative and qualitative
- Uncertain, given that the future cannot be predicted

4.13   At strategic level the information system is likely to be informal, in the sense that it is not possible always to quantify or program strategic information, and much of the information might come from environmental sources. The MIS will provide summary high level data from transactions processing. Human judgement is used more often at this level, as many strategic decisions cannot be programmed

4.14   A table showing typical inputs, processes and outputs at each level of a management information system is provided below.

	Inputs	*Processes*	*Outputs*
Strategic	Plans Competitor information Market information	Summarise Investigate Compare Forecast	Key ratios Ad hoc market analysis Strategic plans
Tactical	Historical data Budget data	Compare Classify Summarise	Variance analyses Exception reports
Operational	Customer orders Programmed stock control levels	Update files Output reports	Updated files Listings Invoices

Other ways of classifying information requirements

4.15   There are many other ways of classifying the information held in a management information system. One approach involves a consideration of the framework within which the information is used. It identifies five levels of information.

(a)   *International information*, for example information on global energy resources or on foreign exchange rates.

(b)   *National information*, for example population trends and the rate of inflation in a national economy.

(c) *Corporate information*, for example a company's market capitalisation and its earnings per share.

(d) *Departmental information*, for example branch turnover or departmental return on capital.

(e) *Individual information*, for example an employee's rate of pay or the price of a particular product.

Exercise 2

Taking an organisation with which you are familiar, such as an employer or college, give a further example of information which it collects in each of the above categories.

Solution

There is clearly a wide range of possible solutions to this exercise and you may well have different ideas of your own. A college might not collect international information; examples in the remaining categories could be as follows.

(a) *National information:* Population trends, including number of school leavers and numbers embarking on courses of further education or higher education.

(b) *International information* on educational trends abroad and educational demand, particularly with a view to attracting foreign students.

(c) *Corporate information:* College funding; college property owned.

(d) *Departmental information:* Student enrolments for individual courses; exam pass rates.

(e) *Individual information:* Lecturers' salaries; student registration details.

Past, present and future information

4.16 Another useful categorisation of information is between past, present and future information.

Past information

4.17 This is record keeping, the storing of information about what has been done or what has happened in the past. This historical information will subsequently be used again at some time in the future. Much past information is information of a transaction processing nature. Recording transactions is a function of the operational level of management.

(a) In the case of a company, there is a statutory requirement of the Companies Act for a company to maintain proper accounting records of past transactions.

(b) Records that are kept of past transactions might be used to generate further routine operations at a later date. For example, a record of a sale to a customer, and details of the invoice sent out, will be kept, and if the customer does not pay on time, a statement or reminder will be sent out, chasing payment.

Present information

4.18 This is information about what is happening now, so that decisions can be taken about what, if anything, to do next. Present information is therefore most readily associated with control information, which is the feedback in a management information system. Much control information relates to the comparison of historical with current data.

4.19 This is information about what is expected to happen in the future. It is most readily associated with planning decisions, possibly for a budget, but also for longer term strategic information. Future information is also likely to include a significant proportion of environmental information, because the future of any organisation will not be secure unless it continues to adapt to changes in its environment.

4.20 Past information should be the most accurate of the three categories, and future information the least accurate of the three. The degree of accuracy expected from information should therefore vary according to whether it is past, present or future.

Quantitative and qualitative information

Exercise 3

Information may be quantitative or qualitative. Quantitative information is measurable in numerical terms, such as money or physical quantities (labour hours or weight of materials), while qualitative information is difficult (or even impossible) to measure in quantitative terms. Examples of qualitative information may be employee morale, motivation, customer loyalty, attitudes of the general public, goodwill or badwill - qualitative information is often concerned with attitudes.

Using these examples, why do you think it might be important to attempt to measure qualitative information? (For example, an organisation might wish to measure goodwill for the purpose of agreeing the sale price of a business.)

Solution

(a) The cost of poor employee morale might have an effect on labour turnover (and the cost of training and recruitment).

(b) Poor motivation might result in lost output and profits.

(c) Customer loyalty might allow a company to charge more for its products than its rivals.

(d) Attitudes of the public (non-customers) might affect the company's ability to recruit or to increase its market share.

4.21 Quantitative information is preferred to qualitative information because it can be built into mathematical models and formulae. Mathematical computer models (such as financial planning models, operation research models and simulation models) which are used extensively by management, require some method of quantifying 'variables' in the situation under review.

4.22 Qualitative information depends on the experience and judgement of a manager, whereas quantitative information simply depends on the accuracy of the measured data and the assumptions used in a mathematical formula or a computer model.

4.23 When qualitative factors will influence a decision, the manager has two options.

(a) To use his or her judgement in reaching the final decision, trying to balance quantitative and qualitative factors.

(b) To use a technique, if one is available in the organisation, for converting qualitative values into quantitative values, and making the decision on the strength of estimated quantified costs and benefits. This is the principle underlying so-called 'cost-benefit analysis' or CBA, which is sometimes used by a government to make decisions (for example about road-building) by putting money values to social costs and benefits.

4.24 In certain areas progress has been made in creating quantitative information by measuring qualitative information. For example:

(a) uncertainty, which inevitably surrounds any decision, can be measured in terms of sensitivity analysis, probability distributions or a 'margin of safety'; or

(b) attitudes can be measured according to their strength. For example, a scale of 0-6 might be used to quantify the motivation of employees, with 0 representing poor morale and 6 high morale.

5 MANAGEMENT BY EXCEPTION 12/96

5.1 *Management by exception* is an approach to planning and control based on 'exception' principles: 'a system of reporting based on the exception principle which focuses attention on those items where performance differs significantly from standard or budget'

5.2 In other words the information is provided, 'by exception', on performance measures that differ significantly from the pre-set budget or standard. This enables management to concentrate attention on matters which are critical to the overall success of the organisation. Therefore, instead of trying to deal with a mass of badly presented and overly detailed information, management can receive clear information showing deviations from expected targets.

5.3 Slight variations between actual results and the plan may be considered acceptable, and corrective action is only applied when results exceed certain established tolerance levels. For example, a factory has six production departments and the production manager uses efficiency ratios as tolerance limits in his scheme of control. If the efficiency ratio for any department is below 95% or above 110% each week, he wishes to investigate the reasons for the low or high performance in order to decide whether control action is needed. In one week, he might receive the following report (assuming that reporting by exception did not exist).

Department	Efficiency ratio	Comments
1	99	Acceptable ...
2	103	Supplier discounts were ...
3	94	Machine failure caused ...
4	106	Large production runs ...
5	98	Set-up time was ...
6	102	Acceptable ...
Overall	100	

5.4 The manager would only be interested in the poor performance of department 3. Time and effort would be saved in preparing the report, as well as for the manager, if reporting by exception were used.

> Department 3 had an efficiency ratio of 94
>
> Reasons: Problems with machine B led to ...

5.5 In the example shown, there is only a very simple control system using one measurement of performance. As a system gets larger, the volume of data being processed also increases, and the principle of exception reporting becomes more efficient and more necessary. Exception reporting is a very important element of a good management information system.

Trend, materiality and controllability

5.6 Variance analysis does not stop once the figures have been calculated. The point of comparing budgeted and actual figures is to see what corrective action, if any, is needed to ensure that the plan will be successfully completed. Thus every variance needs to be considered to see whether it should prompt control action.

5.7 Three important points should be kept in mind.

    (a) *Materiality*. Small variations in a single period are bound to occur occasionally and are unlikely to be significant. Obtaining an 'explanation' is likely to be time-consuming and irritating for the manager concerned. The explanation will often be 'chance', which is not helpful in any case. For such variations further investigation is not worthwhile.

    (b) However, small variations that occur consistently may need more attention. *Variance trend* is more important than a single set of variances for one period. Trend analysis provides information which gives an indication as to whether a variance is fluctuating within acceptable control limits or not.

    (c) *Controllability* must also influence the decision whether to investigate further. If there is a general worldwide price increase in the price of an important raw material there is nothing that can be done internally to control the effect of this. If a central decision is made to award all employees a 10% increase in salary, staff costs in A division will increase by this amount and the variance is not controllable by A division's manager. Uncontrollable variances call for a change in the plan, not an investigation into the past.

Variance trend

5.8 If, say, an efficiency variance is £1,000 adverse in month 1, the obvious conclusion is that the process is out of control and that corrective action must be taken. This may be correct, but what if the same variance is £1,000 adverse every month? The *trend* indicates that the process is in control and the standard has been wrongly set. Suppose, though, that the same variance is consistently £1,000 adverse for each of the first six months of the year but that production has steadily fallen from 100 units in month 1 to 65 units by month 6. The variance trend in absolute terms is constant, but relative to the number of units produced, efficiency has got steadily worse.

6 TYPES OF INFORMATION SYSTEM

Transaction processing systems

6.1 Transactions processing systems, or data processing systems, could be said to represent the lowest level in an organisation's use of information systems. They are used for routine tasks in which data items or transactions must be processed so that operations can continue. Handling sales orders, purchase orders, payroll items and stock records are typical examples.

6.2 Most organisations generate a large volume of transactions which need to be processed efficiently and effectively. Computerised transactions processing systems have clear cost and performance advantages over manual systems for all but the most trivial applications. Even small businesses are now using PCs to provide these functions just as larger companies earlier acquired mainframe computers for these purposes.

6.3 Transactions processing systems provide the raw material which is often used more extensively by management information systems, databases or decision support systems. In other words, transactions processing systems might be used to produce management information, such as reports on cumulative sales figures to date, total amounts owed to suppliers or owed by debtors, total stock turnover to date, value of current stock-in-hand, and so on, but the main purpose of transaction processing systems is operational, as an integral part of day-to-day operations.

Management information systems   *6/95, 12/98, 6/99*

6.4 Organisations need not only information, but an information system to provide it. The term management information system (MIS) can be defined as follows

'A system to convert data from internal and external sources into information and to communicate that information, in an appropriate form, to managers at all levels in all functions to enable them to make timely and effective decisions for planning, directing and controlling the activities for which they are responsible.'

(Lucey, *Management Information Systems*)

6.5 The purpose of an MIS, potentially, is to satisfy all the informational needs of management. Whether this is possible will depend to some degree on the nature and type of information provided.

6.6 An MIS is good at providing regular formal information gleaned from normal commercial data. For example, an MIS relating to sales could provide managers with information on the following.

(a) Gross profit margins of particular products.
(b) Success in particular markets.
(c) Credit control information (aged debtors and payments against old balances).

6.7 It may be less efficient at presenting information which is relatively unpredictable, or informal, or unstructured. So, for example, an MIS could not provide information relating to the sudden emergence of a new competitor into the market.

6.8 While an MIS may not, in principle, be able to provide all the information used by management, it should however, be sufficiently flexible to enable management to incorporate unpredictable, informal or unstructured information into decision-making processes. For example, many decisions are made with the help of financial models (such as spreadsheets) so that the effect of new situations can be estimated easily.

What are the features of an effective information system?

6.9 Examination questions frequently ask what are the features of an effective information system that will support the business described n the question scenario. The whole of the rest of this book may be considered to be the answer to this question, with features selected as appropriate to the particular scenario. For instance if the information handling skills of staff are apparently poor, training and development (Chapter 12) may be part of the solution. If systems are being developed in house CASE tools (Chapter 9) may be beneficial. In other cases a database approach may be desirable, or there may be particularly urgent environmental scanning needs. These matters are also dealt with in subsequent chapters.

6.10 In other words, although an information system should always support the overall objectives of the organisation and should always provide information that displays the well-known 'good' qualities, it is not possible to prescribe an all-purpose answer to this question: it depends on the information you are given in the scenario.

7 DECISION SUPPORT SYSTEMS AND MODELS   12/99

7.1 Decision support systems (DSS) are a form of management information system. Decision support systems are used by management to assist in making unstructured decisions on issues do not allow the easy application of many of the techniques or systems developed for more well defined problems or activities. Decision support systems are intended to provide a wide range of alternative information gathering and analytical tools with a major emphasis upon flexibility and user-friendliness.

7.2 The term decision support system is usually taken to mean computer systems which are designed to produce information in such a way as to help managers to make better decisions. They are now often associated with information 'at the touch of a button' at a manager's PC. DSS can describe a range of systems, from fairly simple information models based on spreadsheets to expert systems.

Exercise 4

You should have studied spreadsheets and their features for Foundation Level *Information Systems*.

Suggest what features of spreadsheets make them useful for modelling, and what possible drawbacks spreadsheets may have.

Solution

The only pre-ordained structure imposed on the end user of a spreadsheet is the grid of rows and columns. This gives the spreadsheet great flexibility and it is this that users find so valuable in decision making.

Spreadsheets are particularly useful at tactical level. Much tactical management involves the analysis and interpretation of operational information. The *'what if?'* manipulation of data, for example, is probably the most important facility in a spreadsheet package.

For instance, a manager planning activities for the next six months might want to know how his department's cash flow would be affected if interest rates changed. It is a simple matter to set up a spreadsheet so that the interest rate is entered in a separate cell and treated as a variable in the cash flow calculations. The value in this cell can then be changed at will to see *what* happens to cash flow *if* the rate is 5%, 6%, 7% and so on.

Other features that make spreadsheets useful are their ability to *import* data from and *export* it to other packages, the ability to *sort* information in a wide variety of ways (eg by the use of Pivot Tables), the availability of *graphics* features to aid presentation and understanding of data, and the ability to write *macros* to automate commonly performed analysis tasks.

However, because spreadsheets are essentially single-user packages and because each one is designed from scratch, there are risks in their use.

(a) Although users are sometimes trained in how to use a spreadsheet, they are rarely trained in *spreadsheet discipline* or *best practice*. This means that spreadsheets may be *badly designed*, increasing the risk of errors or inefficiency.

(b) Users are unlikely to *document* the workings of their spreadsheet, as they consider it 'obvious'. This makes it difficult for other staff (temporary replacement or permanent successor) to understand, use or modify the model.

(c) The *'macro'* is an important feature of all but the simplest spreadsheets. Macros can be *difficult to write and to understand* and are not as conducive to tight control as the use of a programming language.

(d) The *lack of a proper audit trail* can be a disadvantage. Because the user works with a spreadsheet in memory (RAM), only saving it at certain intervals, it is unlikely that a record of the intermediate stages will be maintained, even if output from the intermediate stages is important. Even when a spreadsheet is saved, the previous version is usually overwritten.

7.3 Decision support systems do not *make* decisions. The objective is to allow the manager to consider a number of alternatives and evaluate them under a variety of potential conditions. A key element in the usefulness of these systems is their ability to function interactively. This is a feature, for example, of spreadsheets. Managers using these systems often develop scenarios using earlier results to refine their understanding of the problem and their actions.

7.4 Some decision support computer systems are composed of three elements. These subsystems then combine to provide the capabilities required for an effective decision support system.

(a) A *language subsystem* used by the manager to communicate interactively with the decision support system.

(b) A *problem processing subsystem* which provides analytical techniques and presentation capabilities.

(c) A *knowledge subsystem* which holds internal data and can access any needed external data.

7.5 Many decision support systems have been developed so that they support implementation on a wide range of hardware: full featured systems require mainframe or minicomputers while less powerful or specialised applications may quite comfortably be used on microcomputers. The most common implementation uses distributed processing systems with all types of hardware so that several users may easily use the system.

7.6 The need for the information provided by decision support systems has always existed. It was not possible to economically provide until several prerequisites were first established: database systems are a central feature of the knowledge subsystem, the computer speed and memory required by language processors was not earlier available, the telecommunications required by distributed systems was expensive and unreliable, and managers themselves were unfamiliar with computers and many of the quantitative and analytical methods available.

7.7 A decision support system integrates many of the functions supplied by information systems so that managers may use them more easily and on a wider range of both structured and unstructured problems. Examples of the types of decisions which they might support include the following.

(a) Decision on whether to lease or buy company cars.
(b) Examination of options as to capital structuring and consequences of alternatives.
(c) Decisions on introduction of share option scheme.

Exercise 5

A building society intends to convert from mutual company to a public limited company.

Briefly outline the steps that might be taken to ensure that the MIS supports the decision making process following the conversion.

Solution

Steps that may be taken include the following.

(a) *Check on legislative requirements that affect the new company.* Systems need to be set up to alert management if there is any danger that the new rules will be broken and to inform decisions on how to rectify the situation.

(b) *Check on the system's ability to meet financial reporting requirements.* Reporting requirements will be quite different and this may entail significant reorganisation of accounting systems.

(c) The system will need to include a function to maintain the *register of shareholders*.

(d) The system may need to *link into other networks*, for instance banking networks for clearing of funds or automated teller machine networks, and this may have implications for staffing levels needed to support the system, monitoring of system usage and security matters.

(e) A shareholder telephone helpline should be provided.

Models   6/94, 12/97, 6/98

7.8 A model can be defined as an abstract of a real system which permits the exploration of the behaviour of the system under various different circumstances.

7.9 Most management models tend to be symbolic, have a mathematical base, and incorporate measures of risk and/or uncertainty, with the objective of supplying management with information for policy determination, planning, control and decision-making. A mathematical business model can be defined as the representation in mathematical terms and symbols of the relationship between the significant variables in the business situation to which the model relates.

7.10 The value of models depends on:

    (a) How extensive the database is. Models rely on data. A comprehensive, up-to-date and accurate database is required.

    (b) Flexibility in the use of data on the database files. Computerised databases and different software packages for accessing and using data should be utilised.

    (c) Their accessibility. Relevant data should be available to all staff who require it to make better-informed decisions.

Why use a model?

7.11 A model is used to provide managers with information for decision making. A model is used in most cases because it would be impossible to experiment with the physical, 'real-world' system itself. This may be for any of three reasons.

Reversibility of results

7.12 The effect of experimenting with the system itself may be irreversible. For example, if a company wishes to analyse the effects of granting a large pay rise to all its employees, it could either:

    (a) pay the extra money and wait and see what the effects are; however, having paid the higher wages, the work force will not agree to a subsequent reduction in earnings; or

    (b) experiment with a financial model, to assess the consequences of higher pay on profits, cash flows, ROCE etc.

Creation of artificial conditions

7.13 The system may not exist. For example, if a government wishes to decide on the nature of its future energy policies, the future circumstances for which a policy is required would not yet exist to be experimented with.

Cost

7.14 The costs of experimenting with the physical system might be prohibitively expensive, and many of the experimental items developed might fail to work. Thus an aeroplane manufacturer would test a new design by constructing a model rather than building a prototype straight away in the hope that it will fly.

Examples of models

7.15 Examples of models include a balance sheet, a linear programming model, a DCF net present value statement and a budget. These are used by managers to make planning or control decisions, they are mathematical representations of the 'real world' and so they are models. Simple models can be constructed without the aid of computers, but complex models, or models which require numerous computations to produce output information, or models where the user wants to try variations in the values of inputs, will probably be computer-based.

7.16 Many models which are built relate to a particular area of a company's operations.

    (a) Market models may be used to forecast sales demand. The variables which affect demand must be identified, quantified and set in some mathematical relationship with each other, so as to build a sales forecasting or market model. The variables affecting demand include:

        (i) Past and current sales, where trends or cycles are discernible.

        (ii) Market conditions - ie size of the market, market segments, taxation, new technology.

    (iii)   Consumer spending patterns.

    (iv)   Competition.

    (v)   Sales promotion and advertising expenditure.

    (vi)   Market research findings, product design and development, etc.

(b) Cost prediction models and financial models (for example cash flow models).

(c) Transportation models, or models to help decisions about siting factories, warehouses etc.

(d) Departmental models, covering the design of products, production scheduling and control, stockholding, distribution and sales within a department or division of a company.

(e) Technical models used, for example, in product design.

Sensitivity analysis 6/98

7.17 Different managers will have different assumptions and views about what they think will happen or ought to happen. Operating managers, for example, frequently disagree with finance staff. All of them will want to see the effect on the outcome of future events if things turn out better or worse than expected. This can be done through either sensitivity analysis or risk analysis.

7.18 Sensitivity analysis involves asking 'what if?' questions. By changing the value of different variables in the model, a number of different scenarios for the future will be produced. For example, wage increases can be altered to 10% from 5%; demand for a product can be reduced from 100,000 to 80,000, the introduction of new processing equipment can be deferred by 6 months, on the revised assumption that there will be delays, and so on.

7.19 One form of sensitivity analysis is to produce 'worst possible outcome', 'best possible outcome' and 'most likely outcome' scenarios.

7.20 Sensitivity analysis can be formalised by:

(a) Identifying key variables in the model.

(b) Changing the value of each, perhaps in progressive steps. For example, wage costs might be increased in steps by 5%, 7½%, 10%, 12½% and 15% and the effect on profits and cash flows under each of these five wage cost assumptions can be tested.

7.21 In this way, a full picture would emerge of how the achievement of planning targets would be affected by different values for each key variable. Once the most critical variables have been established, management can then follow a number of courses of action.

(a) *Apply the most stringent controls to the most critical variables*, to ensure that plans are achieved and the variable does not get out of control.

(b) *Alter the plans so that the most critical variables are no longer as critical.* For example, if a car manufacturing company's marketing management are planning to stop producing an old model of car and switch production resources to an entirely new model, sensitivity analysis might show that its profitability will be critically dependent on the speed with which the new model gains acceptance in the market. If the risk seems too great, management might re-think their plans and opt to introduce the new model in smaller numbers to begin with, and to continue producing the old model as well in some numbers until the new model is more established.

(c) *When different planning options are available, choose a lower-risk plan.* For example, if a London-based company has the choice of expanding its operations into either the rest of the UK or into parts of mainland Europe, it might find that Continental operations would offer prospects of bigger profits, but the risk of failure might be bigger too and so it might opt to expand in the UK instead.

7.22 In summary, sensitivity analysis helps managers to know which items they must concentrate on in terms of refining the planning assumptions, assessing risk and subsequent control if the plan is approved.

Risk analysis

7.23 Like sensitivity analysis, risk analysis is more easily carried out with the aid of computer models. Risk analysis is an extension of sensitivity analysis. Models which use probability distributions for risk analysis are sometimes referred to as stochastic models.

Risk analysis packages   6/98

7.24 Spreadsheets can be built that show the flow-on effect of changing certain variables. But spreadsheets have limitations when complex risk analysis is required.

(a) Spreadsheets need precise values for imprecise and vague variables.

(b) Spreadsheet calculations and 'what-if?' analyses are unwieldy if the number of variables becomes large, as the number of possible permutations increases. For example, assume you are manufacturing a product whose profitability depends on four variables.

(i)   Materials cost, which can either be high or low, depending on the market.
(ii) Exchange rates, which can be high or low.
(iii) The market which can be tough or easy.
(iv) The world economy which can be good or bad.

You would need 2^4 or 16 spreadsheet models to analyse every situation, or you would have to change the data 16 times.

7.25 Risk analysis software aims to cope with this uncertainty, by dealing with it using a probability distribution. The advantage of such a package is that not only factual uncertainty is dealt with (the future is generally unpredictable), but that it is possible to build in the possibly conflicting objectives of a number of different strategies.

Strategic planning models   6/98

7.26 Strategic planning models are sometimes referred to as business planning models. In large groups of companies, it is not uncommon for the strategic planning process to begin at the subsidiary company level, or sub-subsidiary level, with individual companies preparing their own business plans using a strategic business planning computer model, and then for the plan to be fed into the planning model of the parent company, which can co-ordinate the plans of its different subsidiaries, and amend them as necessary. Modelling helps to speed up the co-ordinating and decision-making process between companies in the group.

Econometric models for medium-term forecasting

7.27 Econometrics is the study of economic variables and their interrelationships, using computer models. Short-term or medium-term econometric models might be used for forecasting. Such models, incorporating mathematical techniques such as regression analysis, may well be useful for medium-term forecasting.

Forecasting packages

7.28 Software packages that prepare forecasts from historical data are available for all sizes of computer, from mainframe to micro, varying in complexity (and cost). These packages take historical data fed in by the computer user, and conduct correlation analysis and regression analysis to produce forecasts and information about the degree of confidence that can be placed in them.

BPP
PUBLISHING

Optimisation models

7.29 Once long-term forecasts have been made, and the framework of strategic plans agreed, managers will know what assumptions they are expected to make about future environmental conditions and resource availability. Given such assumptions about the constraints within which the organisation will be operating, other types of models, referred to collectively as either mathematical programming models, or optimisation models, can be used.

7.30 Examples of optimisation models are:

(a) *Linear programming models*, which seek to maximise the value of an objective function (eg. profits, or sales revenue) or minimise its value (eg. costs), given certain constraints, such as a known limitation on the availability of resources.

(b) *Critical path analysis*, or *PERT analysis*, which seeks to minimise the timescale for completion of a project, perhaps within the framework of resource limitations and/or cost controls.

Ad hoc decision models

7.31 A further type of model is a decision model, which can be used to enable managers to make 'ad hoc' or 'one-off' decisions, as distinct from routine and repetitive decisions such as budget planning. Examples of decision models are the following.

(a) Discounted cash flow (DCF) models for capital expenditure appraisal.

(b) Lease versus buy decision models.

(c) Models to enable decisions to be taken about new products or new markets.

(d) Shutdown decision models to decide whether or not to close down an operating division.

(e) Models for sell-off decisions or acquisition decisions, where a company is faced with an unforeseen opportunity to sell or acquire a new subsidiary.

(f) Game theory models. Game theory is a form of statistical decision-making technique for marketing decisions, involving an assessment of different courses of action, given uncertainty about the competitive measures or responses that might be taken by major competitors to any course of action taken by the organisation.

Deterministic models

7.32 A *deterministic model* is a model in which the values of each 'input variable' are known with certainty, and the way in which the variables inter-react is also certain and predictable. For example, an economic order quantity model will be deterministic if:

(a) The cost of ordering, the cost of holding stocks per unit per period, the periodic demand for stock items and the re-order supply lead time are all known stated values; and

(b) It is predicted with certainty that stockholding costs are the stockholding cost per unit multiplied by one half the order quantity.

7.33 The resulting formula for the economic order quantity is $Q = \sqrt{\dfrac{2cd}{h}}$

Stochastic models

7.34 A stochastic model is one that recognises that some variables might have any value from a certain range of 'outcomes', although a probability distribution for such outcomes can be estimated and used in the model. For example, in a stock control system, demand for a stores item may vary from day to day, so that the demand variable may be quantified as:

38

(a) 0.2 probability of 4 units
0.6 probability of 6 units
0.2 probability of 8 units

(b) An average demand of 6 units per day with a standard deviation of 0.4 units.

7.35 Alternatively, the inter-relationship between variables can be expressed as a probability distribution; eg. if A happens, then there is a 25% probability that B will happen and a 75% probability that C will happen.

7.36 A stochastic model could be designed to produce 'solutions' in one of two ways.

(a) As an *expected value*, (or weighted average probability) with some statistical analysis of the possible variation around the EV.

(b) As a *range of possible outcomes*.

Behavioural models

7.37 Some experiments have been carried out to develop behavioural models which attempt to analyse and predict customer or buyer behaviour by:

(a) Recognising what factors influence a buyer's purchasing decision, and assigning a points 'score' or weighting to each factor within the behavioural model.

(b) Assessing how well the organisation's products and marketing mix can tap the buyer's purchasing motives.

7.38 The model can then be used to experiment with the marketing mix to decide what mix is most likely to be successful in creating sales.

Exercise 6

What are the benefits of modelling?

Solution

In broad terms, the advantages of models are:

- The ability to explore more alternatives
- Improved decision making
- More effective planning
- Faster decision making
- More timely information
- More accurate forecasts
- More extensive information, and ready access to information
- Flexibility in the production of control reports
- Cost savings, possibly as a result of the other benefits

---

8 EXECUTIVE INFORMATION SYSTEMS

8.1 An executive information system (EIS) provides the executive with the underlying performance facts and figures which have traditionally been under the control of middle managers. It is a *type of DSS*, and takes the form of computer workstations on top of executives' desks. An executive information system is an 'information system which gives the executive easy access to key internal and external data'. EISs have been made possible by the increasing cheapness and sophistication of personal computer and network technology. An EIS is likely to have the following features.

(a) Provision of summary-level data, captured from the organisation's main systems (which might involve integrating the executive's desk top micro with the organisation's mainframe).

(b) A facility which allows the executive to 'drill-down' from higher levels of information to lower).

(c) Data manipulation facilities (for example comparison with budget or prior year data, trend analysis).

(d) Graphics, for user-friendly presentation of data.

(e) A template system. This will mean that the same type of data (eg sales figures) is presented in the same format, irrespective of changes in the volume of information required.

8.2 The basic design philosophy of executive information systems is as follows.

(a) They should be easy to use ('idiot-proof' not just user friendly) as an EIS may be consulted during a meeting, for example.

(b) They should make data easy to access, so that it describes the organisation from the executive's point of view, not just in terms of its data flows.

(c) They should provide tools for analysis (including ratio analysis, forecasts, what-if analysis, trends).

(d) They should provide presentational aids so that information can be conveyed 'without bothering the executive with too many trivial choices of scale, colour and layout.'

8.3 At the heart of an executive information system is a corporate model, which holds key information about the organisation. A database is used to store the underlying data and the corporate model holds such information as organisational structure including consolidation and sub-consolidation groupings, performance indicators including ratios, and reporting cycles as appropriate. This model provides the interface between the database and the executive, who as a result does not have to define how information should be displayed. The corporate model contains rules as to how the information should be presented and aggregated. The model can be amended if required.

8.4 Executive information systems have also been more generally described as *executive support systems* (ESS). Typical applications include the following. (Only the first is really within the domain of an *EIS*.)

(a) Provision of data on the performance of the organisation. This would include actual, budget and forecast figures for key areas such as sales, production and profitability.

(b) Provision of internal communications facilities. This would include storage and retrieval of personal correspondence, minutes of meetings and financial and other reports.

(c) Environmental scanning. As we have already seen, an organisation needs data on the political and economic environment. It might also collect competitor and market intelligence.

8.5 An ESS, by supporting all the major responsibilities and activities of senior executives, can be used for strategic planning. It is instructive to note the reasons why Executive Information Systems are installed. They can be viewed as a means of attacking a *critical business need* in order to ensure the future well-being of the organisation. Secondly, there may be a strong *personal desire* by one or more executives to have an EIS in order to:

(a) Access information faster than at present.
(b) Access a broader range of information than at present.
(c) Retrieve selected information in a more focused way.
(d) Display output in a graphical form.

8.6 Thirdly, installing an EIS may simply be seen as *the thing to do*. It is an example of a current management practice and to that extent may appear attractive to some organisations, the rationale being that it will improve the performance of executives and reduce time wasted in information search activity. This can be a 'risky' justification: Watson identifies five problem areas which should be avoided in developing an EIS.

(a)   A lack of executive support is a particular problem for EIS, because executives are not merely the sponsors but also the users of the system.

(b)   A lack of defined systems objectives is likely, as executives are dazzled by the technology, convenience and power of the EIS.

(c)   Information requirements may be poorly defined, as much of the information required is ad hoc, non-routine and subjective in nature.

(d)   Support staff may not have the required understanding of the business or of the nature of work of executives.

(e)   EIS are not developed, delivered and maintained in the same way as traditional systems. Rather they evolve in a gradual way.

9   ARTIFICIAL INTELLIGENCE AND EXPERT SYSTEMS   *6/96, 12/96*

9.1   Artificial intelligence has been called the study of how to make computers do things at which, at the moment, people are better. For example, people are much better than computers at:

(a)   Learning from experience.

(b)   Making sense out of information that seems to be ambiguous or contradictory.

(c)   Responding in an appropriate way to a completely new situation.

(d)   Recognising the relative importance of different aspects of a situation.

(e)   Understanding other people's behaviour, which may not always be rational or which may be motivated by things that are not part of the problem as defined.

9.2   Artificial intelligence software works by creating a knowledge base that consists of facts, concepts and the relationships between them and then searches it using pattern-matching techniques to 'solve' problems.

(a)   Rules of thumb or ('heuristics') are important. A simple example might be 'milk in first' when making a cup of tea: this is a rule of thumb for tea making that saves people having to rethink how to make a cup of tea every time they do so. A simple business example programmed into many accounting packages might be: 'Don't allow credit to a customer who has exceeded their credit limit'.

(b)   Pattern-matching finds similarities between objects, events or processes that may not be clear if items are only understood in terms of their differences. Tea and coffee are different things but they both serve the same purpose if the problem is that you want a refreshing hot drink. Conventional computer systems are not programmed to make this sort of logical leap.

Case example: Neural networks

Unlike conventional computing techniques, neural computing is modelled on the biological processes of the human brain and has many human like qualities. For example, neural computers can learn from experience and do not need to be programmed with fixed rules or equations. The can analyse vast quantities of complex data and identify patterns from which predictions can be made. They have the ability to cope well with incomplete or "fuzzy' data , and can deal with previously unspecified or new situations. As such they are ideally suited to real world applications and can provide the solution to a host of currently impossible or commercially impractical problems.

IBM has, for example, integrated neural network and artificial intelligence technology into software applications such as data mining packages. Such techniques enable businesses to sift through vast quantities of raw data in order to spot hidden trends or anomalies which might otherwise be missed.

At best information analysis was done manually - perhaps as much as 90 per cent of analysts' time was spent gathering information, leaving only 10 per cent of the time to digest and analyse the data. With IBM's business intelligence technology, however, customers are now able to save millions of dollars, enter new markets, retain customers, track fraud and generally be more competitive.

9.3 Artificial intelligence is still in its infancy but some applications have been developed in a variety of fields, such as linguistics, psychology, and optics. The main commercial applications however, are known as expert systems.

Expert systems

9.4 Expert systems are a form of DSS that allow users to benefit from expert knowledge and information. The system will consist of a database holding specialised data and rules about what to do in, or how to interpret, a given set of circumstances.

9.5 For example, many financial institutions now use expert systems to process straightforward loan applications. The user enters certain key facts into the system such as the loan applicant's name and most recent addresses, their income and monthly outgoings, and details of other loans. The system will then:

(a) Check the facts given against its database to see whether the applicant has a good previous credit record.

(b) Perform calculations to see whether the applicant can afford to repay the loan.

(c) Match up other criteria, such as whether the security offered for the loan or the purpose for which the loan is wanted is acceptable, and to what extent the loan applicant fits the lender's profile of a good risk (based on the lender's previous experience).

9.6 A decision is then suggested, based on the results of this processing. This is why it is now often possible to get a loan or arrange insurance over the telephone, whereas in the past it would have been necessary to go and speak to a bank manager or send details to an actuary and then wait for him or her to come to a decision.

9.7 There are many other business applications of expert systems.

(a) Legal advice.

(b) Tax advice.

(c) Forecasting of economic or financial developments, or of market and customer behaviour.

(d) Surveillance, for example of the number of customers entering a supermarket, to decide the number of checkouts that need to be open.

(e) Diagnostic systems, to identify causes of problems, for example in production control in a factory, or in healthcare.

(f) Project management.

(g) Education and training (diagnosing a student's or worker's weaknesses and providing or recommending extra instruction as appropriate).

(h) Credit scoring systems used to access loan applications.

Exercise 7

If you are studying at a college you might like to annoy your tutor by having a class discussion about whether he or she could be replaced by an expert system!

9.8   An organisation can use an expert system when a number of conditions are met.

   (a)   The problem is reasonably well defined.

   (b)   The expert can define some rules by which the problem can be solved.

   (c)   The problem cannot be solved by conventional transaction processing or data handling.

   (d)   The expert could be released to more difficult problems, in the case of certain types of work. (An actuary in an insurance company is an example. Actuaries are very highly paid.)

   (e)   The investment in an expert system is cost justified.

9.9   This is a diagram of an expert system.

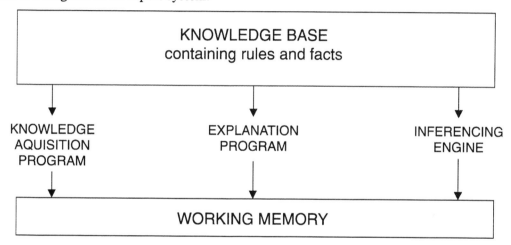

   (a)   The knowledge base contains facts (assertions like 'a rottweiler is a dog') and rules ('if you see a rottweiler, then run away'). Some facts contradict rules, of course, or even each other ('all birds can fly' is contradicted by the existence of ostriches and kiwis).

   (b)   The knowledge acquisition program is a program which enables the expert system to acquire new knowledge and rules.

   (c)   The working memory is where the expert system stores the various facts and rules used during the current enquiry, and the current information given to it by the user.

   (d)   The inferencing engine is the software that executes the reasoning. It needs to discern which rules apply, and allocate priorities.

Advantages and limitations of expert systems

9.10   Advantages include the following.

   (a)   Artificial intelligence and expertise is permanent, whereas human experts may leave the business.

   (b)   It is easily copied, so that one bank branch say, can have access to the same expertise as any other branch.

   (c)   It is consistent, whereas human experts and decision makers may not be.

   (d)   It can be documented. The reasoning behind an expert recommendation produced by a computer will all be recorded. Experts may have what seem to them to be inspired ideas out of the blue, not fully realising the thought processes that they have been going through while they have been mulling the problem over.

BPP PUBLISHING

(e) Depending on the task the computer may be much faster than the human being.

9.11 There are severe limitations, however.

(a) Systems are expensive, especially if they have to be designed from scratch, as they often would be.

(b) The technology is still in its infancy in many areas. Understanding of how the human mind works is also still fairly limited.

(c) It is very difficult to develop a system in the first place, and the system will need extensive testing and debugging before it can be trusted.

(d) People are naturally more creative. If a computer system can be creative at all, it can only be so to the extent that creativity has been programmed into it: arguably this is not creativity at all.

(e) Systems have a very narrow focus, whereas human experts can bring the whole of their experience to bear on a problem.

(f) Managers will resist being replaced by computers, or at least will sometimes be reluctant to believe the advice of an expert system.

Chapter roundup

- An organisation's information requirements can be analysed into five categories. Information is required for planning, for controlling, for recording transactions, for measuring performance and for decision-making.

- Anthony broke down planning and control activities into a three-level hierarchy. Strategic planning is concerned with the long-term goals of the organisation. Management control involves ensuring that resources are used effectively and efficiently to achieve those goals. Operational control ensures that specific tasks are carried out effectively and efficiently.

- One of the key uses of information is in decision making. The making of a decision has a number of identifiable stages. Decisions must be taken in response to choices and options regarding how an organisation responds to its environment and runs its internal activities.

- The information required for planning and control may be classified as strategic, tactical and operational, matching the three levels of the Anthony hierarchy. Similarly, different types of management information system can be discerned.

- Transaction processing systems are used for routine operational information processing. They provide the raw material used more extensively in management information systems.

- A management information system can be described as a system which provides information to management to assist them in decision-making in their roles of planning and controlling.

- Decision support systems are a form of management information system. They are used by management to provide assistance in decision making. A DSS does not make decisions itself. An example of a DSS is the spreadsheet. Spreadsheets are used by end-users, who can create the required model, input the data, manipulate the data and read or print the output themselves. Spreadsheets are particularly well suited to sensitivity analysis.

- A model is an abstract of a real system which permits the exploration of the behaviour of the system under various different circumstances. Models are used for planning and forecasting and to provide managers with information for decision making. Modelling is the process of representing the real entity by analogy, so that conclusions can be drawn about the entity under examination. A model that allows this is an attempt to describe the business as a set of relationships. Sensitivity analysis involves asking 'what if?' questions. Variables in the model can be changed and the overall effect of such changes reviewed.

- Executive information systems are a form of management information system designed to give senior executives easy access to data. They typically include a 'drill-down' facility, graphics and data manipulation facilities for rapid and simple retrieval of the required data.

- Expert systems use artificial intelligence, the concept that computers can be programmed to imitate certain features of human reasoning. Expert systems can be used where problems are reasonably well defined and can be solved by reference to a set of rules.

Test your knowledge

1 What are the information requirements of an organisation? (see para 1.1)

2 What are the three areas of decision-making identified by Anthony? (2.2)

3 What are the six stages in making a decision? (3.5)

4 What are the characteristics of operational information? (4.4)

5 What are the characteristics of strategic information? (4.12)

6 Explain 'management by exception' (5.1 - 5.3)

7 What is a DSS? (7.1, 7.2)

8 Give two reasons why managers use models. (7.11 - 7.14)

9 List four areas of a company's operations which might be successfully modelled. (7.16)

10 What is sensitivity analysis? (7.18)

11 What is a strategic planning model? (7.26)

12 Give two examples of decision models. (7.31)

13 What are the features of an EIS? (8.1)

14 How does artificial intelligence software work? (9.2)

15 Give four examples of expert systems (9.7)

Now try illustrative questions 3, 4 and 5 at the end of the Study Text

BPP PUBLISHING

Chapter 3

ORGANISATIONAL INFLUENCES ON SYSTEMS DEVELOPMENT

This chapter covers the following topics.

1   Ways of looking at organisations

2   Business Process Re-engineering

3   Hard and soft problems

4   The socio-technical approach

5   Technological change and its effect on people

6   Managing change

7   The hybrid manager

Introduction

This chapter briefly revisits certain ideas that will be familiar from your earlier studies such as organisation structure and culture, but principally it is concerned with the need to consider the impact of introducing new information systems on old ways of working and on the people who make up organisations. To get the *full* picture this chapter needs to be read in conjunction with the Chapter 4 on technological and environmental issues and Chapter 5 which deals with long-term business strategy, networks, groupware, teleworking and so on.

1   WAYS OF LOOKING AT ORGANISATIONS   6/94

1.1   You should have studied organisations quite extensively already, for Foundation level *Information Systems* and *Organisation and the Human Resource*, and for *Management Principles* at Pre-Professional level. This section therefore gives only a brief resumé of the main ideas. These are relevant because an organisation described in a *Managing Information Systems* exam scenario is likely to fit into one of the older style categories and be looking to change, and you would need to recognise this in formulating your exam answers.

Exercise 1

Make sure you understand terms such as 'tall' and 'flat' organisation, matrix organisation, functionally based organisations, delayering and empowerment. If not go back to your earlier study material.

Organisation theories

1.2   Organisation theories are really 'approaches', offering ways of looking at issues such as organisational structure and culture, motivation and management functions. They can provide helpful and thought-provoking ways of analysing organisational phenomena, and 'frameworks' within which practical problems and situations can be tackled, or 'models' which can be used to isolate the basic characteristics of organisations. They provide useful, accessible language for describing and discussing organisations, but there are no rights and wrongs.

1.3   The main early theorists who put forward ways of understanding organisations identified 'principles' of organisation, applicable in a wide range of situations. Their approach was essentially prescriptive: it attempted to suggest what is good - or even best - for organisations. Later writers *describe* different approaches, rather than *prescribe* a universal 'best' approach.

Scientific management

1.4   The *scientific management* movement, pioneered by Taylor, argued that management should be based on 'well-recognised, clearly defined and fixed principles, instead of depending on more or less hazy ideas'. This involved the development of a 'true science of work', where all the knowledge gathered and applied in the work should be investigated and reduced to 'law' and techniques.

1.5   The practical application of the approach was the use of work study techniques to break each job down into its smallest and simplest component parts: these single elements became the newly-designed 'job'. Workers were selected and trained to perform their single task in the *most efficient way* possible, as determined by techniques such as time and motion study to eliminate 'wasted motions' or unnecessary physical movement. Workers were paid incentives on the basis of acceptance of the new methods and output norms.

1.6   A summary of scientific management, in Taylor's own words, might be as follows.

(a)   'The man who is fit to work at any particular trade is unable to understand the science of that trade without the kindly help and co-operation of men of a totally different type of education.'

(b)   'It is one of the principles of scientific management to ask men to do things in the right way, to learn something new, to change their ways in accordance with the science and in return to receive an increase of from 30% to 100% in pay....'

1.7   One major weakness of scientific management is that by breaking work down into its elementary parts, and analysing a job as a series of consecutive 'motions', the solution to management problems often provided is that each separate 'motion' within the entire job should be done by a separate worker. This is profoundly dissatisfying to workers, and treats them like (poorly designed) 'machine tools': operations *should* be analysed in this way, but then *reintegrated* into a whole job.

Scientific management today

1.8   In spite of this it is notable that scientific management enjoyed something of a resurgence in the late 1980s and early 1990s when high unemployment meant that companies could more easily attract and retain staff. Some organisations may persist in attempting to create 'satisfying' jobs for their workers, but others are inclined to return to molecularised work design, involving minimal training for workers, close supervision and tightly-timed work activities.

The classical school

1.9   The *classical* school of management thought was primarily concerned with the structure and activities of the formal organisation and the rational principles by which they could be directed most effectively. Fayol is the best known representative.

1.10   Among his fourteen principles of management, Fayol listed the following.

(a)   *Division of work*, ie specialisation.

(b)   *Authority and responsibility*:

(c)   *Discipline.*

(d) *Unity of command*: for any action, staff should receive orders from one boss only.

(e) *Unity of direction*: there should be one head and one plan for each activity. Unity of direction relates to the organisation itself, whereas unity of command relates to the personnel in the organisation.

(f) *Subordination of individual interests*: the interest of one employee or group of employees should not prevail over that of the general interest of the organisation.

(g) *Remuneration* should be 'fair', satisfying both employer and employee alike.

(h) *Scalar chain*: the scalar chain is the term used to describe the chain of superiors from lowest to highest rank.

(i) *Esprit de corps*: team spirit.

(j) *Initiative*.

The human relations approach

1.11 The *human relations* approach emphasised the importance of human attitudes, values and relationships for the efficient and effective functioning of work organisations. It was developed mainly by social scientists - rather than practising managers - and was based on research into human behaviour, with the intention of describing and thereafter predicting behaviour in organisations. Like classical theory, it was essentially prescriptive in nature.

1.12 The human relations approach concentrated mainly on the concept of 'Social Man' (*Schein*): man is motivated by 'social' or 'belonging' needs, which are satisfied by the social relationships he forms at work.

1.13 These ideas were followed up by various social psychologists (for example, Maslow and Herzberg) but with a change of emphasis (the *neo-human relations school*). People were still considered to be the crucial factor in determining organisational effectiveness, but were recognised as having more than merely physical and social needs. Attention shifted towards man's 'higher' psychological needs for growth, challenge, responsibility and self-fulfilment.

1.14 The human relations approaches contributed an important awareness of the influence of the human factor at work (and particularly in the work group) on organisational performance. Most of its theorists attempted to offer guidelines to enable practising managers to satisfy and motivate employees and so (theoretically) to obtain the benefits of improved productivity.

1.15 However, the approach tends to emphasise the importance of work to the workers without really addressing the economic issues: there is still no proven link between job satisfaction and motivation, or either of these and productivity or the achievement of organisational goals.

The contingency approach

1.16 The contingency approach to organisation developed as a reaction to prescriptive ideas of the classical and human relations schools, which claimed to offer a universal 'best way' to design organisations, to motivate staff, to introduce technology and so on.

1.17 Research by a variety of writers indicated that different forms of organisational structure could be equally successful, that there was no inevitable correlation between classical organisational structures and effectiveness, and that there were a number of variables to be considered in the design of organisations. Essentially, 'it all depends'.

1.18 The contingency school rejected the universal 'one-best-way' approach, in favour of analysis of the internal factors and external environment of each organisation and the design of organisational structure as a best fit between the tasks, people and environment *in the*

particular situation. As Buchanan and Huczynski put it: 'With the coming of contingency theory, organisational design ceased to be "off-the-shelf", but became tailored to the particular and specific needs of an organisation.'

Current theory: the new organisation

1.19 Much current organisation 'theory' derives from the widespread influence of management 'gurus' such as Tom Peters, Henry Mintzberg, Charles Handy, Hammer and Champy, and from management consultants attempting to profit from implementing their brand of one or other of the gurus' ideas.

1.20 The writings of such people on organisations and management in the past decade have certain recurring themes.

   (a) Everything is now 'global'.

   (b) Everything is 'new'. Change is the norm.

   (c) Everything has to be done more quickly or differently.

   (d) Departments have been reduced to 'teams' engaged in 'processes'.

   (e) Jobs are multi-dimensional: people in empowered roles must seek to find better and better ways of completing processes.

   (f) People work for their customers, not their old-style bosses.

   (g) The boss is the team coach, *enabling* and motivating people to do their work, not barking out commands.

Culture - a new school of thought?   6/99

1.21 Thus, if you look through the 'management' pages of a modern newspaper you are not likely to find much reference to human relations theory, contingency theory or any other theory. You will find that the issues being discussed are 'global markets', 'leanness', 'flexibility', 'quality', 'business process re-engineering', 'customer service', 'employee empowerment' and, above all, *corporate culture*.

1.22 You could simply regard these as sexier names for the old contingent variables - environment, tasks and people. However, as Buchanan and Huczynski say, 'Many writers ... treat culture as a new school of thought within organization theory'.

1.23 Again , organisational culture is a topic that you should have studied in depth for subjects such as *Organisation and the Human Resource* and *Management Principles* and you are referred to your study material for those subjects for more detail.

Information culture

1.24 As you probably remember, Charles Handy sums up culture as 'that's the way we do things round here'. For Edgar Schein, it is 'the pattern of basic assumptions that a given group has invented, discovered, or developed, in learning to cope with its problems of external adaptation and internal integration, and that have worked well enough to be considered valid and, therefore, to be taught to new members as the correct way to perceive, think and feel in relation to these problems.'

1.25 An *information* culture can therefore be defined as 'the values, attitudes and behaviour that influence the way people sense, collect, organise, process, communicate and use information'. (Donald A Marchand, *Financial Times Mastering Management* series, 1995-96).

1.26 Marchand identifies four common types of information culture.

    (a) A *functional culture,* where information is used as a way to exercise influence or control over others. This is the 'need to know' approach, often used in practice to build mini-empires within organisations, since people protect their own expertise and are unwilling to share it.

    (b) A *sharing culture,* where managers and employees trust each other enough to use information to adapt and improve processes and performance.

    (c) An *inquirng culture,* where managers and employees try to improve their understanding of future trends and enquire how they can best change to meet the challenges ahead.

    (d) A *discovery culture,* where managers and employees are open to new ways of thinking about crisis and radical challenge. These companies deliberately shed old ways of doing business and seek new perspectives and ideas.

1.27 Marchand also identifies four types of dysfunctional information *behaviour.*

    (a) *Control fixation,* where managers do not seek new information when new problems arise but use more of the same control-oriented information that they have always used. This takes up a great deal of senior management time and reinforces a defensive, wait and see attitude among employees.

    (b) *Behavioural regression* exists when managers facing new problems ask for even lower levels of information. Marchand gives the example of a senior manager who, responds to a downturn in company performance by asking for expense claims to be submitted in more detail and reviewed by him personally.

    (c) *Mindset paralysis* occurs when accepted ways of using information block a manager's ability to alter his approach to doing business or anticipating change.

    (d) *React* mode occurs in times of crisis. Managers develop action plans before they really know whether these actions will make matters worse or better ('Fire! Ready, Aim', as Marchand puts it.)

2   BUSINESS PROCESS RE-ENGINEERING

2.1 From the early 1990's it became common for management in many organisations to focus their attention inwards and to consider how inefficient business processes can be redesigned or re-engineered. This process can involve fundamental changes in the way an organisation functions. In particular, it has been realised that processes which were developed in a manual processing environment may not be suitable for an environment which is underpinned by IT.

2.2 The main writing on the subject is Hammer and Champy's *Reengineering the Corporation* (1993), from which the following definition is taken.

> Reengineering is 'the fundamental rethinking and radical redesign of business processes to achieve dramatic improvements in critical contemporary measures of performance, such as cost, quality, service and speed.'

2.3 The key words here, as identified by Hammer and Champy, are 'fundamental', 'radical', 'dramatic' and 'process'. The first two indicate that BPR is somewhat akin to zero base budgeting: it starts by asking basic questions such as 'why do we do what we do', without making any assumptions or looking back to what has always been done in the past. 'Dramatic' means that BPR should achieve 'quantum leaps in performance', not just marginal, incremental improvements.

Processes

2.4 The most important word is 'process', by which Hammer and Champy mean 'a collection of activities that takes one or more kinds of input and creates an output that is of value to the customer.' For example, order fulfilment is a process that takes an order as its input and results in the delivery of the ordered goods. Part of this process is the manufacture of the goods, but under BPR the aim of manufacturing is not merely to *make* the goods. Manufacturing should aim to *deliver* the goods that were *ordered*, and any aspect of the manufacturing process that hinders this aim should be re-engineered. The first question to ask might be 'Do they need to be manufactured at all?'

2.5 A re-engineered process has certain characteristics.

(a) Often several jobs are combined into one.
(b) Workers make decisions.
(c) The steps in the process are performed in a natural order.
(d) The same process has different versions depending on the market, or the inputs etc.
(e) Work is performed where it makes most sense.
(f) Checks and controls are reduced.
(g) Reconciliation is minimised.
(h) A case manager provides a single point of contact.
(i) The advantages of centralised and decentralised operations are combined.

Most of these points are illustrated in the example that follows.

Example: BPR

2.6 This example is based on a problem at Ford, described in Hammer and Champy's book.

A company employs 25 staff to perform the standard accounting task of matching goods received notes with orders and then with invoices. About 80% of their time is spent trying to find out why 20% of the set of three documents do not agree.

One way of improving the situation would have been to computerise the existing process to facilitate matching.

This would have helped, but BPR went further: why have invoices in the system at all?

> 'What if all the orders are entered onto a database on the computer? When goods arrive at the goods inwards department they either agree to goods that have been ordered or they don't. It's as simple as that. Goods that agree to an order are accepted and paid for. Goods that are not agreed are *sent back* to the supplier. There are no files of unmatched items and time is not wasted trying to sort out these files.'
>
> (Alan Lewin, 'Business process re-engineering', *CIMA Student,* February 1996)

2.7 Lewin notes the gains for the company: fewer staff wasting time, quicker payment for suppliers, lower stocks, and lower investment in working capital.

Principles of BPR

2.8 Hammer presents seven principles for BPR.

(a) Processes should be designed to achieve a desired *outcome* rather than focusing on existing *tasks*.

(b) Personnel who use the *output* from a process should *perform* the process. For example, a company could set up a database of approved suppliers; this would allow personnel who actually require supplies to order them themselves, perhaps using on-line technology, thereby eliminating the need for a separate purchasing function.

(c) Information processing should be *included* in the work which *produces* the information. This eliminates the differentiation between information gathering and information processing.

(d) Geographically *dispersed* resources should be treated as if they are *centralised*. This allows the benefits of centralisation to be obtained, for example, economies of scale through central negotiation of supply contracts, without losing the benefits of decentralisation, such as flexibility and responsiveness.

BPP PUBLISHING

(e) Parallel activities should be *linked* rather than *integrated*. This would involve, for example, co-ordination between teams working on different aspects of a single process.

(f) 'Doers' should be allowed to be *self-managing*. The traditional distinction between workers and managers can be abolished: decision aids such as expert systems can be provided where they are required.

(g) Information should be captured *once* at *source*. Electronic distribution of information makes this possible.

IT and BPR

2.9 Hammer and Champy are keen to emphasise that simply throwing IT at a problem does not cause it to be re-engineered. As illustrated above, merely computerising existing ways of doing things (such as processing invoices) is not necessarily the best solution.

2.10 IT is not the solution in itself, it is an *enabler*. BPR uses IT to allow a business to do things that it is *not* doing already. For example teleconferencing facilities might be introduced with the idea of cutting down on the costs of travelling to meetings, but a re-engineering approach takes the view that teleconferencing allows *more frequent* meetings. As Hammer and Champy put it, 'It is this disruptive power of technology, its ability to break the rules that limit how we conduct our work, that makes it critical to companies looking for competitive advantage.'

2.11 Here are the examples given by Hammer and Champy. (More details on databases, expert systems and so on, are given elsewhere in this text.)

(a) *Shared databases* mean that information can appear simultaneously in as many places as it is needed.

(b) *Expert systems* mean that a generalist can do the work of an expert.

(c) *Telecommunications networks* mean that businesses can simultaneously reap the rewards of centralisation and decentralisation.

(d) *Decision support tools* mean that decision making is part of everyone's job.

(e) *Wireless data communication and portable computers* mean that field staff can send and receive information wherever they are.

(f) *Interactive videodisks* mean that personal contact with buyers can be replaced by *effective* contact with buyers.

(g) *Automatic identification and tracking technology* means that things (such as distribution vehicles) tell you where they are, without you having to find out.

(h) *High performance computing* means that plans get revised instantaneously, not periodically.

Exercise 2

Think of a business application of each of the above 'disruptive technologies'.

Problems with BPR

2.12 Business process re-engineering received a great deal of attention in the mid 1990s and there are now concerns that it has been 'hyped' to such an extent that it has become misunderstood. According to a recent independent study of 100 European companies, the Cobra report, BPR has become allied in managers minds with narrow targets such as reductions in staff numbers and cost-cutting measures.

2.13 Champy suggests that management itself should be re-engineered. Managers are not, according to Champy, used to thinking in systems terms, so, instead of looking at the whole picture (which might affect their own jobs), they tend to seize on individual aspects of the organisation, such as re-engineering of processes.

2.14 It is argued that process re-engineering is really only a part of the wider picture. A report on an unnamed company suggests that the organisation sees four sets of parallel changes as being all-important to the transformation from a company which *satisfies* customers to a company that *delights* them and from a company which is a *competent* leading player to a company which is the *best* in its industry.

> '... first, breaking down barriers between its different disciplinary specialists and national units by a series of procedural and structural steps, of which the re-engineering of cross-unit processes is only one; second, developing an explicit set of values and behaviour guidelines which are subscribed to (or "shared") by everyone in the organisation; third, redefining the role of management in order to foster much more empowerment, responsibility and decisiveness at every level. All this requires the creation of the fourth factor: an unprecedented degree of openness and trust among managers.'
>
> *(Financial Times)*

2.15 Most commentators (including Hammer and Champy) now accept that BPR initiatives often failed, not because the emphasis on processes rather than the old functional hierarchies was wrong, but because BPR shows too little concern for human issues. The remaining sections in this chapter, and parts of the two chapters that follow, consider a variety of approaches and movements intended to redress this problem.

3 HARD AND SOFT PROBLEMS   12/94

3.1 Systems and the problems of systems design have both hard and soft properties. For instance when installing a new computer system, decisions about the *financial* effects of buying different sorts of equipment and software or about the logistics of installing cabling in an old office building are *hard* problems. *Soft* elements would include the effect of the new system on staff morale and the resultant changes in working practices.

Hard properties	Soft properties
Problem can be defined	Often difficult to define problem
Objectives/data can be objectively assessed	Taste, values, judgement, opinions concerned
Problem self-contained	Problem is fuzzy-edged
Information needs known	Unsure what is known and what is needed
Solution can be recognised	Unsure what solution would look like
'Things' oriented	'People' oriented
Standard solution techniques often available	No standard solution techniques available

Humans and soft systems

3.2 One of the principal characteristics of soft systems is that they incorporate, and depend on, some element of human behaviour. As noted above, they are 'people' oriented. The presence of people means that systems cannot be guaranteed to behave in a predictable manner. On the one hand, it is quite possible that humans will pursue goals which are not consistent with the goals of the organisation. On the other hand, there are constraints on the ability of humans to process information and make decisions.

Goals

3.3 Just as a system has goals, so too can subsystems. The subsystems of a business organisation will inevitably have their own objectives, which may conflict with the objectives of other subsystems, and even with the objectives of the system as a whole. *Sub-optimisation* or *sub-optimality* occurs when subsystems pursue their goals to the detriment of the system as a whole. It is important to note that a subsystem can be working at its highest level of efficiency, yet still be operating in a way which is harmful to the goals of the wider system of which it is a part.

3.4 Some examples of sub-optimality will illustrate this point.

   (a) A factory might use high technology plant in its operations, but if, as a consequence, employees are neither expected to use any skill nor able to work in a group with others, the optimisation of the technological subsystem would affect the social and psychological structure and lead to inefficiency amongst employees (low productivity or poor quality of output) so that sub-optimisation of the factory system might be the result.

   (b) A production manager might wish to operate at the same level of capacity each week, so as to avoid the costs of under-capacity working (idle time etc) and also of over-capacity (overtime premium etc) in any week. This level of operations would minimise production costs and help to maximise the efficiency of the production department. As a consequence, there may be inadequate stocks of goods to meet peak sales demand so that some sales volume might be lost; or else high volumes of finished goods stocks must be held, at considerable cost, so as to ensure that sales demand can always be met. If the savings in production costs are less than the contribution forgone from lost sales, or the extra costs of stockholding, the optimisation of the production subsystem would result in sub-optimality for the business as a whole.

3.5 Whenever a business organisation is divided into different parts (for example profit centres or divisions in a company, or different factories each producing the same items) there will always be a danger that managers will put all their effort into optimising the results of their subsystem (subsidiary, profit centre, factory etc) to the detriment of the results of the system as a whole (ie the company overall).

3.6 Sub-optimisation might be avoided by properly defining the aims of the overall system, and assigning objectives to subsystems which will help the overall system aims to be achieved. Where this is done, compromises will be made between the goals of the differing individual subsystems.

Humans, information and decision making   6/00

3.7 Davis and Olson, in summarising the works of a number of researchers, identify the following factors as having an effect on the way in which humans use information in the decision-making process and their approach to decision making itself.

   • Locus of control (internal - external)
   • Dogmatism (low - high)
   • Risk-taking propensity (low - high)
   • Extroversion - introversion
   • Tolerance for ambiguity (low - high)
   • Intelligence (low - high)
   • Quantitative abilities (low - high)
   • Verbal abilities (low - high)
   • Experience in decision-making
   • Task knowledge (low - high)
   • Age
   • Management level

3.8 The first four of these items can be explained as follows.

(a) The *locus of control* relates to the extent to which the individual perceives events as being controlled by internal operations rather than by external pressures. The individual is more likely to search for information for use in the decision-making process where he perceives events as being within the internal locus of control.

(b) Individuals who possess a higher degree of *dogmatism*, that is who hold firm beliefs and opinions and express them with conviction, are more likely to be confident in decision-making and less likely to search for information to use in making a decision.

(c) Those who are more willing to take risks, that is individual with a higher *risk-taking propensity*, are more likely to engage in information search activity.

(d) *Extroverts*, who are more likely to inter-react with the external environment than with their own emotions, are seen as having a better retention of information over short periods than introverts, and a lower degree of long-term retention.

Exercise 3

For each of the factors from (e) to (l) listed above, explain how you think that the characteristic in question affects the individual's decision-making behaviour.

Solution

(a) Individuals with a low *tolerance for ambiguity* are likely to require a higher volume of information and to make use of more concrete information.

(b) More *intelligent* individuals are often quicker at processing information and making decisions.

(c) Individuals who possess *quantitative abilities* (ie are more able to perform computations and use numeric reasoning) are more likely to use short-term memory and less likely to use long-term memory.

(d) Individuals with higher *verbal abilities* may have a more effective short-term memory.

(e) Those with more *experience* in formal decision-making situations may select information more effectively, but may be less confident.

(f) Those with a high degree of *task knowledge* may engage in less information search activity.

(g) *Older* individuals may engage in more information search activity and require more time in which to reach a decision.

(h) Individuals at a higher *level of management* may take decisions faster than those at lower levels.

4 THE SOCIO-TECHNICAL APPROACH   *12/95, 12/97*

4.1 A business organisation is not simply an organisational structure. The business structure is just one subsystem of the overall organisation. Trist and his associates at the Tavistock Institute suggested that an organisation is a *structured socio-technical system*, and that it consists of at least three subsystems.

(a) An *organisation structure*, including methods of working. For example, in a business organisation, a subsystem of the organisation structure is the accounts department, and subsystems of the accounts department will include sales ledger work, purchase ledger work, payroll, cash book, nominal ledger and management accounts.

(b) A *technological system* concerning the work to be done, and the machines, tools and other facilities available to do it.

(c) A *social system* concerning the people within the organisation, the ways they think and the ways they interact with each other.

4.2 A development of this is the Leavitt model, which describes the organisation as consisting of four interrelated components.

    (a) Task
    (b) Technology
    (c) Structure
    (d) People

4.3   There is a high degree of interdependence between these components. A change in one inevitably affects the others, in both predictable and unpredictable ways. (Some writers on management theory add a fifth component, culture.)

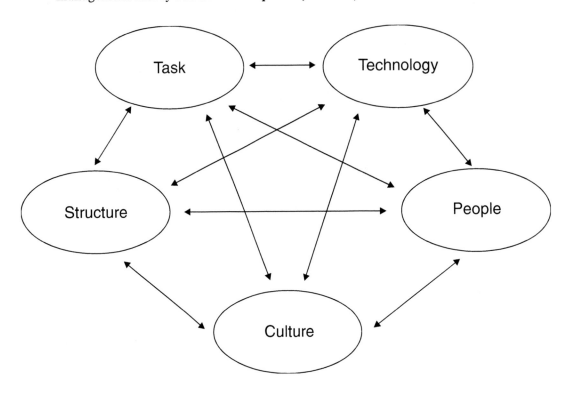

Implications

4.4   Where a 'hard' approach to systems development is used, the tendency is to emphasise the technology component and the task component. The structure component may be considered, but the people component and culture components are all too frequently overlooked.

4.5   As we shall see in more detail in the next section, employees are liable to think that a new system will put them out of a job, because the computer will perform routines that are currently done manually, and so reduce the need for human intervention. New systems might disrupt the established 'social system' or 'team spirit' in the office. Individuals who are used to working together might be separated into different groups, and individuals used to working on their own might be expected to join a group.

4.6   The socio-technical approach to planning and implementing organisational change recognises that people and the way they behave affects the organisation. Human characteristics such as attitudes, values and beliefs may affect such matters as productivity, adaptability and overall quality. The socio-technical approach is:

> 'a design philosophy that produces productivity, quality, co-ordination and control; but also provides a work environment and task structure in which people can achieve personal development and satisfaction'.   (Mumford, *Participative Systems Design*)

4.7   The approach is based on the principles of participation. The goal is not simply the production of a technically efficient system, but also the creation of conditions supporting a high level of job satisfaction. The socio-technical design process is shown in the diagram below.

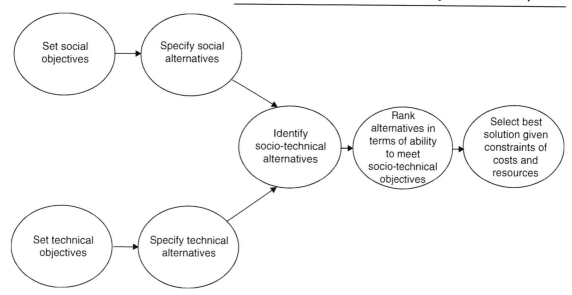

4.8 An assessment of the existing (pre-development) social system can be carried out by 'measuring' the job satisfaction of the individuals and groups to be affected. Social objectives can then be set with the aim of improving job satisfaction. Alternatives may involve the identification of different work groups, various approaches to task allocation and redesign of jobs/roles.

4.9 It may be felt that this type of approach is considered to be too indulgent towards staff, but good reasons for adopting the approach include the following.

(a) *Ethics*, adopting the principle that people have an inalienable right to control their own destinies and applying this to life in the workplace.

(b) *Expediency*, based on the experience that people who participate in the making of decisions are more likely to be committed to them.

(c) *Expertise*, in that the people who actually carry out tasks are the experts on those tasks.

(d) *Motivation*, as people are motivated by participation.

5 TECHNOLOGICAL CHANGE AND ITS EFFECT ON PEOPLE 12/97, 12/98

5.1 As indicated in the previous section, the consequences of technological changes are particularly felt in the world of work.

(a) *Semi-skilled jobs* will be taken over by robots and computers. There will be fewer jobs or more part-time jobs, and so less need for supervision.

(b) There may be *degrading of old skills*, or an ending to the need for old skills. New skills will be needed, and there will be more pressure on managers to provide training or re-training for staff. Management development too will be more important, to keep managers up-to-date, and to motivate them as advancement gets harder.

(c) As equipment becomes simpler to use, there could be opportunities for *greater flexibility* in manning, with one worker able to carry out more varied tasks. In manufacturing, there may be more continuous shift work working (24 hours a day), to keep expensive assets in constant use.

(d) Since more jobs will be *part-time*, there will be less need for full-time employees. More work will be sub-contracted, and full-time jobs axed. Managers will have to deal with external contractors instead of issuing directions to their own staff.

(e) Better communications systems, portable computers etc reduce the need for people to work together in an office. There will be more *working at home*. Several managers can then share the same small office, and to into work only occasionally.

BPP PUBLISHING

(f) Working at home is likely to speed up the progression towards 'sub-contracting', and some managers might become self-employed *consultants* with a 'main client' (their erstwhile employer) and a number of smaller clients who are picked up as the individual gradually markets his services more widely.

(g) Improved information systems should help managers to *plan and control* work more effectively (for example using databases and models for planning, and obtaining fast feedback for better control).

(h) Better information systems open up opportunities for more *centralisation* of decision making by top management and a reduced need for *middle managers*. The size of the middle management workforce might be reduced.

Behavioural issues

Job security and status

5.2 Employees might think that the new system will put them out of a job, because the computer will perform routines that are currently done manually, and so reduce the need for human intervention. An office staff of, say, 10 people might be reduced to 8 say, and the threat of being out of work would unsettle the entire office staff. Even when there is no threat of losing a job, a new system might make some staff, experienced in the existing system, feel that all their experience will be worthless when the new system goes live, and so they will lose 'status' within the office.

5.3 In some cases, the resistance to a new system might stem from a fear that it will result in a loss of status for the department concerned. For example, the management of the department concerned might believe that a computer system will give 'control' over information gathering and dissemination to another group in the organisation. *Dysfunctional behaviour* might therefore find expression in:

(a) Interdepartmental squabbling about access to information.

(b) A tendency to disregard the new sources of information, and to stick to old methods of collecting information instead.

Career prospects

5.4 In some instances, managers and staff might think that a new system will damage their career prospects by reducing the opportunities for promotion. When the effect of a system is to reduce the requirement for staff in middle management and supervisory grades, this could well be true. On the other hand, today's successful manager should be able to adapt to information technology, and to develop a career means having to be flexible, accepting change rather than resisting it.

Social change in the office

5.5 New systems might disrupt the established 'social system' or 'team spirit' in the office. Individuals who are used to working together might be separated into different groups, and individuals used to working on their own might be expected to join a group. Office staff used to moving around and mixing with other people in the course of their work might be faced with the prospect of having to work much more in isolation at a keyboard, unable to move around the office as much. Where possible, new systems should be designed so as to leave the 'social fabric' of the workplace undamaged. Group attitudes to change should then be positive rather than negative.

Bewilderment

5.6 It is easy for individuals to be confused and bewildered by change. The systems analyst must explain the new system fully, clearing up doubts, inviting and answering questions, etc from a very early stage in systems investigation onwards through the design stages to eventual implementation.

Fear of depersonalisation

5.7 Staff may be afraid that the computer will 'take over' and they will be reduced to being operators chained to the machine, losing the ability to introduce the 'human touch' to the work they do.

5.8 Dysfunctional behaviour might manifest itself in the antagonism of operating staff towards data processing specialists who are employed to design and introduce a computer system. It might take the form of:

(a) An unwillingness to explain the details of the current system, or to suggest weaknesses in it that the new system might eradicate. Any such antagonism would impair the system design process.

(b) A reluctance to be taught the new system.

(c) A reluctance to help with introducing the new system.

5.9 A new system may reveal weaknesses in the previous system. If individuals feel that they are put under pressure by the revelation of any such deficiencies, they might try to find fault with the new system too. When fault-finding is not constructive - ie not aimed at improving the system - it will be dysfunctional in its consequences.

5.10 In extreme cases, dysfunctional behaviour might take a more drastic, aggressive form. Individuals might show a marked reluctance to learn how to handle the new equipment, they might be deliberately slow keying in data, or they might even damage the equipment in minor acts of vandalism.

6 MANAGING CHANGE   *6/97, 12/98, 6/00*

6.1 To overcome the human problems with systems design and implementation, management and systems analysts must recognise them, and do what they can to resolve them. The following checklist is suggested as a starting point.

Keeping staff informed

6.2 Employees should be kept fully informed about plans to install the new system, how events are progressing and how the new system will affect what people do.

Explanations

6.3 It should be explained to staff why 'change is for the better'.

Participation

6.4 User department employees should be encouraged to participate fully in the design of the system, when the system is a tailor-made one. Participation should be genuine.

(a) Their suggestions about problems with the existing system should be fully discussed.

(b) The systems analyst's ideas for a new system should be discussed with them.

(c) Their suggestions for features in the new system should be welcomed.

Nature of the work

6.5 Staff should be informed that they will be spared boring, mundane work because of the possibility of automating such work and so will be able to take on more interesting, demanding and challenging work.

Skills

6.6   Employees should be told that they will be able to learn new skills which will make them more attractive candidates either for internal promotion or on the external labour market. For example, experience with using databases or spreadsheet models could greatly enhance an office worker's experience.

Training

6.7   A training programme for staff should be planned in advance of the new systems being introduced. If there are to be job losses, or a redeployment of staff, these should be arranged in full consultation with the people concerned.

Work patterns

6.8   Careful attention should be given to:

(a)   The design of work organisation.
(b)   The developments or preservation of 'social work groups'.
(c)   The inter-relationship between jobs and responsibilities in the new system.

Planning

6.9   Change should be planned and managed. Reductions in jobs should be foreseen, and redundancies can be avoided if plans are made well in advance (eg staff can be moved to other job vacancies in the organisation). Training (and retraining) of staff should be organised.

Office experts, Help Desks and Information Centres

6.10   A member of the staff should be appointed as the office expert or 'guru' in the system, to whom other members of staff can go to ask for help or advice. When the software is bought as an off-the-shelf package, this office expert should be made the person who contacts the software supplier about any problems with the system. Larger organisations have Help Desks or Information Centres, described in more detail in Chapter 5.

The systems analyst

6.11   When systems are designed in-house, the systems analyst should:

(a)   Produce changes gradually, giving time for personnel to accept the changes.
(b)   Build up a good personal relationship with the people he or she has to work with.
(c)   Persuade management to give sound guarantees for the future.
(d)   Work towards getting employees to accept change as a matter of course.
(e)   Be willing to listen to and act on criticisms of the system under design.

Familiarisation

6.12   The system should not be introduced in a rush. Users of the system should be given time to become familiar with it. Implementation by means of 'parallel running' might be advisable.

Confidence

6.13   Confidence between the systems analyst and operational staff should be built up over time.

Management support

6.14   The systems analyst should have the full and clearly expressed support of senior management. There should be no danger that his authority could be undermined.

Case example: Change Management at Abbey National plc

There have been many internal changes in Abbey National since becoming plc.

- Change from 49 to 5 mortgage administration centres
- Set up of 3 Teleservice Centres
- Introduction of postal accounts
- Reduction in the number of branches
- Combine administrations of Scottish Mutual and Abbey National Life under same customer service structure and systems

People do not resist change - they resist what they perceive that they will lose. Perception = reality.

Communication is critical and should be planned and managed by those who are communicating change. **The effects of good communication:-**

- Reduces uncertainty
- Builds commitment
- Shapes assumptions
- Involve the people in the process

COMMUNICATE TO GAIN COMMITMENT - DON'T GET THE COMMUNICATION WRONG!

The communication process

Step 1.   Project team 'sell' concept to managers and supervisors

Step 2.   Supervisors present to their team with support from project team

Step 3.   Two day briefing/training for supervisors

Step 4.   On-ground support for supervisors throughout implementation

Step 5.   Remove support gradually

Step 6.   Continuous improvement course

Step 7.   Formal handover to managers

Change issues encountered at Abbey National plc

- Supervisors confidence destroyed (security blanket removed)
- No PC experience to operate spreadsheets
- Task of planning day takes too long, no time to do other work
- This would not work in our area because we are different
- Frightened of raising issues
- Focus on backlogs - no time to do process management

Summary

- Involve the people who are impacted al all stages
- Caveat on initial stages or market sensitive projects
- Communicate, communicate, communicate - tailored, early, often - if you have nothing to say people may believe you have a hidden agenda
- Consider the cultural differences
- Do not forget managers

What if you do not have the time to go through all the stages and give the level of support people require?

- Anticipate as many issues as possible
- Mobilise maximum power
- Expect/prepare for resistance

Source: *CIMA articles database*

6.15 The case example below provides a good illustration of some of the *barriers* to innovation in many companies. You may have some sympathy with it if you have ever had a good idea, only to see it ignored by more senior management.

Case example: Encouraging innovation

Whatever happened to your last brilliant idea? Maybe it was nurtured and developed and is now making your company lots of money as a new product, service or improved way of doing things.

More likely it shrivelled and died, leaving you feeling slightly jaded and that much less enthusiastic about suggesting the next brilliant idea.

One of three reasons was probably behind the failure.

- The idea was greeted with managerial contempt

- It ran into departmental opposition

- It expired through boredom after being subjected to months of time-wasting scrutiny by a 'taskforce'

Just one company in 10 can claim to be truly innovative, found research jointly conducted by government and industry in the UK four years ago. Since then, innovation has become a tediously over-used buzzword - part of the standard preamble to every chief executive's set-piece speech on remaining competitive.

Differences in performance cannot be accounted for by sector ... but are down to, among other factors, organisational culture and well-defined 'idea management processes'.

Chris Satterthwaite, an HHCL partner, believes ground rules for encouraging innovation within a company are very important. An 'anything goes' culture 'allows everything but gets nowhere,' he says. These rules seek to minimise the three main barriers to new thinking.

First, if managerial contempt is one reason for the failure of new ideas, simply take away the managers, he says: 'At HHCL, the responsibility for generating strategy and ideas is shared equally among a project team of equals ... The rule within this group is always to demonstrate positive intent. Ideas can be dismissed *only* by someone having a better one.'

Second, if departmental opposition is another hurdle, abolish departments. Project teams at the agency 'always have mixed blood ... each person reports to the team, not to a departmental head', thus avoiding hidden departmental agendas.

Finally, if lethargy and time-wasting, in the form of taskforces and protracted research are the killers, do without them. Instead, find ways of keeping close to the customer through constant contact.

Financial Times

6.16 To a large extent, encouraging innovation is a matter of changing the culture of an organisation. This has to be done *from the very top* – the senior managers who have the power to veto new developments or to refuse to allow inventive people adequate time to develop their ideas – *to the very bottom* – the junior members of staff who complain about the way things are done now, rather than *seeing* that things could be done differently, *bothering* to develop new ideas, and having the energy to convince management of the desirability of their ideas.

6.17 Innovation depends on *research* and ready *access* and *receptiveness* to new technology and ideas. Therefore *information systems* can help to encourage innovation in a variety of ways.

(a) The use of communications hardware and software - such as fax machine, e-mail, the Internet, and cellular phones - facilitates dialogue among employees.

(b) Given that new technologies such as the Internet are one of the chief sources of new ideas for new ways of doing business the rate of technology diffusion in a company (in other words the company's takeup of improved products and processes, such as software that can automatically generate web pages) is a key factor in what new ideas come forward.

(c) Formal systems can be set up to help staff to watch the competition and assess their own operations in comparison.

(d) The system needs to provide a research base. For instance information about the size and customer profile of different market sectors is crucial to the design of a new product; so is information about the costs of different approaches. Ideas that are good in principle could easily end up being vetoed because the inventor did not have access to key information that is used in the decision making process.

(e) Formal communication links can be set up with known providers of research information (for instance trade journals, university departments).

(f) Staff need to be *trained* in creative confrontation or healthy disagreement: divergent thinking stimulates creativity. The information system may help either by offering formal 'on-line' training material, or simply by being the medium through which debates are carried on.

(g) Systems development 'methodologies' that may generate new ideas (such as soft systems methodology or business process engineering) are heavily dependent upon good information systems and good systems for analysing information (good in the sense that they provide 'good' information, in all senses of the term.)

7 THE HYBRID MANAGER

7.1 The term *hybrid manager* was invented by Michael Earl of Templeton College, Oxford, who noticed that whenever an IT project was successfully implemented, there was a person at the heart of the development who displayed certain experience and characteristics.

(a) An understanding of the business and what was required within the business

(b) A technical competence that enabled them to understand what was required in technical terms, including the scope of what was being planned.

(c) Excellent social skills, listening, understanding, negotiating and persuading.

7.2 In the 1990s the term was much used, but it is less often seen today. This may be because it is no longer particularly unusual for people to combine familiarity with IT with other managerial and change agent skills. However, the frequency of failed IT projects, or projects that do not deliver what was expected, suggests otherwise.

7.3 Anne Brackley ('Whatever happened to hybrid managers? The short history of the hybrids', *The Computer Bulletin*, December 1996) makes a case for the hybrid manager.

> It is time for a redefinition of the project manager's role, and I believe that managerial hybridisation is still a key requirement. However, this hybridisation will combine familiarity with IT and appreciation of its strategic importance to organisations (now de rigeur for successful managers) with knowledge of ... *human and organisational* factors, in particular the principles of *good job design*. Two more characters have come onto the stage, both of whom are in archetypal managerial roles: the organisation's HR manager, and the specialist behavioural scientist who will provide a resource of expertise just as the IT specialist will.

BPP PUBLISHING

Chapter roundup

- Organisational theories are models of the way organisations actually behave, looking at issues such as structure, culture, motivation and management functions. Examples include scientific management, the classical school, the human relations approach and the contingency school. 'New' theories are put forward every day on themes such as change, empowerment, customer focus and so on.

- Corporate culture is seen by some as a new school of thought in management theory. Common information cultures are the functional culture, the sharing culture, the inquiring culture and the discovery culture.

- Business process re-engineering describes an approach to doing away with old-fashioned and inefficient business processes. It can involve a fundamental redesign of the way in which an organisation functions. The focus is on desired outcomes rather than on tasks.

- The unstructured problems encountered in organisations are sometimes referred to as soft problems. It is usually difficult to define soft problems, because many issues, revolving around such matters as differing interpretations or differing objectives, come into play.

- Soft systems incorporate, and depend on, some element of human behaviour. They are 'people' oriented.

- The socio-technical approach recognises that a business structure is not simply an organisational structure, but is composed of three interrelated subsystems: the organisation structure, the technological system and the social system. The Leavitt model identifies four interrelated components: task, technology, structure and people. A fifth element, culture, is sometimes added. It is apparent that many organisations emphasise only the task and technology components.

- The socio-technical approach is a participative approach to systems design. It focuses as much on job satisfaction as on technical performance.

- Technological change has a marked effect on the working environment. Staff are likely to have a number of concerns, raising from fear of redundancy to dislike of new working patterns and methods.

- There are many ways in which systems analysts can try to overcome such concerns, including good communication, training, good job design, sensitive handling of redundancies and so on.

- The 'hybrid' IT manager combines familiarity with IT and appreciation of its strategic importance to organisations with knowledge of and skills in dealing with human and organisational factors.

Test your knowledge

1   What do organisation theories attempt to do? (see para 1.2)

2   What are the characteristics of the 'new' organisation? (1.20)

3   Identify four types of dysfunctional information behaviour. (1.27)

4   What is a process? (2.4)

5   What are seven principles of BPR? (2.8)

6   Why have BPR initiatives failed? (2.14)

7   Distinguished between hard and soft problems (3.1)

8   How do people vary in their use of information? (3.7)

9   What are the three sub-systems identified by the socio-technical approach? (4.1)

10   How might people respond to change? (5.2 - 5.10)

11   Suggest six features of good change management (6.2 - 6.14)

12   What is a hybrid manager? (7.1)

Now try illustrative questions 6, 24, 35 and 36 at the end of the Study Text

Chapter 4

TECHNOLOGICAL AND ENVIRONMENTAL INFLUENCES

This chapter covers the following topics.

1   The information technology environment

2   Human-computer interaction

3   Communications

4   Multimedia

5   The Internet

6   Environmental scanning

Introduction

In this chapter we look at a number of general technological developments that are having an impact upon information systems, and also briefly consider the effect of other environmental influences. You studied office automation at Foundation level for *Information Systems*, but you probably need to update your knowledge, particularly on the subject of telecommunications developments and the Internet.

It would be possible to write a whole book on the important topic of *human computer interaction*. Here we concentrate on two key issues: dialogue design and user-friendliness.

More technological developments that give rise to strategic choices are considered in Chapter 5.

---

1   THE INFORMATION TECHNOLOGY ENVIRONMENT   6/98

Manual systems v computerised systems

1.1   There are a number of reasons why, in many situations, manual office systems are less beneficial than computerised systems.

(a)   Labour productivity is usually lower, particularly in routine processing tasks.

(b)   Processing is slower where large volumes of data need to be dealt with.

(c)   Slower processing means that information that could be provided, such as statistical analyses, will not be provided at all, because there is not time.

(d)   The risk of errors is greater, especially in repetitive work like payroll calculations.

(e)   Information is generally less accessible. Unless there is a great deal of duplication of records access to information is restricted to one user at a time. Paper files can easily be mislaid or buried in in-trays, in which case the information they contain is not available at all. This can mean inconvenience and wasted time internally and may prevent the organisation from providing its services to customers.

(f)   It is difficult to make corrections or alterations. If a document contains errors or needs updating it is often necessary to recreate the whole document from scratch, rather than just a new version with the relevant details changed. If several copies of a paper record are stored in different places each of them will need to be changed: this can easily be overlooked and so some parts of the system will be using out of date or inaccurate data. Unless changes are dated, it may not be clear which is the correct version.

(g) Quality of output is less consistent and not as high as well-designed computer output. At worst, handwritten records may be illegible and so completely useless. Badly presented information may fail to communicate because key points will not have their intended impact.

(h) Paper based systems are generally very bulky both to handle and to store, and office space is expensive.

Information technology

1.2 Many of an organisation's MIS activities are enhanced through the use of information technology. Information technology is a term used to describe the coming together of *computer* technology with *data transmission* technology, to revolutionise information systems. Cheap computer hardware, based on microchip technology with ever-increasing power and capacity, has been harnessed to an extensive telecommunications network. IT can be said to involve the electronic acquisition, storage and dissemination of vocal, pictorial, textual and numerical information.

1.3 Computers are able to 'talk' to each other over telecommunications links, or can transmit data to and from remote terminals. Remote terminals can send data to a computer and receive output messages. Small computers have spread rapidly in the home and the office. Information technology also involves other equipment and information transmission systems, not just computers; for example, there is electronic mail, facsimile transfers, cable television, teletext, electronic telephone exchanges, satellite communications and data transmission using laser technology.

1.4 The emergence of the *electronic office* means that management information can be provided quicker and more cheaply than before, and that managers can obtain greater involvement in information production and report design.

Exercise 1

Describe the main features of the two most widely used pieces of 'office' software, the spreadsheet and the word processor.

Solution

You should have covered this for your Foundation level *Information Systems* exam.

2 HUMAN-COMPUTER INTERACTION

2.1 In spite of the above, people *like* manual methods of working and often find it more convenient to jot down notes with pen and paper or tap out a few figures with a calculator than to use a computer. This is especially true of people who have not been brought up with computers: at present in the UK this means almost everybody over the age of about 25, the bulk of the working population.

2.2 People also prefer communicating face to face with their colleagues, not just to fulfil their social needs but also because it remains the most effective means of communication for many everyday tasks.

2.3 Computers can waste time, especially if the user is not properly trained or if the system has deficiencies such as limited access to printers.

2.4 For this reason one of the key concerns in modern information systems design is to make it easy and 'natural' to use a computer.

Case example

Consider this extract from a review of a book called *The Squandered Computer* by Paul Strassmann.

For every success story - for every Federal Express and SABRE - just how many IT failures have arisen from popular delusions about computers? For every large-scale project that has been implemented successfully, how many have been cancelled or have ended inconclusively?

The answers are chilling, as Strassmann shows in his extrapolations from survey data about failed software projects.

Indeed, employees can misuse computers in a number of ways. How many times can people revise a word-processing document, manipulate a spreadsheet, or polish a presentation before they hit the point of diminishing returns on their time? Is productivity really increased in this context? When you multiply all those diminishing returns by the tens of thousands of personal computers in a large company, what is the real value-to-waste ratio?

The human computer interface   *12/97*

2.5   Most people operate computers using a keyboard and a screen. The important thing about screen and keyboard is the capacity for 'feedback' between user and computer that they provide, allowing the system to be highly flexible, interactive and conversational.

2.6   The way the keyboard is used, and what you would expect to see on the screen, will therefore depend on the particular strategy for 'screen dialogue' that the software adopts.

2.7   This dialogue between the system and its users might be a central feature of the running of a program, and the term conversational mode describes a method of operation in which the operator appears to be carrying on a continual interactive dialogue with the computer, receiving immediate replies to input messages.

2.8   Broadly speaking, there are three ways of using a keyboard with VDU to input data. Any system is likely to use a combination of the three.

(a)   By selecting options from a menu.
(b)   By filling in a form.
(c)   Using a graphical user interface.

Menu selection

2.9   A menu is a list of items to choose from. For example, the menu for a sales ledger system might include the following options - shown as icons.

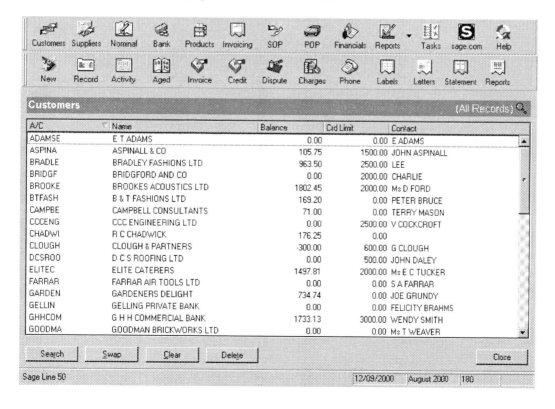

BPP
PUBLISHING

Form filling

2.10 With form filling the screen is landscaped for specific user requirements. Relevant data fields may be set up within an on-screen skeleton form.

2.11 Screen formatting for this purpose usually includes several features.

- Different colours for different screen areas
- Larger characters for titles
- Paging or scrolling depending on the volume of information
- Input boxes or fields for each item

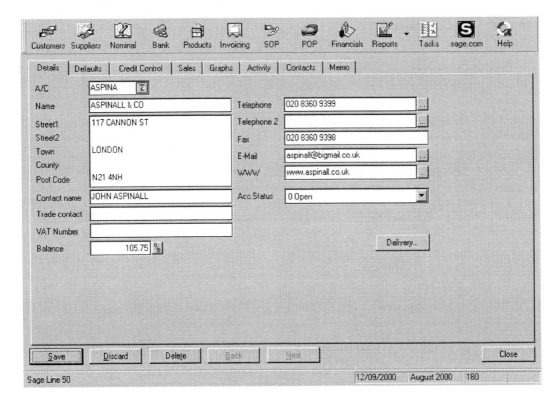

Graphical user interfaces

6/99

2.12 Graphical user interfaces (GUIs) were designed to make computers more 'user-friendly'.

2.13 A GUI involves the use of two design ideas and two operating methods which can be remembered by the abbreviation WIMP. This stands for 'Windows, Icons, Mouse, Pull-down menu' and is an environment which offers a method of accessing the computer without using the keyboard. Dialogue is conducted through images rather than typed text.

2.14 Graphical user interfaces have become the principal means by which humans communicate with machines.

Windows (the generic term rather than the operating system)

2.15 This basically means that the screen can be divided into sections, 'windows' of flexible size, which can be opened and closed. This enables two or more documents to be viewed and edited together, and sections of one to be inserted into another. For instance figures from an Excel spreadsheet can be pasted directly into a Word word-processing document.

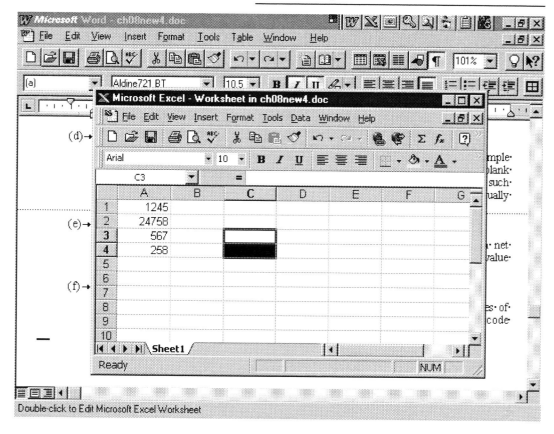

Icons

2.16   An icon is an image of an object used to represent a function or a file in an obvious way. For instance Windows based packages use a picture of a printer which is simply clicked to start the printing process.

2.17   Both icons and windows are shown in the illustration over the page.

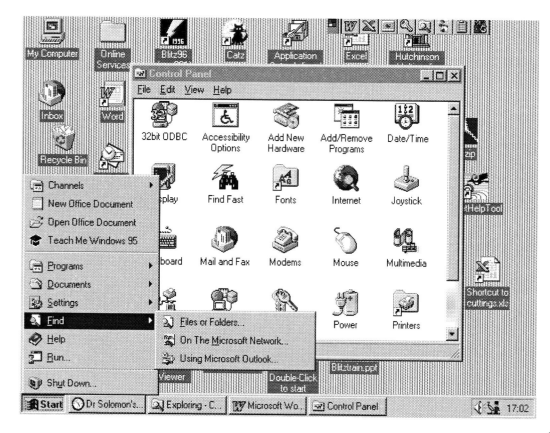

BPP
PUBLISHING

Mouse

2.18 As the mouse moves around on the desktop a *pointer* (cursor) on the screen mimics its movements. A mouse can be used to pick out and activate an icon or button, to highlight a block of text for deletion/insertion, or to drag data from one place on the screen to another. It also has buttons which are clicked to execute the current command.

The cursor

2.19 The cursor (an arrow, line or 'blob') shows you on screen the point in your text that will be affected (written on, deleted, moved etc.) by your keyboard entries.

2.20 The cursor is a 'marker' of where the computer's 'attention' is at any given moment. It is generally moved about the screen by means of direction keys on the keyboard or a mouse.

Pull-down menu

2.21 A menu-bar across the top of the screen is a feature of many software packages. Using the mouse to move the pointer to the required item in the menu, the pointer 'pulls down' a subsidiary menu. The pointer and mouse can then be used to select (input) the required item (output) on the pulled-down menu, which may lead to more menus.

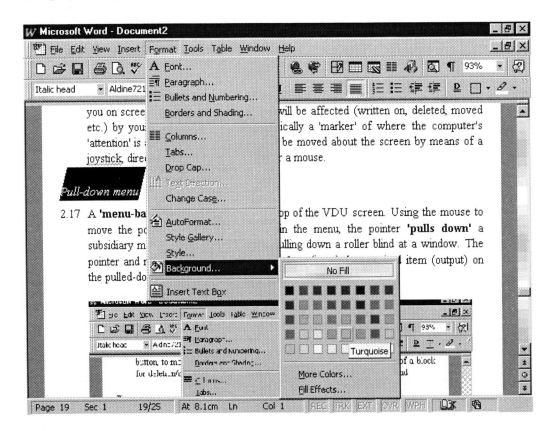

User-friendliness

2.22 The following features all improve the user-friendliness of a system.

Ease of data entry

2.23 It must be easy for the user to input data into the system. This has several aspects.

(a) The data entry screen should be designed in the same logical order as the input form (source document).

The user should be able to work down the form in a logical order with the screen cursor moving down the screen to the next input field in the same order. Data entry will be inefficient if the user has to search around for the item to go into the next field.

(b) The data entry screen should be clearly designed, so that, for example, input fields are highlighted, perhaps by colour, flashing or reverse colouring. The position of the cursor should be clear.

Titles of fields should be easy to read and should match the titles used on source documents.

(c) Default entries should be provided for items such as the date (usually today's date) or the standard VAT rate.

The defaults will then be entered automatically unless the user wishes to change them. This can speed up data entry considerably.

Intuitiveness

2.24 It should be possible for users to make reasonable guesses about what they need to do.

2.25 For example in Windows a program is started simply by double-clicking on an icon that represents that program in an obvious way ('W' for Microsoft Word; a letter tray for e-mail). The user does not need to know where the program is stored on disk or have to type in command words to start up the application.

Design principles consistent with other modules/packages

2.26 Many computer users use more than one part of a system. Even in a non-accounting environment, an increasing number of users must be able to operate a spreadsheet and WP, and, in an accounting environment, it is useful for staff to have 'transferable' skills.

2.27 This means that the more systems can 'look and feel' the same and operate in a similar way (eg F1 is always 'Help', F2 is always 'Save' etc), the easier it will be for users to switch between packages/modules without going through a huge learning curve.

2.28 One of the advantages of the Windows environment is that packages specifically written for Windows are generally similar in design. This reduces training time and costs and makes skills transferable.

On-screen help

2.29 It is increasingly common to find software pre-loaded onto computers without manuals being provided or to find that, when manuals *are* provided, they are rarely referred to. This is because packages invariably include on-screen help.

2.30 If a user requires help, he or she requests it at the touch of a single key (eg F1) or by clicking on 'Help' on a pull-down menu. The help screen is usually context specific, so that, for example, if a particular dialogue box in a package is open, the system will offer help related to relevant functions and options. Problems can be resolved more quickly and productivity improved.

2.31 Help files are often written in hypertext, which provides links between topics. The user can click on words that are underlined and move directly to another topic.

Use of dialogue boxes and on-screen prompts

2.32 The more critical the potential effect of a command issued by the user, the more important it is that the user is not allowed simply to start a process by mistake.

BPP
PUBLISHING

2.33   Thus where commands such as delete a file, format a disk or update a ledger are being made, user-friendly software should issue a warning that such an operation is about to be carried out, *after* the initial command is entered.

2.34   This gives the user a second chance to confirm that the command was intended and that the computer is indeed required to carry out the specified process.

2.35   In turn this means that users will spend less time attempting to reverse the effects of unintentionally-used commands.

Escapability

2.36   An inexperienced user, or someone 'exploring' in a hit-or-miss way to try to find the right command, might find himself or herself faced with a command which he or she *knows* to be the wrong one.

2.37   It is important that an option is available which offers a harmless alternative to following the unwanted route. Thus in Windows there is usually a 'Cancel' button next to the 'OK' button in each dialogue box. Selection of 'Cancel' enables the user to return to where he or she was before the wrong path was taken. An alternative is often the 'Esc' key on the keyboard. These options are to be preferred to simply switching off the machine, which can have catastrophic consequences.

Customisation

2.38   Many users find that they perform the same series of actions so frequently that it becomes tedious to click their way through menus and dialogue boxes. User-friendly software will recognise this and offer fast alternatives.

   (a)   'Shortcut keys' (typically pressing the Ctrl key together with one or more other keys) can be assigned to standard actions so that they are performed literally at the touch of a button.

   (b)   A series of actions can be 'recorded' as they are done in the form of 'macros', which can then be activated using a shortcut key or user-defined button.

Exercise 2

Look at the various illustrations of screens in this chapter and elsewhere in this book. How many 'user friendly features' can you identify?

Solution

Look at the buttons, menus, keyboard shortcut hints (eg File means press Alt + F on the keyboard to bring up the file menu), scalability of windows, system messages, Help facilities, and so on. You may have found lots of other examples.

---

3   COMMUNICATIONS
6/99

3.1   Some people have referred to the past decade as the 'telecoms revolution'. Developments in communications and computing technology have converged changing the ways in which many of us communicate with each other.

Exercise 3

You should be able to explain certain telecoms terms like 'modem' and 'ISDN' from your earlier studies for *Information Systems* at Foundation level, and you should also be able to describe the features of, say, fax and Electronic Data Interchange (EDI).

Mobile communications

3.2 Radio networks for portable telephone communications, also known as 'cellular phones', started up in the late 1980s and have boomed since.

3.3 Digital networks are gradually replacing analogue transmission systems. These are better able to support data transmission then the older analogue networks, with higher transmission speeds and less likelihood of data corruption.

3.4 This means that a salesperson out on the road can send or receive a fax or e-mail. A laptop PC (with internal modem) could be connected to a cellular phone for this purpose. Alternatively, a combined palmtop computer and cellular phone device, or a WAP cellular phone, could be used.

3.5 The mobile services available are increasing all the time. Here are some examples.

(a) Messaging services such as: voice mail; short message service (SMS) which allows text messages of up to 160 characters to be transmitted over a standard digital phone; and paging services.

(b) Call handling services such as: call barring, conference calls and call divert.

(c) Corporate services such as: integrated numbering, so that people have a single contact number for both the phone on their desk and for their mobile; and virtual private networks that incorporate mobile phones as well as conventional desktop phones, so that users can dial internal extension numbers directly.

(d) Internet access is possible, through Wireless Application Protocol (WAP) or similar technology, although the speed of transmission when downloading information is relatively slow at present.

(e) The 'roam' functionality provided on many cellular phone networks allows people to contact each other at a modest cost using a mobile phone from virtually any point on Earth.

Electronic mail (E-mail)

3.6 The term 'electronic mail', or e-mail, is used to describe various systems of sending data or messages electronically via a telephone or data network and a central computer.

BPP PUBLISHING

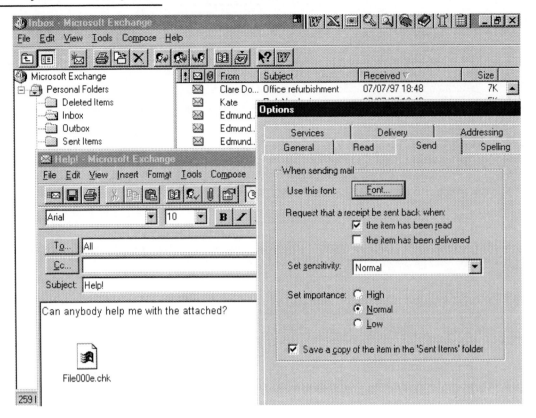

3.7 E-mail has the following advantages.

    (a) Speed (transmission, being electronic, is almost instantaneous). E-mail is far faster than post or fax. It is a particular time-saver when communicating with people overseas.

    (b) Economy (no need for stamps etc). E-mail is reckoned to be 20 times cheaper than fax.

    (c) Efficiency (a message is prepared once but can be sent to thousands of employees at the touch of a button).

    (d) Security (access can be restricted by the use of passwords).

    (e) Documents can be retrieved from word-processing and graphics packages.

    (f) Electronic delivery and read receipts can be requested.

    (g) E-mail can be used to send documents and reports as well as short memos, for instance by 'attaching' a file.

3.8 Typically information is 'posted' by the sender to a central computer which allocates disk storage as a 'mailbox' for each user. The information is subsequently 'collected' by the receiver from the mailbox.

    (a) Senders of information thus have documentary evidence that they have given a piece of information to the recipient and that the recipient has picked up the message.

    (b) Receivers are not disturbed by the information when it is sent (as they would be by face-to-face meetings or phone calls), but collect it later at their convenience.

3.9 Each user will typically have password protected access to his own inbox, outbox and filing system. He can prepare and edit text and other documents using a word processing function, and send mail using standard headers and identifiers to an individual or a group of people on a prepared distribution list.

3.10 E-mail systems may serve one department or the whole organisation. It is also possible to connect an e-mail system to outside organisations.

3.11 E-mail is now widely used both within organisations and between them. (See the Internet section later this chapter.) A recent development is on-line chat that enables instant text communication in private chat-rooms when both users are on-line.

Exercise 4

E-mail can also be abused, a topic of some concern in businesses at present. Can you think how?

Solution

One problem is that employees can look as if they are working hard at their computers whereas in fact they are just exchanging office gossip, jokes and so on, with their colleagues.

A more serious problem is 'flame mail', where abusive -mail is used to harass colleagues or bully subordinates.

Voice mail

3.12 Voice mail (or v-mail) systems enable the caller's message to be recorded at the recipient's voice mail box (similar to a mail box in an e-mail system).

3.13 The main advantage of the system is that it only requires a telephone to be used. No typing or keying in is necessary. A voice mail message is basically a spoken memo: for the person sending the message it is much more convenient than typing it or having it typed and then faxing it.

3.14 Voice mail can be used for different situations.

 (a) To contact sales representatives 'in the field'.
 (b) To leave messages in departments in different time zones.
 (c) In organisations where employees might be working away at a client's premises.

Voice messaging

3.15 This is a kind of switchboard answerphone that takes the place of a human receptionist, or at least relieves the receptionist of the burden of dealing with common, straightforward calls.

3.16 Typically, when a call is answered a recorded message tells the caller to dial the extension they want if they know it, or to hold if they want to speak to the operator. Sometimes other options are offered, such as 'press 2 if you want to know about X service and 3 if you want to know about Y'.

3.17 Such systems work well if callers frequently have similar needs and these can be accurately anticipated.

3.18 They can be frustrating for callers with non-standard enquiries, however, and many people find the impersonality of responding to an answerphone unappealing. Badly set up systems can result in the caller being bounced about from one recorded message to another and never getting through to the person they want to deal with.

Case example: Interactive voice response (IVR)

Several pharmaceutical companies have installed sophisticated interactive voice response systems to deal with enquiries from doctors, chemists or patients. For example some allow the caller to press a number on their handset and have details of possible side effects sent back to them by fax.

Computer Telephony Integration (CTI)

3.19 Computer Telephony Integration (CTI) systems gather information about callers such as their telephone number and customer account number or demographic information (age, income, interests etc). This is stored on a customer database and can be called up and sent to the screen of the person dealing with the call, perhaps before the call has even been put through.

3.20 Thus sales staff dealing with hundreds of calls every day might appear to remember individual callers personally and know in advance what they are likely to order. Order forms with key details entered already can be displayed on screen automatically, saving time for both the sales staff and the caller.

3.21 Alternatively a busy manager might note that an unwelcome call is coming in on the 'screen pop' that appears on her PC and choose to direct it to her voice mail box rather than dealing with it at once.

3.22 As another example, a bank might use CTI to prompt sales people with changes in share prices and with the details of the investors they should call to offer dealing advice.

Computer conferencing and bulletin boards

3.23 A computer conferencing system is similar to e-mail but more expensive, in that there is a huge central mailbox on the system where all persons connected to the system can deposit messages for everyone to see, and, in turn, read what other people have left in the system.

3.24 Computer conferencing can be appropriate for a team of individuals at different locations to compare notes. It becomes a way of keeping track of progress on a project between routine team meetings.

3.25 Computer conferencing systems can become organisation-wide bulletin boards, where members can leave messages of general import. A bulletin board system can be a way of re-establishing some of the social ties of office life which are alleged to have suffered from computerisation.

Videoconferencing

3.26 Videoconferencing is the use of computer and communications technology to conduct meetings in which several participants, perhaps in different parts of the world, are linked up via computer and a video system. (Conference calls on a telephone system, where several people can converse at the same time, are a precursor of teleconferencing.)

3.27 Videoconferencing has become increasingly common as the ready availability of chips capable of processing video images has brought the service to desktop PCs at reasonable cost. More expensive systems feature a separate room with several video screens, which show the images of those participating in a meeting.

3.28 Even if the technology used is expensive, it is far cheaper when compared to the cost in management time and air fares of business travel.

Digital TV

3.29 Digital television started in the UK in 1998, with two suppliers Sky-digital and On-digital. Transmitting by digital signal rather than by conventional (analogue) dramatically increases the number of services which can be delivered.

3.30 Digital broadcasting allows viewers greater choice over how and when they watch, and allows them to interact with programmes. Using digital flexibility and extra capacity, broadcasters are able to offer additional programmes, information, sound and graphics, to complement what is being shown. The first application of this technology was seen with Sky Sports interactive service launched in July 1999. This allows viewers to select camera angles, view on-demand replays and access a range of related statistical information through on-screen menus and their remote control.

3.31 The take-up rate for digital television has been slower than expected. This is largely because the vast majority of televisions require a set-top box to be fitted to be able to receive digital broadcasts At present only top of the range televisions are manufactured with in built digital receivers. However, as the range of digital services expands, the public is expected to increasingly buy digital capable television sets, and analogue broadcasts are expected to cease completely within ten years.

3.32 The concept of interactive television with on-screen menus, and the imminent availability of Internet availability through digital television providers will see the blurring of the distinction between PCs and televisions.

4 MULTIMEDIA   *6/00*

4.1 The concept of multimedia is the delivery of text, sound and pictures using communications and computer technology. Examples of multimedia technology are found on CD-ROMs, DVDs and many websites. (These terms are explained later this chapter.)

4.2 Examples of multimedia applications include the following.

(a) Provision of computer based training, by use of interactive training materials and film demonstrations.

(b) Provision of computerised brochures and reports which could include audio introductions and video clips of personnel, products and processes.

(c) Enabling workgroup collaboration. If a camera is installed (as used in video phones), users can see each other but because a PC screen is used they can also share computer files on screen.

(d) Virtual reality type applications, where the user puts on a headset and an electronic glove and seems to be in a different physical world, are used in design and training.

4.3 Multimedia can only enhance human-computer interaction in the long-term (usually not very long in the IT world), because it engages more of the senses. However, quite considerable computer power is needed. At the time of publication the average new PC still cannot cope particularly well with TV quality moving pictures, although the new version of Windows (Windows 2000) and a new generation of TV-enabled PCs is likely to change this.

CD-ROM

4.4 It should be noted that although CD-ROM is an integral element of multimedia, CD-ROM and multimedia are not the same thing. CD-ROM is suited to storage of large volumes of data, whether encyclopaedias or archived transactions information. Multimedia is concerned with the way in which information is communicated.

BPP PUBLISHING

DVD

4.5 In a few years time the CD format is likely to be entirely superseded by DVD (Digital Versatile Disk). CD-Roms hold 650 megabytes of data, which only a few years ago was considered enough for any application. However, the advent of multimedia files with video graphics and sound encouraged the development of a new storage technology- DVD.

4.6 Digital Versatile Disk (DVD) technology can store almost 5 gigabytes of data on one disk. Access speeds are improved as is sound and video quality. DVD is sometimes referred to as Digital Video Disk. Many commentators believe DVD will not only replace CD ROMS, but also VHS cassettes, audio CDs and laser discs. Read the case example below.

Case example: DVD

DVD or Digital Versatile Disk is the storage media of the future according to figures from industry analyst Dataquest.

But DVD is essentially the same technology as its older sibling the CD-ROM. The pits and groves in a disk are read by a laser which converts the pits into digital data. In order to squeeze in more data than on traditional CDs the pits on a DVD disc are smaller and the tracks are closer together. The most significant difference is that DVDs can be two-sided and double layered giving the format up to 25 times more storage space than a CD.

DVD players come in two types: the set-top box linked to the TV like a VCR, or more popular at present, a drive for PCs. And while the battle between DVD drives looks set to escalate over the next year or so it could be overshadowed by the battle between rival DVD formats. Whereas CD ROM had a long period of grace before the CD rewriters arrived, DVD RAM is already competing with DVD ROM as the next generation format. The difference is simple: DVD ROM can only read data whereas DVD RAM can read, write, rewrite and erase.

Creative's European brand manager Franco de Bonis thinks the battle between ROM and RAM will be won on price. 'Whereas a DVD ROM drive is available for under £100, an equivalent RAM drive will cost about £500,' he says. 'Rewriteable technology is incredibly complicated'. The format would have mass appeal, allowing a DVD player to perform the same tasks as a VCR.

An at a glance guide to the formats:

DVD ROM

The read only format.

DVD RAM

Vendors are very excited about the possibilities of this format.

DVD + RW

Primarily with only Sony behind it, some industry commentators accuse the format of being a distraction in the market. It is effectively a direct competitor to DVD RAM.

DVD R

A write-once standard with limited applications. Useful for organisations which do a lot of archiving or need to store huge amounts of data that won't need to be altered. Currently drives are prohibitively expensive at around £5000.

From an article posted on www.zdnet.co.uk

---

5 THE INTERNET
6/00

5.1 The Internet is the name given to the technology that allows any computer with a telecommunications link to exchange information with any other suitably equipped computer.

5.2 Terms such as 'the net', 'the information superhighway', 'cyberspace', and the 'World Wide Web (www)' are used fairly interchangeably, although technically the 'web' is what makes the 'net' user-friendly (rather like Windows did for MS-DOS).

Websites

5.3 As you are no doubt aware, most companies of any size now have a 'site' on the Net. A site is a collection of screens providing information in text and graphic form, any of which can be viewed simply by clicking the appropriate button, word or image on the screen.

5.4 The user generally starts at the site's 'home page', which sets out the contents of the site. For instance, here is Microsoft's home page.

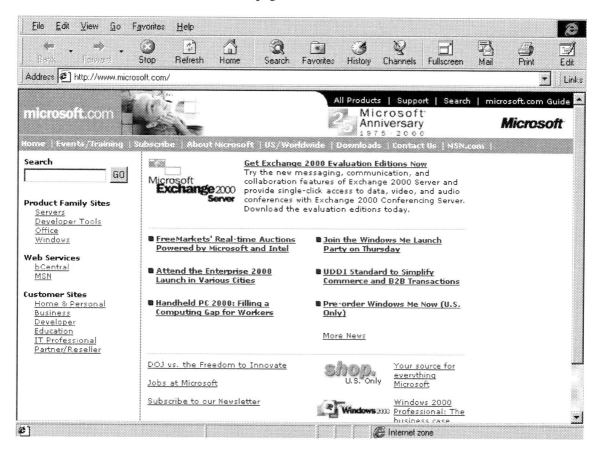

5.5 The main part of the page offers *news* about what is happening at the company. Other buttons in the page take the user to other pages where they can:

(a) Find out more details about individual Microsoft *products*.

(b) Carry out a *Search* of the site.

(c) Consult pages that offer technical *Support* for Microsoft products, perhaps including *FAQs* (frequently asked questions and their answers) and files to *download* such as *free demonstrations* of products or *fixes* for problems with Microsoft software.

(d) Order products.

(e) Contact Microsoft.

(f) Subscribe to the site and thereby receive updated information via e-mail.

5.6 As another example here is an illustration of a *page* from the BPP site bpp.com.

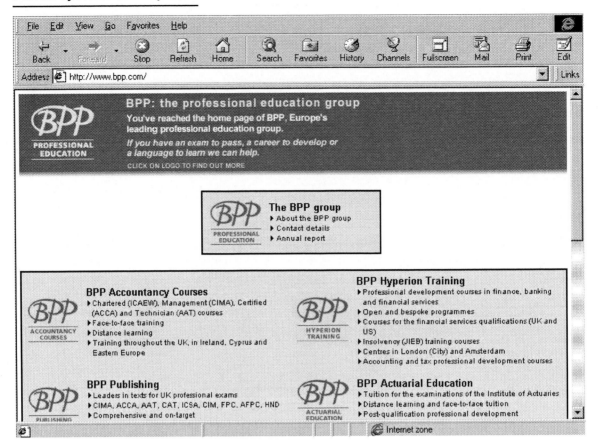

Internet Service Providers (ISPs)

5.7 Connection is made via an Internet Service Provider (ISP). Many ISPs offer free access to the Internet, meaning users pay only the local telephone charges incurred during connection. Free ISPs include Virgin Net, Freeserve and Freedom Online. AOL is one of the few ISPs that still charges a small monthly subscription fee, justified (they say) by superior service. Unmetered access via 'Freephone' telephone numbers (in return for a subscription fee) has recently been introduced.

5.8 Most ISPs provide their own services, in addition to Internet access and e-mail capability. For instance, AOL also offers a main menu with options such as Life, Travel, Entertainment, Sport, Kids.

Browsers and search engines

5.9 The Internet is viewed through interface programs called browsers. The most popular and best known is Microsoft Internet Explorer.

5.10 Searching the Net is done using a search engine such as Yahoo!, Excite or AltaVista. These guide users to destinations throughout the world: the user simply types in a word or phrase like 'beer' to find a list of thousands of websites that contain something connected with beer.

5.11 Companies like Yahoo! make money by selling advertising space. For instance if you type in 'beer', an advertisement for Miller Genuine Draft will appear, as well as your list of beer-related sites. If you click on the advertisement you are taken to the advertiser's website.

5.12 The advertiser may get you to register your interest in the product so that you can be directly targeted in future. At the very least advertisers know exactly how many people have viewed their message and how many were interested enough in it to click on it to find out more.

5.13 An Internet development that has created a good deal of excitement is known as 'push' technology. This describes the process whereby relevant information is 'pushed' to an individual – usually via e-mail. An example of this is websites (or user groups) that allow users to register an interest in a subject. Any future material that meets the criteria set by the user is e-mailed to them.

5.14 Browser software packages provide a facility to store Internet addresses so that users can access frequently-visited sites without having to go through a search process.

Case example: How to search the web

First, it help to understand the basics of how search engines get their listings. There are two main ways: human beings or automated 'crawlers'.

Yahoo is an example of a search engine that uses human beings. Its editors classify websites into different categories. So a search for 'travel' reveals categories such as Travel Booksellers, Travel Companies and Hawaiian travel. Clink on a topic and you'll be shown a list of sites that an editor has selected for that particular category.

In contrast, a search engine like AltaVista sends robot crawlers out across the web to read automatically a large number of pages. The text is stored in what you can think of as a big book. So when you search for 'travel', AltaVista flips through its book to display links to all the individual web pages it has found with those words.

In general, use a human powered search engine when looking for answers to something general. But for something specific, such as 'places to stay in Fort William', a crawler based search engine may be more helpful.

It is also helpful to understand the basic search engine 'maths'. This means that by using symbols such as + or -, you can get better search results. For instance, say you were looking for 'football' and kept getting answers about the NFL, the National Football League in the United States. Try searching again like this: football-nfl. The minus symbol tells the search engine to look for pages that say football then to subtract any pages that contain the word NFL. That makes it more likely that you'll get pages about Liverpool FC rather than the Miami Dolphins!

In fact, you can use the + symbol to get even closer to Liverpool. Try a search like this: football+liverpool. That tells the search engine to find all the pages with football on them, then to show you only pages that also say liverpool.

Using quote marks" " around a series of words tells the search engine to return only with pages with that exact phrase on them, in that exact order.

By searching in lower case, you'll find both lower and upper-case versions of your words. So save your fingers and stay off the shift key! Another search tip is to always be specific. For instance, if you want to buy tickets for Liverpool matches online, then search that way, such as: Where can I buy tickets for liverpool matches online? It's fine to use natural language queries like this on any search engine - you don't need to use Boolean commands or even the maths commands described above. Just start with a specific query, and you may find what you are looking for without having to resort to other attempts.

Another way to get better results can be to use multiple search engines. No two search engines are exactly the same. You can even send your query to multiple search engines at the same time, using metasearch engines. Also called metacrawler, these sites save you time by forwarding your query to several major search engines then bringing back the results to one place. There is even metasearch software that brings back answers from multiple places to sort through.

Finally, have you ever looked for something to do with Britain and come back with loads of results that made you feel like the entire web is American? Next time, try a British search engine. These services make an extra attempt to ensure the sites they list are either British or about Britain. Just be sure to use the UK option usually located near the search box.

The best places to start looking

Yahoo: www.yahoo.co.uk
The oldest major human powered search engine on the web.

AltaVista: www.altavista.co.uk

BPP
PUBLISHING

Crawler based service that's an excellent choice for finding unusual of very specific information. Offers the ability to search within the UK or across the entire web.

Google: www.google.com
Crawler based service with a unique ranking system that finds great answers, even when seeking general information.

Excite: www.excite.co.uk
Crawler based service with UK or webwide abilities.

Ask: www.ask.co.uk
Many like its unusual style of asking you questions to get you to the right website. Also a metasearch engine.

Northern Light: www.northernlight.com
Crawler-based service popular with researchers. Good place to look for hard-to-find information.

UKMax: www.ukmax.com
Crawler based search engine for both UK and worldwide.

SearchUK: www.searchuk.com
Crawler based search engine specifically for the UK.

UK Plus: www.ukplus.co.uk
The only major human powered service produced for the UK, in the UK.

Looksmart: www.looksmart.co.uk
Human powered service that classifies sites into categories, helpful for finding general information. Search within the UK or across the word.

Lycos: www.lycos.co.uk
A crawler based search engine with UK or webwide search abilities.

Virgin Net: www.virgin.net
Search the web with a special edition of the Google engine, with extra listings for the UK.

FAST: www.alltheweb.com
Crawler based service with a large number of listings. Good for unusual information.

Go2Net: www.go2net.com
Meta search site that lets you query many popular search engines at once.

SavvySearch: www.savvyseach.com
Another popular meta search site.

Source: The Guardian, January 2000

Going directly to an Internet address (URLs)

5.15   You may know the precise address of an Internet site that you wish to visit, perhaps because you have seen or heard it on TV or radio or read it in a newspaper or magazine. Typically the format is something like '*http://www.bbc.co.uk*'.

5.16   The address is called a *URL* or *Uniform Resource Locator*

URL element	Explanation
http://	*Hypertext Transfer Protocol*, the protocol used on the World-Wide Web for the exchange of documents produced in what is known as 'hypertext mark-up language' (HTML). A common alternative to *http* is *ftp* (file transfer protocol) explained briefly later. The two forward slashes after the colon introduce a 'host name' such as *www*.
www	This stands for *World Wide Web*. As noted before, to put it simply the web (via its use of HTML), is what makes the Internet user-friendly
bbc	This is the *domain name* of the organisation or individual whose site is located at this URL
co	This part of the URL indicates the type of organisation concerned. The Internet actually spans many different physical networks around the world including commercial (*com* or *co*), university (*ac* or *edu*) and other research networks (*org*, *net*), military (*mil*) networks, and government (*gov*) networks.
uk	As you can probably guess, this indicates that the organisation is located in the UK

Other Internet services

5.17 Here are three other terms that you are likely to encounter frequently in connection with the Internet.

(a) *File Transfer Protocol (FTP)* is the facility on the Internet that allows users to *copy files from one computer to another across the network*. Using an FTP program, information and applications residing on distant computers can be accessed and retrieved. A wide range of files are available via system called 'Anonymous FTP'. This lets users connect to a remote computer and *download files* from a public area of its disk. Many companies maintain such a site to allow customers to download new versions of software and product information.

(b) *Telnet* is an application that allows a user to establish a connection to a *remote computer*, perhaps on the other side of the world, as if it were on the next desk. Once connected the telnet software acts as an intermediary, translating the user's keyboard strokes so that the distant computer can understand them and interpret the information the distant computer sends back. In effect, it is as if a *keyboard and screen* on this side of the world were *directly connected* to the computer on the other side of the world.

(c) *Usenet* is short for User's Network, a series of open conferences or *discussion groups* on a multitude of topics. People who register with a Usenet newsgroup receive copies of all messages and articles posted by other members of the group. For instance there is a Usenet group called *uk.finance*.

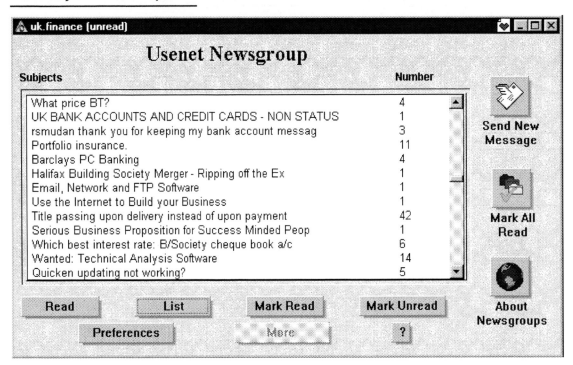

Internal communication

5.18 Internet technology is now being used extensively within organisations who create their own 'intranets'. Intranets are described in more detail in the next chapter in the context of group working.

Current uses of the Internet

5.19 The scope and potential of the Internet are still developing. Its uses already embrace the following:

(a) Dissemination of information.

(b) Product/service development - through almost instantaneous test marketing.

(c) Transaction processing - both business-to-business and business-to-consumer.

(d) Relationship enhancement - between various groups of stakeholders, but principally (for our purposes) between consumers and product/service suppliers.

(e) Recruitment and job search - involving organisations worldwide.

(f) Entertainment - including music, humour, art, games and some less wholesome pursuits!

(g) Distribution. The Internet can be used to get certain products directly into people's homes. Anything that can be converted into digital form can be uploaded onto the seller's site and then downloaded onto the customer's PC. The Internet thus offers huge opportunities to producers of text, graphics/video, and sound-based products. Much computer software and music products are now distributed in this way.

5.20 It is estimated that over 32% of households in the UK will have Internet access by the year 2001, with the figure rising to 40 per cent by 2002.

5.21 The Internet provides opportunities to organise for and to automate tasks which would previously have required more costly interaction with the organisation. These have often been called low-touch or zero-touch approaches.

5.22   Tasks which a website may automate include:

(a)   Frequently-Asked Questions (FAQs): carefully-structured sets of answers can deal with many customer interactions.

(b)   Status checking: major service enquiries (Where is my order? When will the engineer arrive? What is my bank balance?) can also be automated, replacing high-cost human service processes, and also providing the opportunity to proactively offer better service and new services.

(c)   Keyword search: the ability to search provides web users with opportunities to find information in large and complex websites.

(d)   Wizards (interview style interface) and intelligent algorithms: these can help diagnosis, which is one of the major elements of service support.

(e)   E-mail and systems to route and track inbound e-mail: the ability to route and/or to provide automatic responses will enable organisations to deal with high volumes of e-mail from actual and potential customers.

(f)   Bulletin boards: these enable customers to interact with each other, thus facilitating self-activated customer service and also the opportunity for product/service referral. Cisco in particular has created communities of Cisco users who help each other - thus reducing the service costs for Cisco itself.

(g)   Call-back buttons: these enable customers to speak to someone in order to deal with and resolve a problem; the more sophisticated systems allow the call-centre operator to know which web pages the users were consulting at the time.

Exercise 5

(a)   Use a PC with Internet access to experience these things for yourself.

(b)   If you have Internet access at work, how does it help you (or your colleagues) to do a better job?

Problems with the Internet

5.23   To a large extent the Internet has grown organically without any formal organisation. There are specific communication rules, but it is not owned by any one body and there are no clear guidelines on how it should develop.

5.24   Inevitably, also, the quality of much of the information on the Internet leaves much to be desired.

5.25   Speed is a major issue. Data only downloads onto the user's PC at the speed of the slowest telecommunications link - downloading data can be a painfully slow procedure. A number of faster services have recently become available, or will do so in the next few years eg ADSL (Asymmetric Digital Subscriber Line) and ISDN (Integrated Systems Digital Network).

5.26   Interactive electronic purchasing (e-commerce) was initially slow to catch on in the United Kingdom. Somewhat illogically, people were reluctant to supply their credit card details over the Internet, although they will gladly do so over the telephone, and happily transcribe the details onto a bill that they are paying by post. Logical or not, some consumers require further reassurance about security before interactive purchasing really takes off.

5.27   Technological developments such as 'secure websites', utilising encryption techniques, have already provided some reassurance. Once people are used to this method of buying it is likely to become the norm for many transactions.

5.28   The range of products and services being bought over the Internet includes books, holidays, cinema tickets, train tickets, shares, banking, betting and even the weekly groceries.

Case example

(1) Airlines

The impact of the web is seen clearly in the transportation industry. Airlines now have a more effective way of bypassing intermediaries (ie travel agents) because they can give their customers immediate access to flight reservation systems. British Airways aims to sell at least half of its tickets on-line by the year 2003; one of the new low-cost airlines in the UK, EasyJet, has become the first airline to have over half of its bookings made on-line.

(2) Travel agents

The web has also produced a new set of on-line travel agents who have lower costs because of their ability to operate without a High Street branch network. Their low-cost structure makes them a particularly good choice for selling low margin, cheap tickets for flights, package holidays, cruises and so forth.

These low-cost travel agents have been joined, furthermore, by non-travel-agents who simply specialise in opportunistic purchasing (eg lastminute.com).

(3) Tesco

In another arena, Tesco is already the world's largest Internet grocery business, but other companies are rapidly developing new initiatives. Waitrose@work allows people to order their groceries in the morning (typically through their employer's Intranet communication system) and then have them delivered to the workplace in the afternoon: this approach achieves significant distribution economies of scale so far as Waitrose is concerned.

(4) Financial services

The impact of the Internet is especially profound in the field of financial services. New intermediaries enable prospective customers to compare the interest rates and prices charged by different organisations for pensions, mortgages and other financial services. This means that the delivering companies are losing control of the marketing of their services, and there is a downward pressure on prices, especially for services which can legitimately be seen as mere commodities (eg house and contents insurance).

5.29   So much information and entertainment is available that employers worry that their staff will spend too much time browsing through non-work-related sites.

5.30   Security is perhaps the biggest worry of all. Security aspects of the Internet are discussed in Chapter 14.

Case example: Business and the Internet

The Internet is turning business upside down and inside out. It is fundamentally changing the way companies operate, whether in high-tech or metal-bashing. This goes far beyond buying and selling over the Internet, or e-commerce, and deep into the processes and culture of an enterprise.

Some companies are using the Internet to make direct connections with their customers for the first time. Others are using secure Internet connections to intensify relations with some of their trading partners, and using the Internet's reach and ubiquity to request quotes or sell off perishable stocks of goods or services by auction.

The Internet is helping companies to lower costs dramatically across their supply and demand chains, take their customer service into a different league, enter new markets, create additional revenue streams and redefine their business relationships.

The Economist quotes with approval the claim by Andy Grove, Chairman of Intel, that in five years time all companies will be Internet companies or they won't be companies at all. Andy Grove has also argued that companies can be either 'brick' or 'click' businesses, but they can't be both: if they are a 'brick' operation - ie they have real premises, real shops, real factories and warehouses - then their culture will make it impossible for them fully to assimilate the drastic changes required in order to operate successfully in a 'click' environment. It is no accident, therefore, that companies like Prudential Assurance have initiated their Internet activities through stand-alone enterprises, using newly-recruited people situated in geographically-distinctive locations.

The Economist, June 1999

6   ENVIRONMENTAL SCANNING   6/94, 6/96, 6/97, 6/00

The wider organisational environment

6.1   Besides technology a wide number of other elements have an impact on an organisation's information needs and information systems design.

   (a)   The *marketplace* consists of customers and trends in design and consumer tastes.

   (b)   The *competition* includes both existing competitors and new competitors.

   (c)   *Government* determines financial and political policies and has an effect on the macro-economic environment within which the organisation operates.

   (d)   The *general public* reflects changes in the behaviour and expectations of society as a whole. The growth of 'ethical' investment funds reflects a new pressure on corporate activity.

   (e)   *Ecology*, or the natural environment, is affected by the organisation's activities.

Exercise 6

Each of the above topics is covered in much more depth in other Pre-Professional papers notably *Management Principles*.

See if you can expand an item in the list into a full paragraph explaining the possible impact of each on the design of an information system.

Consult your other BPP study material for ideas if necessary. To focus your mind you may wish to think about the issues in terms of the six key tasks of information management - see the first paragraph of Chapter 1 in this book.

6.2   Sources of information (besides information received directly from the environment such as letters of complaint, suppliers brochures etc) include the following.

   (a)   The *Internet*, as already described: a vast and ever more important resource for information on every subject. Older services, such as the Prestel 'viewdata' service provided by British Telecom, now offer Internet alternatives (Prestel Online).

   (b)   *The government*. The Department of Trade and Industry is the most obvious example in central government, but other departments may be contacted as appropriate. Local government bodies frequently provide information and assistance, particularly to encourage new business ventures. The government and its various departments and agencies also publish information through the Stationery Office.

   (c)   *Advice or information bureaux*. These provide enquirers with information in their own particular field, in the form of advice, or information leaflets and fact sheets. Examples include Consumer Standards Offices, Offices of Fair Trading, Law Centres, Tourist Information bureaux and so on.

   (d)   There are also *consultancies* of all sorts. You will have heard of general market research organisations like MORI and Gallup. There are also a great many specialist market research companies providing market intelligence for specific industries. Accounting firms have management consultancy divisions. Many organisations have their own information 'desk' which can be contacted for detailed of a non-confidential nature about themselves or their field.

(e) *Newspaper and magazine publishers*. The quality press is a vital source of general economic information. Most industries are also served by several trade journals and magazines.

(f) There may be *specific reference works* which are used in a particular line of work. In a tax department of a firm of accountants, for example, you would use published lists of dividends and fixed interest payments for publicly quoted securities. If you worked for a car dealer your 'bible' might be Glass's Guide which lists secondhand values for vehicles by make and model.

(g) *Libraries and information services*. These may be part of the free public library system, or associated with a learned or professional institution like the ICSA.

(h) Increasingly businesses can use *each other's systems* as sources of information, via electronic data interchange (EDI) which, in simple terms, involves the exchange of routine business documents between the computers of suppliers and their customers. Major retailers such as Tesco, for example, have automated their business chain to such an extent that orders, invoices and payments are all triggered off by shoppers passing through supermarket check-outs.

(i) *Television and radio* offer news services, business programs and general interest programs of a wide variety. This is likely to increase with the introduction of digital services, and in time TV, telecoms and computers may merge into a single information source.

6.3 Environmental scanning might be formally delegated to particular individuals, such as a market research manager; it might also be 'informal'. Informal gathering of information from outside sources goes on all the time, consciously or unconsciously, because the employees of an organisation learn what is going on in the world around them - from newspapers, television, experience or other people.

Case example: environmental scanning!

Microsoft sparked a tempest in 1995 when it was revealed that its Registration Wizard, which allowed users of Windows 95 to register on-line, was automatically collecting information about customers' software without their knowledge or permission. When users registered with Microsoft, going on-line for the first time, Microsoft took the opportunity to 'read' the configuration of their PCs. The company gained instant knowledge, subscriber by subscriber, of the major software products running on its customers' systems. When members of the on-line world got wind of what Microsoft was doing, they protested publicly. Microsoft quickly abandoned the practice. *Harvard Business Review*, Jan/Feb 1997

Chapter roundup

- Information technology is commonly described as the convergence of computer technology and communications technology. It involves the electronic acquisition, storage and dissemination of vocal, pictorial, textual and numerical information.

- Computerised systems offer advantages such as higher productivity, faster processing, greater information access, greater accuracy, ease of correction, higher quality output and less bulk.

- Spreadsheets are versatile tools that can be used for a wide variety of tasks, especially at tactical level. There are potential drawbacks due to overuse and poor practice. Word processing is probably the most widespread feature of the electronic office. It uses a computer system to produce and edit typed letters and documents and store them on magnetic storage media.

- Dialogue design refers to the messages that the computer system displays on screen and the ways that users can respond. Modern systems use menus, form-filling and graphical user interfaces.

- User friendliness is enhanced by good input screen design, intuitiveness, consistency between packages, on-screen help, dialogue boxes, escapability and customisation.

- The electronic office may allow communications by a number of media including telex, teletex, fax, e-mail, voice mail, computer conferencing and teleconferencing.

- The Internet connects millions of computers worldwide and is having a major impact on ways of communicating and doing business. Concepts to understand include Internet Service Providers, Websites, Browsers and Search Engines.

- Environmental scanning is a process of obtaining information from external sources. Externally generated information may be more difficult to assimilate or to input into an information system, but is just as important to management as internal information.

- Sources include the Internet, research agencies, the government and the media

Test your knowledge

1 Why are computerised systems preferable to manual ones? (see para 1.1)

2 What is form filling? (2.10 - 2.11)

3 Describe seven features of user-friendliness (2.22 - 2.38)

4 What are the advantages of e-mail? (3.8)

5 What is CTI? (3.20 - 3.23)

6 Give four examples of multimedia applications (4.3)

7 What is a website? (5.3)

8 What is push technology? (5.14)

9 Give three commercial uses of the Internet (5.20 - 5.26)

10 List six sources of environmental information (6.2)

Now try illustrative questions 7 and 30 at the end of the Study Text

Chapter 5

INFORMATION SYSTEMS STRATEGY AND ORGANISATION

> **This chapter covers the following topics.**
>
> 1 Information strategy
>
> 2 Developing a strategic plan
>
> 3 Information management at board level
>
> 4 Identifying users' needs
>
> 5 Centralisation and decentralisation
>
> 6 Interoperability, standards and quality
>
> 7 Computer supported co-operative working
>
> 8 Homeworking
>
> 9 Outsourcing the IS function
>
> **Introduction**
>
> In this chapter we look at a variety of issues that are of great strategic importance to all organisations (although not all organisations yet consider them to be this important). The first four sections look at the formulation of IS strategy, while the remainder consider the key information strategy issues facing organisations in the late 1990s.

1 INFORMATION STRATEGY

12/94, 6/96, 6/97

Information strategy

1.1   A strategy is a general statement of long-term objectives and goals and the ways by which these will be achieved. An *information* strategy deals with the integration of an organisation's information requirements and information systems planning with its long-term overall goals (customer service etc).

1.2   Here are some reasons justifying the case for a strategy for information systems (IS) and information technology (IT).

(a)   Information systems involve high costs.

(b)   Information systems are critical to the success of many organisations.

(c)   Information systems are now used as part of the commercial strategy in the battle for competitive advantage.

(d)   Information systems involve many stakeholders, not just management, and not just within the organisation.

A high cost activity

1.3   Many organisations invest large amounts of money in IS, but not always wisely. The importance is not how much is spent but how well the funds are spent.

1.4 The problem is made more acute because individual components of an information system are now not particularly expensive. A very powerful PC can be bought for less than £1,000, and much software can be downloaded for free or at very little cost from the Internet.

1.5 However, the unmanaged proliferation of IT is likely to lead to chaos: no two users would have the same equipment or use the same processing methods or software, and the two key benefits of IT - the ability to share information and the avoidance of duplication - would be lost.

1.6 All IT expenditure therefore needs rigorous scrutiny to ensure that it enhances rather than detracts from the overall information management strategy.

Critical to the success of many organisations

1.7 In developing a strategy a firm should assess how important IT actually is in the provision of products and services. IT may be any of the following.

(a) A support activity (for example providing ad hoc responses to queries) which is useful but not critical to organisational success.

(b) A 'factory' activity where information systems are crucial to current operations and their management but not at the heart of the company's strategic development.

(c) A turnround activity in which IT is seen as crucial to a firm's business development, and is used to open up new opportunities (for example information technology acquired to enhance flexibility of marketing and production of consumer goods).

(d) A strategic activity, where without IT the firm could not function at all (for example many financial services companies depend on computers, telecommunications and databases, just like a manufacturing company depends on raw materials or a transport company depends on vehicles).

A strategic weapon

1.8 IT can be used as a strategic weapon in the following ways.

(a) IT can be used to develop new businesses (for example Reuters created an electronic market place where subscribers could trade via Reuters terminals).

(b) IT is a potential supplier of competitive advantage to an organisation.

Competitive advantage   *12/95*

1.9 An organisation can employ three basic strategies to obtain competitive advantage.

Strategy	Comment
Overall cost leadership	This involves becoming the most cost efficient producer. IT can reduce costs by: (a) Reducing labour costs (for example production control systems, clerical work) (b) Reducing manufacturing costs by efficient scheduling etc (for example computer integrated manufacturing, better monitoring of raw materials usage to reduce wastage)
Product differentiation	This involves making a unique product or a product which appears different from your competitors', and hence more attractive. Information technology can be used to: (a) Design new products speedily (Computer Aided Design) (b) Enable customisation of a product to a customer's particular specification (Computer Integrated Manufacturing)

BPP
PUBLISHING

Strategy	Comment
	(c) Differentiate the product by using IT-based components to make it unique (for example, one travel company has introduced multimedia booths so customers can get a better idea of different holiday destinations).
Focus on a market niche.	A market niche is a group of consumers who have particular needs. (a) Use sales data to identify customer preferences and spot unusual trends. (b) Use IT to analyse market research and statistical information.

Exercise 1

Think about the role of Information Technology in securing an advantage over competitors. Try to think of an example of each of the following.

(a) The use of IT to 'lock out' competitors.

(b) The use of IT to commit customers to investment, reducing the likelihood of their changing suppliers.

(c) The use of IT to secure a straightforward performance advantage.

(d) The use of IT to generate a new product or service.

Solution

(a) An example is an airline booking service. Let's take a fictitious airline: British Transatlantic Airways (BTA). A passenger wishes to fly BTA from the UK to New York, and then from New York to Minneapolis. BTA is not allowed to make internal flights in the USA. However, several American airlines fly from New York to Minneapolis. BTA's booking system is interlinked with that of one American airline, whose flights are always chosen for connections by the BTA booking system. The IT system is thus a barrier to competition, as alternative flights from New York to Minneapolis are not offered by BTA.

(b) Once a bank customer has gone to the effort and expense of installing a home banking system, he or she is unlikely to make a decision to change banks (which requires a switch to another system).

(c) Efficient stock control systems (for example just-in-time) might make an organisation more dependent on efficient suppliers, resulting in its stopping trading with less efficient companies which hamper its own ability to deliver.

(d) An outstandingly successful example in the financial services sector is simple insurance policies approved over the telephone (using expert systems).

Stakeholders

1.10 A stakeholder is a person or organisation that has an interest in an enterprise. An organisation must take steps to manage these external stakeholders. Parties interested in an organisation's use of IS are as follows.

(a) Other businesses for example, for common standards for electronic data interchange. These can form into lobbying groups for a particular industry.

(b) Governments (for example, data protection regulation).

(c) Consumers (for example in testing technology-based products such as teleshopping).

(d) Employees and internal users (as IS affect work practices).

2 DEVELOPING A STRATEGIC PLAN   12/97

2.1 An information strategy must deal with three issues.

(a) The organisation's overall business needs, and IT needs as a consequence.

(b) The organisation's current use of IT.

(c) The potential opportunities that IT can bring.

2.2 Each of these three issues involves different personnel, and requires a slightly different approach. A diagrammatic representation of strategy development is given below.

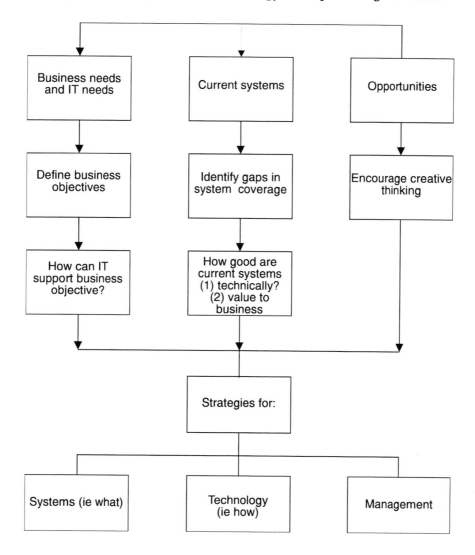

Identifying business needs

2.3 The identification of business needs and the information technology framework to satisfy them is at the heart of a strategy for information systems and information technology. The IS and IT strategies should be part of the overall strategy for the organisation and so the IS strategy should be considered whenever the organisation prepares its long-term marketing or production strategies.

2.4 Techniques for identifying business needs include SWOT analysis and the use of *critical success factors* (CSFs). Such techniques are covered in the Pre-Professional paper *Management Principles*.

Evaluating current systems

2.5 This part of the strategy study is necessary so that the organisation might have some idea where it is starting from, as, later, it will aid in the targeting of resources. For example, an organisation with good financial reporting systems may have no marketing information systems. Gaps in the IS coverage are identified here.

BPP PUBLISHING

2.6 Secondly, the efficiency of current systems coverage is also evaluated. Are users happy? Is the system reliable?

Opportunities

2.7 Opportunities cannot always be identified from the two processes above. Instead, creative thinking in the organisation should be encouraged. The organisation should foster innovation, by encouraging and supporting new ideas from its staff, and consulting users and customers. The strategic plan may not be able to identify small, incremental improvements to systems. Users should be encouraged to develop their own ideas by providing them with the technological tools to do so.

Information strategies

2.8 An information strategy for an organisation can be said to cover three areas.

Information systems strategy

2.9 This has been defined as the long-term directional plan. It is seen to be business-led, demand-oriented and concerned to exploit IT either to support business strategies or create new strategic options. An IS strategy therefore deals with the integration of an organisation's information requirements and information systems planning with its long-term overall goals (customer service etc).

Information technology strategy

2.10 This leads on from the IS strategy above, in that it deals with technologies.

   (a) Computing.
   (b) Communications.
   (c) Data.
   (d) Application systems.

2.11 This provides a framework for the analysis and design of the technological infrastructure of an organisation. For example, this might involve guidelines for makes of computers purchased and so forth.

Information management strategy

2.12 This refers to the basic approach an organisation has to the management of its information systems, including the following.

   (a) Planning IS developments.

   (b) Organisational environment of IS (for example the role of the information director, in many organisations the board member responsible for IS)

   (c) Control (for example cost control).

   (d) Technology (for example systems development methodologies).

2.13 The strategy will therefore affect all an organisation's information systems and information technology activities.

3   INFORMATION MANAGEMENT AT BOARD LEVEL   6/95, 6/97

3.1 In a small company information systems may be the responsibility of the finance director, the company secretary or the chief executive. There may be an *information director* (or 'Head of Systems' or 'Chief Information Officer') in larger organisations. The point is not so much that there should be a designated individual on the board with specific IT responsibilities but rather that IT issues relating to strategy, planning and so forth should be considered at board level.

3.2 An information director needs these skills.

    (a) General management ability.

    (b) Good understanding of organisational activities and the way the organisation operates.

    (c) Good technical expertise in developing and running information systems.

3.3 The reason why such generalist skills are needed can be best understood in the context of the role the information director is supposed to play. This includes the following.

Corporate objectives

3.4 Ensuring that the organisation's acquisition and use of information technology and computer systems fits in with the goals and objectives of the organisation as a whole. The information systems strategy should tie in with the overall organisation strategy.

Information infrastructure

3.5 Furthermore, the information director should ensure that IT systems activities undertaken by users should firstly satisfy user demands and secondly not be sub-optimal to the overall system goals and organisational objectives. This activity will include overall responsibility for the construction of an information infrastructure comprising:

    (a) technical standards (for example only buy from one supplier);
    (b) software standards (for example only use Lotus 1-2-3 for spreadsheet applications);
    (c) establishment of corporate as opposed to departmental or functional databases;
    (d) providing an information systems service function.

Liaison

3.6 Liaison between information systems professionals and the rest of the organisation is a key role. Such functions include the following.

    (a) Provision of technical assistance.

    (b) Informal discussions with users as to their needs before detailed feasibility studies are carried out, which can also include discussions as to the payoffs of a particular IS investment.

    (c) Advice on the impact of information systems on organisational structure, working environment and so forth.

The environment   *6/00*

3.7 Interaction with the environment is important. This is essential for a strategic perspective. An organisation's information systems can affect the way it trades, as there are a growing number of information systems connections between different organisations. The information director will seek to dovetail these types of facility into the organisation's overall commercial strategy.

3.8 Links with external organisations can also be important if the organisation takes over another. Incompatible information systems between merged organisations can add significantly to the cost of the merger. Information system flexibility is therefore a desirable aim. A suitable approach to public relations is desirable to convince customers and suppliers of the benefits to them of new information systems.

3.9 The information director will gather information relating to the legal environment of information systems. This includes handling the impact of data protection legislation, rules governing transborder dataflows, and ensuring that other areas of legislation are accounted for in information systems development.

Constraints

3.10 There are a variety of problems facing senior information systems managers, and their job may require them to implement the organisation's information system strategy within the framework of certain inevitable constraints.

(a) Shortage of skilled staff.

(b) Backlogs in application development caused by (a) above, and also the fact that much programming time is spent repairing old applications rather than developing new ones.

(c) The need to ensure continued growth.

Exercise 2

Draft a job description for an information director.

Solution

Role

Director of Information responsible to the Board of Directors for the establishment, maintenance and review of a management information system (MIS) to support the strategy and objectives of the group.

To report to the Board on all matters relating to the management of information technology as a corporate resource including technology, systems design/development and staff.

To participate fully in the presentation and evaluation of information at all board meetings.

Duties

To serve the information needs of management and staff at all levels to enable them, with confidence, to make timely and effective decisions for all matters for which they are responsible.

(1) To set up, maintain and review an effective MIS for the group to reflect the group policy of highest quality customer service.

(2) To work to an agreed MIS budget and deliver cost-effective information.

(3) To recommend the purchase of appropriate hardware, software and communications to serve the group network.

(4) To build a high performing MIS team within agreed staff budgets.

(5) To carry out staff development and monitor results for the MIS team.

(6) To maintain full security of all information systems.

Skills

(1) General management skills acquired in a service focused environment.
(2) Leadership, innovation and team management skills.
(3) High level personal communication and social skills.
(4) Organisational skills reflecting a good understanding of the group functions.
(5) Technical skills for developing, operating and ongoing planning of MIS.

---

4   IDENTIFYING USERS' NEEDS

Users and new systems

4.1 There are many computer installations that have failed to achieve the performance standards expected of them. A common reason for this is that the investigation and analysis of existing systems was inefficiently carried out and inadequately controlled. Another common problem has been the failure to accurately define user requirements. This is not generally the fault of the users: systems professionals need to be able to communicate with users and *establish* their needs.

4.2 The starting point for a decision to build a new system or improve an existing one varies from one situation to another. Users might feel that a problem in an existing system can be eliminated, or a process improved, by the introduction of a new system. Alternatively, the organisation may wish to gain competitive advantage, for example by improving the speed of its customer service procedures.

4.3 The aim of this preliminary activity, sometimes referred to as *problem definition*, is to define, in overview, the information processing routine which is to be the subject of development or improvement. The problem definition should include some indication of the advantages which are expected to result if the problem is solved.

4.4 It is possible that at any one time an organisation may have a list of desired projects. These may have come from any of a number of sources, described in this section.

Requests from user departments

4.5 Most project proposals are initiated by user departments. Users are a good source of proposals, since they are the 'customers' of the system. However, it is important to ensure that user requests or suggestions do not cause a conflict with the overall objectives of the organisation.

The information centre approach   *12/95, 12/99*

4.6 An information centre (IC) is a small unit of staff with a good technical awareness of computer systems, whose task is to provide a support function to computer users within the organisation.

4.7 An IC usually offers some kind of *Help Desk* to help staff solve IT problems. Help may be via the telephone, using an e-mail system or, if necessary, face-to-face. Common problems and their solutions can be posted on a bulletin board for all to read

4.8 The IC will maintain a *record of problems*, eventually building a database of all calls/queries received. This can be used to help establish user training requirements.

4.9 Problems with the *system itself* should also become apparent through analysing this information.

4.10 The IC can also consider the viability of *suggestions for improvements* to the system and brings these into effect, where possible, for all users who stand to benefit.

4.11 The IC is also likely to be responsible for setting, and encouraging users to conform to, common *standards*. For instance data processing standards ensure that certain conventions such as the format of file names are followed throughout the organisation. This facilitates sharing and storage and retrieval of information by as many users as possible.

4.12 The IC may help to preserve the security of data in various ways, for instance by developing utility programs and recommended procedures for company-wide use, to ensure that back-ups are made at regular intervals.

User-developed applications

4.13 Modern software packages such as Microsoft Word, Excel and Access have powerful 'macro' facilities that enable users to automate frequently performed tasks, and in some cases to develop quite complex applications.

4.14 These programs are typically difficult to modify – being understood only by the individual who developed the system. This is undesirable from the organisation's viewpoint: a great deal of time and energy is going into producing inefficient programs which are unusable by anyone other than their developer.

4.15 An IC can help to remedy this situation by providing technical guidance to the developers and to encourage comprehensible and documented programs. Understandable programs can be maintained or modified more easily by people other than the system developer. Documentation then provides a means of teaching others how the programs work. These efforts can greatly extend the usefulness and life of the programs that are developed.

New opportunities

4.16 Information technology is developing at such a rate that new possibilities are presenting themselves every year. Developments such as the Internet and corporate intranets and the convergence of computer and telecommunications technology mean that businesses are continually finding new ways of doing business and new opportunities to develop. User needs are continually changing in line with this.

Outside sources

4.17 However talented and creative a systems analyst is, he is unlikely to be able to develop a full range of 'perfect' systems simply by examining his own organisation. A review of what *competitors* and *other organisations* in similar sectors or areas of business are doing may give rise to useful ideas. Similarly, suggestions may be made by auditors or management consultants or trends may be identified by the relevant trade association.

5   CENTRALISATION AND DECENTRALISATION   6/97

5.1 Broadly speaking, the Information Systems function may be centralised or decentralised.

Centralised processing

5.2 Centralised processing means having the data/information processing done in a central place, such as a computer centre at head office. Data will be collected at 'remote' (ie geographically separate) offices and other locations and sent in to the central location, by post, by courier or by telecommunications link. Processing could be in either batch processing mode or on-line.

5.3 At the central location there will be:

(a) A central computer, probably a large mainframe computer.
(b) Central files, containing all the files needed for the system.

Exercise 3

Think of examples of types of business that have 'remote' offices/locations.

Solution

Obvious examples include banks and building societies, chains of supermarkets, high street chains, hotel chains, pubs.

5.4 The advantages of centralised processing are as follows.

(a) There is one set of files. Everyone uses the same data and information.

(b) It gives better security/control over data and files. It is easier to enforce standards.

(c) Head office is in a better position to know what is going on.

(d) An organisation requires a very large central computer, with extensive processing capabilities that smaller 'local' computers could not carry out.

(e) There are economies of scale available in purchasing computer equipment and supplies.

(f) Computer staff are in a single location, and more expert staff are likely to be employed. Career paths may be more clearly defined.

5.5 The disadvantages of centralised processing are as follows.

(a) Local offices might have to wait for data to be processed centrally.

(b) Reliance on head office. Local offices have to rely on the central processing unit to provide the information they need.

(c) If the central computer breaks down, or the software develops a fault, the entire system goes out of operation.

Decentralised processing

5.6 Decentralised processing means having the data/information processing carried out at several different locations, away from the 'centre' or 'head office'. Sometimes this is referred to as distributed processing. There will be several unconnected computers in the various offices, each with its own files.

5.7 The advantages of decentralised processing are set out below.

(a) Each office can introduce an information system specially tailored for its individual needs. Local changes in business requirements can be taken into account.

(b) If data originates locally it might make sense to process it locally too.

(c) Each office has control over its own data.

(d) There is likely to be easy/quick access to information when it is needed.

(e) Any breakdowns in the system are restricted to just one part of the system.

(f) It fits in with the organisation structure, and responsibility accounting systems (profit centres).

(g) It allows staff to concentrate on business objectives rather than being constrained by IT objectives.

5.8 The disadvantages of decentralised processing are set out below.

(a) Many different and uncoordinated information systems will be introduced.

(b) Decentralisation encourages lack of co-ordination between departments.

(c) One office might be unable to obtain additional information from the information system of another office.

(d) There might be a duplication of data, with different offices holding the same data on their own separate files.

Distributed processing

5.9 In practice, information systems do not have to be entirely centralised or entirely decentralised. Distributed processing links several computers together. A system might consist of a mainframe, minicomputer or a powerful 'server' PC, with PCs as intelligent terminals, and a range of peripheral equipment. Files may be either held centrally or at dispersed sites.

Advantages and disadvantages of distributed processing

5.10 The advantages of using a distributed processing system compared with having a centralised mainframe computer are as follows.

(a) There is greater flexibility in system design. The system can cater for both the specific needs of each local user of an individual computer and also for the needs of the organisation as a whole, by providing communications between different local computers in the system.

(b) Since data files can be held locally, data transmission is restricted because each computer maintains its own data files which provide most of the data it will need. This reduces the costs and security risks in data transmission.

(c) Speed of processing for both local branches and also for the central (head office) branch.

(d) There is a possibility of a distributed database. Data is held in a number of locations, but any user can access all of it for a global view.

(e) The effect of breakdowns is minimised, because a fault in one computer will not affect other computers in the system. With a centralised processing system, a fault in the mainframe computer would put the entire system out of service.

(f) The fact that it is possible to acquire powerful PCs at a 'cheap' price enables an organisation to dedicate them to particular applications. This in turn means that the computer system can be more readily tailored to the organisation's systems, rather than forcing the organisation to change its systems to satisfy the requirements for a mainframe computer.

(g) Decentralisation allows for better localised control over the physical and procedural aspects of the system.

(h) Decentralised processing may facilitate greater user involvement and increase familiarity with the use of computer technology. The end user must accept responsibility for the accuracy of locally-held files and local data processing.

5.11 Distributed processing has certain disadvantages, some of which might be overcome by future technological developments.

(a) The minicomputers and PCs of the past did not have enough storage capacity to support the high-level language programs needed for distributed processing. This disadvantage has largely been eliminated by the development of more powerful small machines.

(b) There may be a duplication of data on the files of different computers. If this is the case, there may problems with data redundancy and synchronisation.

(c) A distributed network can be more difficult to administer and to maintain with service engineers.

(d) The items of equipment used in the system must, of course, be compatible with each other.

Networks

5.12 A network is an interconnected collection of autonomous processors.

5.13 There are two main types of network, a local area network (LAN) and a wide area network (WAN).

5.14 The key idea of a network is that users need equal *access* to resources such as data, but they do not necessarily have to have equal computing *power*. LANs, WANs and this 'client-server' concept are perhaps the most important trends in modern computing.

Local area networks (LANs)

5.15 A *local area network* (LAN) is a network of computers located in a single building or on a single site. The parts of the network are linked by computer cable rather than via telecommunications lines. This means that a LAN does not need modems.

Network topologies

5.16 Network topology means the physical arrangement of nodes in a network. A node is any device connected to a network: it can be a computer, or a peripheral device such as a printer.

5.17 There are several types of LAN system configuration. For example, in a bus structure (shown below), messages are sent out from one point along a single communication channel, and the messages are received by other connected machines.

5.18 Each device can communicate with every other device and communication is quick and reliable. Nodes can be added or unplugged very easily. Locating cable faults is also relatively simple.

Bus system

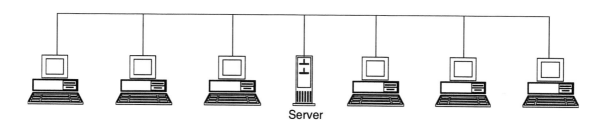

Server

5.19 Local area networks have been successful for a number of reasons. First of all, personal computers of sufficient power and related software (for example UNIX) were developed, so that network applications became possible. Networks have been made available to computer users at a fairly low price. Some computer users who could not afford a mainframe or minicomputer with terminal links have been able to afford a LAN with personal computers and software packages.

Wide area networks (WANs)

5.20 Wide area networks (WANs) are networks on a number of sites, perhaps on a wide geographical scale. WANs often use minicomputers or mainframes as the 'pumps' that keep the data messages circulating, whereas shorter-distance LANs normally use PCs for this task.

5.21 A wide area network is similar to a local area network in concept, but the key differences are as follows.

   (a) The geographical area covered by the network is greater, not being limited to a single building or site.

   (b) WANs will send data over telecommunications links, and so will need modems. LANs, in contrast, will use direct cables only for transmitting data.

   (c) WANs will often use a larger computer as a file server.

(d) WANs will often be larger than LANs, with more terminals or computers linked to the network.

(e) A WAN can link two or more LANs, using gateways.

    (i) Connections may be leased. This is the preferred option where there is a high volume of inter-office communication.

    (ii) Connections may be made over the public telephone network. Standard call charges will apply, so this is beneficial where communication levels are relatively low.

Client-server computing

5.22 The term client-server computing has gained widespread usage. This is a way of describing the relationship between the devices in a network. With client-server computing, the tasks that need to be carried out are distributed among the various machines on the network.

5.23 A client is a machine which requests a service, for example a PC requesting a printing job be processed by the print server.

5.24 A server is a machine which is dedicated to providing a particular function or service requested by a client. Servers include file servers (see below), print servers, e-mail servers and fax servers.

5.25 A client-server system allows computer power to be distributed to where it is most needed. The client, or user, will use a powerful personal workstation with local processing capability. The server provides services such as shared printers, communications links, special-purpose processing and database storage.

5.26 This approach has a number of benefits.

(a) It reduces network communications costs.

(b) It allows the central computer to be used for administrative tasks such as network management.

(c) The technological flexibility of this type of system allows the use of sophisticated applications such as multimedia and DIP.

5.27 A server computer (or file server) may be a powerful PC or a minicomputer. As its name implies, it serves the rest of the network offering a generally-accessible hard disk file for all the other processors in the system and sometimes offering other resources, such as a shared printer for the network.

5.28 Clients on a network generally have their own hard disk storage capability. The server's hard disk can also be partitioned into separate drives for use by each node, and programs or data (eg a database) for common use can be stored on the file server. Accounting packages written for small businesses are usually available in a multi-user version for this purpose.

File servers

5.29 File servers must be powerful enough to handle multiple user requests and provide adequate storage. File servers are typically classified as 'low end' or 'high end'.

(a) A low end file server might be used in a network of around six users running WP software and a database. A low end server might be a dedicated machine or might be a highly specified standard PC. Once it is asked to support more than 10 users, it will probably need replacing and can be 'demoted' for use as a desktop PC.

(b) It might be replaced by a 'mid range server'. A mid range server might support 20-30 users.

(c) A high end file server might be used in a large department network of about 50-100 users handling transaction processing and an accounting system. High end servers have now been joined by superservers and 'enterprise servers' (effectively, mainframes). These are either departmental or organisation-wide, running sophisticated mission-critical systems and offering fault tolerance features. They might support upwards of 250 users.

The advantages of client/server computing

5.30 The advantages of the network approach using the client/server model are as follows.

Advantage	Comment
Greater resilience	*Processing is spread* over several computers, so client/server systems are more resilient. If one server breaks down, other locations can carry on processing.
Scalability	They are highly *scalable*. In other words instead of having to buy computing power in large quantities you can buy just the amount of power you need to do the job. When you need more you simply add another server.
Shared programs and data	*Program and data files* held on a file server can be *shared* by all the PCs in the network. With stand-alone PCs, each computer would have its own data files, and there might be unnecessary duplication of data.
	A system where everyone uses the same data will help to improve data processing and decision making. The value of some information increases with its availability.
Shared work-loads	Each PC in a network can do the *same work*.
	If there were separate stand-alone PCs, A might do job 1, B might do job 2, C might do job 3 and so on. In a network, any PC, (A, B or C) could do any job (1, 2 or 3). This provides flexibility in sharing work-loads. In a peak period for job 1, say, two or more people can share the work without having to leave their own desk.
Shared peripherals	*Peripheral* equipment can be *shared*. For example, in a LAN, five PCs might share a single on-line printer, whereas if there were stand-alone PCs, each might be given its own separate printer. If resources are scarce (for example fast laser printers) this is a significant benefit.
Communication and time management	LANs can be linked up to the office *communications network*, thus adding to the processing capabilities in an office. Electronic mail can be used to send messages, memos and electronic letters from node to node. Electronic calendar and diary facilities can also be used.
Compatibility	Client/server systems are more likely than centralised systems to have Windows *interfaces*, making it easier to move information between applications such as spreadsheets and accounting systems.
Ad hoc enquiries	They enable information to be moved to a separate server, allowing managers to make *ad hoc* enquiries without disrupting the main system.

The disadvantages of client/server computing

5.31 Not everybody is convinced of the value of the client/server approach.

   (a) Mainframes are better at dealing with very large volumes of transactions.

   (b) It is easier to control and maintain a system centrally. In particular it is easier to keep data secure.

   (c) It may be cheaper to 'tweak' an existing mainframe system rather than starting from scratch: for example it may be possible to give it a graphical user interface and to make data exchangeable between Windows and non-Windows based applications.

Network computers: thin clients

5.32 A widespread criticism at present is that there is now far more computing power on the desktop than is really necessary and a compromise is needed to control costs and simplify computing for end-users.

5.33 The Network Computer (NC) was touted by rivals to Microsoft and Intel such as Oracle and Sun Microsystems as a more efficient method of using computer technology. An NC is intended to be used for similar purposes to the PC but it does not have a hard disk (hence the name 'thin client'): its applications are downloaded when needed from powerful ('fat') servers on the organisation's own network or from a public network such as the Internet.

5.34 This saves on hardware costs, because the machine itself is less packed with expensive electronics, and on software and support costs, because there is no need to buy and install a separate copy of each application for each machine.

5.35 The main example to date is the JavaStation launched by Sun in 1996. The response has not been great, as people are reluctant to give up their processing power. The future may see a compromise with 'hybrid' software applications using programs stored partly on the users PC hard disk, *and* on a 'fat' server.

6   INTERORPERABILITY, STANDARDS AND QUALITY

Interoperability

6.1 Interoperability allows an individual or organisation to readily share and exchange information with another individual or organisation without having to use the same service provider or technology platform as the other party. Interoperability means concerns over data structures are able to be kept to a minimum.

Backward compatibility

6.2 A new version of a program is said to be backward compatible if it can use files and data created with an older version of the same program. Computer hardware is said to be backward compatible if it can run the same software as previous models.

6.3 Backward compatibility is important because it eliminates the need to start afresh when upgrading to a newer product. A backward-compatible word processor, for instance, allows users to edit documents created with a previous version of the program. In general, manufacturers try to keep their products backward compatible. Sometimes, however, it is necessary to sacrifice backward compatibility to take advantage of a new technology.

Legacy system

6.4 A legacy system is a computer system or application program which continues to be used because of the prohibitive cost of replacing or redesigning it and often despite its poor competitiveness and compatibility with modern equivalents. The implication is that the system is large, monolithic and difficult to modify.

6.5 Legacy *software* may only run on antiquated *hardware*, and the cost of maintaining this may eventually outweigh the cost of replacing both the software and hardware. The non Year 2000 compliance of many legacy systems forced their replacement.

Open systems

6.6 As organisations have developed computerised systems over a period of time, perhaps focusing on different functions at different times, a number of consequences have become apparent.

(a) They may have networks or other equipment supplied by a range of manufacturers.
(b) Data is duplicated in different areas of the business.
(c) Software may have become inefficient and out of date.

6.7 *Open systems* aim to ensure compatibility between different makes of equipment, enabling users to choose on the basis of price and performance. An open systems approach has a number of characteristics. The first is vendor independence. Applications can be 'ported' from one system to another. An open systems infrastructure supports organisation-wide functions and allows interoperability of networks and systems. Authorised users would be able to access applications and data from any part of the system.

Case example: Pure Java v Microsoft Java

Depending on who you talk to, Java is three things. Firstly, it is a programming language: a scaled down version, some would even argue a derivative, of C++. Java has the benefit of being a write-once-run-anywhere language, or so its creators claim.

Secondly, Java is a platform all of its own. It runs on any computer that has a Java Virtual machine - embedded code that recognises and reads Java code as it is downloaded onto the machine. Java is a single unifying platform for organisations with heterogeneous computing environments, which is most companies. Finally, Java has assumed the role as the ultimate IT panacea, 'Java-as-lifestyle'. number of industry heavyweights are jostling for position in their attempts to dominate the Java field. First up, naturally, is Sun. Creator and progenitor of Java, Sun appears to be betting the company jewels on Java. Definitely belonging to the 'Java-as-lifestyle' element, Sun has even committed itself to a '100% Pure Java' initiative, a bid to get programmers to write for and in native Java without calling on any local machine code, such as Windows APIs, for extra functionality.

Behind the Java evangelists are the two companies with most to gain from Java as a platform: IBM and Oracle. Although IBM has publicly chided Microsoft for not supporting the 100% Pure Java initiative, it is the Java as middleware idea that would appear to drive IBM's interest. Firstly, it has many different platforms to unify. Vendors are also increasingly wary of committing to proprietary security, messaging and transaction software from IBM, because they have been burned in the past and because they now demand the inter-operability and openness that the Internet exemplifies. ...

And then there is Microsoft, both contrary and dominant simultaneously. Microsoft has been anything but slow in developing Java. Its own Java VM is the fastest available. Yet Microsoft insists that Java is just a language. And to demonstrate its ambivalent attitude towards Java, it will make its breakaway move whilst attempting to win plaudits for development the fastest Java VM. ... This sort of commitment to developing Java tools and code for its other products, but endless re-iteration of how Java itself is only a poor rival to C++, is why so many of Microsoft's opponents accuse it of hypocrisy.

Microsoft came under more scrutiny when UK manager Jeremy Gittins commented on the likelihood of Microsoft splitting from the Java standard. Although Microsoft has yet to endorse these comments, it seems that the company is gearing itself up for a split. Microsoft claims

---

BPP
PUBLISHING

publicly that the Sun standard for Java will only run on 42 per cent of systems before making calls to the operating system, and that the cross-platform Java claim is simply not true except for trivial applets. So, the 'Java-as-extension-of-Windows' model is one that Microsoft appears committed to follow.

Source: *Information Week*, September 1997

The operating system

6.8 An *operating system* is like a 'silent partner' for the computer user, providing the interface between the computer hardware and both the user (via keyboard) and the other software. An operating system or operating software can be defined as a program or suite of programs which provide the 'bridge' between *applications* software (such as word processing packages, spreadsheets or accounting packages) and the hardware. For example, access to data files held on disk during the processing of a business application would be managed by the operating system.

Network operating systems

6.9 To carry out the administrative tasks connected with operating a network a special operating system is required. This establishes the links between the nodes of the network, monitors the operation of the network and controls recovery processes when the system or part of it breaks down. The main examples are Novell Netware, Microsoft Windows NT, and UNIX , which tends to be used on larger systems.

UNIX v Windows NT

6.10 The UNIX operating system was developed in 1969 as a non-proprietary multitasking operating system that could be portable to different computer architectures. By the 1980s it had been developed far enough for commercial users to take an interest in it. UNIX works equally well in a network environment as in a multi-user system. Particular areas where UNIX has demonstrated its capabilities are *communications*, where the ability to accommodate PC operating systems in the UNIX environment supports the use of electronic mail, and *engineering*, where UNIX's capabilities are suited to driving high-resolution graphics systems.

6.11 UNIX comes in 'flavours', depending who is selling it. For instance IBM's version is known as AIX; Hewlett Packard's Unix is called HP-UX. SCO is another well-known variety.

PC operating systems

6.12 In the PC market (stand alone and networked) the most widely used operating system is Microsoft Windows. Early incarnations of Windows, culminating in Windows 3.x (Windows 3.1 and Windows for Workgroups 3.11), were not genuine operating systems in their own right, but were really an operating *environment* for an older Microsoft system called MS-DOS.

6.13 **Windows NT** is a complete operating system in its own right, designed for **networks**, and now providing strong competition for other network operating systems like Novell NetWare.

6.14 For PCs and smaller networks there is **Windows 95**, and its upgrade **Windows 98**. **Windows 2000** (replacing NT) and **Windows Millennium Edition** (replacing 98) have recently been launched, but are not yet in widespread use.

6.15 Features of Windows 95/98 and NT include the following.

(a) A '**desktop**', from which everything in the system branches out. Disk drives, folders (directories), applications and files can all be placed on the desktop.

(b) A 'taskbar' which includes a **Start** button and buttons representing every open application.

(c) **Long file names** are supported (up to 256 characters).

(d) There is a **Recycle Bin** for easy deletion and recovery of files.

(e) Easy integration with widely used **networking** software is possible.

(f) **Multitasking** is available. It is described as 'true' or pre-emptive multitasking, under which each program is allocated a time slice and tasks switch whenever the operating system dictates.

(g) The **Microsoft Internet Explorer** browser is included.

6.16 Although it has bugs and irritations for the experienced user, Microsoft Windows provides a **comprehensive working environment**, managing programs specifically written for it. This makes it **easier for beginners** to learn how to use PCs, as most new applications tend to look and 'feel' the same as existing ones.

6.17 Other features of Windows 98 and Windows NT are explained in the table below.

Area	Comments
User-friendly	User interface enhancements include easier navigation, such as **single-click launching** of applications, icon highlighting, forward/backward buttons, and an easy to customise Start Menu.
Reliability	(a) Windows 98 can be set up to regularly **test** the user's hard disk, system files, and configuration information to increase the system reliability, and in many cases fix problems automatically. (b) Enhanced **backup** and **restore** functions.
Web integration	There are a variety of features designed to enhance **Internet access** and use of Internet facilities and technologies, and integrate them with the users system.
More entertaining	Windows 98 has better **graphics** and **video capabilities** and better support for **games** hardware such as joysticks. It supports **digital versatile disks** (DVD) and technologies connected with **digital television.**
More manageable for businesses	Tools such as Dr. Watson and System Information Utility make it easier for IT support staff to **diagnose and correct problems.**

6.18 Microsoft Windows CE is a **scaled down operating system** for small communications, entertainment and mobile-computing devices. Windows CE allows **non-PC devices** to communicate with each other, share information with Windows-based PCs, and connect to the Internet.

6.19 These include **handheld** PCs, 'wallet' PCs, wireless-communication devices such as digital information **pagers** and **cellular phones**, entertainment and multimedia consoles including **DVD players,** and purpose-built Internet access devices such as **Internet TVs,** digital set-top boxes and Internet 'Web phones.'

6.20 There are some computer users, particularly those working in design and graphics, who prefer the **Apple Macintosh** system. For an organisation that already has many Apple Macs and many staff familiar with them the best option may be to continue to use them.

6.21 Other competitors to Windows exist, such as **IBM's OS/2** but, since the majority of PC manufacturers send out their products with Windows pre-loaded, this is the system that is likely to predominate.

BPP PUBLISHING

Communications standards

6.22 One of the big problems in transmitting data down a public or private telephone wire is the possibility of distortion or loss of the message. There needs to be some way for a computer to:

   (a) detect whether there are *errors* in data transmission (eg loss of data, or data arriving out of sequence, ie in an order different from the sequence in which it was transmitted);

   (b) take steps to *recover* the lost data, even if this is simply to notify the computer or terminal operator to telephone the sender of the message that the whole data package will have to be re-transmitted. However, a more 'sophisticated' system can identify the corrupted or lost data more specifically, and request re-transmission of only the lost or distorted parts.

6.23 The mechanism used to detect and usually then to correct errors is known as a communications protocol. Protocol is defined as 'an agreed set of operational procedures governing the format of data being transferred, and the signals initiating, controlling and terminating the transfer.'

6.24 Factors covered by a protocol include the following.

   (a) Mode of transmission: synchronous or asynchronous.
   (b) Speed of transmission.
   (c) Full or half duplex transmission.
   (d) Format of the data.
   (e) Error detection and correction procedures.

6.25 One Standards body which has been influential is the Consultative Committee for International Telephone and Telegraphy (CCITT), which produced a series of Standards, numbered X1 to X29 and V1 to V57. X25 is the standard for packet switching systems, and V24 is the Standard for terminals connected to modems. X25 is compatible with the bottom three layers of the OSI model, which is also compatible with British Telecom's digital telephone exchange system, System X. The physical layer protocol (level 1) of X25 can only handle digital signals, so in those areas of the public network where analogue exchanges are still in use, a separate interface is necessary.

The ISO OSI

6.26 One set of protocols has been developed by the International Standards Organisation (ISO). It is known as open systems interconnection (OSI). Protocol was divided into seven functions in a *seven-layer reference model*.

6.27 Layers 1 to 4 handle the movement of data from one place to another. Layers 5 to 7 deal with the exchange of data between applications.

Layer	Explanation
1	The *physical layer* sets out specifications for the electrical connections. This includes matters such as the size and shape of plugs, the number of pins on the connector, the speed of transmission and so on.
2	The *data link layer* checks the data that flows into and out of each device and makes sure that no data loss occurs and corrects errors in data transmission.

Layer	Explanation
3	The *network layer* ensures that individual messages are switched and routed properly through the network, by establishing, maintaining and terminating connections. It also collects data related to billing for network services.
4	The *transport layer* controls the quality of transmissions and synchronises fast and slow equipment so that transmission takes place at a speed that the system can handle. If an incoming message arrives out of sequence the transport layer will put the data back into the right order.
5	The *session layer* deals with users opening and closing communications between two computers (open, close, read, write, etc). It establishes the connections between different applications and acts as a moderator, seeing that messages are sent as directed and allowing or prohibiting interruptions. If there is a failure the session layer re-establishes the connection. The session layer is also used for administrative tasks such as security.
6	The *presentation layer* translates data to and from standard formats used in the application layer, enabling different computer equipment to communicate. For instance it makes sure that the display shows the right number of characters per line.
7	The *application layer* deals with the interconnection of user programs and applications. This level makes sure that the right screens, headers and menus appear on the user's screen. It also controls checks such as signing on and passwords.

6.28 This indicates the *types* of protocols that are needed. However, the OSI standard itself has not been widely adopted and many suppliers are instead adopting TCP/IP (Transmissions Control Protocol/Internet Protocol).

TCP/IP

6.29 TCP/IP was developed in the US defence community and was accepted by the vast academic computer base in the US. It is regarded as cheaper and easier to implement than the OSI model and, because of the exponential growth of the Internet, it has become the *de facto* industry standard.

TCP/IP was initially successful because it delivered a few basic services that everyone needs (file transfer, electronic mail, remote logon) across a very large number of client and server systems. Several computers in a small department can use TCP/IP (along with other protocols) on a single LAN.

6.30 The IP component provides routing from the department to the enterprise network, then to regional networks, and finally to the global Internet. It is designed to be robust and automatically recover from any node or phone line failure. This design allows the construction of very large networks with less central management. However, because of the automatic recovery, network problems can go undiagnosed and uncorrected for long periods of time.

6.31 IP is responsible for moving packets of data from node to node. IP forwards each packet based on a four byte destination address (the IP number). IP operates on 'gateway' machines that move data from department to organisation to region and then around the world.

6.32   TCP is responsible for verifying the correct delivery of data from client to server. Data can be lost in the intermediate network. TCP adds support to detect errors or lost data and to trigger retransmission until the data is correctly and completely received.

Quality issues

6.33   An important modern management philosophy is Total Quality Management . TQM is the process of applying a zero defect philosophy to the management of *all* resources and relationships within the firm as a means of developing and sustaining a culture of *continuous improvement* which focuses on *meeting customers' expectations.'*

6.34   One of the basic principles of TQM is that the cost of preventing mistakes is less than the cost of correcting them once they occur. The aim should therefore be to *get things right first time.*

6.35   A second basic principle of TQM is the idea of continuous improvement: dissatisfaction with the *status quo* and the belief that it is always possible to improve. The aim should be to 'get it *more* right next time'.

6.36   Eight key requirements of quality may be listed as follows.

   (a)   Accept that the only thing that matters is the customer, whether the 'customer' is somebody who buys things from your organisation or an internal customer (ie a colleague).

   (b)   Recognise the all-pervasive nature of the customer-supplier relationship, including internal customers: passing sub-standard material down to another division is not satisfactory.

   (c)   Move from relying on inspecting to a predefined level of quality to preventing the cause of the defect in the first place.

   (d)   Each operative or group of operatives must be personally responsible for defect-free production or service in their domain.

   (e)   There must be a move away from acceptable quality levels to defect levels measured in parts per million.

   (f)   All departments should try obsessively to get things right first time: this applies to misdirected telephone calls and typing errors as much as to production.

   (g)   Quality certification programmes should be introduced.

   (h)   The cost of poor quality should be emphasised: good quality generates savings.

6.37   When quality improvements are achieved by introducing new technology that makes it easier for people to do their jobs effectively, or by introducing new practices that are designed to help workers to take more care, then *training* to show people how to use the new technology or implement the new practices will be required.

6.38   However, workers themselves are frequently the best source of information about how (or how not) to improve quality. 'Training' means training workers to *want* to improve things: it is a matter of changing attitudes.

   (a)   Workers can be *motivated* by a positive approach to quality: producing quality work is a tangible and worthwhile objective. Also, where responsibility for quality checking has been given to the worker himself (encouraging self-supervision), job satisfaction may be increased: it is a kind of job enrichment, and also a sign of trust and respect, because imposed controls have been removed.

   (b)   Cultural orientation (the deep 'belief' in quality, filtered down to all operatives) and work group norms and influence can be enlisted. Inter-group competition to meet and beat quality standards, for example, might be encouraged. Quality circles may be set up, perhaps with responsibility for implementing improvements which they identify.

6.39 You are probably aware of the ISO 9000 (formerly BS 5750) group of quality standards from your other studies. ISO 9001 is the international standard for quality management systems which was formally extended to cover software production in 1991 with the publication of ISO 9000-3.

TickIT

6.40 The UK developed a 'sector certification scheme' for the software sector. This was christened TickIT. TickIT builds on ISO 9001, in particular by including the international interpretation of the ISO 9001 (ISO 9000-3) requirements for the software development environment, by requiring that auditors of software development should be appropriately trained and experienced, and by requiring that a quality management system must be fully reassessed for continuing relevance every three years.

7   COMPUTER SUPPORTED CO-OPERATIVE WORK   12/97

Integrated management

7.1 Stephen Alter (*Information Systems: A Management Perspective*)points out that business processes may be completely unrelated or may be integrated at any one of five levels.

(a) *Common culture:* people involved in the two separate processes share the same general beliefs and expectations about how people communicate and work together.

(b) *Common standards:* for instance, two business processes may both use Microsoft Office software for administration, but otherwise operate independently. This offers the possibility of closer integration in the future.

(c) *Information sharing:* two different business processes share some of the same information. For instance a sales department and a production department may both be able to access a database showing what production capacity was spare and available for new orders.

(d) *Co-ordination:* different business processes pass information to one another to co-ordinate efforts towards a shared objective. For instance the marketing department tell the production department what customers want and the production tell the marketing department what it is possible to produce. A compromise is reached that is achievable by both parties, who then go about their separate activities.

(e) *Collaboration:* a this level different processes merge part or all of their identity. For instance production experts spend part of their time on marketing activities or *vice versa.*

7.2 It is possible for systems to be *too* tightly integrated (or too 'closely coupled', to use the terminology of systems theory). For example, if a procurement system is so closely integrated with an order processing system that new items are assumed by order processing to be available for despatch the instant they are delivered, the system is likely to collapse if put under time pressure. In reality the items may need to be repacked, put into bundles with a variety of other items, weighed, checked for quality or whatever, and a certain amount of delay in the linked systems is quite acceptable, or perhaps even desirable.

7.3 However, since organisations by their very nature rely upon people working together and co-operating with each other, it should be obvious that information systems should be designed to help people to do this. This is the principle behind Computer Supported Co-Operative Working (CSCW).

CSCW and groupware

7.4 Computer supported co-operative (or 'collaborative') working is a term which combines the understanding of the way people work in groups with the enabling technologies of computer networking and associated hardware, software, services and techniques.

7.5 Internal telephone networks are perhaps the most obvious example of the use of technology to facilitate group working. Other examples, such as video-conferencing and e-mail, were discussed in Chapter 4.

7.6 *Groupware* is a term used to describe a collection of IT tools designed for the use of co-operative or collaborative work groups. Typically, these groups are small project-oriented teams that have important tasks and tight deadlines. Groupware can involve software, hardware, services, and/or group process support.

7.7 Perhaps the best known groupware product at present is Lotus Notes. However, there are many related products and technologies.

7.8 At the *individual* level groupware is similar to an electronic personal organiser. Features might include the following.

(a) A scheduler (or diary or calendar), allowing users to keep track of their schedule and plan meetings with others.

(b) An electronic address book to keep personal and business contact information up-to-date and easy to find. Contacts can be sorted and filed in any way.

(c) To do lists. Personal and business to-do lists can be kept in one easy-to-manage place, and tasks can quickly be prioritised.

(d) A journal, which is used. Record interactions with important contacts, record Outlook items (such as e-mail messages) and files that are significant to you, and record activities of all types and track them all without having to remember where you saved each one.

(e) A jotter, for jotting down notes as quick reminders of questions, ideas, directions, and so on.

7.9 There are clearly advantages in having information such as this available from the desktop at the touch of a button, rather than relying on scraps of paper, address books, corporate telephone directories. However, it is when groupware is used to share information with colleagues that it comes into its own. Here are some of the features that may be found.

(a) *Messaging*, comprising an *e-mail* in-box which is used to send and receive messages from the office, home, or the road and *routing* facilities, enabling users to send a message to a single person, send it sequentially to a number of people (who may add to it or comment on it before passing it on), or sending it to every one at once.

(b) Access to an information database, and customisable 'views' of the information held on it, which can be used to standardise the way information is viewed in a workgroup.

(c) *Group scheduling*, to keep track of colleagues itineraries. Microsoft Exchange Server, for instance offers a 'Meeting Wizard', which can consult the diaries of everyone needed to attend a meeting and automatically work out when they will be available, which venues are free, and what resources are required.

(d) *Public folders*. These collect, organise, and share files with others on the team or across the organisation.

(e) One person (for instance a secretary or a stand-in during holidays or sickness) can be given '*delegate access*' to another's groupware folders and send mail on their behalf, or read, modify, or create items in public and private folders on their behalf.

(e) *Conferencing*. Participation in public, online discussions with others.

(f) *Assigning tasks.* A task request can be sent to a colleague who can accept, decline, or reassign the task. After the task is accepted, the groupware will keeps the task status up-to-date on a task list.

(g) *Voting* type facilities that can, say, request and tally responses to a multiple-choice question sent in a mail message (eg 'Here is a list of options for this year's Christmas party').

(h) *Hyperlinks* in mail messages. The recipient can click the hyperlink to go directly to a Web page or file server.

(i) Workflow management (see below) with various degrees of sophistication.

7.10 The groupware package may also link directly in with other decision support packages used in the organisation.

Workflow

7.11 Workflow is a term used to describe the defined series of tasks within an organisation to produce a final outcome.

7.12 Sophisticated workgroup computing applications allow the user to define different workflows for different types of jobs. For example, in a publishing setting, a document might be automatically routed from writer to editor to proofreader to production.

7.13 At each stage in the workflow, one individual or group is responsible for a specific task. Once the task is complete, the workflow software ensures that the individuals responsible for the next task are notified and receive the data they need to execute their stage of the process.

7.14 Workflow systems can be described according to the type of process they are designed to deal with. There are three common types.

(a) *Image-based workflow systems* are designed to automate the flow of paper through an organisation, by transferring the paper to digital "images". These were the first workflow systems that gained wide acceptance. These systems are closely associated with "imaging" (or 'document image processing' (DIP))technology, and empathise the routing and processing of digitised images.

(b) *Form-based workflow systems* (formflow) are designed to route forms intelligently throughout an organisation. These forms, unlike images, are text-based and consist of editable fields. Forms are automatically routed according to the information entered on the form. In addition, these form-based systems can notify or remind people when action is due. This can provide a higher level of capability than image-based workflow systems.

(c) *Co-ordination-based workflow systems* are designed to facilitate the completion of work by providing a framework for co-ordination of action. The framework is aimed to address the business processes, rather than the optimisation of information or material processes. Such systems have the potential to improve organisational productivity by addressing the issues necessary for customer satisfaction, rather than automating procedures that are not closely related to customer satisfaction.

Intranets

7.15 The idea behind an 'intranet' is that companies set up their own mini version of the Internet, using a combination of the company's own networked computers and Internet technology. Each employee has a browser and a server computer distributes corporate information on a wide variety of topics, and also offers access to the global Net.

7.16 Potential applications include daily company newspapers, induction material, online procedure and policy manuals, employee web pages where individuals post up details of their activities and progress, and internal databases of the corporate information store.

7.17 Most of the *cost* of an intranet is the staff time required to set up the system. The *benefits* of intranets are diverse.

(a) A considerable amount of money can be saved from the elimination of storage, printing and distribution of documents that can be made available to employees on-line.

(b) Documents on-line are more widely used than those that are kept on shelves, especially if the document is bulky (for instance company information handbooks, finance manuals and procedures manuals) and needs to be searched. This means that there are improvements in productivity and efficiency.

(c) It is much easier to update information in electronic form.

(d) Wider access to corporate information should open the way to more flexible working patterns. For instance if bulky reference materials are available on-line then there is little need to be in the office at all.

Case example: Swiss Bank Corporation

One of the biggest users of intranets is Swiss Bank Corporation. In fact it has so many - around 100 - that it has just appointed a head of intranets to co-ordinate them all.

At Swiss Bank Corporation intranets are used for:

Corporate accounting and credit information
Publishing research internally, and to a select group of 50 external clients
Trading information
Ordering information technology equipment
IT project management
Informing staff of regulatory changes

The job of Marie Adee, the company's new head of intranets, is to unify the disparate sites so that employees can find information easily. The sites will also be given a common look and feel. All the company's sites can be searched using the Netscape Navigator Web browser, but the company is also standardising on Lotus Domino software.

This software will sit on the server computers that store the intranet information. Domino incorporates Lotus Notes information sharing software. So employees will be able to input information to Web sites either through Notes or through their Web browsers. It will also be possible for SBC to set up workflow applications - which control the flow of work between users in a team.

Extranet

7.18 An extranet is an intranet that is partially accessible to authorised outsiders. Authorised outsiders are allocated a username and password, which allows entry and determines which parts of the extranet are able to be viewed. Extranets are becoming a very popular means for businesses (eg customer and supplier) to share information.

8 HOMEWORKING

8.1 Advances in communications technology have, for some tasks, reduced the need for the actual presence of an individual in the office. This is particularly true of tasks involving computers.

(a) The worker can, for example, do 'keying in' tasks at home.
(b) The keyed-in data can be sent over a telecommunications link to head office.

8.2 The advantages to the organisation of homeworking are as follows.

(a) Cost savings on space. Office rental costs and other charges can be very expensive. If firms can move some of their employees on to a homeworking basis, money can be saved.

(b) A larger pool of labour. The possibility of working at home might attract more applicants for clerical positions, especially from people who have other demands on their time (eg going to and from school) which cannot be fitted round standard office hours.

(c) If the homeworkers are freelances, then the organisation avoids the need to pay them when there is insufficient work, when they are sick, on holiday etc.

8.3 The advantages to the individual of homeworking are as follows.

(a) No time is wasted commuting to the office. Perhaps commuting time is more a problem of the congested metropolis of London than in some other areas, but commuting can often take up over two hours a day.

(b) The work can be organised flexibly around the individual's domestic commitments (eg school trips).

(c) Jobs which require concentration can sometimes be done better at home without the disruption of the office.

8.4 The problems for the organisation are chiefly problems of control. Managers who practise close supervision will perhaps feels a worrying loss of control. Managers might view homeworking as an opportunity for laziness and slack work (more 'tele' than work!)

8.5 Other 'problems' for the organisation might be as follows.

(a) Co-ordination of the work of different homeworkers. The job design should ensure that homeworkers perform to the required standard.

(b) Training. If a homeworker needs a lot of help on a task, this implies that the task has not been properly explained.

(c) Culture. A homeworker is relatively isolated from the office and therefore, it might be assumed, from the firm. However, questions of loyalty and commitment do not apply for an organisation's sales force, whose members are rarely in the office.

8.6 Problems for homeworkers are as follows.

(a) Isolation. Work provides people with a social life, and many people might miss the sense of community if they are forced to work at home.

(b) Intrusions. A homeworker is vulnerable, by definition, to other interruptions (eg from members of his or her family forgetting that the worker is *working* at home, in time that the employer is paying for).

(c) Adequate space. It is not always possible to obtain a quiet space at home in which to work.

(d) In practice many homeworkers, especially if they are freelances, have fewer employment rights. They are not entitled to sick pay or holiday pay. They have limited security, as the firm can dispense with their services at whim.

9 OUTSOURCING THE IS FUNCTION   6/00

9.1 Many organisations do not employ specialist IS staff because they cannot justify the costs of full time professionals. Other organisations might employ some specialist staff but not enough for all their requirements. In some cases, organisations will not even possess the equipment to do their own computerised processing.

9.2 If an organisation does not wish (or cannot afford) to have its own in-house IS management it may prefer to use external resources.

BPP PUBLISHING

Computer bureaux

9.3 Computer bureaux are organisations which provide computing facilities to their clients. As the cost of hardware has reduced during over the past decade, the importance of computer bureaux has reduced.

Facilities management

9.4 Facilities management, also referred to as outsourcing, is not a concept which is limited to the arena of computing. Any company which contracts out necessary services to a third party is using facilities management (FM) in one form or another.

9.5 Buying in services is seen as a better way of managing resources and of obtaining access to specialists in particular fields. The practice has been firmly established for years in such activities as sandwich-making, laundry services and office cleaning.

9.6 As the significance of IT grew through the 1980s, it became clear that a large proportion of many companies' workforces were engaged in IT activities and that IT expenditure was frequently in excess of budget. This experience clashed with the belief held by many executives that IT should be a critical but subordinate function of the core business, whether operating in international financial markets or running a UK county council.

9.7 Facilities management has enabled many organisations simply to pick a supplier, draw up a contract and hand over the entire responsibility for running the organisation's IT function.

9.8 The third party supplier, or FM company, usually takes over the employment contracts of the organisation's IT staff. Their terms and conditions of employment are protected by legislation in the form of the Transfer of Undertakings (Protection of Employment) Regulations, or TUPE. It may also take over the organisation's computer centre.

9.9 FM companies operating in the UK include Andersens, Cap Gemini, EDS and CFM.

9.10 The advantages of facilities management are as follows.

(a) A small organisation may have substantial data processing requirements, but not have the staff, management time or expertise to cope with them.

(b) Facilities management is an effective form of cost control, as there is a contract where services are specified in advance for a fixed price. If the facilities management supplier is inefficient, the extra costs will not be borne by the 'host' organisation.

(c) A facilities management company has economies of scale. If two organisations employ the same FM company, the FM company's research into new products on the market or new technologies can be shared between them.

(d) Similarly, FM companies can employ staff with specific expertise which can be shared between several clients. FM is a way of coping with the widespread skills shortage, widely felt to be a feature of the IS labour market.

9.11 The drawbacks, however, can be quite considerable.

(a) It is arguable that information and its provision is an inherent part of management. Unlike office cleaning, or catering, an organisation's IS services are too important to be contracted out. They are at the heart of management.

(b) Technologies which play a strategic role in an organisation's success cannot be handed over to outsiders. The FM company has strategic objectives of its own, which are different from (though probably not conflicting with) the strategic objectives of the host. An IS function run by an FM company will be even more separate from the overall business functions than an organisation's own IS department.

(c) Once an organisation has handed over its computing to an FM company, it is locked in to the arrangement. The decision is very difficult to reverse. Should the FM company supply unsatisfactory levels of service, then the effort and expense and organisation would have to incur to rebuild its own computing function and expertise would be enormous.

(d) The use of FM does not encourage a proper awareness of the potential costs and benefits of IT amongst managers '...many managers naturally lean towards FM because they are technophobic and frightened by their jargon-spouting DP departments. The result...is that they opt for the easy if short-sighted route' (*Financial Times*).

9.12 A vital aspect of any FM contract is the service level contract (SLC). This should specify clearly minimum levels of service to be provided. It should also contain arrangements for an exit route, addressing what happens if the contract is handed over to another contractor or brought in-house. The responsibilities of the outgoing FM company should be clearly specified.

Other organisations

Software houses

9.13 Software houses concentrate on the provision of services including feasibility studies, systems analysis and design, development of operating systems software, provision of application program packages, 'tailor-made' application programming, specialist systems advice, and so on.

Consultancy firms

9.14 The use of consultancy services enables management to learn directly or indirectly from the experience of others. The success of an individual consultancy project will depend largely on the expertise of the firm approached and more particularly on the individual consultant or consultants employed. Many larger consultancies are owned by big international accountancy firms; smaller consultancies may consist of one or two person outfits with a high level of specialist experience in one area.

Computer manufacturers

9.15 Computer manufacturers or their designated suppliers will provide the equipment necessary for a system. They will also provide, under a maintenance contract, engineers who will deal with any routine servicing and with any breakdown of the equipment. In addition they may supply the operating systems software and very often application programs. They may also undertake to 'tailor' the application programs to fit into the client's system. On supplying the equipment and software, the manufacturer will normally offer a training course for the client's staff, the cost of which may be included in the total price, or may be charged separately.

Problems in dealing with third parties   *6/94, 6/00*

9.16 Some organisations experience difficulties in their relationship with facilities managers, consultants and the like. Possible reasons for a breakdown in relationships are as follows.

(a) The company may not have taken sufficient care in *selecting* a third party suitable for the job. Firms vary widely in expertise and specialisation, from the large firms of management consultants operating as part of international accountancy partnerships through to small firms with a high degree of specialisation in particular areas. Sometimes a small specialist consultancy or facilities manager may have expertise in just the right area; alternatively an organisation might need advice in a number of related areas, in which case it might ask its audit firm's consultancy wing to tender for the work.

(b) The company and/or the third party may not have invested enough time, effort and suitable tools in clearly *defining the 'problem(s)'*, ie company needs.

(c) There are a number of possible reasons why *communications* may be damaged.

(i) The third parties' language may be inappropriate (possibly too technical).

(ii)   Methodology may not be user-oriented - leading to users feeling distanced from the development.

(iii)   Company unwilling to participate - possibly lacking confidence in their ability to contribute.

(iv)   Lack of agreement on precise terms of reference at the start of the project.

(v)   Failure to identify a specific person within the organisation to liaise with the third party.

(vi)   Failure to set regular progress meetings, measurable and deliverable stages and approval to continue.

9.17   Steps to try to overcome these problems would include the following.

(a)   A careful selection process based on their experience, evidence of previous success and, most important, their willingness to listen and understanding the company's needs.

(b)   A clear problem definition stage with suitable tools to enable the needs to be fully explored by the company and consultants together, eg conceptual models, dataflow diagrams.

(c)   Again, a suitable methodology and/or tools will help with communications but good communication requires mutual trust and understanding. Thus a willingness to listen, understand and respond is essential. Open, basic and direct questions should be asked and answers required to be in a similar vein. A disciplined communications and reporting structure should be set up from the start.

Factors to considering when selecting third party firms

12/94

9.18   An organisation should consider the following in choosing a suitable consultant.

(a)   Are we sure of the objectives of our proposed computerised information systems?

(b)   Is the third party able to understand our business objectives and formulate a strategy for the information system to support them?

(c)   Does he/she have experience and a successful record in dealing with businesses of this type?

(d)   Is he/she independent of any computer supply company and thus able to give impartial advice?

(e)   What qualifications and/or professional membership(s) does the consultant have which support his/her knowledge and professional competence?

(f)   Has the third party responded in a positive, prompt and helpful manner to our request for discussions?

(g)   Does he/she have relevant recent experience in our type of business?

9.19   Once the company has met prospective suppliers of services, the following questions should be asked.

(a)   Did they communicate in a language and style to which we could relate?

(b)   Did they show a positive attitude and a real understanding of our problems?

(c)   Are they available to give sufficient time and attention to our needs?

(d)   Did they offer evidence and examples of completed work?

(e)   Do they have a suitable network of expert support?

(f)   Are they willing to prepare a full proposal for the study complete with costing to a tight deadline?

(g)   Will they be able to establish a good working relationship with their key contact(s) in the company? Individual relationships are very important at this level, and if any of the organisation's key staff took a dislike to the supplier, this should be discussed before appointment.

Chapter roundup

- A strategy is needed for information management because IT involves high costs, it is critical to the success of many organisations, it can be used as a strategic weapon and it affects stakeholders in the organisation.

- There are three elements to the development of any strategy. It must review how IT fits into the overall business needs of the organisation, it must consider the current use of IT and it must address the potential opportunities that IT can bring.

- An organisation may appoint an information director, whose role is to ensure that IT issues relating to strategic planning are considered at board level. An information director can ensure that IT activities support overall organisational strategy and objectives.

- The starting point for a decision to build a new system or improve an existing one varies from one situation to another. Users might feel that a problem in an existing system can be eliminated, or a process improved, by the introduction of a computer-based information system. Alternatively, the organisation may wish to gain competitive advantage, for example by improving the speed of its customer service procedures. It may be that new possibilities are presented by advances in available technology.

- An important issue in systems development is the question of centralisation or decentralisation. Centralisation allows the use of a single set of files and offers better security and control. Disadvantages include the extent of local office reliance on head office and the risk of delays in processing.

- A local area network is a system of interconnected PCs (and other devices, such as printers and disks) which are connected by special cable. LANs can have a server computer holding files used by more than one computer, and providing storage capacity to the other computers in the network. In a LAN, data processing tasks can be shared between a number of PCs, and single items of peripheral equipment can be accessed by all of them.

- A wide area network is a network of computers which are dispersed on a wider geographical scale than LANs. They are connected over the public telecommunications network. A WAN will normally use minicomputers or powerful PCs.

- Client-server computing is a configuration in which desktop PCs are regarded as 'clients' that request access to the services available on a more powerful server PC, such as access to a file, e-mail, or printing facilities.

- Interoperability means that it is possible to share and exchange information and facilities with others without having to use the same service provider or technology platform and with a minimum of concern about data structures, and a minimum need for new skills. A key issues in the open systems debate at present are the choice of UNIX or Windows NT as an operating system. Standards tend to be imposed through commercial dominance of a market (Windows) or through practicality (TCP/IP).

- Computer supported co-operative working combines the understanding of the way people work in groups with the enabling technologies of computer networking and associated hardware, software, services and techniques. Groupware and workflow software are key products. Internal versions of the Internet called Intranets are the current fashion.

- Outsourcing or facilities management entails contracting out the management of information systems to a third party. This is an increasingly common trend, but needs to be carefully managed.

BPP
PUBLISHING

1   In what ways may IT be important to an organisation? (see para 1.7)

2   How can IT help a business to win competitive advantage? (1.9)

3   What three areas may an information strategy cover? (2.8)

4   Explain three roles of an information director (3.4 - 3.9)

5   What does an information centre do? (4.6 - 4.12)

6   What are the advantages of client-server computing? (5.30)

7   What does 'interoperability' mean? (6.1)

8   What is TCP/IP? (6.29 - 6.32)

9   How may business processes be integrated? (7.1)

10   What are typical group working features of groupware? (7.9)

11   What are the three common types of workflow system? (8.4 - 8.6)

12   What are the benefits of intranets? (7.17)

13   What problems does home working cause? (8.4 - 8.6)

14   What are the advantages and disadvantages of facilities management? (9.10 - 9.11)

Now try illustrative questions 8, 22 and 29 at the end of the Study Text

Part B
Systems analysis and design

Chapter 6

THE SYSTEMS DEVELOPMENT LIFECYCLE

This chapter covers the following topics.

1   Systems development

2   Identifying projects

3   The feasibility study

4   Areas of feasibility

5   Costs and benefits

6   The feasibility study report

7   Systems investigation

Introduction

In this chapter we turn our attention to the systems development life cycle, a framework for the development of information systems. We shall concentrate on the feasibility study, the first stage, and systems investigation, the second stage, examining the common techniques of systems investigation, including the use of interviews and questionnaires.

---

1   SYSTEMS DEVELOPMENT

6/00

1.1   Managing information systems *development* is a major operation involving large parts of an organisation and elements of its environment.

1.2   Two approaches to the description of the development process can be distinguished.

     (a)   A model is a framework which identifies the various stages through which the organisation or department passes. It is intended to be predictive and to be of value to management in developing techniques to deal with each stage.

     (b)   A *methodology* is a structured approach to the management of IS development. It is a collection of tools, techniques and procedures used by systems development staff in implementing a new information system.

1.3   Two *models* will be introduced here. Chapter 7 is concerned with methodologies.

The stage hypothesis

1.4   Richard Nolan developed a model to reflect the acquisition and use of computers in the organisation. His *stage hypothesis* can be used as a planning tool for the future development of systems. The six stages include phases where progress is made and phases of consolidation.

BPP
PUBLISHING

Stage	Comment
Initiation	This stage covers the organisation's first steps in computerisation. Systems are selected because the more technically-minded staff are keen to acquire them, not because they are necessarily cost effective.
Contagion	The wider benefits of computerisation are perceived by a range of potential users, and the organisation is committed to large-scale investment, not necessarily in a co-ordinated manner. End-users begin to influence the development process.
Control	Following the contagion stage, there is user dissatisfaction with systems and it becomes apparent that the organisation's resources are finite. This may be the point at which it is realised that investment in computers should not be undertaken solely for financial reasons. Controls may be introduced in the form of steering committees, project management teams and the introduction of development controls.
Integration	The role of the controls which have been implemented becomes clear. User involvement in development and IT issues generally increases.
Data administration	It becomes apparent that data is an important resource of the organisation. Even if there is no corporate database, data management becomes an important concept. A database administrator may be appointed.
Maturity	Information flows in the organisation mirror the real-world requirements of the organisation. Data resources are flexible, permitting their use in any application. It is acknowledged that this final stage may not be reached in practice.

1.5 An organisation will *never be at a single point in this process*. It is far more likely that different departments will be at different points of development at the same time. The stage hypothesis helps management to identify the stage which a department or operating unit has reached, so that development activities can be *monitored and controlled*.

The systems development lifecycle   12/96, 6/00

1.6 The systems development lifecycle was developed in the 1960s by the National Computing Centre.

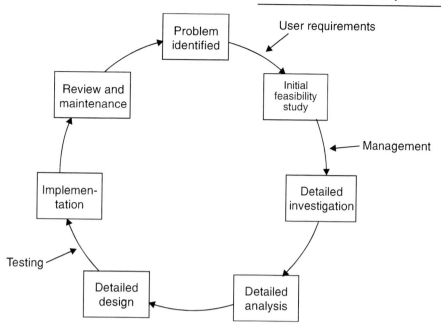

Stage	Comment
Identification of a problem	In the case of the development of a new information system, this stage will involve an analysis of the organisation's information requirements. Such an analysis should be carried out in conjunction with users, so that their *actual* requirements can be identified, rather than their *likely* requirements.
Feasibility study	This involves a brief review of the existing system and the identification of a range of possible alternative solutions. One will usually be recommended on the basis of its costs and benefits, although it is possible for a decision not to proceed to result.
Systems investigation	This is a fact finding exercise which investigates the existing system to assess its problems and requirements and to obtain details of data volumes, response times and other key indicators.
Systems analysis	Once the workings of the existing system have been documented, they can be analysed. This process examines why current methods are used, what alternatives might achieve the same, or better, results, what restricts the effectiveness of the system and what performance criteria are required from a system.
Systems design	This is a technical phase which considers both computerised and manual procedures, addressing, in particular, inputs, outputs, program design, file design and security. A detailed specification of the new system is produced.
Systems implementation	This stage carries development through from design to operations. It involves acquisition (or writing) of software, program testing, file conversion or set-up, acquisition and installation of hardware and 'going live'.
Review and maintenance	This is an ongoing process which ensures that the system meets the objectives set during the feasibility study, that it is accepted by users and that its performance is satisfactory.

Criticisms of the systems development lifecycle

1.7 The systems development lifecycle approach to systems development was adopted by many organisations. While it has some advantages, it has a number of *drawbacks* if incorrectly applied.

(a) The information needs of *middle and senior management* could be ignored if computerisation is just seen as a means of speeding up high-volume routine transaction processing, not providing information for decision-making.

(b) When computer systems are first introduced, they may be modelled after the manual systems they were replacing. If the computerisation is ambitious, it might lead to a potentially beneficial *rethink* of the way the organisation carries out its activities with a view to *improving* the system. There is more on this later.

(c) *User requirements* may be poorly defined and so new systems do not live up to users' expectations.

(d) System *documentation* may be written for programmers and specialists and be more of a technical manual than a guide for the user. Problems could also occur, if inadequately documented modifications lead to 'bugs' elsewhere in the system.

(e) Routine transaction processing systems may not be able to cope with *unusual situations*, and so some complicated processing will still be performed manually.

2 IDENTIFYING PROJECTS

12/99

A planned approach

2.1 A planned approach is needed when identifying and selecting new computer projects. The following actions should be considered.

(a) IT is critical to the success of many organisations. This means that an *IT strategy* should form a *core part of the overall corporate strategy* and should be developed/updated whenever the organisation's strategy is reviewed or as otherwise necessary. IT needs can then be identified in the context of *overall business needs*.

(b) Because IT is critical, it requires adequate *representation at senior management level*. It is no longer suitable for IT to be under the control of the MD, FD or computer centre manager. It really needs a separate Board level person responsible, such as an *Information Director* or an *IS director*. This will help to ensure that IT is given adequate consideration at strategic level.

(c) The IT development can no longer function as a subsystem of accounting, administration or finance. Its importance means that it should be given *separate departmental or functional status* in the organisation with its own reporting lines and responsibilities. It is no longer simply an organ of the accounts department: as more departments use IT, there is less reason for it to be organised by one department.

(d) Once the IT department has been set up, its *funding* must be considered. A simplistic approach would be to treat it as an overhead; this is simple but inefficient. There are various approaches possible to the recovery of IT costs from user departments, and the IT department may even operate as a commercial concern providing services to third parties at a profit.

(e) A *strategic plan for the use of IT* should be developed. This should take in separate elements such as information technology and information systems. It should also acknowledge the importance of the organisation's information resource.

(f) If new computer systems are to be introduced regularly, the organisation may set up a *steering committee* to oversee *systems development*. A steering committee can also be set up for a one-off project. The role of the steering committee includes approving or rejecting individual projects and where appropriate submitting projects to the Board for approval. The composition and determination of terms of reference for the steering committee must be agreed.

(h) The *approach* of the organisation to individual projects must be decided. Will it follow the traditional *life cycle* or will it use a *methodology*? Commercial methodologies impose discipline and have a number of advantages.

(i) Procedures for *evaluating and monitoring performance* both during and after a project need to be put in place. Many methodologies require formal sign-off of each stage, but this does not obviate the need for good project management or for post-implementation evaluation.

(j) Details of the *systems development procedures* must be agreed. If a commercial methodology is used, much of this will be pre-determined, but, for example, decisions must be made on the approach to *feasibility studies*, methods of *cost-benefit analysis, design specifications* and conventions, *tools and techniques* which will be used, *reporting* lines, contents of standard *invitations to tender*, drawing up of *supplier conditions* and procedures for *testing and implementation*.

3 THE FEASIBILITY STUDY   *12/95, 6/96, 6/00*

3.1 The feasibility study is the first stage of systems development in the systems development lifecycle. A *feasibility study* is a formal study to decide what type of system can be developed which meets the needs of the organisation.

3.2 Steps, in outline, are as follows. These are explained in more detail in the remainder of this chapter.

(a) Establish the objectives of the new system and their relationship to organisational goals, in particular noting any concerns of management and users about deficiencies in the current system.

(b) Gain an understanding of the present organisation structure and communication channels.

(c) Examine and evaluate the existing system and its costs and benefits.

(d) Compare the implications of up-grading the existing system with building a new one.

(e) Formulate the objectives of the new system and set performance criteria or benchmark standards.

(f) Establish technical needs (hardware, software, communications (network) software).

(g) Evaluate staff expertise/development requirements.

(h) Consider other human factors such as working environment and ergonomics.

(i) Consider the security implications of the new system.

(f) Prepare a detailed cost/benefit analysis to include all tangible and intangible items.

(g) Submit a report and recommendations to include:

   (i) a clear recommendation of the most suitable systems;

   (ii) a full justification of anticipated benefits in terms of company needs, pressure of competition, growing complexity and decision making (marketing in particular);

   (iii) a detailed budget including capital and revenue items;

   (iv) an operational plan for investigation, analysis, design, development, implementation, testing, maintenance and review of the system;

   (v) membership of the steering group to manage the project.

   Methods used for fact gathering may include interviews, questionnaires, documents, meetings and observation, described later in this chapter.

3.3 Some of the work performed at the feasibility study stage may be similar to work performed later on in the development of the project. This is because some of the information necessary to decide whether to go ahead with a project or trying to define a problem is common to both phases. Amongst factors which may be considered as part of the feasibility study which might also feature in a later stage in the systems development are *investigation and analysis work*, a *cost-benefit analysis* and the identification of *user requirements*, at least in outline.

3.4   Among the reasons for having a feasibility study are that new systems can *cost* a great deal to develop, be very *disruptive* during development and implementation in terms of the opportunity cost of management time, and have far reaching consequences in a way an organisation conducts its business or is structured.

3.5   *Project management* skills are necessary from an early stage. Project management is considered in Chapter 11.

Terms of reference

3.6   The terms of reference for a feasibility study group must be set out by a steering committee, the information director or the board of directors, and might consist of the following items.

   (a)   To *investigate* and report on an *existing system*, its procedures and costs.
   (b)   To define the *systems requirements*.
   (c)   To establish whether these requirements are being met by the *existing* system.
   (d)   To establish whether they could be met by an *alternative* system.
   (e)   To specify *performance criteria* for the system.
   (f)   To recommend the *most suitable system* to meet the system's objectives.
   (g)   To prepare a detailed *cost budget*, within a specified budget limit.
   (h)   To prepare a draft *plan for implementation* within a specified timescale.
   (i)   To establish whether the hoped-for *benefits* could be realised.
   (j)   To establish a detailed design, implementation and operating *budget*.
   (k)   To *compare* the detailed budget with the costs of the current system.
   (l)   To set the *date* by which the study group must *report back*.
   (m) To decide which *operational managers* should be approached by the study group.

3.7   The remit of a feasibility study may be narrow or quite wide. The feasibility study team must engage in a substantial effort of fact finding. These facts may include matters relevant to the project which are not necessarily of a data processing nature.

Problem definition

3.8   In some circumstances the 'problem' (for example the necessity for a real-time as opposed to a batch processed application) may be quite *exact*, in others it may be characterised as 'soft' (related to people and the way they behave).

3.9   The problem definition stage should result in the production of a set of documents which define the problem.

   (a)   A set of *diagrams* representing, in overview:

      (i)   the current physical flows of data in the organisation (*documents*); and
      (ii)   the activities underlying them (*data flows*).

   (b)   A description of all the people, jobs, activities and so on (*entities*) that make up the system, and their relationship to one another.

   (c)   The *problems/requirements* list established from the terms of reference and after consultation with users.

The problems/requirements list

3.10 The problems/requirements list or catalogue can cover, amongst other things, the following areas.

(a) The data *input* to the current system.
(b) The nature of the *output* information (contents, timing etc).
(c) Methods of *processing*.
(d) The expected *growth* of the organisation and so *future volumes* of processing.
(e) The systems *control* in operation.
(f) *Staffing* arrangements and organisational *structure*.
(g) The *operational costs* of the system.
(h) *Type of system* (batch, on-line).
(i) *Response times*.
(j) Current organisational *problems*.

Project identification
12/99

3.11 This stage involves suggesting a number of *options* for a new system, evaluating them and recommending one for adoption. It concludes with a final *feasibility study report*.

Step 1. Create the *base constraints* in terms of expenditure, implementation and design time, and system requirements, which any system should satisfy.

(a) *Operations* (for example faster processing, larger volumes, greater security, greater accuracy, better quality, real-time as opposed to other forms of processing).

(b) Information *output* (quality, frequency, presentation, eg GUIs, database for managers, EIS facilities).

(c) *Volume of processing*.

(d) *General system requirements* (eg accuracy, security and controls, audit trail, flexibility, adaptability).

(e) *Compatibility/integration* with existing systems.

Step 2. Create outlines of *project options*, describing, in brief, each option. The number will vary depending on the complexity of the problem, or the size of the application, but is typically between three and six.

Step 3. Assess the *impact* each proposal has on the work of the relevant user department and/or the organisation as a whole.

Step 4. *Review* these proposals with users, who should indicate those options they favour for further analysis.

System justification

3.12 A new system should not be recommended unless it can be justified. The justification for a new system would have to come from:

(a) an evaluation of the *costs and benefits* of the proposed system; and/or
(b) other *performance criteria*.

4   AREAS OF FEASIBILITY
6/00

4.1 There are four key areas in which a project must be feasible if it is to be selected.

(a) Technical feasibility
(b) Operational feasibility
(c) Social feasibility
(d) Economic feasibility

Technical feasibility

4.2   The requirements, as defined in the feasibility study, must be technically achievable. This means that any proposed solution must be capable of being implemented using available *hardware, software and other equipment*. The type of requirement which might depend for success on technical feasibility might be one of the following.

(a)   *Volume* of transactions which can be processed within a given time
(b)   *Capacity* to hold files or records of a certain size
(c)   *Response times* (how quickly the computer does what you ask it to)
(d)   *Number of users* which can be supported without deterioration in the other criteria

Operational feasibility

4.3   Operational feasibility is a key concern. If a solution makes technical sense but *conflicts with the way the organisation does business*, the solution is not feasible. Thus an organisation might reject a solution because it forces a change in management responsibilities, status and chains of command, or does not suit regional reporting structures, or because the costs of redundancies, retraining and reorganisation are considered too high.

Social feasibility

4.4   An assessment of social feasibility will address a number of areas, including the following.

(a)   *Personnel* policies
(b)   Redrawing of *job specifications*
(c)   Threats to *industrial relations*
(d)   Expected *skills requirements*
(e)   *Motivation*

Social feasibility is sometimes considered to be an aspect of operational feasibility, but it deserves separate serious consideration because it is an aspect that has frequently been neglected in the past, leading directly to systems failure.

Economic feasibility

4.5   A system which satisfies all the above criteria must still be economically feasible. This means that it must be a 'good investment'. This has two strands.

(a)   The project selected must be the 'best' of the *computerisation* projects under consideration.

(b)   The project selected *must compete with other projects in other areas* of the business for funds. Even if it is projected to produce a positive return and satisfies all relevant criteria, it may not be chosen because a *new warehouse* is needed or the head office is to be relocated, and available funds are allocated to these projects instead.

5   COSTS AND BENEFITS   *6/94, 12/94, 6/95, 6/96, 12/96, 6/98, 12/99*

The costs of a proposed system

5.1   In general the best cost estimates will be obtained for systems bought from an *outside vendor* who provides a cost quotation against a specification. Less concrete cost estimates are generally found with development projects where the work is performed by the organisation's own employees.

5.2   The costs of a new system will include costs in a number of different categories.

Cost	Example
Equipment costs	• Computer and peripherals • Ancillary equipment • The initial system supplies (disks, tapes, paper etc)
Installation costs	• New buildings (if necessary) • The computer room (wiring, air-conditioning if necessary)
Development costs	These include costs of measuring and analysing the existing system and costs of looking at the new system. They include software/consultancy work and systems analysis and programming. Changeover costs, particularly file conversion, may be very considerable.
Personnel costs	• Staff training • Staff recruitment/relocation • Staff salaries and pensions • Redundancy payments • Overheads
Operating costs	• Consumable materials (tapes, disks, stationery etc) • Maintenance • Accommodation costs • Heating/power/insurance/telephone • Standby arrangements, in case the system breaks down

Capital and revenue costs

5.3   The distinction between capital costs and revenue costs is important.

(a)   To establish the *cash* outflows arising from the system, the costs/benefit analysis of a system ought to be based on *cash flows and DCF*.

(b)   The annual charge against *profits* shown in the financial accounts is of interest to *stakeholders*.

5.4   *Capital* items will be capitalised and depreciated, and revenue items will be expensed as incurred as a regular annual cost.

5.5   Items treated as *one-off revenue costs* are costs which would usually fall to be treated as revenue which, by virtue of being incurred during the period of development only and in connection with the development are one-off.

5.6   In practice, *accounting treatment* of such items may *vary widely* between organisations depending on their accounting policies and on agreement with their auditors.

Exercise 1

Draw up a table with three headings: capital cost items, one-off revenue cost items and regular annual costs. Identify at least three items to be included under each heading. You may wish to refer back to the preceding paragraphs for examples of costs.

BPP PUBLISHING

Solution

Capital cost items	'One-off' revenue cost items	Regular annual costs
Hardware purchase costs	Consultancy fees	Operating staff salaries/wages
Software purchase costs	Systems analysts' and programmers' salaries	Data transmission costs
Purchase of accommodation (if needed)	Costs of testing the system (staff costs, consumables)	Consumable materials
Installation costs (new desks, cables, physical storage etc)	Costs of converting the files for the new system	Power Maintenance costs
	Staff recruitment fees	Cost of standby arrangements Ongoing staff training

The benefits of a proposed system

5.7 The benefits from a proposed new system must also be evaluated. These ought to consist of benefits of several types.

(a) *Savings* because the *old system* will no longer be operated. The savings will derive from simpler administration and more productive use of time, and should include:

   (i)   savings in *staff costs*;
   (ii)   savings in *other operating costs*, such as consumable materials.

(b) Extra *savings* or revenue benefits because of the improvements or enhancements that the *new system* should bring:

   (i)   possibly *more sales revenue* and so additional contribution;

   (ii)   *better stock control* (with a new stock control system) and so fewer stock losses from obsolescence and deterioration;

   (iii) further savings in *staff time*, resulting perhaps in reduced future staff growth.

(c) Possibly, some one-off revenue benefits from the *sale of equipment* which the existing system uses, but which will no longer be required. Second-hand computer equipment does not have a high value, however! It is also possible that the new system will use *less office space*, and so there will be benefits from selling or renting the spare accommodation.

5.8 Some benefits might be *intangible*: difficult or impossible to give a precise money value to.

(a) Greater *competitive edge*, through increased ability to respond to changing markets, improved image and links to wider (global?) markets. (This may be measurable to an extent, in terms of profitability and market share.)

(b) Greater *customer satisfaction*, arising from a more prompt service (eg because of a computerised sales and delivery service), and better information (for instance statements with a detailed breakdown of expenditure and usage).

(c) Improved *staff morale* from working with a 'better' system, following more effective procedures and using higher skills.

(d) *Better decision making* is hard to quantify, but may result from better MIS, DSS or EIS. These might offer better quality information that is available more quickly, and more sophisticated modelling facilities.

Investment appraisal

6/94

5.9 There are three principal methods of evaluating a capital project.

Method	Comment
Payback period	This method of investment appraisal calculates the length of time a project will take to recoup the initial investment; in other words how long a project will take to pay for itself. The method is based on *cash flows*.
Accounting rate of return	This method, also called *return on investment*, calculates the profits that will be earned by a project and expresses this as a percentage of the capital invested in the project. The higher the rate of return, the higher a project is ranked. This method is based on *accounting* results rather than cash flows.
Discounted cash flow (DCF)	This is a method which may be sub-divided into two approaches. (a) *Net present value (NPV)*, which considers all relevant cash flows associated with a project over the whole of its life and adjusts those occurring in future years to 'present value' by discounting at a rate called the 'cost of capital'. (b) *Internal rate of return (IRR)*, which involves comparing the rate of return expected from the project calculated on a discounted cash flow basis with the rate used as the cost of capital. Projects with an IRR higher than the cost of capital are worth undertaking.

5.10 You will study the mathematics involved for other ICSA subjects such as *Introduction to Accounting, Corporate Finance and Taxation* and *Management Accounting*, so we shall not go into details here. There has never been a numerical question in the *Managing Information Systems* exam.

6 THE FEASIBILITY STUDY REPORT

6.1 Once the outline project specifications are prepared, these are presented to *users* who, with the assistance of technical staff will evaluate each option and make a *final choice*. This stage is much more intensive than when the original options were first examined. All the systems specified in the project specifications are feasible and it is simply a matter of *weighing up the advantages and disadvantages* of each.

6.2 One option may be to *carry on with the existing system* as it is, with no development option being chosen. If the feasibility study has been quite a lengthy one, circumstances beyond the control of the study teams may render any systems development inappropriate. For example, interest rates may rise increasing the organisation's cost of capital, and in this context the cost/benefit analysis might render the proposed system uneconomic.

6.3 This is the final step of the feasibility phase. A number of projects were mooted. A few favoured ones were examined and specified in more detail, and a choice made after evaluation. The results of these deliberations are included in a *feasibility study report*. This should contain the following points.

(a) The *introduction* will contain the study's terms of reference and details as to how and when the study was carried out.

(b) The *problem definition* will contain material from the problem definition stage, as outlined earlier.

(c) *Outline project specifications* are summaries of the detailed project specifications prepared for a number of project options.

(d) *Reasons for selection of preferred project option* may include cost/benefit analyses, or any of the non-economic criteria noted above.

(e) *Specification of selected project option* will include:

    (i)   outline *data flow diagrams* and processes of the new system;

    (ii)   a description of the *entity model*;

    (iii)   an updated *problems/requirements list*;

    (iv)   a brief description of the system's *physical implementation*.

6.4   We shall explain what data flow diagrams and entity models are in Chapter 12.

Exercise 2

You are the member of a feasibility study group with responsibility for preparing the first draft of the report so that this can be circulated to the other group members for their comments before your next meeting. List the sections of the report.

Solution

A typical report might include:

(a)   terms of reference;

(b)   description of existing system;

(c)   system requirements;

(d)   details of the proposed system;

(e)   cost/benefit analysis;

(f)   development and implementation plans; and

(g)   recommendations as to the preferred option.

---

7   SYSTEMS INVESTIGATION   6/95

Fact finding

7.1   The systems investigation is a detailed *fact finding* exercise about the areas under consideration.

    (a)   The project team has to determine the inputs, outputs, processing methods and volumes of the current system.

    (b)   It also examines controls, staffing and costs and reviews the organisational structure.

    (c)   It should also consider the expected growth of the organisation and its future requirements.

A *top down approach* to the exercise would focus first on the top management viewpoint and then examine the operational information needed to implement their strategies.

7.2   The stages involved in this phase of systems development are as follows.

    (a)   *Fact finding* by means of questionnaires, interviews, observation, reading handbooks, manuals, organisation charts, or from the knowledge and experience of members of the study team.

    (b)   *Fact recording* using flowcharts, decision tables, narrative descriptions, organisation and responsibility charts.

    (c)   *Evaluation*, assessing the strengths and weaknesses of the existing system.

If the investigation is being conducted by outsiders such as systems consultants, the confidentiality of the information gathered should be maintained at all times.

Improving the system

7.3   The purpose of the investigation is not merely to find out what needs to be computerised. The emphasis in each case is on the potential for *improvement* of the system *before* it is automated.

7.4 For instance, the activities in a process could be assessed by asking five sets of questions.

Purpose	What is being done? Why is it being done? What else can be done? What else should be done?
Place	Where is it being done? Why there Where else could it be done? Where else should it be done?
Sequence	When is it done? Why then? When else could it be done? When should it be done?
Person	Who does it? Why that person or department? Who else might do it? Who else should do it?
Means	How is it done Why that way? How else could it be done? How should it be done

Work-centred analysis (WCA)

7.5 As an alternative approach you may like to consider what Stephen Alter (*Information Systems: A Management Perspective* (1996)) calls 'work-centred analysis (WCA)'. This is a framework combining modern ideas form a number of sources, such as BPR, TQM and systems theory.

7.6 WCA looks at business processes from six points of view.

(a) The internal or external customers of the process
(b) The products or services produced by the process
(c) The steps involved in the process itself
(d) The participants who perform the process
(e) The information the process uses and/or creates
(f) The technology used in the process

7.7 The only aspect of this process that cannot be *changed* or *improved* is the customer. If the customer is not happy with the product, the product must be improved and this may have implications for each of the other changeable components. If the participants cannot perform as required then they must change through training, motivation or replacement. If the information needed is not available it must be collected and analysed.

Gathering data   *6/94, 12/94, 6/97, 6/98*

Interviews

7.8 Interviews with members of staff are undoubtedly the *most effective method* of fact finding. If properly conducted, an interview should enable the analyst (investigator) to *overcome the fears and resistance* to change that may be felt by the employee, in addition to finding out facts about his work.

7.9 There are some helpful *guidelines* as to the approach and attitude to be adopted by the investigator who is conducting a fact finding interview.

(a) The interviewer must appreciate that he is dealing with many different individuals with different attitudes and personalities. He must be able to *adapt his approach* to suit the individual interviewee, rather than follow a standard routine.

(b) The interviewer should be *fully prepared* for the interview, having details of the interviewee's name and job position, and a plan of questions to ask.

(c) Employees ought to be informed before the interview that a systems investigation is taking place, and its *purpose explained.*

(d) The interviewer must ask questions at the *level appropriate* to the employee's position within the organisation (for example top management will be concerned with policy, supervisors with functional problems).

(e) The interview should *not be too formal* a question and answer session, but should be allowed to develop into a *conversation* whereby the interviewee offers his opinions and suggestions.

(f) The interviewer must *not jump to conclusions* or confuse opinions with facts. He should accept what the interviewee has to say (for the moment) and refrain from interrupting or propounding his own opinions.

(g) The interviewer should *gain the interviewee's confidence* by explaining in full what is going on and not giving the impression that he is there solely to find fault. This confidence can also be obtained by allowing the interview to take place on the interviewee's 'home ground' (desk or office) and by ensuring that the interviewee has no objection to notes being taken.

(h) The interviewer should arrange interviews so that he *moves progressively* through the system, for example from input clerk to supervisor to manager.

(i) The interviewer should refrain from making *off the record* comments during the course of the interview, for example about what he is going to recommend.

(j) The interview should be *long enough* for the interviewer to obtain the information he requires and to ensure that he understands the system but *short enough* to ensure that concentration does not wander.

(k) The interview should be *concluded* by a resumé of its main points (so that the interviewee can confirm that the interviewer has obtained what he should have done) and the interviewer should thank the interviewee for his time and trouble.

Exercise 3

Draw up a checklist of do's and don'ts for conducting fact finding interviews.

Solution

A useful checklist for guidance in conducting interviews is suggested by Daniels and Yeates in *Basic Training in Systems Analysis* as follows:

Do	Don't
Plan	Be late
Make appointments	Be too formal or too casual
Ask questions at the right level	Interrupt
Listen	Use technical jargon
Use the local terminology	Confuse opinion with fact
Accept ideas and hints	Jump to conclusions
Hear both sides	Argue
Collect documents and forms	Criticise
Check the facts back	Suggest
Part pleasantly	

7.10 Interviews can be *time consuming* for the analyst, who may have several to conduct, and therefore expensive.

7.11 If conducted effectively, however, they allow the interviewer to *provide information* as well as obtain it. In an interview, *nuances and attitudes* not apparent from other sources may be obtained, and *immediate follow up* to unsatisfactory/*ambiguous replies* is possible. Interviews are particularly appropriate for *senior management*, as other approaches may not be appropriate at executive levels.

Questionnaires

7.12 The use of questionnaires may be useful whenever a *limited amount of information* is required from a *large number of individuals*, or where the organisation is decentralised with many 'separate entity' locations.

7.13 Questionnaires may be used *in advance of an interview* to save the analyst's and employee's time, but it should be remembered that they must be properly introduced.

(a) Employees ought to be informed before receiving the questionnaire that a systems investigation is to take place, and its *purpose* explained.

(b) *Questions* must be designed to *obtain exactly the information necessary* for the study. This is a very difficult task.

7.14 It must be stressed that questionnaires, by themselves, are an *inadequate* means of fact finding, and should usually be followed up by an *interview* or *observation*.

7.15 Whenever possible, questionnaires should be *designed* with the following in mind.

(a) They should *not contain too many questions* (people tend to lose interest quickly and become less accurate in their answers).

(b) They should be *organised in a logical sequence*.

(c) They should include an occasional *question* the answer to which *corroborates the answers* to previous questions.

(d) Ideally, they should be designed so that each question can be answered by either *'yes' or 'no' or a 'tick'* rather than sentences or paragraphs.

(e) They should be *tested independently* before being issued to the actual individuals. The test answers should enable the systems analyst to establish the effectiveness of his questions and help determine the level of subsequent interviews and observations.

(f) They should take into account the *sensitivity of individuals* in respect of their job security, change of job definition etc. Staff may prefer *anonymity*, but this prevents follow-up of 'interesting' responses.

Exercise 4

Next time you receive a questionnaire of any sort, study it carefully to see how well it adheres to these design principles.

Observation

7.16 Once the analyst has some understanding of the methods and procedures used in the organisation, he should be able to *verify* his findings and *clarify* any problem areas by an observation of operations.

7.17 Observation is a useful way of *cross-checking* with the facts obtained by interview or questionnaire. Different methods of recording facts ought to produce the same information, but it is not inconceivable that staff do their work in one way, whilst management believe that they do something different. A possible way of reconciling differences is to use *deployment flowcharting*, described in more detail in Chapter 9.

7.18 It should be noted that staff *may act differently from normal* if they know that they are being observed: whereas there might normally be a lack of adherence to procedures laid down in manuals, these might be rigorously followed in the presence of a systems analyst.

Document review

7.19 The systems analyst must investigate the *documents* that are used in the system. This may be a wide ranging investigation, using for example organisation charts, procedures manuals and standard operational forms.

7.20 One way of recording facts about document usage is the *document description form*. This is simply a standard form which the analyst can use to describe a document. It includes certain details about any document.

(a) A list of *all the items* on the document.

(b) The *size* of each data item (fixed length or variable length field).

(c) The *format* of the item, in terms of alphabetic, numeric or other characters, eg:
    A(15)   means 15 alphabetic characters
    ANN   means a letter followed by two numbers

(d) The *person responsible for entering the data item* on the document.

(e) *Source* and *destination* of each copy of the document.

(f) *Purpose* of the document.

(g) *Name* of the document.

(h) Space for the system analyst to make any *further notes* (for example price or discount allowed on a sales invoice, whether the completed document is checked and authorised by a supervisor etc).

7.21 The overriding risk is that staff do not follow documented policies and procedures or that these documents have not been properly updated, so this method is *best used in tandem with one or more other techniques*.

External reports

7.22 It may be possible to make use of reports on the system prepared for other purposes, for instance by auditors(internal and external) or insurers. These may not be accurate or up to date, however, so they should not be relied upon exclusively.

Reliable data

7.23 *Reliability* will largely depend on choosing a combination of the above methods, using them sensitively and evaluating the result carefully. Statistical tests may be used to make the evaluation process more rigorous eg to identify trends. Results can be further evaluated by *soft systems* modelling (see the next chapter) which may help to clarify contentious factors.

Exercise 5

How would you investigate an existing operational system in a company which operates through a network of regional branches controlled from a centrally located head office?

Solution

Because the company operates through a network of regional branches controlled from a centrally located head office, it may be appropriate for the systems analysis team to visit head office and a single representative branch. Interviews will be used with key head office staff and on the branch visit, where document analysis and observation can be used for corroborative purposes. Questionnaires can then be designed for use at other branches and, if necessary, followed up if the results do not appear compatible with those obtained by direct contact/observation at the branch visited.

Chapter roundup

- The systems development life cycle was developed by the National Computing Centre in the 1960s to add discipline to many organisations' approach to system development. It is a model of how systems should be developed. It has a number of drawbacks, among which is the criticism that it fails to recognise the importance of the user.

- The feasibility study is the *first stage of systems development* in the systems development lifecycle. Some of the work undertaken may overlap with elements of the systems investigation and system analysis stages.

- The *feasibility study* is a formal study to decide what type of system can be developed which meets the needs of the organisation.

- Work carried out includes the production of *diagrams* showing *data and document flows*, a description of all the *entities* in the system (people, activities etc) and a *problems/requirements list*. This is the problem definition phase.

- The second phase of the study is project identification, during which a number of options for a new system are evaluated and one recommended.

- There are four key areas in which a project must be feasible if it is to be selected. It must be justifiable on *technical, operational, social* and *economic* grounds.

- One of the most important elements of the feasibility study is the *cost-benefit analysis*.

  - *Costs* may be analysed in different ways, but include equipment costs, installation costs, development costs, personnel costs and running costs.

  - *Benefits* are usually somewhat more intangible, but include cost savings, revenue benefits and qualitative benefits.

- There are three principal methods of evaluating a capital project, *payback, accounting rate of return*, and *DCF techniques*.

- The feasibility study culminates with a *feasibility study report*, reflecting all of the above analysis and recommending and giving a specification for the selected option.

- The systems investigation is a detailed fact finding exercise which involves investigating and recording the current system. Methods employed include the use of interviews and questionnaires. Care should be taken in planning how to carry out an investigation of this type, to ensure the most useful response.

Test your knowledge

1   What are Nolan's six stages? (see para 1.4)

2   Explain the stages of the SDLC (1.6)

3   Suggest four actions that might be considered to ensure a planned approach to IS projects. (2.1)

4   Define a feasibility study. (3.1)

5   What might be covered in a problems/requirements list? (3.10)

6   Suggest four steps in project identification. (3.11)

7   What is meant by technical feasibility and social feasibility? (4.2, 4.4)

8   What sort of costs might a new system have? (5.2)

9   What benefits might a new system have? (5.7, 5.8)

10 Describe the contents of a feasibility study report. (6.3)

11 What is work-centred analysis? (7.5, 7.6)

12 What are five ways of gathering data? (7.8 - 7.22)

Now try illustrative questions 9 and 10 at the end of the Study Text

Chapter 7

METHODOLOGIES AND DEVELOPMENT TOOLS

This chapter covers the following topics.

1   Methodologies

2   Soft Systems Methodology

3   Structured Systems Analysis and Design Methodology (SSADM)

4   Data driven methodologies

5   User involvement

6   Fourth Generation Languages

7   Object oriented methods

Introduction

The systems development life cycle brought considerable improvements to the development process. However, as we saw in the last chapter, it had a number of drawbacks. From the 1970s, companies began to adopt methodologies as their standard approach. Methodologies were developed to add discipline to the process, to improve reliability and to maximise efficient use of resources.

A variety of methods are available to promote *user involvement* in the analysis and design process, including structured walkthroughs, joint applications development and prototyping.

Methodologies such as SSADM are now sometime themselves described as 'traditional'. In the early 1980s, fourth generation languages and prototyping permitted more rapid development and since the late 1980s object-oriented development has introduced a new approach to development of complex applications such as graphical user interfaces, multimedia and database design.

---

1   METHODOLOGIES

6/97

1.1   A systems development 'methodology' is a collection of procedures, techniques, tools and documentation aids which will help systems developers in their efforts to implement a new information system.

Characteristics of methodologies

1.2   Many methodologies work on the assumptions that the *logical design* is to be distinguished from the *physical design* of a system, and is carried out first.

1.3   That is to say, there is no use in buying a computer and then trying to find a system that will be compatible with it if the system does not meet the needs of users. A better approach is to begin by defining what a system is supposed to do, and the data items it will deal with.

1.4   Hardware and software are therefore acquired for the system, rather than a system acquired to fit in with the purchased hardware and software. On the other hand, technological constraints cannot be ignored.

140

1.5 A second issue is whether a methodology is *process-driven* or *data-driven* . Process-driven methodologies concentrate on the processes which the system performs. Data-driven methodologies focus on the data items regardless of the processes they are related to, on the grounds that the type of *data* an organisation needs is less likely to change than either the processes which operate on it or the output information required of it.

1.6 Thirdly, within the organisation, the needs of *users* as expressed in the outputs or potential outputs required of the system are considered prior to hunting for input data. The user's information requirements and potential requirements should determine the type of data collected or captured by the system.

Comparing and evaluating methodologies   *6/94, 6/95, 12/96, 12/99*

1.7 Jayaratna (*Understanding and Evaluating Methodologies*, 1994) estimates that there are over 1,000 brand named methodologies in use in the world. Clearly this book cannot cover all of them. The aim is to illustrate some general principles that may help you to hold your own if you ever come into contact with systems analysts and designers.

1.8 We will be going on later to look at to look at two methodologies in particular - Soft Systems Methodology and the UK government's SSADM - not because it these are necessarily the 'best' methodologies but because they are specifically mentioned in the syllabus, they have featured in exam questions, and they are well-known and much written about. Arguably, approaches such as BPR could also be described as 'methodologies'. See Chapter 3.

1.9 Before going into further detail, however, it will be useful to review some of the main conclusions reached by Jayaratna about methodologies.

(a) All methodologies *evolve* over time as their creators and users use them in practice and revise them as appropriate.

(b) All methodologies are underpinned by a set of *philosophical beliefs*. For instance, some are based on the belief that systems development is based on unchangeable and *objective facts*, while others take the view that the 'facts' may be *interpreted* differently depending on one's viewpoint. A sales target may be simply a figure, or it may be 'part of a political process which negotiates between sales personnel, management and directors', possibly with 'far reaching implications relating to people's lives, remuneration, job satisfaction' etc (Avison and Fitzgerald, *Information Systems Development*).

The point is that if you don't subscribe to the philosophy behind a methodology there is a good chance that you will not get the system that you want. Methodologies measure *success* in terms of their underlying philosophy.

(c) Different methodologies emphasise different aspects of the development process. For example, soft systems methodology concentrates on the *problem formulation* stage, while structured methodologies such as SSADM emphasise the design of *solutions*.

1.10 All methodologies seek to facilitate the 'best' solution. But 'best' may be interpreted in a number of ways, such as most rapid or least cost systems. Some methodologies are highly prescriptive and require rigid adherence to stages whilst others are highly adaptive allowing for creative use of their components. The former may be viewed as following a recipe and the latter as selecting suitable tools from a toolkit.

1.11 In choosing the most appropriate methodology, an organisation must consider the following questions.

(a) How open is the system?
(b) To what extent does it facilitate participation?
(c) Does it generate alternative solutions?
(d) Is it well documented, tried, tested and proven to work?
(e) Can component 'tools' be selected and used as required?
(f) Will it benefit from CASE tools and prototyping?

1.12 It is not necessary to be restricted to the tools offered by just one methodology. For instance soft system methodology may be useful at the outset, to get a system well-defined, and subsequently to review its performance. Elements of harder techniques and possibly prototyping might usefully be employed during development.

1.13 Ultimately it is important to remember that whilst methodologies may be valuable in the development their use is a matter of great skill and experience. They do not, by themselves, produce good systems solutions.

Exercise 1

Why does it matter how 'open' a system is?

Solution

An open system is much affected by unpredictable and rapidly changing environmental factors (a hospital admissions system, for instance) and it needs an approach that takes account of 'soft' problems. A highly stable system, such as a payroll system, simply needs to follow predefined rules (payroll rules change, but even the changes are relatively predictable) and may have less need for 'soft' thinking.

Advantages and disadvantages

1.14 The advantages of using a standard approach such as a methodology are as follows.

(a) The documentation requirements are rigorous.

(b) Standard methods allow less qualified staff to carry out some of the analysis work, thus cutting the cost of the exercise.

(c) Using a standard development process leads to improved system specifications.

(d) Systems developed in this way are easier to maintain and improve.

(e) Users are involved with development work from an early stage and are required to sign off each stage (see the previous chapter).

(e) The emphasis on diagramming makes it easier for relevant parties, including users, to understand the system than if purely narrative descriptions were used.

(f) The structured framework of a methodology helps with planning. It defines the tasks to be performed and sets out when they should be done. Each step has an identifiable end product. This allows control by reference to actual achievements rather than to estimates of progress.

(g) A logical design is produced that is independent of hardware and software. This logical design can then be given a physical design using whatever computer equipment and implementation language is required.

(h) Techniques such as dataflow diagrams, logical data structures and entity life histories allow information to be cross-checked between diagrams and ensure that the system delivered is what was wanted. These techniques are explained in the next chapter.

1.15 The use of a methodology in systems development also has *disadvantages*.

(a) Methodologies are generally tailored to large, complex organisations. Only recently, as in Micro-SSADM, are they being adapted for PC-based systems.

(b) It has been argued that methodologies are ideal for analysing and documenting processes and data items are operational level, but are perhaps inappropriate for information of a strategic nature that is collected on an ad hoc basis.

(c) Some are a little too limited in scope, being too concerned with systems design, and not with their impact on actual work processes or social context of the system.

(d) The conceptual basis of some is not properly thought out. Many methodologies grew out of diagramming conventions.

(e) Arguably methodologies are just as happy documenting a bad design as a good one.

2.1   A way of describing 'soft systems' has been provided by Checkland's Soft Systems Methodology (SSM). SSM is a way of analysing the 'problem situations' in open systems (organisations). It provides an organised methodology which can be used to tackle unstructured and poorly defined (often people-related) problems in the real world. As a methodology, it is a highly organised and *structured* approach, but it is necessarily flexible and applicable to a broad range of situations.

2.2   SSM was first developed in the early 1980s and has undergone a process of revision and refinement up to the present day. It is based on a number of assumptions about the 'real world'.

Exercise 2

What is a 'soft' problem?

Solution

Refer back to Chapter 3 if you cannot remember.

Meaning

2.3   Human beings will attempt to place a meaning on their observations and experiences. This is 'human nature'. The existence of world religions can be interpreted as being evidence of man's desire to find solutions to fundamental questions. The meaning which an individual attributes to an event or situation is that individual's *interpretation* of the event or situation. His interpretation is derived from his experience of the real world.

Intention

2.4   Once an interpretation has been placed on experience, it is possible to form intentions. An intention represents a decision to follow a particular course of action.

Action

2.5   When an individual has decided to follow a particular course of action, he can be described as taking *purposeful action*. This is any action which is deliberate. Purposeful action has the effect of changing the real world. This in turn means that the event or situation upon which an interpretation was placed is altered, creating a cycle of activity.

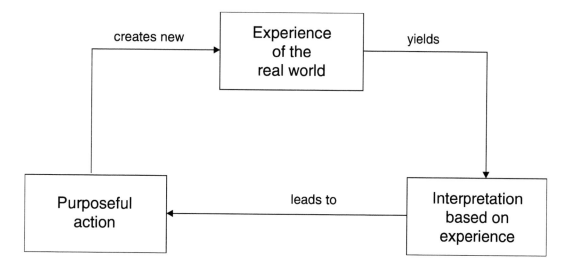

BPP
PUBLISHING

2.6 The purpose of SSM, therefore, is to enhance understanding of human situations that are perceived as problematic and, as a consequence, where improvements are aimed at. The learning is about a complex social situation which entails *many divergent perspectives* on the issues to be dealt with. There is no such thing as the 'real world', just different perspectives on it.

2.7 SSM involves a process of enquiry which leads to action, but this action is not ever regarded as an end point unless the participants in the process choose to make it one. SSM recognises that taking action changes the problem situation: this means that enquiry can continue in a learning process that remains open for new findings.

The 'stages' of SSM

2.8 The learning process of SSM cycles between learning and action and follows a set of seven stages.

   (a) In the first stage the problematical situation is entered into. This very step is viewed as an intervention (being itself problematic and as such analysable).

   (b) Secondly, the problem situation is expressed in three analytical steps (intervention, prevalent culture, and power relationships).

   (c) The third stage involves a representation of these findings in a set of 'root definitions', in other words systems thought to be relevant to a deeper exploration of the problem situation which will lead to action in order to improve it.

   (d) Conceptual models are built in stage four where the verbal concepts previously defined are logically structured by use of arrows to form relevant combinations of an operational and a monitoring and control system.

   (e) By comparing models and reality (real-world actions) stage five aims at inducing learning steps in the participating group which in general leads to a reiteration of the preceding stages.

   (f) The purpose of the sixth stage is then to achieve a common understanding regarding possible changes of the real-world situation which could improve it.

   (g) The last stage of SSM is concerned with taking action and putting the changes in place – thus changing the problem situation itself and restarting the cycle.

2.9 This approach tended to lead to the (restricting) belief that SSM was a stage by stage process, which is not intended. The current representation is as developed by Checkland in 1988. can be represented in diagrammatic form.

BPP PUBLISHING

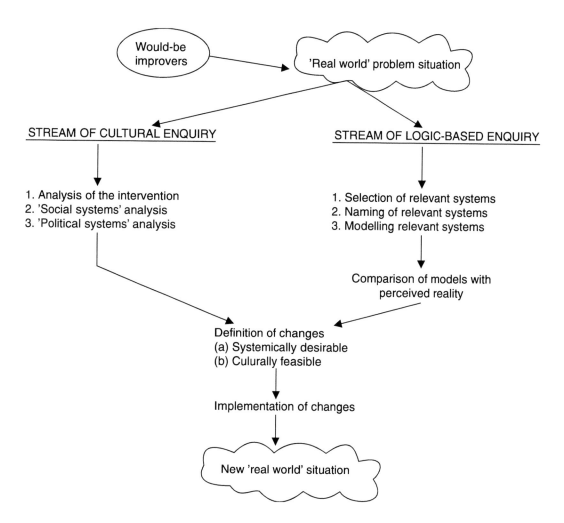

2.10 The logic-driven stream of enquiry uses models of 'human activity systems' to analyse the problem situation. The models are compared with the perceived real world, thereby generating debate about changes which could be implemented. As noted earlier in this chapter, the human element is at the heart of soft systems. The second stream of enquiry, interacting with the first, seeks to take account of this human element.

The logic-driven stream of enquiry

2.11 The first stage of this stream is the selection of 'relevant systems'. This is a subjective choice: it is never possible to identify a particular human activity system as automatically relevant to a given problem situation. Two types of relevant system can be chosen.

(a) The primary-task system is a system which coincides with a real world system, for example a warehousing system.

(b) The issue-based system does not necessarily have a real world equivalent, for example a system to develop an internal transfer pricing mechanism.

Root definition: CATWOE   *12/95*

2.12 Once relevant systems have been selected they must be named. The name of a system becomes its root definition. This expresses the *core purpose* of the system. The recommended approach to formulating the root definition is to consider the mnemonic CATWOE. This has the following elements.

(a) *Customers*. These are the people or groups who benefit or suffer from the system.

(b) *Actors*. Actors are those who will carry out the transformation process.

(c) *Transformation process*. This is the conversion of input to output.

(d) *Weltanschauung*. This is the 'world view' which underlies the assumptions behind the root definition.

(e) *Owners*. These are people who could stop the transformation process.

(f) *Environmental constraints*. These are fixed elements outside the system.

2.13 Root definitions can vary. For example, a root definition for a prison could be one of the following.

(a) A system to punish criminals by locking them up in order to deter others.

(b) A system to rehabilitate offenders by showing them the error of their ways in order to help them adjust to society.

(c) A system to train criminals by bringing them into contact with one another in order to share their skills.

(d) A system to produce mail-bags by using a captive workforce in order to utilise cheap labour.

(e) A system to store people by keeping them in cells in order to ease the housing shortage.

2.14 Root definitions frequently utilise the same' a system to ... by ... in order to' structure. Finally the model of the relevant system is created. This is an account of the activities which the system will perform. It is process-oriented and set out in chronological order. The success or failure of the transformation process in the model is assessed by reference to three factors.

(a) Efficacy. This checks whether the means chosen produces the required output.
(b) Efficiency. This ensures that the process makes minimum use of resources.
(c) Effectiveness. This tests whether long-term objectives are being met.

2.15 The conceptual model must be compared to the real world. This is not simply in order to establish the correctness of the model, but to stimulate debate among the participants as to whether changes can be made to improve the problem situation. There are four possible approaches to this, the first being the most commonly used.

(a) Formal questioning, asking questions about the situation based on the model.

(b) Informal discussion, asking how the model differs from the current situation.

(c) Event reconstruction, considering what might have happened in the past using the system modelled.

(d) Model overlay, comparing the model with a conceptual model of the existing system.

The cultural stream of enquiry

2.16 The first stage in this stream is an analysis of the intervention. Three groups must be considered. The *client* is the person or group who initiated the study. The *would-be problem solver*, who may be the client, wishes to take some action in respect of the problem situation. The *problem owner* role is the third key role. A *rich picture* is developed which shows these three roles together with the role of problem solver. It displays relationships and attempts to provide the 'feel' of the situation by incorporating value judgements. The analysis of the intervention is referred to as Analysis One.

2.17 Analysis Two assumed that a social system consists of an evolving set of relationships between roles, norms and values. A *role* may be defined formally, for example 'data processing manager' or informally, for example 'office joker'. The behaviour expected from a person in a particular role is the *norm*. Behaviour of a person in a particular role is assessed by reference to values, which are the local yardsticks of performance measurement.

2.18 Analysis Three considers the political dimension. The focus is on understanding how power is expressed.

2.19 Once the two streams of enquiry have been followed, it is necessary to define the changes which would improve the problem situation. SSM then addresses implementation of the changes, which may be categorised as *systemically desirable* or *culturally feasible*.

SSM and information systems

2.20 SSM is highly relevant to the development of information systems. Whereas information system *design* can be seen as a 'how' problem, a hard problem, there is a fundamental soft problem to be considered. This is the question as to which information systems should be developed, the 'what' problem.

2.21 At its simplest, an information system might be considered as a system which transforms input (data) by manipulating (processing) it to give output (information). However there is a human element, because users will attribute particular meaning to the output in the light of their own perceptions of the world.

2.22 Checkland and Scholes suggest the following series of questions once a relevant system has been identified.

(a) What information is necessary to enable the activity to be carried out?

(b) From where can the information be obtained, in what form and with what frequency?

(c) What information will be generated when the activity is carried out?

(d) To whom should the information be sent, in what form and with what frequency?

Advantages and disadvantages of SSM

2.23 The features of soft systems methodologies which may be of particular benefit to an organisation developing a revised MIS are as follows.

(a) Soft systems methodologies address the inherent 'soft' nature of the complex problems faced by all organisations.

(b) Using a methodology based on the soft systems approach will recognise the number of issues, points of view and potential conflicts in a problem situation. Identifying systems and sub-systems helps to place the new system in its wider context.

(c) The methodology should allow for a thorough exploration of the problem situation and the human activity system within which it resides. This will enhance understanding of the problem and the subsequent needs for sensitive management of change.

(d) Agreements may be reached among the key 'players' associated with the new MIS (this would be in the form of *root definitions*)

(e) Using systems thinking tools, models may be generated of *alternative strategies* for MIS development.

(f) The methodology should help the system developers to discover the best way forward; as distinct from being driven towards a solution by the relative rigidity of the chosen methodology.

(g) There is the opportunity to review the relationship between company objectives, contractors' objectives, individual and MIS objectives.

2.24 In any organisation, changing the work practices and structure will require much foresight and sensitivity. Managing the changes in information systems will be equally challenging and there is often a clear need for a people oriented methodology which can help define the problems, recognise opinions and the cultural context and promote appropriate solutions.

BPP PUBLISHING

2.25 However, soft systems methodology has many critics.

    (a) *Technically oriented critics* complain that SSM doesn't actually tell you how to build a system, that there is no real 'method', though proponents would reply that what is really needed is a way of securing commitment and taking into account a variety of interests.

    (b) *Management oriented critics* worry that the open ended nature of SSM makes it impossible to manage.

    (c) *Radical (and traditional socialist) critics* say that SSM assumes that all members of the enterprise have equal choice. SSM ignores issues of power.

    (d) Critics also argue that SSM imposes values of openness and 'niceness' which are more suitable to middle class academics than to managers or workers. These criticisms do indicate that SSM has a fairly simple understanding of society.

3 STRUCTURED SYSTEMS ANALYSIS AND DESIGN METHODOLOGY (SSADM)

12/95, 6/96, 6/98, 12/99

Structured methods

3.1 Structured methodologies represent an approach to systems analysis and design which:

    (a) emphasises the logical design of a system (what types of data item there are, the relationships between them, what processing operations they undergo and so on) before physical implementation (before programs are written, hardware specified);

    (b) proceeds from the general to the particular via a series of modules, stages and steps (so the system as a whole is designed before individual applications or programs);

    (c) is heavily documented in a standard way using techniques to show the links between data, processes, functions, customers etc such as dataflow diagrams (DFDs) and entity relationship models (see the next chapter).

3.2 There are a number of methodologies based around the principles of structured analysis. Structured Systems Analysis and Design Methodology (SSADM) was developed in conjunction with the UK government's Central Computer and Telecommunications Agency, and it is revised regularly to take account of new developments.

SSADM

3.3 SSADM is a widely used methodology, and the structure it supplies forms the basis of much discussion of systems analysis and design. SSADM has several features.

    (a) It describes how a system is to be developed.

    (b) It reduces development into stages, and each stage contains a number of steps. The work done in one stage is refined and developed in the next.

    (c) It is self-checking, and can be tailored to a number of applications.

3.4 The structure of SSADM in a system development lifecycle is outlined below. This structure is the one used in SSADM Version 4. (The latest version at the time of publication is SSADM 4+ Version 4.3, published in October 1996 to address the issue of Graphical User Interfaces.)

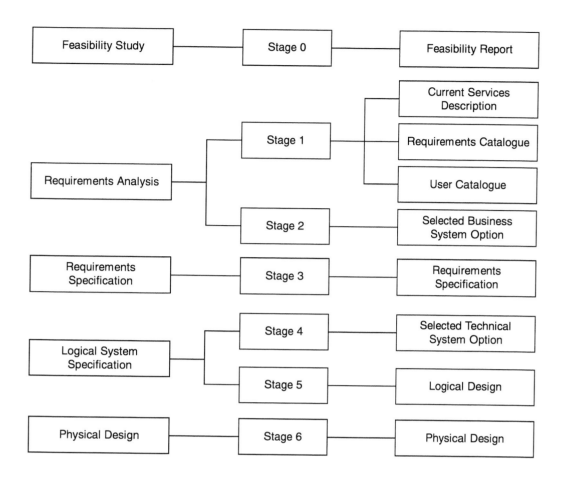

Stage 0: Feasibility study

3.5 This stage, although not mandatory in many SSADM projects, is to examine the 'case' for undertaking a particular project in terms of its technical, operational and economic feasibility. This was discussed in Chapter 10.

3.6 As we have seen, this stage is divided into four steps.

   (a) Prepare for the feasibility study, taking a preliminary view and setting out plans for the rest of the study.

   (b) Define the problem, where a problem (some deficiency in the system as it is now running, or an anticipated future deficiency) is identified. Information about it is gathered and the new requirements are set out in a Problem Definition Statement.

   (c) Select feasibility options: a series of options are identified for solving, or at least coping with the problems defined. Each potential project identified will have an outline specification and will be costed.

   (d) The results of this stage are formalised into a feasibility study report, which should also contain costings for the next phase.

Stage 1: Investigation of current environment

3.7 In this stage the current system is investigated, described and analysed using the techniques of observation, questionnaires, document description forms and so forth (see later in this chapter). Some of the work may have been done already during the feasibility study.

3.8 A major requirement of this phase is that the current system is properly documented in dataflow diagrams and the logical data structure (entity-relationship model) is described.

3.9 A further product from this stage (building on work done during the feasibility study) is a detailed problems/requirements list or requirements catalogue.

(a) Problems could be encountered over a range of areas, including data input, poor controls, volumes higher than the system can cope with, poor user interface, slow response times and inflexibility in processing.

(b) Requirements can in fact be solutions to the problems identified in the current system, but could also imply a completely new way of doing things, (for example replacing batch by on-line processing). Users are invited to describe:

(i) what they want a system to do;
(ii) what items of data are required for it to deal with;
(iii) what information is required.

Exercise 3

List areas likely to be covered by the problems/requirements list.

Solution

Refer back to Chapter 7 if you have forgotten this.

Stage 2: Business system options

3.10 This involves the specification of the requirements of the new system, where what users actually require is laid down in detail. Any solution offered must satisfy these requirements. There will normally be a number of possible solutions and those considered the best will be put forward to users as Business System Options.

(a) Six options, say, are suggested, from which a shortlist is created. For each option on the shortlist there is drawn up a level-1 DFD, function descriptions (the basic processes that transform data), a logical data structure (entity model), a cost/benefit analysis (in brief) and an assessment of the impact of the proposed system.

(b) Users are then asked to make a choice.

Stage 3: Requirements specification

3.11 At this stage, the team takes the results of the previous stage, and arrives at a requirements specification. This stage has several steps. (Terms like entity life history are, again, explained in depth in the next chapter.)

(a) The chosen option is defined more precisely.

Detailed DFDs etc are drawn up, and the required system matched with the current system to ensure that all necessary processing has been performed. The DFDs are modified by the solutions to the problems/requirements identified earlier.

(b) Specifications for input and output from the chosen system are prepared.

These input/output descriptions detail what appears on screen, or on a document. An input/output description of a sales statement will list what should appear on the statement (eg customer number, name, address, statement date, transaction type, transaction data, balance brought forward).

(c) A relational data analysis is performed on the input and output descriptions.

This is to identify any entities that might not have been noticed, or drawn in enough detail, in the existing logical data structure (entity model). Whereas production of the logical data structure is a top down view, the analysis carried out here is a bottom up complement to it.

(d) Entity life histories are drawn up.

What has been missing so far is a means of matching the DFDs (which show flows of data through the system and what happens to it), with the logical data structure (which denotes the building blocks of the system). An entity life history is a technique which indicates what happens to an entity ie what functions (processes) it is subjected to, and so forth.

Stage 4: Technical system options

3.12 At this point users are asked to make choices concerning the means by which they would like the system to be implemented: there might be a number of ways of implementing a system physically. These can include:

(a) hardware configuration (for example mainframe, mini, PC; centralised or distributed processing); and

(b) software (use of a database or a conventional file structure).

Some of the technical options may have been outlined in brief at the feasibility study stage.

3.13 Users are presented with the various options outlined, and the implications of each are stated, so that the decision is an informed one. Once this is achieved, these details are incorporated into the required logical system design. Performance objectives are then specified in detail so that these can be followed in the actual design of the system.

Stage 5: Logical design

3.14 In this stage, the data and file structures for the entire new system are designed. The input to this stage are the descriptions of input and output from stage 3, and functions and processes that act upon or use data items are specified.

(a) Update is a function which alters in some way the contents of a file.

(b) Enquiry is simply accessing a record to see what it is.

3.15 This stage includes the development of output formats, and specifying the type of dialogue that users will have with the system, to ensure that it is consistent with what has been prepared so far.

Exercise 4

What does 'dialogue' mean?

Solution

This term refers to the messages that appear on screen (such as 'Are you sure you want to delete this file?') and the responses that the user makes - often just clicking on OK or Cancel. See Chapter 14 for more on this aspect of design.

Stage 6: Physical design

3.16 Physical design involves the following tasks.

(a) Initial physical design (obtaining the design rules from the chosen database, and applying them to the logical data design drawn up in the previous stages).

(b) Further define the processing required. For instance requirements for audit, security and control are considered. Briefly, these can include:

(i) controls over access to the system;
(ii) controls incorporated within programs (eg data validation, error handling);
(iii) recovery procedures, in case processing is interrupted.

(c) Program specifications are created. These provide in detail exactly what a particular program is supposed to achieve. Structured English may be used. Each process may be designated batch or on-line.

(d) Program specifications are assessed for their performance when implemented. For example, it should be possible to make some estimate of the times that some programs will take to run. These may initially fall below the targets originally set, and so there may have to be some changes to the specifications or users may have to accept some deficiencies in required performance, or the equipment may have to be changed.

(e) File and database specifications are designed in detail, and will contain, typically:

(a) name;
(b) contents;
(c) record size, types, fields per record etc.

(f) Operating instructions are drawn up (user documentation). These will include such items as error correction and detailed instructions for operators and users (eg the sort of screen format that will appear).

Systems Development Template

3.17 SSADM 4+ includes a framework called the Systems Development Template (SDT). This is used to determine user requirements, analyse information needs and then design and specify systems.

3.18 The SSADM user establishes which parts of the SDT are important and then adapts the components of SSADM to suit the specific project.

Exercise 5

(a) Glance forward to Chapters 8 and 9 and get a rough idea of what is meant by the terms dataflow diagram, entity relationship model, entity life history, normalisation and Structured English.

Then find each of the above terms in the summary of SSADM given above.

(b) What is meant by logical design?

Solution

(a) Either do this now, or else come back to this section after you have studied Chapters 8 and 9. You will find it makes a lot more sense.

(b) See paragraphs 1.2 to 1.3.

Assessment of SSADM

3.19 Organisations may wish to adopt SSADM for the following reasons.

(a) It incorporates clear stages with instructions as to how to proceed from one stage to the next. This has the advantage of simplicity and uniformity throughout the two large organisations.

(b) Standard methods make it cheaper and quicker to train staff and consequently save project costs.

(c) All stages are rigorously defined and fully documented, making systems easier to maintain and improve.

3.20 However, too great a rigidity in the application of the methodology may lead to disregard for the social and organisational context of the system. This may produce systems which are technically satisfactory but do not satisfy the users. They reduce the need for creative thinking and this could affect staff well-being and motivation.

3.21 Users may be reluctant to be involved with what they may regard as complex methods - they may be unfamiliar with techniques such as DFDs, and possibly suspicious of the procedures.

3.22. SSADM should therefore be used in a highly open and participative manner if it is to help an organisation to produce a widely accepted and valued system.

4   DATA-DRIVEN METHODOLOGIES

4.1   Whilst SSM and SSADM emphasise *processes*, which are broken down into logically defined segments of a system, other approaches to system design emphasise the *data* used by a system. Even if applications change, the data already collected may still be relevant. This, in many respects, is the approach behind database design.

Information Engineering

4.2   Information Engineering is an information systems development methodology which starts with a strategic planning exercise, to identify important information systems required by the business, and then develops chosen priority systems through successively detailed analysis and design, through to implementation.

(a) *Strategic management planning* uses any *existing* strategic or tactical statements that may exist and/or a management questionnaire to gather information about business strategy. It then goes on to identify and define *potential* goals (critical success factors) and issues, and defines strategies to deal with each. This part of the process concludes with the creation of the strategic agenda and formal documentation of strategic decisions, rationale, assumptions, conclusions and alternatives.

(b) *Information strategy planning* documents the business objectives in terms of information required. The key document produced is the information system development strategy, looking at the current information requirements and analysing business functions, data types, technical support for systems.

(c) *Business area analysis* further analyses areas of the business in terms of data used and the relationships between different types of data (entity analysis), and functions and processes.

(d) *Business system design* is the logical design of the new system and will include how the data in the database will be structured, the use of data flow diagrams to map the processes of a business and planning for technical design (for example screen dialogue, reports).

(e) *Implementation* is technology dependent, and is carried out using suitable CASE and other development tools.

4.3   Information engineering has a strong strategic perspective at the outset, but in later stages it suffers from many of the problems identified with structured methodologies such as SSADM. For instance it could be said to be too limited in scope, too concerned with systems design and not with the impact of systems on actual work processes or the social context of the system. It could be said to reduce the need for creative thinking. Moreover, users may be reluctant to get to grips with what they regard as complex ideas about 'entity modelling' and the like, and suspicious of techniques such as DFDs and normalisation.

5   USER INVOLVEMENT   *6/99, 6/00*

5.1   In the preceding sections there have been frequent references to the importance of user involvement in the development process. This section looks at a number of approaches intended to ensure that this happens.

Structured walkthroughs   *12/94, 6/96, 6/00*

5.2   Structured walkthroughs are a technique used (often in conjunction with SSADM) by those responsible for the design of some aspect of a system (particularly analysts and programmers) to present their design to interested *user groups* – in other words to 'walk' them through the design. Structured walkthroughs are formal meetings, in which the

BPP
PUBLISHING

documentation produced during development is reviewed and checked for errors or omissions.

5.3 These presentations are used both to introduce and explain the new systems to users and also to offer the users the opportunity of making constructive criticism of the proposed systems, and suggestions for further amendments/improvements, before the final systems specification is agreed.

5.4 Users are involved in structured walkthroughs because their knowledge of the desired system is more extensive than that of the systems development personnel. Walkthroughs are sometimes referred to as user validation.

The importance of signing off work

5.5 At the end of each stage of development, the resulting output is presented to users for their approval. There must be a formal sign-off of each completed stage before work on the next stage begins.

5.6 This minimises reworking, as if work does not meet user requirements, only the immediately preceding stage must be revisited. More importantly, it clarifies responsibilities and leaves little room for later disputes.

(a) If the systems developers fail to deliver something that both parties formally agreed to, it is the developers' responsibility to put it right, at their own expense, and compensate the user for the delay.

(b) If users ask for something extra or different, that was not formally agreed to, the developers cannot be blamed and the user must pay for further amendments and be prepared to accept some delay.

Personnel involved in structured walkthroughs

5.7 Although the number and types of staff who attend a walkthrough may change, there are several roles which have become fairly standardised.

(a) *Chairperson*

The chairperson will control the overall direction of the walkthrough, ensuring that the agenda is adhered to.

He or she will also have overall responsibility for administrative matters such as inviting various representatives to the meeting.

The chairperson needs to be highly technically competent and thoroughly familiar with the particular project and the business's requirements.

The chairperson is also likely to responsible for formally signing off the project.

(b) *Author*

The author is the person who has created the system under discussion. Clearly this person must be present to offer explanations as appropriate. Other systems staff may also be present if they have particular areas of expertise.

Sometimes the role of the author is also to *present* and explain the material which is being walked through, although it may be better to choose someone else, since authors can be sensitive to suggestions which may imply criticism

(c) *Recorder*

The recorder ensures that all agreed action points are noted and follows them up. The author might fulfil this role.

(d) *User representatives*

Users will obviously be present because their knowledge of the desired system is more extensive than that of the systems development personnel.

Their chief responsibility is to approve the system when they are satisfied that they understand it and that it will do what they want it to do.

Users will include not only people who will actually be operators of the system in their day-to-day work, but also those interested its output, such as internal or external auditors, and senior management who will want to ensure that their organisation's money is being well spent, and that their information needs will be met.

(e) *Reviewers*

These people get an advance working model of the material being walked through (or detailed documentation of the system that is about to be built) and their role, in essence, is to try and break it!

They are expected to have worked through the proposed system, checking it against a list of criteria and noting any respects in which it is likely to fall short of the required quality.

Reviews will be completed and passed to those leading the meeting (notably the author and chairperson) in advance of the actual meeting, but reviewers will also attend the meeting, in case any points need clarification, and to learn about how the problems they identified are going to be dealt with (as a basis for their *next* review).

Exercise 6

What, besides identification of mistakes (errors, omission, inconsistencies etc), would you expect the benefits of a walkthrough to be?

Solution

(a) Users become involved in the systems analysis process. Since this process is a critical appraisal of their work, they should have the opportunity to provide feedback on the appraisal itself.

(b) The output from the development is shown to people who are not systems development personnel. This encourages its originators to prepare it to a higher quality and in user-friendly form.

(c) Because the onus is on users to approve design, they are more likely to become committed to the new system and less likely to 'rubbish' it.

(d) The process focuses on quality of and good practice in operations generally.

(e) It avoids disputes about who is responsible for what.

Joint applications development

12/94, 6/96, 6/98

5.8 Joint applications development is based on a partnership between users and IT specialists. When this was originally pioneered in the 1970s, it involved developers and users specifying an entire application in just a few days, right down to detailing screen layouts, by participating in day-long design sessions. Specific steps were followed to ensure that the design process was completed in those few days, and accomplished its goal, largely by bringing the decision makers together into one place at one time.

5.9 Joint Applications Development (JAD) was originally developed by *IBM* to promote a more participative approach to systems. The potential value to an organisation may be as follows.

(a) It creates a pool of expertise comprised of interested parties from all relevant functions.

(b) Reduced risk of systems 'imposed' by computer systems personnel.

(c) This increases the corporate ownership and responsibility for systems solutions.

(d) Emphasises the information needs of users and their relationship to business needs and decision making.

5.10 There are a number of possible risks affecting the potential value of JAD.

(a) The relative inexperience of many users may lead to misunderstandings and possibly unreasonable expectations/demands on the system performance.

(b) The danger of lack of co-ordination leading to fragmented, individual, possibly esoteric information systems.

5.11 The shift of emphasis to applications development by end-users must be well managed and controlled. An organisation may wish to set up an information centre to provide the necessary support and co-ordination.

Rapid applications development

5.12 JAD may also be used as a tool for users and IT specialists to build software using rapid applications development (RAD). RAD can be described as a quick way of building software. It combines a new management approach to systems development with the use of modern software tools such as graphics-based user interfaces and object oriented design methods. RAD also involves the end-user heavily in the development process.

5.13 At the start of the process, users and systems designers meet to identify the overall business objectives and to discuss the technology required to support these objectives. They produce a detailed definition of the required application, a description of the planned implementation and an indication of the flexibility required.

5.14 The approach is dependent upon an efficient infrastructure within the organisation; this is likely to be based on open systems, networks and a corporate database. This provides the components for the hardware, while software may be developed using the object oriented approach, which is based upon a static and dynamic view of organisations. The dynamic view is concerned with processes and activities; the static view considers the structural objects which perform or are performed upon by processes. These objects are seen as behaving in a predictable way and can be re-used by different applications.

Prototyping   *12/94, 6/96*

5.15 Another way of ensuring full user involvement in, and commitment to, design is the technique of prototyping.

5.16 A prototype is a model of all or part of a system, built to show users early in the design process how it will appear. As a simple example, a prototype of a formatted screen output from a system could be prepared using a graphics package, or even a spreadsheet model. This would describe how the screen output would appear to the *user*. The user could make suggested amendments, which would be incorporated into the next model.

5.17 Using prototyping software, the programmer can write an application program quickly. (Much software production is repetitive, and this makes the development of prototyping software feasible.) He or she can then check with the data user whether the prototype program that has been designed appears to meet the user's needs, and if it doesn't it can be amended. Any number of 'prototype' programs can be made for the user to sample, and it is only when the program does what the user wants that the final version of the program is ready.

5.18 The *advantages* of prototyping are as follows.

(a) It makes it possible for programmers to present a 'mock-up' version of a program to a data user, to see how it works, before anyone has to commit substantial time and money to the project. The data user can judge the prototype before things have gone too far to be changed.

(b) It makes it more economical for data users to get 'custom built' application software, instead of having to buy off-the-shelf application packages which may or may not suit their particular needs properly.

(c) It makes efficient use of programmer time by helping programmers to develop programs more quickly. Prototyping may speed up the 'design' stage of the systems development life-cycle.

(d) A prototype does not necessarily have to be written in the language of what it is prototyping (as an analogy, you can make a prototype car out of wood), and so prototyping is not only a tool, but a design technique.

5.19 There are some *disadvantages* with prototyping too.

(a) Many prototyping software tools assume that the data user is about to computerise an application for the first time. This may not be so: some data users might want to transfer an application from an 'old' program to an updated new one, and so transfer data from existing files on to files for the new program.

(b) Many prototyping software tools produce programs that are tied to a particular make of hardware, or a particular database system, and cannot 'travel' from one system to another without further use of prototyping.

(c) It is sometimes argued that prototyping tools are inefficient in the program codes they produce, so that programs are bigger and use up more computer memory than they would if they had been written by programmers without the aid of prototyping.

(d) Computer users may be unimaginative, and the resulting system may be too similar to what has been the case before.

(e) Some specialised program demands cannot be 'automated' and have to be hand-written. Not all prototyping tools allow programmers to insert hand-written codes into a program.

(f) A serious criticism is that prototyping tools allow programmers to produce a bigger quantity of shoddy programs at a high speed.

(g) Many prototyping tools do not produce suitable program documentation for the user.

Evolutionary prototyping
6/95

5.20 Prototyping is often described as an evolutionary process. It is particularly suited to being used in the evolutionary approach to systems development. In the evolutionary approach, a project is broken down into separate parts and each part in turn is taken through the development process.

'The emphasis is on a learning process, whereby users and developers refine the requirements or learn more about the possibilities of the technology, from the experience of developing and testing a given part, and then use this knowledge to shape the development of the next part.'(Flynn, *Information Systems Requirements*)

5.21 The evolutionary approach requires a new first phase to be inserted. This can be described as 'define separate parts'. Once developed, each part will either add to the functionality of an earlier part or be integrated into the evolving system.

BPP PUBLISHING

5.22 The advantages of the evolutionary approach are as follows.

(a) The task of project control becomes easier, as the tackling of individual parts is less complex than working on the whole.

(b) It is not necessary to 'freeze' requirements for all parts at the outset (unlike traditional systems development).

(c) Each part can be developed relatively quickly.

(d) As with prototyping, users are able to see the effects of their decisions and the results of their requirements before the whole system is developed. This provides greater flexibility and responsiveness to changing user needs and enables greater user participation in development.

5.23 There are also a number of disadvantages to the evolutionary approach.

(a) A mistake in an early part may significantly affect later work.

(b) A project is likely to take longer from inception to completion than with traditional methods.

(c) If key phases are tackled early, the risk that changes may be necessitated by changing requirements will be increased.

User groups

5.24 A user group is a forum for users of particular hardware or, more usually, software, so that they can share ideas and experience and, on occasions, acting as an arbiter in disputes with the supplier. The term is more commonly associated with users of existing packaged software who wish to contribute ideas for the continuing development and improvement of packages.

5.25 User groups are usually set up either by the software manufacturers themselves (who use them to maintain contact with customers and as a source of new product ideas) or by groups of users who were not satisfied with the level of support they were getting from suppliers of proprietary software.

5.26 Users of a particular package can meet, or perhaps exchange views over the Internet to discuss solutions, ideas or 'short cuts' to improve productivity. An (electronic) newsletter service might be appropriate, based view exchanged by members, but also incorporating ideas culled from the wider environment by IT specialists.

5.27 Sometimes user groups are set up within individual organisations. Where an organisation has written its own application software, or is using tailor-made software, there will be a very small knowledge base initially, and there will obviously not be a national user group, because the application is unique.

5.28 'Interested parties', including, as a minimum, representatives from the IT department and users who are familiar with different parts of the system can attend monthly or quarterly meetings to discuss the operation of the system, make suggestions for improvements (such as the production of new reports or time-tabling of processing) and raise any queries.

6 FOURTH GENERATION LANGUAGES

6.1 A fourth generation language is a programming language that is easier to use than languages like COBOL, PASCAL and C.

6.2 The term fourth generation language (4GL) loosely denotes software which enables systems designers, and even users, to develop their own systems. A 4GL offers the user an English-like set of commands and simple control structures in which to specify general data processing or numerical operations. These programs are then translated into a conventional high-level language such as COBOL or C.

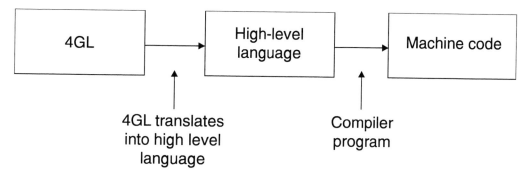

6.3 4GLs arose partly in response to the applications backlog. A great deal of programming time is spent maintaining and improving old programs rather than building new ones. Many organisations therefore have a backlog of applications waiting to be developed. 4GLs, by stepping up the process of application design and by making it easier for end-users to build their own programs, helps to reduce it.

6.4 Most fourth generation systems use a mixture of text and graphics, often a graphical user interface. A fourth generation system should have the following features.

(a) It should be easy to learn and use.

(b) It should contain on-line 'help' facility for users.

(c) It should be usable interactively.

(d) It should be 'fault' tolerant (ie any mistakes in data entry should be dealt with easily).

(e) It should be suitable for document design work.

Case example: Informix

The following is an extract from current marketing material on the Informix website.

The INFORMIX-4GL Product Family, comprised of INFORMIX-4GL Rapid Development System, INFORMIX-4GL Interactive Debugger, and INFORMIX-4GL Compiler, is a comprehensive fourth-generation application development and production environment that provides power and flexibility without the need for third-generation languages like C or COBOL. INFORMIX-4GL version 4.1 provides more enhancements to the product line than any other release since 4GL was introduced in 1986 giving you more functionality than ever before!

Wouldn't you like to find a self-contained application development environment that:

- provides rapid development and interactive debugging capabilities;

- offers high performance in the production environment;

- integrates all the functionality you could possibly need for building even the most complex applications;

- doesn't require the use of a third-generation language;

- allows you to easily maintain your applications for years to come;

- is based on industry-standard SQL; and

- is easily portable?

Look no further. You've just described INFORMIX-4GL.

The INFORMIX-4GL Product Family gives you all the tools you need to create sophisticated database applications in three easy packages with one consistent interface. Used together, INFORMIX-4GL Rapid Development System and INFORMIX-4GL Interactive Debugger provide the optimal environment for developing applications, while INFORMIX-4GL Compiler provides high-performance application execution in the production environment.

Whether you're building menus, forms, screens, or reports, INFORMIX-4GL performs all development functions, and allows for easy integration between them, eliminating the need for external development packages. Because our INFORMIX-4GL products are source-code compatible, portability is ensured.

Application generators

6.5 An application generator is a type of 4GL used to create complete applications programs. The user describes what needs to be done and the data and files which are to be used. The applications generator then translates this description into a program.

6.6 The basis for this process is the recognition that many of the functions such as data input, sorting, searching, file management, report writing and the like are quite similar in operation even when these program segments are found in quite different applications programs.

6.7 The objective is to use a number of standardised program segments to provide these common functions. This is analogous to the use of interchangeable parts in manufacturing which helped stimulate the industrial revolution. Programs no longer need to be entirely custom made since the appropriate use of common modules may significantly reduce the cost and time involved in creating programs.

6.8 The usefulness of application generators lies in their ability to provide much of the program quickly and relatively easily. The major drawback to using these systems results from their inability to cover all possible program requirements. As a consequence application generators are used in two modes.

   (a) They may be used to provide relatively simple programs in a finished form, this would be appropriate for non-programmers with undemanding requirements.

   (b) As programs become more complex or use less common analytical methods the program generators become less useful. In these cases the generators provide common segments while a programmer then adds the specialised program segments. This combination of man and machine takes advantage of the relative abilities of each to provide a finished system.

6.9 Application generators can be used by non-programmers to develop their own program though some experience or training in programming generally aids the creation process and also allows the user to add in any specialised program segments when needed. Application generators are useful but limited tools.

Report generators

6.10 An example of a tool which is particularly useful for PC users is a report generator. This is a program which gives the non-specialist user a capability of producing reports from one or more files, through easily constructed statements.

6.11 Many software packages (for example for database systems or accounting systems) include a report generator which can be used by non-technical users. The value of a report generator is that it enables PC users to extract information from their files - for example in a database or spreadsheet package - in the form of tabulated reports which can be presented to management.

Advantages and disadvantages

6.12 The use of 4GLs has the following advantages.
   (a) It enhances end-user computing, so limiting the work of IS staff.
   (b) It taps user creativity.
   (c) It diffuses IT throughout the organisation.
   (d) It vastly increases programmer productivity, even though it uses more hardware resources.

6.13 There are also potential problems with 4GLs.

   (a) Over-enthusiastic use by users might overload the main hardware resources.

   (b) The information systems department might get overloaded by training requirements.

   (c) Programs written in a 4GL do make less efficient use of computer processing power and memory. This can have the effect of slowing down the execution of a program to unacceptable levels.

7 OBJECT ORIENTED METHODS
12/98

7.1 The object oriented approach to analysis, developed in the last decade, is based on a static *and* a dynamic view of the organisation. The static view considers the structural objects which interact with processes by initiating them or by being operated on by them. The dynamic view focuses on the processes themselves.

7.2 Under the object oriented approach (OOA) a specification consists of one type of component only: the object. This is really an object *together with* the processes which involve that object. The advantages of this approach are as follows.

   (a) A specification can be agreed upon more readily, as there is likely to be agreement on identification of the objects.

   (b) A library of objects can be assembled, from which specifications can be created.

   (c) Maintenance costs are reduced as it is relatively easy to change objects.

7.3 There are also disadvantages. In particular a process which affects more than one object may be difficult to 'fix'.

Object-oriented development

7.4 *Object-oriented development* differs from traditional development in a number of ways.

   (a) Instead of treating *data* and *processes* separately, it packages them together as *objects* to create a model of the business. When an object-oriented system runs, it simulates the operation of the business.

   (b) In traditional programming, programs are *active* and data is *passive*. In object-oriented programming, the data is active and is able (within objects) to perform work on itself.

   (c) *Re-use* of existing components is an inherent part of object-oriented programming.

7.5 The packaging together of data and processes into an object is referred to as *encapsulation*. An object includes some *data* and a set of *operations* ('methods') which can access that data. When a message is received by an object, it:

   (a) chooses the operation which implements the request contained in the message;
   (b) executes the chosen operation; and
   (c) sends the result of the operation to the source of the request.

7.6 Encapsulation has the effect of surrounding each piece of data with code. The messages received by the object specify *what* should be done and the object decides *how* to execute the chosen operation. Software which has been written using encapsulation is highly tolerant of change, because a change in one part of the software need not affect other areas. Another concept in object-oriented programming is *inheritance*. This involves the re-use of existing material by taking characteristics of existing objects and using these to inform the development of new classes of objects.

161

7.7 Object-oriented development (OOD) requires more work at the outset, but the benefits available from re-use of components are considerable. OOD is widely used in three areas at present.

(a) Graphical applications, particularly the user interface.
(b) Multimedia applications, because of the wide variety of data handled.
(c) Complex systems, where it can reduce multiple dependencies between functions.

Chapter roundup

- A methodology is a collection of procedures, techniques, tools and documentation aids which are designed to help systems developers in their efforts to implement a new system. Methodologies are usually broken down into phases. Methodologies may be process-driven or data-driven. Process-driven methodologies are based on the processes which are performed, rather than the data which is the subject of the processing. Data-driven methodologies focus on data, the rationale being that the type of data in a system is less likely to change than the processes through which it passes.

- Checkland's Soft Systems Methodology provides a way of analysing the problem situations in open systems. SSM is based on the meaning-intention-action cycle inherent in human activity. SSM involves the following of two interrelated streams of enquiry, the logic-driven stream of enquiry and the cultural stream of enquiry. These are drawn together in the final stages of change definition and change implementation.

- SSADM breaks the systems development process down into stages. Each stage is further broken down into steps and tasks. Each stage requires a number of documents to be provided, as a sign that it has been completed, and to ensure that the outputs from one stage are used as the inputs to a later stage. Logical design and physical design are separated, with as much design work as possible being done on paper before there is any commitment to implement it.

- Data-driven methodologies emphasise the data used by a system. The steps involved in database design usually follow this type of approach. Information engineering is an example of a data-driven methodology. Data needs are identified before processing options.

- One way of ensuring full user involvement in and commitment to design is the technique of prototyping. Prototyping assists programmers by helping them to write application programs much more quickly and easily, and they involve little coding effort on the part of the programmer.

- Structured walkthroughs are a technique used by those responsible for systems design to present their design to interested user groups. A structured walkthrough is a meeting in which the output from a phase or stage of development is presented to users for discussion and for formal approval.

- Joint applications development is an approach to development based on a partnership between users and IT specialists.

- A fourth-generation language is software which enables a systems developer or an end-user to develop his or her own system.

- Object-oriented development is widely used, particularly for graphical user interfaces.

Test your knowledge

1   What is a methodology? (see para 1.1)

2   What factors need to be considered when choosing a methodology? (1.11)

3   What are the disadvantages of using a methodology? (1.15)

4   Explain CATWOE (2.12)

5   What are the advantages of SSM? (2.22)

6   What are the stages of SSADM? (3.4)

7   What does physical design involve? (3.16)

8   What are the phases of information engineering? (4.2)

9   What is a structured walkthrough: (5.2)

10   What are the advantages and disadvantages of prototyping? (5.18, 5.19)

11   What are the advantages of OOA? (7.2)

12   How does object-oriented development differ from traditional development? (7.4)

Now try illustrative questions 11, 12, 21, 23 and 25 - 27 at the end of the Study Text

BPP
PUBLISHING

Chapter 8

SYSTEMS ANALYSIS TECHNIQUES

> **This chapter covers the following topics.**
>
> 1 Data flow diagrams
>
> 2 Entity modelling
>
> 3 Entity life histories
>
> 4 Normalisation
>
> 5 More techniques
>
> **Introduction**
>
> This is the first of two chapters in which we examine some of the techniques and tools used in systems analysis and design. Some of this is likely to be familiar from your earlier studies for the *Information Systems* exam. We are mostly concerned with *data* analysis in this chapter, whereas in the next chapter we are more concerned with the *logic* of processes.

1 DATA FLOW DIAGRAMS

12/98

1.1 A useful way of recording the ways in which data is processed, without bothering with the equipment used, is a data flow diagram. The production of a data flow diagram is often the first step in a structured systems analysis, because it provides a basic understanding of how the system works.

1.2 Four symbols are used in data flow diagrams. See the diagram on the next page. These symbols should *not* be confused with any type of flowcharting symbols that you have learned for other subjects.

   (a) An *entity* is a source or destination of data which is considered external to the system (not necessarily external to the organisation). It may be people or groups who provide data or input information or who receive data or output information. An example would be a customer.

   (b) A *data store* is a point which holds data, and receives a data flow. Examples of data stores are transaction records, data files, reports and documents.

   (c) A *data flow* represents the movement or transfer of data from one point in the system to another. A data flow could be 'physically' anything - for example a letter, a telephone call, a fax message, a link between computers, or a verbal statement.

   (d) *Data processes* are processing actions carried out from a data store, or which produce a data store. The processes could be manual, mechanised or automated/ computerised. A data process will use or alter the data in some way.

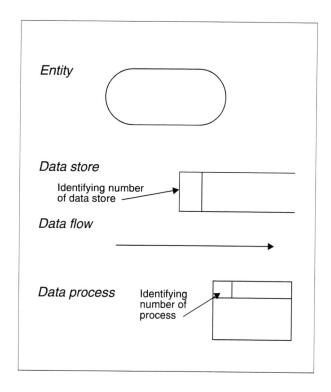

1.3   *Data stores* are not restricted as to their form, and might be held in a computer's memory, in the form of various magnetic media, or in the form of documents in a filing cabinet, or microfiche.

1.4   A *data flow* may involve a document transfer or it may simply involve a notification that some event has occurred without any detailed information being passed. When a data flow occurs a copy of the data transferred may also be retained at the transmitting point.

1.5   An example of a *process* which simply uses the data would be an output operation, where the data held by the system is unchanged and it is merely made available in a different form, for example printed out.

1.6   A process which alters the data would be a mathematical computation or a process such as sorting in which the arrangement of the data is altered.

1.7   Systems vary widely in the amount of data processing which they perform. Some systems are dominated by the amount of data movement which they provide, whilst others are intensively concerned much more with transforming the data into a more useful form.

Levelled DFDs

1.8   The complexity of business systems means that it is impossible to represent the operations of any system by means of a single diagram.

1.9   At the top level, an overview of the different systems in an organisation can be given, or alternatively the position of a single system in the organisation shown. This might be achieved by means of a context diagram.

1.10   This is in turn 'exploded' by means of a more detailed data flow diagram, known as a Level-1 DFD. Further detail can be represented on a Level-2 DFD, and so on until all individual entities, stores, flows and processes are shown.

1.11 The diagram below illustrates how levels of DFDs are built up.

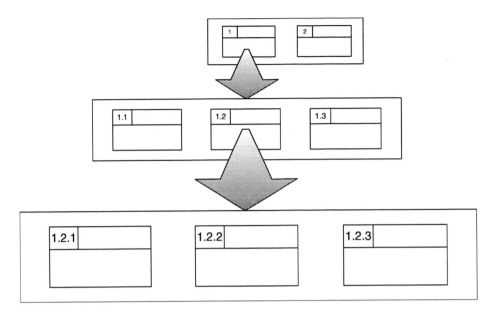

Example: data flow diagram

1.12 The example used here is a system used for purchasing in a manufacturing company. Three data flow diagrams are shown; each is prepared to record a certain level of detail.

Level-0 DFD (context diagram)

1.13 A Level-0 DFD or context diagram summarises the inputs and outputs to the system at a high level.

1.14 The central box represents the system as a whole and (for simplicity in this case) one external entity is shown. (Usually the box would be *surrounded* by external entities, such as different types of suppliers who are dealt with in different ways by the system, and the diagram would look like a spider.)

1.15 Note that we are only showing flows of data. The physical resources (the goods supplied) *can* be shown (by means of broad arrows ⇨), but this tends to overcomplicate the diagram. Also no data stores are shown on the context diagram.

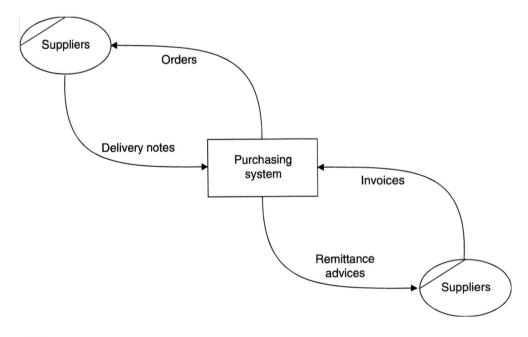

1.16 Within the purchasing system as a whole in this organisation there are two subsystems: the Stores department places requests for purchases and accepts delivery of the goods themselves; the Purchasing department places orders, and receives and pays invoices.

1.17 On the next page is shown a Level-1 DFD for the purchasing department.

1.18 This is not meant to depict an ideal system, if there is any such thing. You may be able to detect flaws or inefficiencies in the system shown on the next page. This is irrelevant at this stage since we are only trying to describe the system as it currently exists.

1.19 Also, for the sake of simplicity, we are only showing purchasing department activities. The supplier would send delivery notes to the Stores department who would carry out their own checks, prepare GRNs, and have other data flows with other subsystems.

1.20 Note the following important points.

(a) Each process is numbered, but this is only for ease of identification: the numbers are not meant to show the strict sequence of events.

(b) The process box also has a heading showing where the process is carried out or who does it. The description of the process should be a clear verb like 'prepare', 'calculate', 'check' (not 'process', which is too vague).

(c) Arrows must always finish at or start from a process. (If you simply remember that data cannot move without intervention (processing) you should never get this wrong.)

(d) Rather than having data flow arrows criss-crossing all over the place it is often simpler to show a symbol more than once on the same diagram, wherever it is needed. When this is done an additional line is put within the symbol. The supplier entity and several of the data stores have extra lines for this reason.

(e) Data stores are given a reference number (again sequence is not important).

This is preceded by an M if it is a manual store and a D if it is a computer store.

(f) There may be little reason to label arrows that go in and out of data stores, because it will be clear enough from the description of the process. (See, for example, process 3 in the example DFD shown: is it really necessary to label the arrows 'invoice', 'invoice details', especially at this level?)

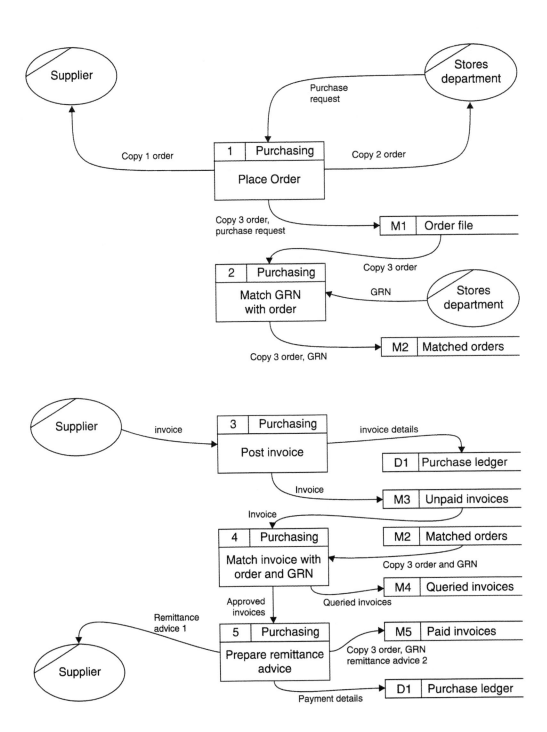

1.21 A separate DFD (Level-2) would then be prepared for each of the numbered processes.

1.22 This is known as decomposing a process. The diagram below, for example, shows the data flows for process 1, placing the order.

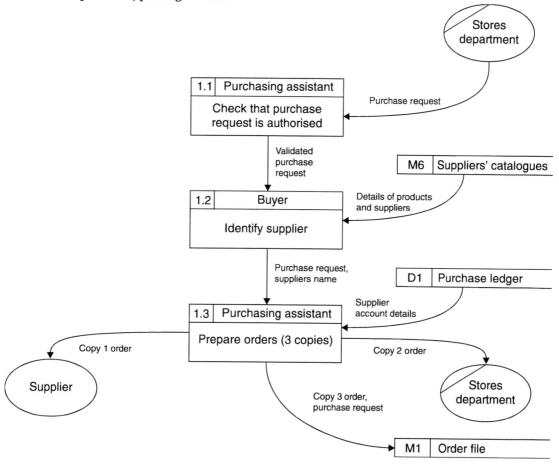

Exercise 1

Compare this diagram with the Level-1 DFD and note how it is possible to trace the same data flows from one level to the next.

1.23 In turn box 1.1 could be further decomposed in a Level-3 DFD, with processes 1.1.1, 1.1.2 and so on, and box 1.2 could be decomposed into processes 1.2.1, 1.2.2 etc. In theory there is no limit to the number of lower levels, but three levels is usually enough.

Exercise 2

Study these diagrams carefully and then try to 'decompose' some of the other processes in the Level-1 DFD into Level-2 DFDs. For example try process 4 and show what might happen if an invoice does *not* match the GRN. You might also like to try to construct a Level-1 DFD for the Stores department.

Solution

There are no right answers, because we have not given you full details of the system: you will **need to make assumptions** based on your knowledge and experience of typical accounting systems. This is to encourage you to have a go without being scared of making mistakes. (Experienced and highly paid systems analysts are likely to make mistakes when they first try to get a system down in DFD form: they will only get it right after discussion and agreement with **users**, which is the whole point of the exercise.)

Drawing data flow diagrams

1.24 The easiest way to prepare a data flow diagram is to work logically through a number of steps. (The following are suggested as a guide; if you evolve your own approach and it works, that is fine!)

The extent of the system

1.25 The first thing to do is to identify the extent of the systems under consideration. You should have a pretty clear idea of this in an examination, as it will be described in narrative form.

Processes

1.26 Next, you need to identify all the processes which are included in the system or the part of the system which you have identified.

Each process should involve an action, for example 'prepare despatch instructions' or 'allocate stock to order'.

Inputs and outputs

1.27 Then you need to identify all the outputs from the processes which you have identified. These are data flows, each of which must be connected to another symbol.

1.28 You also need to identify the input or inputs to each process. The arrow representing each data flow should lead into the process and should start at a point of origin (for which the options are the same as those available for output destinations).

1.29 As already mentioned some connections are not allowed, as summarised in the following table.

	Entity	Process	Store
Entity	No	**Yes**	No
Process	**Yes**	**Yes**	**Yes**
Store	No	**Yes**	No

Exercise 3

What are the *four* destinations to which a data flow leading from a process might lead?

Solution

It can lead to any of the following.

(a) Another process on the same DFD.
(b) A process on another DFD.
(c) An external entity.
(d) A data store.

Entities

1.30 In identifying outputs and inputs, you should also have identified all the external entities, as these will be sources or destinations of data flows (sometimes referred to as 'sources and sinks').

Drawing the diagram

1.31 When drawing data flow diagrams, note the following points.

(a) Use plenty of space on the paper.

(b) If possible use a stencil which includes suitable shapes.

(c) Use a ruler or other straight edge for boxes.

(d) Data flow arrows look nicer as curved lines, as shown above. (They somehow make the system look more human and realistic, less 'techy'.) If you can't do this *neatly*, however, your hand-drawn diagrams will look *very* messy: straight lines drawn with a ruler are better than mess.

(e) Lastly, it should go without saying that you should write legibly.

2 ENTITY MODELLING

12/95

Entities, attributes and relationships

2.1 An entity, as we have seen, is an item (a person, a job, a business, an activity, a product or stores item etc) about which information is stored.

- In a sales ledger system a customer is an entity.
- In a payroll system an employee is an entity.

2.2 An attribute is a characteristic or property of an entity. For a customer, attributes include customer name and address, amounts owing, date of invoices sent and payments received, credit limit etc.

2.3 For any entity we can identify relationships between attributes and relationships between entities. Here are some simple examples. (The diagrams are sometimes called Bachmann diagrams.)

No relationship

2.4 There are no relationships in a printout of customer names. This is simply a list of records. Each address is an attribute.

One-to-one relationship

2.5 The relationship employs exists between *company* and *finance director*. There is one company which can only employ one finance director.

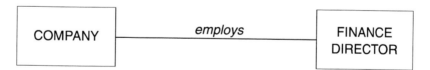

One-to-many relationship

2.6 The relationship employs also exists between *company* and *director*. The company employs more than one director.

Many-to-one relationship

2.7 This is really the same as the previous example, but viewed from the opposite direction. For example, many *sales managers* report to one *sales director*.

Many-to-many relationship

2.8 The relationship between *product* and *part* is many-to-many. A product is composed of many parts, and a part might be used in many products.

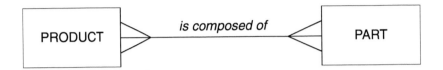

Breaking down relationships

2.9 Many-to-many relationships cause difficulties when designing the software to search for items and they should if possible be broken down so that they are eliminated.

2.10 The relationship depicted above could be amended by the insertion of a new entity called 'job sheet'. Thus a product is manufactured to job sheets and job sheets specify a part.

Entity relationship models

2.11 An entity relationship model (ERM) (also known as an entity model, an entity attribute relationship model or a logical data structure) provides an understanding of the logical data requirements of a system independently of the system's organisation and processes.

2.12 An entity relationship model (ERM) uses one-to-one, one-to-many and many-to-many relationships. These relationships can also be described by the notations: *1:1*, *1:n* and *m:n* respectively.

2.13 The correct classification of relationships is important. If the one-to-many relationship customer order contains part numbers is incorrectly described as one-to-one, the system designed on the basis of this ERM might allow an order to be entered with one item and one item only, thus necessitating the creation of a separate order for each part.

Example: ERM

2.14 An example of a diagram relevant to a warehousing and despatch system is given below. This indicates that:

- a customer may make many orders
- that an order form can contain several order lines
- that each line on the order form can only detail one product, but that one product can appear on several lines of the order.

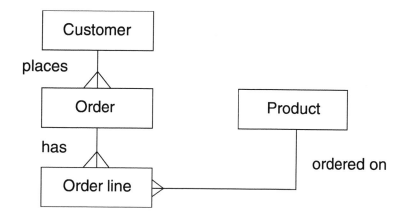

2.15 Another example of an entity model is given below. Note the structure of the accompanying narrative.

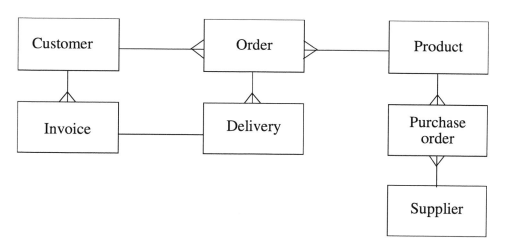

Entity	Relationship	Entity
Customer	Places many	Orders
Order	Has many	Deliveries
Product	Is ordered on many	Orders
Supplier	Supplies many	Products
Product	Is ordered on many	Purchase orders
Supplier	Receives many	Purchase orders
Invoice	Is for one	Deliveries
Customer	Receives many	Invoices

Exercise 4

Customers send orders in to your company. The company send supplies to customers as soon as the order, or part of the order, can be fulfilled. An invoice is raised for each delivery. Draw an entity relationship model to show these procedures.

BPP
PUBLISHING

Solution

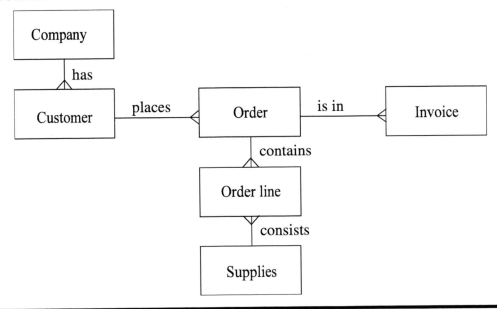

---

3 ENTITY LIFE HISTORIES

3.1 Don't confuse entity life histories (logical data structures) with entity relationship models which take a static view of the data.

3.2 An entity life history (ELH) is a diagram of the *processes* that happen to an *entity*. Data items do not remain unchanged at all times, they may come into existence by a specific operation and be destroyed by another. For example, a customer order forms part of a number of processes, and is affected by a number of different events. An entity life history gives a dynamic view of the data.

3.3 At its simplest, an entity life history displays the following structure.

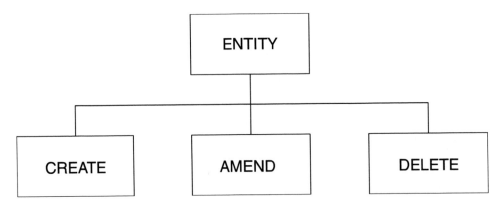

3.4 Entity life histories identify the various states that an entity can legitimately be in. It is really the functions and events which cause the state of the entity to change that are being analysed, rather than the entity itself. The ELH diagram provides a pictorial way of communication that enables users to validate easily the accuracy (or otherwise) of the analysis.

3.5 The following conventions for ELHs are used in SSADM.

(a) Three symbols are used. The main one is a rectangular box. Within this may be placed an asterisk or a small circle. as explained below.

(b) At the top level the first box (the 'root node') shows the entity itself.

(c) At lower levels the boxes represent events that affect the life of the entity.

(d) The second level is most commonly some form of 'create, amend, delete', as shown above (or birth, life, death if you prefer). The boxes are read in sequence from left to right.

(d) If an event may affect an entity many times (iteration) this is shown by an asterisk in the top right hand corner of the box. A customer account, for example, will be updated many times.

(e) If events are alternatives (for example accept large order or reject large order) (selection) a small circle is placed in the top right hand corner.

3.6 Note the three types of process logic:

- Sequence
- Iteration
- Selection

3.7 Here is a very simple example.

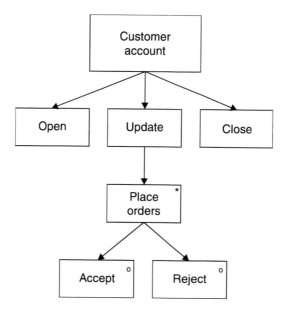

Exercise 5

See if you can expand the diagram to show the iterative event 'Pays bills' and the alternatives 'pays on time' and 'pays late'

Solution

Your diagram should be along the following lines: another (iteration) box coming out of the update box called something like 'Pays'; two selection boxes coming out of the 'Pays' box for 'On time' and 'Late'.

---

4 NORMALISATION

4.1 When thinking about how data should be organised in a computer system two features are particularly desirable.

(a) Links between items of data that are related, such as customer name and customer address, should be preserved.

(b) Duplication of data items should be avoided, so that as little space is taken up as possible, and so that there is as little chance as possible of inconsistencies between examples of the same data stored in different places.

4.2   Normalisation is a way of achieving this. Normalisation is a step-by–step process in which a set of related data fields are refined into new sets having progressively simpler and more regular structure. Normalisation is also called relational data analysis.

4.3   Normalisation is a useful technique for designing 'relational' databases, as we shall see in Chapter 14. You may find it particularly valuable if you are ever expected to use a package such as Microsoft Access at work.

Example: normalisation

4.4   An organisation has the following table of data showing which customers are interested in which products. You are required to convert it to 'Third Normal Form'

Product Code	Product Name	Customer Code	Customer name	Customer Since	Sales Rep Code	Sales Rep name	Credit Status	Discount %
A005	Large	A071	Agassi	02/02/95	145	Singh	A	10
		L015	Laver	05/04/96	145	Singh	C	5
		W006	Wade	31/10/96	172	Michaels	D	5
		B104	Becker	25/11/94	145	Singh	F	0
		W015	Wade	13/07/93	172	Michaels	B	7
A006	Medium	L015	Laver	05/04/96	175	Hempel	E	0
		F094	Frentzen	06/08/95	175	Hempel	B	7
		D149	Dumali	02/03/97	175	Hempel	C	5
A007	Small	F094	Frentzen	06/08/95	175	Hempel	A	10
		W015	Wade	13/07/93	144	Calder	B	7
		S022	Scholes	17/09/96	144	Calder	E	0
		H053	Henman	19/05/97	175	Hempel	C	5

Solution

4.5   In normalisation a row of data is called a row (!), and a column is called a field. The column headings are the names of the fields.

Step 1.   Identify the key field.

The key field is the item of data within a row by which the row can be uniquely identified. This is a term worth highlighting again, although you have met it before.

(a)   Choose a code rather than a text field, if possible

(b)   Choose a field that is not determined by any other field or combination of fields

In this case, product code seems the obvious choice. (In theory it does not matter what you choose: normalisation will always give the same end-result. However, a good choice at the start saves work.)

Step 2.   Convert to First Normal Form by removing repeating groups

A repeating group is a field or set of fields which have data in them more than once for a single value of the key field.

This is easy to see in our example. Each product code has a related product name field that has data in it only once, while each of the other fields have several different data items. There is repeating group of data about customers.

The original table is therefore split into two. The repeating data has the key field appended to it to preserve the link between all data items.

Product Code	Product Name
A005	Large
A006	Medium
A007	Small

Product Code	Customer Code	Customer Name	Customer Since	Sales Rep Code	Sales Rep Name	Credit Status	Discount %
A005	A071	Agassi	02/02/95	145	Singh	A	10
A005	L015	Laver	05/04/96	145	Singh	C	5
A005	W006	Wade	31/10/96	172	Michaels	D	5
A005	B104	Becker	25/11/94	145	Singh	F	0
A005	W015	Wade	13/07/93	172	Michaels	B	7
A006	L015	Laver	05/04/96	175	Hempel	E	0
A006	F094	Frentzen	06/08/95	175	Hempel	B	7
A006	D149	Dumali	02/03/97	175	Hempel	C	5
A007	F094	Frentzen	06/08/95	175	Hempel	A	10
A007	W015	Wade	13/07/93	144	Calder	B	7
A007	S022	Scholes	17/09/96	144	Calder	E	0
A007	H053	Henman	19/05/97	175	Hempel	C	5

Step 3. Identify key fields for the new tables

The Product Code table's key field will clearly be Product Code

However, there are a number of rows in the second table with the same Product Code. A better choice would be Customer Code, but this does not uniquely identify a row. For instance two rows have the code L015.

In this case we use a compound key which is made up of two or more fields which together uniquely identify a row. In this case we can use Product Code and Customer Code.

A simpler way of presenting the story so far is as follows. The key field(s) are shown in bold.

PRODUCT   **Product Code,** Product Name

PRODUCT/CUSTOMER   **Product Code, Customer Code,** Customer Name, Customer Since, Sales Rep Code, Sales Rep Name, Credit Status, Discount %

Step 4. Convert to Second Normal Form by ensuring that EITHER:

(a) The key is a single item OR

(b) Fields that are not key are fully dependent on all of the fields that are key, not just part of them

In our example the PRODUCT table's key is a single item, so it is already in second normal form.

In the PRODUCT/CUSTOMER table, however, some of the non-key items do not depend on both of the key fields.

(a) Customer name and Customer Since could be determined from (in other words they depend on) Customer Code

(b) However Sales Rep Code, Sales Rep Name, Credit Status and Discount % can only be determined by referring to both Product Code and Customer Code.

Exercise 6

If the Customer Code is L015 what is Sales Rep Name?

Solution

It could be either Singh or Hempel. You have to know the Product Code as well as the Customer Code to identify a particular row. Try some other combinations like this for yourself until you are sure you understand.

We can remove the fields that are not fully dependent on both Product Code and Customer Code to their own CUSTOMER table, with Customer Code the clear candidate for key field.

Customer Code	Customer Name	Customer Since
A071	Agassi	02/02/95
L015	Laver	05/04/96
W006	Wade	31/10/96
B104	Becker	25/11/94
W015	Wade	13/07/93
L015	Laver	05/04/96
F094	Frentzen	06/08/95
D149	Dumali	02/03/97
F094	Frentzen	06/08/95
W015	Wade	13/07/93
S022	Scholes	17/09/96
H053	Henman	19/05/97

This leaves the PRODUCT/CUSTOMER table looking like this.

Product Code	Customer Code	Sales Rep Code	Sales Rep Name	Credit Status	Discount %
A005	A071	145	Singh	A	10
A005	L015	145	Singh	C	5
A005	W006	172	Michaels	D	5
A005	B104	145	Singh	F	0
A005	W015	172	Michaels	B	7
A006	L015	175	Hempel	E	0
A006	F094	175	Hempel	B	7
A006	D149	175	Hempel	C	5
A007	F094	175	Hempel	A	10
A007	W015	144	Calder	B	7
A007	S022	144	Calder	E	0
A007	H053	175	Hempel	C	5

Here is another an alternative presentation of the story so far. The <u>key fields</u> are <u>underlined</u>.

<u>Product Code</u> Product name	<u>Product Code</u> <u>Customer Code</u> Sales Rep Code Sales Rep Name Credit Status Discount %	<u>Customer Code</u> Customer Name Customer Since

Step 5. Convert to Third Normal Form by ensuring that BOTH:

(a) all non-key fields are independent of all other non-key fields; AND

(b) all key fields are independent of all other key fields.

The PRODUCT table and the CUSTOMER table are already in third normal form.

In the PRODUCT/CUSTOMER table, however, Sales Rep Name is determined by Sales Rep Code and Discount % is determined by Credit Status (but not vice versa: a discount of 5% is given to both grade C and D credit risks, for instance). There are clearly some non-key dependencies.

As for the key fields in the PRODUCT/CUSTOMER table, there is more than one possible value for Customer Code given a single Product Code, and there is more than one possible value for Product Code given a single value of Customer Code. Neither field determines what the other will be so they are independent.

We can now remove the dependencies in the PRODUCT/CUSTOMER table to give the following final result.

PRODUCT	**Product Code,** Product Name
PRODUCT/CUSTOMER	**Product Code, Customer Code,** Sales Rep Code, Credit Status
CUSTOMER	**Customer Code,** Customer Name, Customer Since
SALES REP	**Sales Rep Code,** Sales Rep Name
CREDIT STATUS	**Credit Status,** Discount %

Notice that the PRODUCT/CUSTOMER table retains the fields Sales Rep Code and Credit Status to preserve the links between the tables.

Exercise 7

Given a particular Customer Code, how would you find out that customer's Discount %?

Solution

You could look up the customer's Credit Status in the PRODUCT/CUSTOMER table, and then look up the Discount % that applied to that status in the CREDIT STATUS table. Again, try any other combinations you can think of.

Summary

4.6 Normalisation is a way of analysing and simplifying the relationships between items of data (it is also called relational data analysis). This is done in three stages, as follows.

First Normal Form (1NF)	Remove repeating groups
Second Normal Form (2NF)	Remove part-key dependencies
Third Normal Form (3NF)	Remove non-key dependencies and inter-key dependencies

5 MORE TECHNIQUES

5.1 More systems analysis techniques are described in the next chapter.

Chapter roundup

- Dataflow diagrams are used to record the ways in which data is processed without taking account of physical factors. There are only four symbols used in dataflow diagrams.

- An entity relationship model provides an understanding of a system's logical data requirements independently of the system's processes. The ERM uses 1:1, 1:n and m:n relationships.

- An entity life history is a diagram of the processes that happen to an entity. It gives a dynamic view of the data, rather than a static view of it. It describes how an entity comes into existence, the processes to which it is subjected and the way in which it is terminated.

- Normalisation is a technique used in the creation of a relational database. It allows the complex relationships between entities to be simplified so that all the data for an entity can be held in two-dimensional tables.

Test your knowledge

1 Draw and label the four symbols used in a data flow diagram. (see para 1.2)

2 What is a context diagram? (1.13)

3 What connections are not allowed in a DFD? (1.29)

4 What three relationships may be found in an entity relationship model? (2.12)

5 How are sequence, iteration and selection depicted in an ELH diagram? (3.5)

6 What is normalisation? (4.2)

7 What is a 'key' or 'key field'? (4.5)

8 What are the three stages of normalisation? (4.6)

Now try illustrative questions 13 and 34 at the end of the Study Text

Chapter 9

MORE SYSTEMS ANALYSIS TECHNIQUES

This chapter covers the following topics.

1   Structured English

2   Decision trees

3   Decision tables

4   CASE tools

5   Deployment flowcharting

Introduction

This chapter is a continuation of the last. Here we look at what are sometimes called process specification tools. These set out in detail the logic behind a data process that might simply be described as 'Process order' in a DFD. As in the previous chapter, you may have met some of these techniques in your earlier studies for *Information Systems*.

---

1   STRUCTURED ENGLISH

1.1   A 'structured narrative' is a systems design tool which describes the logic of a process in a highly detailed narrative form.

1.2   This method uses English as the language but severely limits the available vocabulary and tries to follow the layout and logical operation of a computer program.

1.3   This tool is not particularly easy to use or to understand. It is best suited for describing specific activities or functions, while the broader and more general concerns of system design are typically analysed by using data flow diagrams and decision tables or trees, which are better at simplifying procedures and choices into a presentable format.

1.4   There are several different kinds of Structured English. What is important is that Structured English has the following features.

(a)   It is more like spoken English than normal programming languages and so is easier for programmers and non-programmers to understand.

(b)   It is much more limited than normal speech, as it has to follow a strict logical order.

(c)   There is a variety of conventions for writing it.

1.5   Structured English uses keywords (eg IF, ADD) which, by some conventions, are written in capitals and have a precise logical meaning in the context of the narrative.

1.6   The logical order in which instructions are performed is sometimes expressed in indentation. As we have seen in the previous chapter, there are three basic logical structures.

- Sequencing
- Selection
- Iteration

1.7   The data elements which are the subject of processing are, by some conventions, written in lower case and underlined.

Sequence instruction

1.8   For example, the calculation of gross pay from hours worked and rate of pay could be written in structured English. This type of instruction is known as a sequence instruction.

> MULTIPLY hours worked by pay rate to get gross
> pay

1.9   It is possible to aggregate sequence instructions. For example the computation of gross pay in a program not only involves simple calculation but includes other processes.

(a)   Retrieving master records from a file for the employee reference.

> GET master record

(b)   Counting records so that the next record in sequence is retrieved.

> ADD 1 to counter

Selection instruction

1.10   Most computer programs offer a number of 'choices' and the consequent action taken depends on the choices being made. In structured English, a choice follows this structure.

> IF
>   THEN
> ELSE
>   SO

1.11   For example, a company offers discounts to trade customers only. How would this be expressed in structured English?

> IF the customer is a trade customer
>   THEN give 10% discount
> ELSE (customer is not trade customer)
>   SO no discount given

1.12   Sometimes, decisions are more complicated. Assume that the company only offers a 10% discount to trade customers who have been customers for over one year, but other trade customers receive a 5% discount.

> IF the customer is a trade customer
>   IF customer is customer over 1 year
>   THEN 10% discount given
>   ELSE 5% discount given
> ELSE (customer not a trade customer)
>   SO no discount given

1.13   One particular type of decision is a CASE statement. Cases are a special type of decision structure to indicate mutually exclusive possibilities.

1.14 A case structure is an alternative to the IF-THEN-ELSE-SO structure outlined above, which is satisfactory for making relatively simple decisions, but can become unwieldy when the decision becomes complex.

1.15 For example, we could have expressed the trade credit policy as follows. (END IF ends the case statement.)

```
IF customer a trade customer
        CASE    customer for more than one year
        give 10% discount
        CASE    customer for less than one year
        give 5% discount
END IF
```

Iteration

1.16 Sometimes a block or set of instructions may need to be repeated until a final condition is reached.

For example, assume we have called a given block out instructions the name Block 1. We wish these instructions to be executed until the number of records processed reaches 100. This requirement is a condition, which we can call condition 1. In structured English, this can be written as follows.

```
REPEAT
        Block 1
UNTIL
        Condition 1
```

2   DECISION TREES

2.1 You may have met decision trees as part of your studies for other papers in the context of expected values, probabilities and so on. In the context of systems analysis they are slightly different.

2.2 A decision tree is a design tool which provides a graphic representation of the various choices or decisions which are available, the events which might occur and their consequences.

Example: decision trees

2.3 Consider an order processing system. Whenever an order is received the system should first check to determine if payment has been received with the order. There are two possibilities - yes and no - which lead on to differing responses.

(a) If payment is included with the order, the system would then have to check on the availability of the items ordered. Here there are two further possibilities - the items can be in stock or not.

    (i)   If the items are in stock they would then be shipped or delivered to the customer.

    (ii)   If the item is not in stock a record of the customer's order needs to be made so that the item will be despatched when stock becomes available.

(b) If the customer has not included payment with order a similar set of activities would be undertaken but they would be preceded by credit evaluations.

BPP PUBLISHING

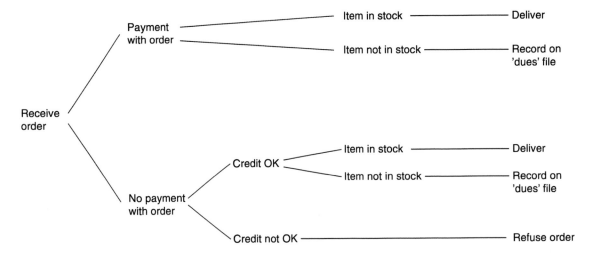

2.4   In the discussion above the focus was upon imposing an order or structure upon the decision-making process so that a computerised system could replicate the sequence of decision-event-decision as necessary.

2.5   In many cases in business the likelihood of various responses or conditions can be predicted or is known. In the example used above, we may know from past experience that most orders are prepaid or are for items held in stock. This information will be useful since it can be used to predict which systems functions may be most heavily used.

2.6   Decision trees are methods used to select the most appropriate or optimum option at each stage in the process. This approach may also be built into an information system. If the likelihood of various subsequent events may be estimated it is then possible to design the system so that it will attempt to select the option which leads to the best outcome.

Drawing decision trees

2.7   It is conventional to draw decision trees from left to right.

2.8   You may also have encountered conventions which use, for example, a box for a decision point and a circle for an outcome point. These are more usually associated with decision trees used for statistical or decision-making purposes, where probabilities and expected values are assigned to each outcome.

2.9   Here, we are concerned with representing the logic of a process and so it is quite acceptable to draw decision trees without such conventions. For example, in the diagram above, the first point does not really represent a decision or an outcome. We are simply showing the two possible states of a customer order: either payment is included with the order or the customer expects to be given credit.

Exercise 1

Draw a decision tree to represent the following procedure for development of new employees in an organisation.

Employees with a relevant degree may either joint the graduate entry programme or, provided they are in the top 15% in special aptitude tests, undergo accelerated management training. Those with other degrees are eligible for the graduate entry programme only. Employees without a degree but with other qualifications join the main intake stream. Employees without any qualifications are taken on at clerical grades.

Solution

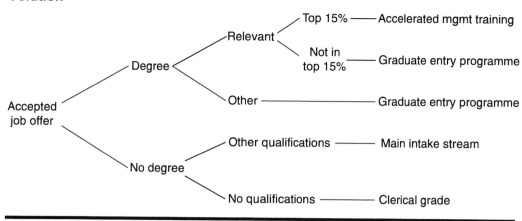

Disadvantages of decision trees

2.10 Decision trees are usually structured so that each decision has a maximum of two outcomes. This leads to potential inefficiencies in the use of decision trees.

(a) An action may result from more than one condition, leading to repetition.

(b) Very long or complex processes will be difficult to adapt to this method because choices could easily be missed or the tree size could become unmanageable.

(c) It might take several runs through the tree to complete all possibilities. In the exercise above, how would you treat a new employee who has a non-relevant degree, a relevant degree *and* other qualifications?

3 DECISION TABLES

3.1 Decision tables are used as a method of defining the logic of a process (ie the processing operations required) in a compact manner. They are more convenient than decision trees in situations where a large number of logical alternatives exist.

3.2 The basic format consists of four quadrants divided by intersecting double lines.

Condition stub	Condition entry
Action stub	Action entry

Simple example: a decision table

3.3 The technique is quite hard to grasp at first so we shall start by considering a very simple decision that most of us face every day: whether to get up or stay in bed.

Suppose you have to get up at around 8 am if you are going to get to work on time. You go to work on Monday to Friday only and have your weekends free. If you woke up one Tuesday morning at 8.02 you would be faced with the following appalling dilemma. An X marks the action you should take.

Conditions	Entry
Is it 8 o' clock yet?	Yes
Is it the weekend?	No
Actions	*Entry*
Get up	
Stay in bed	X

3.4 We can expand this table so that it takes account of all the possible combinations of conditions and shows the action that would be taken in each case.

(a) Because a condition can only apply or not apply (Yes or No), the number of combinations (or 'rules') is 2^n, where n is the number of conditions.

Here there are 2 conditions (n = 2) so the number of combinations is $2^2 = 4$. There are four columns.

	1	2	3	4
Is it 8 o' clock yet?				
Is it the weekend?				
Get up				
Stay in bed				

(b) Because the conditions can either have a Yes or No answer (Y or N) half of the each row must be filled with Ys and the other half with Ns.

(i) Write in Y for the first half of the columns in row 1 (columns 1 and 2) and N for the other half.

(ii) For row 2, write in Ys and Ns alternately, the number in each group of Ys and Ns being half that of each group in the previous row. In this example row 1 has Ys in groups of twos, so row 2 will have Ys in groups of 1.

(iii) If there are more conditions continue halving for each row until you reach the final condition, which will always be consecutive Ys and Ns.

	1	2	3	4
Is it 8 o' clock yet?	Y	Y	N	N
Is it the weekend?	Y	N	Y	N
Get up				
Stay in bed				

(c) Now consider what action you would take if the condition(s) specified in each column applied. For column 1 it is 8 o'clock but it is the weekend so you can stay in bed. For column 2 it is 8 o' clock but it is not the weekend so you must get up. Explain the logic of columns 3 and 4 yourself.

	1	2	3	4
Is it 8 o' clock yet?	Y	Y	N	N
Is it the weekend?	Y	N	Y	N
Get up		X		
Stay in bed	X		X	X

(d) In more complicated problems you may find that there are some columns that do not have any Xs in the Action entry quadrant because this combination of conditions is impossible. You can delete these columns. Exercise 2 will demonstrate this in a moment.

(e) Other columns have different combinations of conditions, but lead to the same action. Columns 1, 3 and 4 in the above example are of this type: they all say you can stay in bed. However, in columns 3 and 4 you can stay in bed because it is not yet 8 o clock.

It is immaterial whether it is the weekend or not: the answer can be Y or N. When a condition is immaterial to the decision we replace the Y or N with a dash – and consolidate columns if possible.

	1	2	3/4
Is it 8 o' clock yet?	Y	Y	N
Is it the weekend?	Y	N	–
Get up		X	
Stay in bed	X		X

(f) This is the final form of the table: it has been simplified as far as possible.

Exercise 2

L Bones woke up one morning and looked at the clock. It was 8.30. 'Oh no!', he thought, 'What day is it?' He lay in a daze for a moment and then realised it was Sunday.

Some hours later when he got up Mr Bones decided to draw up a decision table that he could use to save all this mental activity when he woke up in future. He identified 3 conditions, mirroring his early-morning thought processes, and 2 possible actions.

Conditions   *Is it 8 o' clock yet? Is it a weekday? Is it the weekend?*

Actions   *Get up. Stay in bed.*

Draw up and complete the decision table.

Solution

There are 3 conditions so there will be 2^3 = 8 columns.

	1	2	3	4	5	6	7	8
Is it 8 o' clock yet?	Y	Y	Y	Y	N	N	N	N
Is it a weekday?	Y	Y	N	N	Y	Y	N	N
Is it the weekend	Y	N	Y	N	Y	N	Y	N
Get up		X						
Stay in bed			X			X	X	

Columns 1, 4, 5 and 8 do not have any Xs because, thankfully of course, it cannot be both a weekday *and* a weekend. The impossibility of this combination is intuitively obvious in this simple example, but in more complex or less familiar decision situations it may only become clear that certain combinations are impossible once the table has been drawn up.

In this example we could delete columns 1, 4, 5 and 8 and cross out one or other of conditions 2 or 3, since if one applies the other doesn't. Columns 6 and 7 would be consolidated and we would end up with the same decision table as the one we saw earlier (although with the columns in a different order.)

Check that you understand all of this before continuing. Perhaps try out some other homely examples for yourself.

A more formal explanation

3.5 We can now explain this more formally and look at a business example.

(a) The purpose of the condition stub is to specify the values of the data that we wish to test for.

(b) The condition entry specifies what those values might be.

3.6 Between them, the condition stub and condition entry show what values an item of data might have that a computer program should test for. Establishing conditions will be done within a computer program by means of comparison checks.

3.7 The action entry quadrant shows the action or actions that will be performed for each rule. The columns are marked with an 'X' opposite the actions(s) to be taken. In the computer program, instructions specify the action to take, given the conditions established by comparison checks.

Example: a decision table

3.8 Consider the three conditions which might be encountered by a sales order processing clerk taking a telephone order.

Account overdue?	Y	Y	Y	Y	N	N	N	N
Credit limit exceeded?	Y	Y	N	N	Y	Y	N	N
New customer?	Y	N	Y	N	Y	N	Y	N

3.9 There are eight separate rules (2^3). In this example the three conditions are totally independent, that is, the answer to one will not affect the answer to the others. As we have seen, in some tables the conditions are not totally independent and there will be fewer columns.

3.10 Continuing the above example, suppose that the actions are as follows.

An order should be placed on hold if the customer's account balance is overdue and it exceeds the customer's credit limit. If the order is processed, a reminder should be generated for overdue balances and a reference should be obtained if the customer is a new one. If the customer is not new, then the appropriate level of discount should be given. New customer orders in excess of the credit limit should be referred to the section head.

3.11 From this description we can isolate six actions

(a) 'Place on hold'
(b) 'Process order'
(c) 'Send reminder'
(d) 'Obtain reference'
(e) 'Give discount'
(f) 'Refer to head'

3.12 Consider the fifth rule in the table below. There is no overdue balance on the account, but a new customer wishes to exceed his credit limit. The action entry will therefore show an X against 'Process order'; 'Obtain reference' and 'Refer to head'.

Rule	1	2	3	4	5	6	7	8
Account overdue?	Y	Y	Y	Y	N	N	N	N
Credit limit exceeded?	Y	Y	N	N	Y	Y	N	N
New customer?	Y	N	Y	N	Y	N	Y	N
Place on hold								
Process order					X			
Send reminder								
Obtain reference					X			
Give discount								
Refer to head					X			

3.13 By considering each rule in turn the table can be completed.

Rule	1	2	3	4	5	6	7	8
Account overdue?	Y	Y	Y	Y	N	N	N	N
Credit limit exceeded?	Y	Y	N	N	Y	Y	N	N
New customer?	Y	N	Y	N	Y	N	Y	N
Place on hold	X	X						
Process order			X	X	X	X	X	X
Send reminder			X	X				
Obtain reference			X		X		X	
Give discount				X		X		X
Refer to head	X				X			

Exercise 3

Sales orders are processed and approved by a computer. Management has laid down the following conditions. Construct a decision table to reflect these procedures.

(a) If an order is between £10 and £100 a 3% discount is given, if the credit rating is good. If the customer has been buying from the company for over 5 years, the discount is increased to 4%.

(b) If an order is more than £100 a 5% discount is given, if the credit rating is good. If the customer has been buying from the company for over 5 years, the discount is increased to 6%.

(c) If the credit rating is not good in either case the order is referred to the supervisor.

(d) For orders under £10 no discount is given.

Solution

There are five *conditions*.

(1) Is the order < £10?
(2) Is the order £10 - £100?
(3) Is the order > £100?
(4) Is the credit rating good?
(5) Has the customer been buying > 5 years?

Note that the 'cut-off' values must be precisely stated.

There are seven *actions*: approve, refer on, give one of 5 levels of discount.

32 rules are required (2^5). This results in the following table.

	1	2	3	4	5	6	7	8	9	10	11	12	13	14	15	16	17	18	19	20	21	22	23	24	25	26	27	28	29	30	31	32	33	34
Order < £10	Y	Y	Y	Y	Y	Y	Y	Y	Y	Y	Y	Y	Y	Y	Y	Y	N	N	N	N	N	N	N	N	N	N	N	N	N	N	N	N	N	N
Order £10-£100	Y	Y	Y	Y	Y	Y	Y	Y	N	N	N	N	N	N	N	N	Y	Y	Y	Y	Y	Y	Y	Y	N	N	N	N	N	N	N	N	N	N
Order > £100	Y	Y	Y	Y	N	N	N	N	Y	Y	Y	Y	N	N	N	N	Y	Y	Y	Y	N	N	N	N	Y	Y	Y	Y	N	N	N	N	N	N
Rating good	Y	Y	N	N	Y	Y	N	N	Y	Y	N	N	Y	Y	N	N	Y	Y	N	N	Y	Y	N	N	Y	Y	N	N	Y	Y	N	N	N	N
5 years	Y	N	Y	N	Y	N	Y	N	Y	N	Y	N	Y	N	Y	N	Y	N	Y	N	Y	N	Y	N	Y	N	Y	N	Y	N	Y	N	Y	N
Impossible	X	X	X	X	X	X	X	X	X	X	X	X						X	X	X	X										X	X	X	X
Approve													X	X	X	X																		
0%													X	X	X	X																		
3%																								X										
4%																							X											
5%																												X						
6%																											X							
Refer																									X	X			X	X				

189
BPP
PUBLISHING

This means unwieldy construction (particularly in an examination). Condition 3 can be removed from the decision table. For example, if the answers to conditions 1 and 2 are NO then the answer to condition 3 must be YES, (unless there is an error) and so it need not be tested. In this way the decision table will be reduced to 16 rules.

Condition																
Order < £10?	Y	Y	Y	Y	Y	Y	Y	Y	N	N	N	N	N	N	N	N
Order £10 - £100	Y	Y	Y	Y	N	N	N	N	Y	Y	Y	Y	N	N	N	N
Rating good	Y	Y	N	N	Y	Y	N	N	Y	Y	N	N	Y	Y	N	N
5 years	Y	N	Y	N	Y	N	Y	N	Y	N	Y	N	Y	N	Y	N
Impossible	X	X	X	X												
Approve					X	X	X	X								
0%					X	X	X	X								
3%										X						
4%									X							
5%														X		
6%													X			
Refer											X	X			X	X

In addition, the over 5 year condition is only relevant to orders for £10 or more, and so we need not test this condition when the order is below £10. This cuts the number of rules to 10.

Original rule no	13	15	21	22	23	24	25	26	27	28
Order < £10	Y	Y	N	N	N	N	N	N	N	N
Order £10-£100	N	N	Y	Y	Y	Y	N	N	N	N
Rating good	Y	N	Y	Y	N	N	Y	Y	N	N
5 years	-	-	Y	N	Y	N	Y	N	Y	N
Approve	X	X								
0%	X	X								
3%				X						
4%			X							
5%								X		
6%							X			
Refer					X	X			X	X

Three points arise from the above exercise.

(a) Orders under £10 are processed whether the credit rating is good or not. Although this results in lack of control over small orders, management may feel that the risk is justified by the savings made in processing time.

(b) After the first construction (the draft) the decision table should be redrawn to take into account:

    (i) the impossible combinations - these rules can be removed;

    (ii) take rules which result in identical actions. These indicate which conditions need not be tested by the computer program, and highlight the order in which the conditions should be examined (to save processing time). In the example, rules 13/15 and 23/24 can be combined and it then becomes apparent that credit rating is immaterial if the order is less than £10; but if the credit rating is bad, it is immaterial whether the order is between £10 and £100, or over £100.

(c) For the customer > 5 years check, customers are given an extra 1% discount if they have been with the company over 5 years. Instead of 2 action entries, discount 4% and discount 6%, we can have a single action entry - add 1% to discount. The decision table could be refined still further.

The two-table approach

3.14 Read through the following narrative. (CASE is explained later in this chapter.)

'An organisation which has advertised for a systems analyst has received so many applications that it has devised a set of procedures for drawing up an interview shortlist.

All accredited systems analysts will be interviewed: those with CASE experience during the week commencing 27 June and those without during the following week. A reserve list will be drawn up of applicants with CASE experience but without systems analysis accreditation.

Applicants who are not accredited systems analysts but who have 4GL experience will have their application forms sent to an associated organisation which requires a 4GL expert. Those programmers with 4GL experience in a mainframe environment will be interviewed by this second organisation while others will be placed on a reserve list.

Any other applicants will receive a rejection letter.'

3.15 The standard single table approach to this problem would probably involve the identification of four conditions, as follows.

    (a)   Accredited systems analyst?
    (b)   CASE experience?
    (c)   4GL experience?
    (d)   Mainframe experience?

3.16 This would give $2^4 = 16$ columns, and a total of six actions, as follows.

    (a)   Interview during w/c 27 June
    (b)   Interview during w/c 4 July
    (c)   Reserve list
    (d)   Interview at associated organisation
    (e)   Associated organisation's reserve list
    (f)   Reject

3.17 However, because condition (d) is relevant only to condition (c) and is not independent, and because condition (c) is not relevant if condition (a) applies, this approach is inefficient. For all the situations where the applicant is an accredited systems analyst, it simply does not matter whether he or she has 4GL experience, whether on mainframes or not.

3.18 The recommended approach is therefore to move condition (d) into a separate table, together with any actions which relate solely to that condition. A cross-reference from one table to the other must of course be added.

3.19 This amended approach produces the following tables.

Table A

Accredited systems analyst?	Y	Y	Y	Y	N	N	N	N
CASE Experience?	Y	Y	N	N	Y	Y	N	N
4GL experience?	Y	N	Y	N	Y	N	Y	N
Interview during w/c 27 June	X	X						
Interview during w/c 4 July			X	X				
Reserve list					X	X		
Do *Table B*					X		X	
Reject								X

Reduced Table A

Accredited systems analyst?	Y	Y	N	N	N	N
CASE Experience?	Y	N	Y	Y	N	N
4GL experience?	-	-	Y	N	Y	N
Interview during w/c 27 June	X					
Interview during w/c 4 July		X				
Reserve list			X	X		
Do *Table B*			X		X	
Reject						X

Table B

Mainframe experience?	Y	N
Interview at associated organisation	X	
Associated organisation's reserve list		X

BPP PUBLISHING

Extended entry and mixed entry decision tables

3.20 Decision tables of the type we have just examined are called 'limited entry' decision tables. In these, each condition is posed as a question requiring either a YES, NO or 'immaterial' answer and each action is either taken or not taken.

3.21 In an extended entry decision table the condition and the action stubs are more general, the exact condition or action being specified in the entry quadrants. A mixed entry table consists of both limited and extended entry lines within one table. An example will make this clear.

Example: mixed entry decision tables

3.22 Reservation requests for the flights of the Caviar and Champagne Airline are dealt with according to the following rules. You are required to construct a mixed entry decision table of the procedure.

   (a) All flights contain both first and second class cabins.

   (b) If a seat is available on the flight of the requested class allocate seat and output a ticket for that class.

   (c) If not, where a first class passenger will accept a seat in the second class cabin and one is available, the seat is allocated and a second class ticket is output. Second class passengers are not offered a seat in the first class cabin.

   (d) In cases where no seat is available to meet the request, output 'sorry, no seat' message.

Solution

3.23 A mixed entry decision table is shown below.

Request is for:	1st	1st	1st	1st	2nd	2nd
1st class seat available?	Y	N	N	N		
2nd class acceptable?		Y	Y	N		
2nd class seat available?		Y	N		Y	N
Allocate seat	1st	2nd			2nd	
Issue ticket	1st	2nd			2nd	
Output 'sorry no seat'			X	X		X

3.24 Extended entry and mixed entry decision tables are more compact when constructed, and are useful as a communication method (eg to show the analysed problem to management).

3.25 However they are more difficult than limited entry decision tables to prepare and check for completeness.

The advantages and disadvantages of decision tables

3.26 The main advantages of using decision tables are as follows.
   (a) It is possible to check that all combinations have been considered.
   (b) They show a cause and effect relationship.
   (c) It is easy to trace from actions to conditions (unlike in flowcharts).
   (d) They are easy to understand and copy as they use a standardised format.
   (e) Alternatives can be grouped to facilitate analysis.

3.27 However, there are some disadvantages.
   (a) They are not suited to problems with unclear conditions or actions.
   (b) They do not present the step-by-step logic of a process.

4 CASE TOOLS

12/95, 6/00

4.1 Systems development methodologies are part of a more general trend towards software engineering, which takes the construction of a program to be similar to constructing a large building, requiring detailed plans, blueprints and co-ordination by effective project management. You will have noted that all the methodologies discussed place a heavy reliance on documentation. SSADM makes frequent use of DFDs throughout the development process.

Computer aided software engineering

4.2 CASE techniques aim to automate this document production process, and to ensure automation of some of the design operation.

4.3 A CASE tool is a software package that supports the construction and maintenance of logical system specification models. They are often designed to support the rules and interaction of models defined in a specific methodology, and more sophisticated packages permit software prototyping and code generation.

4.4 There are two types of CASE tool: analysts' workbenches and programmers' workbenches.

Analysts' workbenches

4.5 These are software which perform several analysis tasks.

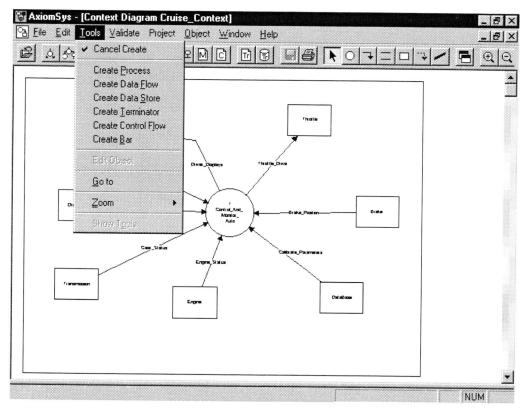

(a) *Create design diagrams (eg DFDs) on screen*

High quality documentation can be produced, and very easily updated. Maintenance of complex models such as DFDs and entity-relationship models is made easy. The diagramming facilities are used with a mouse, in a manner similar to most graphics packages.

Tool kits come with a bank of pre-designed symbols including those used in flowcharts and data flow diagrams and, like graphics packages, allow on-screen editing.

193

Tool kits usually also offer a simple word processing package to assist in the preparation of written material including narrative supporting diagrams, the system specification, program specifications and any other reports produced.

(b) *Check adherence to design and development standards*

Standards define how development will be carried out. A CASE tool will not allow designers to break rules (such as not linking a data store directly to an external entity) that they could easily break accidentally if working manually.

(c) *Consistencies and relationships*

CASE tools can verify that diagrams are consistent with each other and that the relationships are correct.

(d) *Documentation and screens*

CASE tools can help generate specimen input and output documentation (ie from the data flows identified in the diagrams), and also specimen screens, increasing the capacity to prototype the development in close liaison with users.

(e) *Data dictionaries*

CASE tools can create a logical data dictionary (see the next chapter) from the items identified. Entries will be made for entities, data flows, data stores, processes, external entities and individual data items and the dictionary can be easily maintained, checked for consistency, cross-referenced and analysed. For example it will be possible to produce a listing of all the data flows where a particular data item is used, or cross reference the entities of the entity relationship diagram to the data stores of the DFD.

Programmers' workbenches

4.6 These provide similar features to ensure consistency of coding during the later stages of the design cycle.

(a) There is usually a code-generator facility to automate the production of code in a high level language from, say, Structured English.

(b) Diagnostic aids enable subroutines to be tested independently of other programs.

(c) A library of subroutines is also provided. These are often-repeated procedures which can be incorporated into programs.

Advantages of CASE

4.7 Advantages of CASE include the following.

(a) The drudgery is taken out of document preparation and re-drawing of diagrams is made easier.

(b) Accuracy of diagrams is improved. Diagram drawers can ensure consistency of terminology and maintain certain standards of documentation.

(c) Prototyping (see below) is made easier, as re-design can be effected very quickly and the models are always consistent with the actual system.

(d) Blocks of code can be re-used. Many applications incorporate similar functions and processes; if pieces of software are retained in a library they can be used (or modified) as appropriate.

5 DEPLOYMENT FLOWCHARTS OR PROCESS MAPS

5.1 Some people would argue that DFDs, ERMs, decision tables and so on are very difficult for users not familiar with these techniques to understand. Why not call a customer a 'customer', an invoice an 'invoice', and so on. Why analyse all the discretion out of a job and express it as a series of mechanical conditions?

5.2 Deployment flowcharting or process mapping is a more user friendly technique to show a process or procedure as it flows through different departments or uses different resources. Resources or departments are arranged as a background in columns or rows, and the flowchart is drawn on top of the background.

5.3 The symbols used *may* be those that are familiar to you from your earlier studies of program flowcharting: a rectangle for a process or operation, a diamond for a decision and so on.

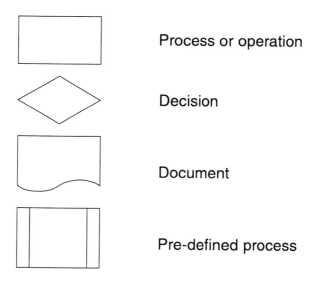

5.4 Increasingly, however, it may be possible and preferable to use more elaborate graphics that are more meaningful to users. Appropriate symbols are readily available in drawing and charting software packages and these can be obtained very cheaply, or even free.

5.5 Here is an example of a deployment flowchart for part of a process that involves customer service staff, production scheduling and purchasing.

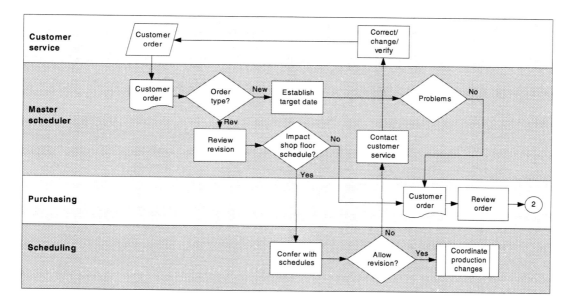

Procedure for deployment flowcharting

5.6 As mentioned in an earlier chapter, there is often a discrepancy between how managers *think* a process is achieved and how it is actually achieved. One of the key aims of process mapping or deployment flowcharting is to bring such discrepancies to light. Here is a possible approach.

BPP PUBLISHING

(a) The manager starts by identifying, by title, the processes for which he or she alone is solely responsible to a superior. The process may be the production of goods, the supply of a service; the provision of technical advice; or the co-ordination of a set of major business processes within a project.

(b) List inputs and outputs relating to each of the processes identified and also list the key characters involved in each process. Depending upon the nature of the process the characters may be other managers or supervisors or operators. But in every case the person identified by name or title will be the person most directly responsible for that part of the process. It could be the director responsible for sign-off or the clerk responsible for issuing the order number.

(c) Draft map the flow of the tasks within each process (as they exist now) and at each step ensure that the person responsible for each task is clearly identified. This exercise, carried out alone by the manager, will reveal how much s/he actually understands about the total process and demonstrate the vital importance of the next step.

(d) Meet with every person in the cast of characters and explain the need to help the manager to gain a better understanding of the details of the process to which they are an integral part. Some resistance may be met at this stage unless there is a reasonable level of trust between the manager and his sub-ordinates.

(e) Prepare a fresh draft of the deployment flowchart and then return it to the process team and gain confirmation of their 'ownership' of the map. In other words, the team confirms that the chart now shows what *really* goes on.

(f) At this stage it is likely that fresh ideas will arise as problems and bottlenecks are identified and individuals share with others their own ways of getting round problems.

5.7 Some of the advantages claimed for deployment flowcharting are evident from this procedure.

(a) The chart or map serves as a starting point for improving the process by rationalisation or simplification.

(b) The procedure removes barriers between people both departmentally and hierarchically.

(c) The chart serves as a basis for process-induction and training of new staff.

(d) The chart sets down the process clearly and graphically, on a minimum of pages and in a user-friendly manner.

(e) The charts may be used as an intermediate tool before the more rigorous conventions of the techniques described earlier in this chapter and the last are brought into play by professional systems analysts.

Chapter roundup

- Structured English is a highly stylised and carefully disciplined version of the English language which seeks to eliminate the ambiguities and complexity of the natural language in order to make it suitable for describing program operations and processes. There are three basic logical structures: sequence, selection and iteration.

- A decision tree is a design tool which provides a graphic representation of the choices or decisions made in a particular process so long as these are not too numerous.

- Decision tables are another method of defining the logic of a process. The basic format consists of four quadrants, with conditions in the top half and the actions taken, when different combinations of conditions apply, in the bottom half.

- CASE techniques attempt to automate the process of producing documentation which is important in many systems development methodologies. Available tools are analysts' workbenches and programmers' workbenches.

- Deployment flowcharting or process mapping is a user friendly technique to show a process or procedure as it flows through different departments or uses different resources. Resources or departments are arranged as a background in columns or rows, and the flowchart is drawn on top of the background. One of the key aims of process mapping or deployment flowcharting is to bring to light discrepancies between what is assumed to happen and what actually happens.

Quick quiz

1   When might Structured English be used? (see para 1.3)

2   Explain the terms sequence, selection and iteration. (1.8 - 1.16)

3   What are the disadvantages of decision trees? (2.10)

4   How do you determine the number of columns in a decision table? (3.4(a))

5   What is meant by 'halving' in decision tables? (3.4(b))

6   When can columns in a decision table be consolidated? (3.4(e))

7   How are the tables in the two table approach to decision tables linked up? (3.18 - 3.19)

8   What are the advantages and disadvantages of decision tables? (3.26, 3.27)

9   What are the advantages of CASE? (4.7)

10   Why is deployment flowcharting used? (5.1, 5.2, 5.6)

Now try illustrative question 14 at the end of the Study Text

BPP PUBLISHING

Chapter 10

THE DATABASE APPROACH

Introduction

Databases have a section of the syllabus to themselves, but because we have been describing many of the techniques and principles of database design, such as normalisation, in the preceding chapters, this is a more logical place to deal with the issues.

1   THE DATABASE APPROACH   12/94, 6/95, 6/96, 12/96, 6/97, 6/98, 12/98, 12/99

1.1   The way in which data is stored and manipulated is an important aspect of information systems design. There are three principal approaches to information handling in computer systems.

(a)   Non-integrated systems.
(b)   Integrated systems.
(c)   Database systems.

As organisational information needs have become more complex, environmental change is ever more rapid, and the need for flexibility ever more crucial to survival, organisations are increasingly adopting a database approach to the storage and manipulation of data.

Non-integrated systems

1.2   A computer application might process only one sort of data. A payroll file would process only payroll data and a stock file only stock data. An organisation might end up with separate files and processing subsystems for each area of the business.

1.3   However, in many cases the underlying data used by each application might be the same. A major consequence is that data items are duplicated in a number of files. They are input more than once (leading to errors and inconsistencies) and held in several files (wasting space).

Integrated systems

1.4   An integrated system is a system where one set of data is used for more than one application. In an accounting context, it might be possible to integrate parts of the sales ledger, purchase ledger, stock control systems and nominal ledger systems, so that the data input to the sales ledger updates the nominal ledger automatically.

198

Database systems

1.5 A database provides a comprehensive file of data for a number of different users. The term database has a strict and a loose meaning.

(a) Strictly speaking, a database is a collection of structured data. The structure of the data is independent of any particular application. Any item of data can be used as a subject of enquiry. The concept is that programs are written around the database rather than files being structured to meet the need of specific programs.

(b) Loosely speaking, a database is a collection of data files which is integrated and organised so as to provide a single comprehensive file system. The data is governed by rules which define its structure and determine how it can be accessed. The purpose of a database is to provide convenient access to the common data for a wide variety of users and user needs.

1.6 A *database management system (DBMS)* is the software that builds, manages and provides access to a database. It is a system which allows a systematic approach to the storage and retrieval of data in a computer.

1.7 The independence of logical data from physical storage, and the independence of data items from the programs which access them, is referred to as *data independence*.

1.8 Duplication of data items is referred to as *data redundancy*.

1.9 You may also encounter the term 'data warehouse', which in essence is a database on a very large scale: a database that collates data stored on other, separate databases.

Case example: Data warehouse

Information derived from a data warehouse suggested to an American retailer, Wal-Mart, that there was a strong correlation between the sale of nappies and beer.

Wal-Mart found that both tended to sell at the same time, just after working hours, and concluded that men with small children stopped off to buy nappies on their way home and picked up some beer at the same time. If the two items were put in the same shopping aisle, sales of both should increase. Wal-Mart tried this and it worked.

The objectives of a database system

1.10 A database should have four major objectives.

(a) It should be *shared*. Different users should be able to access the same data in the database for their own processing applications, and at the same time if required. This removes the need for duplicating data on different files.

(b) The *integrity* of the database must be preserved. This means that one user should not be allowed to alter the data on file so as to spoil the database records for other users. However, users must be able to make valid alterations to the data.

(c) The database system should provide for the needs of *different users*, who each have their own processing requirements and data access methods.

(d) The database should be *capable of evolving*, both in the short term (it must be kept updated) and in the longer term (it must be able to meet the future data processing needs of users, not just their current needs).

The advantages and disadvantages of database systems

1.11 The advantages of a database system are as follows.

(a) *Avoidance of unnecessary duplication of data*

It recognises that data can be used for many purposes but only needs to be input and stored once. The drawback to single entry input is that one department only must accept responsibility for the accuracy of the input.

(b) *Multi-purpose data*

From (a), it follows that although data is input once, it can be used for several purposes.

(c) *Data for the organisation as a whole, not just for individual departments*

The database concept encourages management to regard data as a resource that must be properly managed just as any other resource. The installation of a database system encourages management to analyse data, relationships between data items, and how data is used in different applications.

(d) *Consistency*

Because data is only held once, it is easier to ensure that it is up to date, so that no department in an organisation uses out-of-date data, or data that differs from the data used by other departments. They should not come to different decisions simply because they were based on different data.

(e) *New uses for old data*

Data on file is independent of the user programs that access the data. This allows greater flexibility in the ways that data can be used. New programs can be easily introduced to make use of existing data in a different way.

(f) *New applications*

Developing new application programs with a database system is easier than developing other applications, because the programmer is not responsible for the file organisation, which is already taken care of by the database management software.

1.12 The disadvantages of a database systems relate mainly to security and control.

(a) There are problems of data security and data privacy. The potential for unauthorised access to data creates a serious problem. Administrative procedures for data security must supplement software controls.

(b) Since there is only one set of data, it is essential that the data should be accurate and free from corruption.

(c) Since data is held once, but its use is widespread, there are potential problems of recovery of data in the event of a system failure.

(d) If an organisation develops its own database system from scratch, initial development costs will be high, although the costs of maintaining a database system (keeping the data up to date etc) should be lower than for more traditional systems. 'Off-the-shelf' database management system (DBMS) software packages can be obtained, and so the cost of installing a database can be reduced.

The database administrator   6/96

1.13 However, control over data and systems development can be facilitated by the appointment of a database administrator, who controls and sets standard for the input of data, its definition, storage structures, security and integrity of data and back-up and recovery strategies.

1.14 A Database Administrator (DBA) occupies a core position within the management structure of the organisation and should report directly to the top-level of management. The principal role of a DBA can be described as ensuring that the database functions correctly and efficiently at all times. To achieve these aims the DBA will, as a minimum, carry out a number of tasks that are discussed later in this solution. Before doing so it is worth noting that the DBA must be a person that is technically competent and possesses a good understanding of the business and operational needs of the organisation.

1.15 The DBA must implement procedures that ensure that all data entered onto the system is complete, current and accurate. Techniques that can be used to achieve this are data validation and verification procedures such as batch sampling of entered data, software "traps" to detect the attempted input of wrong data types and completeness checks.

1.16 Database security is another important area for the DBA. The database must be protected from possible physical and logical threats. The DBA should implement logical access controls such as passwords to log-on to the system and, in addition, partition the database so that only authorised users can access relevant data. For example, accounts clerks will be prohibited from accessing medical data. Regular virus checks should be made and the database users should be prohibited from installing their programs onto the system. If the database can be accessed from external sites it will be necessary for the DBA to implement appropriate procedures, such as firewalls, to protect the system from hackers and other unauthorised users.

1.17 Measures to provide physical security will include physical access controls, fire prevention and detection equipment, storage of working media in fireproof locations, the provision of un-interruptible power supplies. It is vital that the DBA introduces, and enforces, a strict back-up routine with a copy of the data stored in a secure location off-site.

1.18 The DBA will actively seek to keep abreast of new technical developments, identify new user requirements and their development, review the performance of the database and take appropriate action to ensure that the database functions correctly. The DBA will implement effective maintenance schedules for the hardware and maintain the database software. An audit trail will be devised and used as an aid to maintaining the database.

1.19 The DBA must make sure that the database is operated legally and complies with the relevant legislation such as the Data Protection Act, the Computer Misuse Act, The Copyright Act and the Health and Safety at Work legislation.

1.20 Finally the DBA will have responsibility for producing system documentation (technical information, the data dictionary, user guides, etc) and developing training programmes for users of the database.

2   DATABASE STRUCTURES   *12/97, 12/99*

2.1 A number of different models are used in databases.
   (a) The hierarchical model
   (b) The network model
   (c) The relational model

The hierarchical model

2.2 Many relationships are one-to-many or many-to-one relationships. Such relationships can be expressed conveniently in a hierarchy. Each data item is related to only one item above it in the hierarchy, but to any number of data items below it.

2.3 In a customer database, for example, the hierarchical model might be used to show customers and customer orders. An extract from a parts department database might be structured as follows.

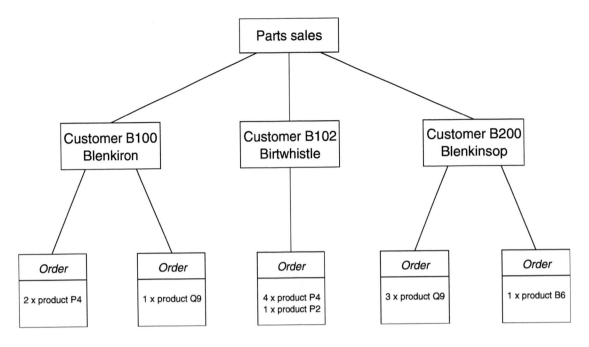

2.4 The biggest drawback to a file organised in hierarchical data structure is that the user is limited in the number of ways he or she can look for records: the file organisation makes it much easier to search for certain items in the file records than for others.

2.5 In the example above, to access an order record it is necessary to specify the customer to which it belongs, which is straightforward. However, let us imagine that you wish to obtain a listing of all customers who have ordered a particular part number. This would require a search of each customer record - a long process.

2.6 If the hierarchical model had been structured so that products were superior to orders and each order contained customer data instead of product data, this would be simpler, but the first process would be harder!

2.7 This asymmetrical character of the hierarchical model makes it unsuitable for many applications, especially where there is not a true hierarchical relationship between the data.

The network model

2.8 Whereas a hierarchical data structure only allows a one-to-many relationship between data items, a *network* database is a database in which the logical data structure allows many-to-many relationships.

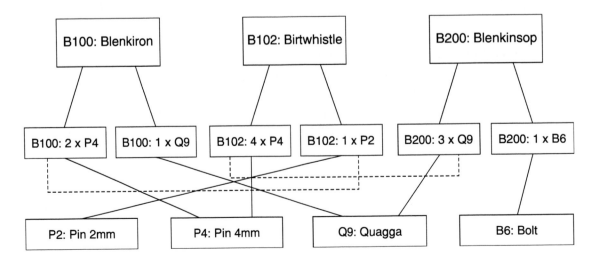

2.9 There is still some redundancy of data at the order level, although the problems inherent in the hierarchical model have been eliminated.

(*Note.* A question in the June 1997 exam used the term 'network*ed* integrated database', meaning any sort of database run across a computer network such as a LAN, not specifically a database designed on the network model.)

The relational model

2.10 Another way of expressing many-to-many and one-to-many relationships is the relational data structure. A relational model organises data elements in a series of two-dimensional tables consisting of rows and columns. A row represents a record, and columns represent part of a record.

2.11 In a relational data structure, the structure of the file is independent of the actual data. The relationships between different entity types have been determined at the outset, and are not embodied in the records themselves. A relational database thus does not have to navigate through other data before reading the required record.

2.12 You will recognise this technique as normalisation, or relational data analysis.

Customer table		Product table		Order table		
B100	Blenkiron	B6	Bolt	B100	P4	2
B102	Birtwhistle	P2	Pin 2mm	B100	Q9	1
B200	Blenkinsop	P4	Pin 4mm	B102	P4	4
		Q9	Quagga	B102	P2	1
				B200	Q9	3
				B200	B6	1

2.13 The redundant data in the network model, ie the customer number and part number in the order relation, has been eliminated. Any data element can be recognised by its record number or field name. The primary key is used to identify a record.

3 DATA DICTIONARIES

3.1 A data dictionary is an index of data held in a database, used to assist in maintenance and any other access to the data.

3.2 A data dictionary is a feature of many database systems. As the term might suggest, it provides a method for looking up the items of data held in the database, to establish the following.

(a) A list of the entity, attribute and relationship types.

(b) A list of the aliases (see below).

(c) A list of all the processes which use data about each entity type.

(d) How to access the data in whatever manner is required (a data dictionary is sometimes called a data directory).

(e) What the data codes and symbols mean.

(f) The origin of the data.

(g) Possible range of values.

(h) Ownership of the data.

(i) Other comments.

3.3 A data dictionary is simply a list or record of each data store in the system and each data flow in the system showing what items of data they contain. It is easy for different users to give data ambiguous names. Thus 'stock number', 'part number' and 'stock code' might be used interchangeably.

Example

3.4 In a payroll system, the data store for the employee name might be included in a data dictionary as follows.

Reference

File: Employee name for payroll system
Ref No of file D2

Data elements

Name:	Employee name
Aliases:	Name
	Staff name
	Employee
Description:	The name of an employee, in the form: Last name, first name, other details
Format:	Character
Related data:	Employee address
	Employee number
Ownership:	Human resources
Users:	Human resources
	Accounting
	Payroll
	Job costing
	Administration

The usefulness of a data dictionary

3.5 The data dictionary is a form of technical documentation; it ensures that everyone in the organisation defines and uses the data consistently. This consistency is extremely important for large projects which involve several programmers. The opportunity for misunderstandings is so high that the data dictionary becomes essential.

3.6 A data dictionary helps with systems analysis, systems design and systems maintenance.

(a) During systems analysis a data dictionary helps the analyst to organise his information about the data elements in the system, where they come from, where they go to, and even whether any key data elements are missing.

(b) During systems design a data dictionary helps the analyst and programmers to ensure that no data elements are missed out if they are really needed.

(c) Once the system is operational, and an amendment is required to a program, a data dictionary will help the programmer to understand what each data element is used for, so that any amendment he makes does not 'spoil' other parts of the program.

3.7 Software packages which automate the creation of dictionaries have been developed. The creation of this reference material is tedious and the availability of a computer tool which can determine basic information about the data has increased their use.

4 USING A DATABASE

4.1 There are four main operations in using a database.

(a) Creating the database structure, ie the structure of files and records.

(b) Entering data on to the database files, and amending/updating it.
(c) Retrieving and manipulating the data.
(d) Producing reports.

Creating a database structure

4.2 Of the four broad operations involved in setting up and using a database, the most crucial is the creation and structure of the database file or files. As we have seen, the person creating the database file must first carry out an analysis of all the data for processing and filing, because a full and accurate analysis of data in the system is crucial to the construction of complete and workable database files.

4.3 It is also necessary to specify what files will be held in the database, what records (entities) and fields (attributes) they will contain, and how many characters will be in each field. The files and fields must be named, and the characteristics of particular fields (for example all-numeric or all-alphabetic fields) should be specified.

Entering and amending data   6/95, 6/96

4.4 When the database structure has been established, the data user can input data and create a file (or files) or derive data from existing records.

Amalgamating existing data

4.5 Problems in amalgamating data originally stored separately are likely to be numerous.

(a) The compatibility between systems is not just a matter of whether one system's files are computer-sensible to another system. It may extend to matters such as different systems of coding, different formats for personal data (with/without a contact name? with/without phone or fax number, and so on), different field sizes.

New standards that apply across the board can be developed, but implementing them is likely to require a great deal of collection of data and inputting. It will be necessary to acquire and test conversion software and ensure that there are sufficient staff to perform and check the conversion.

(b) There is great potential for loss or corruption of data during the conversion process. Depending on the extent of the loss this could mean a small amount of re-keying or it could be a disastrous, permanent loss of valuable information needed for sales management.

Full back-ups should be taken at the start of the process, and back-ups of information on the old system should continue during any period of parallel running.

(c) Existing application-specific systems are unlikely to have sufficient storage space to accommodate the combined data. This can easily be resolved, but it must be resolved with an eye to the future growth of the business and future use of the database to store both existing information and new information that has not been available in the past.

(d) Access to data must not suffer. Operational users will be attempting to extract information from a much larger pool, and the system must be designed in such a way that they do not have to wade through large amounts of data that is irrelevant to them to find what they need. If this aspect is neglected the new system could seriously undermine users' ability to respond to queries.

Those developing the system therefore need to consult widely with users at the sharp end of processing to ensure that their current information needs are understood and can be met by the new data architecture.

(e) As well as offering the potential for new kinds of report the system must continue to support present requirements for management reports that are essential to the smooth running of the business. Amalgamation could inadvertently break down links between data items and make it impossible to pull off a much needed daily report.

Once more, extensive consultation with users is essential.

(f) Once the data has been amalgamated the business faces the task of ensuring that it is secure. A systems failure will now mean that no part of the business can operate, rather than at most just one part.

Dealing with this is likely to mean changes in the role and structure of the IT department. New, centrally administered back-up procedures will be needed, and contingency arrangements must be worked out and put in place to ensure that the risks to the business of systems disasters are minimised.

4.6 The data must be kept up-to-date, and so there will be subsequent insertions of new records, deletions of unwanted records and amendments to existing records. Database packages usually allow the same field in every record on file, or all records with certain characteristics, to be amended in the same way by means of a single command. For example, a single command can arrange for all customers on a sales ledger database file whose account type is type 2, say, to have their credit limit raised by 5%.

Retrieval and manipulation of data

4.7 Data can be retrieved and manipulated in a variety of ways.

(a) Data can be retrieved by specifying the required parameters - for example from a database of employee records, records of all employees in the sales department who have been employed for over 10 years and are paid less than £12,000 pa could be extracted. If there are certain search and retrieve parameters that are used regularly, they can be stored on a search parameters file for future use.

(b) Retrieved data can be sorted on any specified field (for example for employees, sorting might be according to grade, department, age, experience, salary level etc).

(c) Some calculations on retrieved data can be carried out - such as calculating totals and average values.

Query languages

4.8 A database can be interrogated by a query language. A query language is a formalised method of constructing queries in a database system. Basically a query language provides the ways in which you ask a database for data. Some query languages can be used to change the contents of a database.

4.9 SEQUEL (Structured English Query Language) is the name of the original version of SQL (which is pronounced either as separate letters or like 'sequel'). SQL was adopted by the *Oracle* corporation and helped Oracle to become the second largest software company in the world after Microsoft. It is now regarded as the industry standard query language.

Example: SQL

6/95

4.10 A simple query is given below. You are interrogating a database of customer information, and you wish to discover which customers in the database owe you £2,000 or more. You want a list in alphabetical order. You might wish to say the following. 'List all customers who owe £2,000 or more.'

4.11 However, in fact the queries need to be formulated more precisely. Our query might be formulated instead as:

FIND (ACCOUNTS, CUSTOMER-NAME) WHERE (ACCOUNT-BALANCE > = £2,000)

4.12 Here we are specifying the data to be interrogated. We are trying to find out the customers, who are held in the relation ACCOUNTS and who owe £2,000 or more. The relation ACCOUNTS refers to the two-dimensional table(s) where the data is held. There might be two or more tables if linked by the relation ACCOUNTS.

4.13 SQL has the basic structure:

SELECT (ie what data items you are looking for)
FROM (the relation involved in the query)
WHERE (the condition that must be satisfied).

4.14 The example above might be written as

SELECT CUSTOMER-NAME, BRANCH-NAME
FROM ACCOUNTS
WHERE ACCOUNT BALANCE > = £2,000

4.15 A variety of logical functions (including ANDs, NOTs and ORs) and operations (eg averages, maxima, minima, ordering in specified sequence) can be performed. Some menu systems have been devised so that the query could be presented as a list of questions.

Microsoft Access

4.16 The illustration below shows the tools available in Microsoft Access for building queries using Visual Basic-like comments. Access also offers the option of using SQL-type queries.

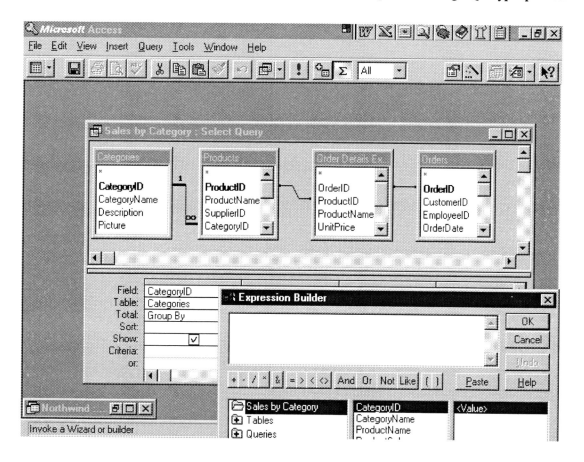

Report production

4.17 Most database packages include a report generator facility which allows the user to design report structures so that information can be presented on screen and printed out in a format which suits the user's requirements and preferences. Report formats can be stored on disk, if similar reports are produced periodically, and called up when required.

Exercise 1

Try to get someone to demonstrate a database package to you - perhaps your marketing department at work uses Access - and if possible learn how to build a query.

---

5 DATA MODELS

5.1 On two occasions now students have been asked to draw a 'data model', which is a diagram that shows the basic structure of the data elements required by a system. There are no hard and fast rules about this. In the examiner's own answers the individual elements have been drawn as labelled rectangles linked by arrows.

5.2 In the examples set so far very little information has been given in the question to help you . This is an advantage in the sense that a wide variety of answers is possible, but a disadvantage in that it is difficult to know where to begin.

5.3 The view of a data model is a highly summarised, top-down view. For instance if you are drawing a data model for an airline, one of your data elements would be 'details about aircraft', another would be 'staff details'. You would probably not have space to break these down further into 'aircraft maintenance details', 'aircraft seating capacity', or 'pilots details', 'cabin crew' details', 'baggage handlers details', 'admin staff details', and so on.

5.4 Don't forget external data elements (eg licences to fly certain routes, legal regulations), accounting and finance elements and monitoring elements.

Exercise 2

See if you can draw a data model describing the organisation that you work for. If you can't, avoid exam questions asking you to do this!

Chapter roundup

- A database has four major objectives. It should be shared, its integrity must be preserved, it should provide for the needs of different users and it should be capable of evolving.

- A database management system organises the storage of data in the most appropriate way to facilitate its use in different applications. It provides the interface between the logical data and the physical data. A database administrator will often be appointed to look after the structure, physical storage and security of the data.

- Three different models are used in databases: the hierarchical model, the network model and the relational model. Each is suitable in different situations.

- Data analysis is vital to the design and construction of database files. It involves identifying the entities in a system, the attributes of those entities and the relationships between them.

- A data dictionary is a feature of many database systems. It provides a method of looking up the items of data held in the database and indicates their meaning. It assists with access to the data and is useful in database maintenance, ensuring that all users define and use the data consistently.

- There are four main operations in using a database. First of all records must be created. Data can then be entered and updated. Amalgamating data from existing sources may be highly problematic. The user can retrieve and manipulate data and, finally, produce reports.

Now try illustrative questions 15, 16 and 31 at the end of the Study Text

BPP
PUBLISHING

Part C
Management control

Chapter 11

PROJECT MANAGEMENT

Introduction

We saw in Chapter 6 how important it is to choose projects carefully. In this chapter the topic of managing projects is analysed.

The importance of good management of projects cannot be exaggerated as certain recurrent problems may frequently be observed. Any one or combination of these failings leads to wasted time, money and effort.

(a)   New systems do not arrive on time.
(b)   New systems often cost a lot more than was budgeted.
(c)   New systems do not meet user requirements.

This chapter looks at these threats in more detail and at the techniques and tools used to overcome them.

1   PROJECT MANAGEMENT   *12/94, 12/96, 12/98, 12/99*

1.1   The following definition will help you to appreciate why it is necessary to manage information systems projects.

> A project is a type of work whose end-product is a single item on a very large scale. Examples include the Channel Tunnel and the Millenium Dome.

1.2   Like these examples, information systems projects involve large numbers of people, long periods of time and large amounts of money.

1.3   However, it is not uncommon for a systems development project to be years late, wildly over budget, and a waste of effort, as the system produced in the end does not deliver the goods. Perhaps the best way of understanding why active management of systems development projects is necessary is by seeing what problems arise when they go wrong.

What can go wrong?

1.4   A number of factors can combine to produce these expensive disasters.

BPP
PUBLISHING

Project managers

1.5 Project managers are usually technicians, not managers. Technical ability for IS staff is no guarantee of management skill. However, often, the only promotion path available is to a management role. An individual might be a highly proficient analyst or programmer, but not a good manager.

1.6 The project manager has a number of conflicting requirements.

(a) The systems manager, usually the project manager's boss, wants the project delivered on time, to specification and within budget.

(b) Users, and the management of the function to which they belong, want a system which does everything they require - but they are not always certain what they want. User input is vital to a project, but user management and staff may not be able to take time off from their normal duties to help out. If the project is late, over budget, and does not do all which is required of it, then users will be vocal critics.

(c) The project manager has to plan and supervise the work of analysts and programmers and these are rather different roles (see later in this chapter).

1.7 The project manager needs to develop an appropriate management style. What he or she should realise is the extent to which the project will fail if users are not consulted, or if the project team is unhappy. As the project manager needs to encourage participation from users, an excessively authoritarian style is not suitable.

Other factors

1.8 Other factors can be identified.

(a) The project manager accepts an unrealistic deadline for having the system up and running. The timescale is fixed too early on in the planning process: the user's idea of when the system would be needed is taken as the deadline, before sufficient consideration is given to the realism of this timescale.

(b) Poor or non-existent planning is a recipe for disaster. Ludicrous deadlines would appear much earlier if a proper planning process was undertaken.

(c) Control is non-existent (ie no performance reviews).

(d) Users change their requirements, resulting in costly changes to the system as it is being developed.

(e) Poor time-tabling and resourcing is a cause of problems. It is no use being presented on day 1 with a team of programmers, when there is still systems analysis and design work to do. As the development and implementation of a computer project may take a considerable length of time (perhaps 18 months from initial decision to operational running for a medium-sized installation) a proper plan and time schedule for the various activities must be drawn up.

Terms of reference

1.9 At the start of a project, once selected, a Project Initiation Document (PID) may be drawn up, setting out the terms of reference for the project. Typical contents might include the following.

(a) The business objectives. Projects should not be undertaken simply for their own sake: the business advantages should be clearly identified and be the first point of reference when progress is being reviewed, to make sure that the original aim is not lost sight of

(b) Project objectives

(c) The scope of the project: what it is intended to cover and what it is not

(d) Constraints, such as maximum amount to be spent and interim and final deadlines

(e) The ultimate customer of the project, who will resolve conflicts as they occur (for example between two different divisions who will both be using the new system) and finally accept it

(f) The resources that will be used – staff, technical resources, finance

(g) An analysis of risks inherent in the project and how they are to be avoided or reduced (for example, the consequences of replacing the old sales ledger system and only discovering after the event that the new one does not work).

(h) A project plan (targets, activities and so on) and details of how the project is to be organised and managed (see the next section)

(i) Purchasing and procurement policy, perhaps specifying acceptable suppliers and delivery details.

Phases of project management

1.10 Every project is different, by definition, and it is impossible to be prescriptive about what a project involves. According to the very recent *Guideline for the Project Management of the Development of Critical Computer Systems* issued by a leading group of European experts, there are twelve phases of project management (following the selection of the project) categorised as follows.

Phase	Comment
1 Preparation 2 Initiation	These phases are likely to involve tasks such as identifying and assembling the project team and any resources (software tools etc) needed; making arrangements with the user of the new system for access to existing systems and staff; agreeing terms of reference and briefing the team on what is to be done.
3 Specification 4 Design 5 Build 6 Integration	This is the development work described in Chapters 6 to 10, probably following a methodology such as SSADM. Integration means pulling the work of all the different people involved in the project together
7 Installation 8 System validation 9 Handover	These phases are described in Chapter 12.
10 Project review 11 Operations and maintenance	See Chapter 13 for more on these phases.
12 Decommissioning and replacement	This point comes when a new system to replace this one has been developed and is about to take over. This phase would roughly coincide with Phases 7 to 9 of the new project. Obviously it is useful to have members of the original team on hand to run down the old system, but this may not be possible in practice.

2 THE PROJECT MANAGER'S ROLE

2.1 A project is affected by a number of factors, often in conflict with each other.

(a) Quality of the system required, in terms of basic system requirements.

(b)   The resources, both in terms of staff recruitment and work scheduling, and technology.

(c)   Time, both to complete the project, and in terms of the opportunity cost of time spent on this project which could be spent on others.

(d)   Costs, which are monitored and controlled, in accordance with the budget set for the project.

2.2   The requirement to keep to a specified time might for example increase costs, if there are delays and new staff have to be employed, or reduce quality if corners are cut.

2.3   It is with these threats in mind that management of the project must be conducted.

Project planning

6/99

2.4   This involves the setting of measurable targets from the stated broad objectives.

(a)   Developing project targets such as overall costs or timescale needed (ie project should take 20 weeks).

(b)   Dividing the project into activities (eg analysis, programming, testing), and placing these activities into the right sequence, often a complicated task if overlapping.

(c)   Developing a framework for the organisational procedures and structures necessary to manage the project (eg decide, in principle, to have weekly team meetings, performance reviews etc).

Detailed planning

2.5   The 'nitty-gritty' of time scheduling and so forth is worked out here, and the exact sequence of individual tasks within activities. Network analysis techniques may be used in this context. There are outputs from the planning process.

(a)   Time budgets for tasks, and for team members.

(b)   Identification of critical activities.

(c)   Allocation of resources to activities (for example computer hardware).

(d)   Arrangement of any training which might be needed for certain members of the project team.

(e)   Establishment of reporting structures and procedures identified in the outline planning phase (ie decide when to have the weekly team briefings).

Communication

2.6   The project manager must let superiors know what is going on, and ensure that members of the project team are properly briefed. Overall staffing structures must support effective communication.

Co-ordination

2.7   Co-ordinating project activities between the project team and users, and other external parties (for example suppliers of hardware and software) is a vital task.

Monitoring and control

2.8   Project management invariably involves a number of control activities.

(a)   Planning and work scheduling.

(b) Establishment of feedback procedures to aid the control and monitoring of the project (timeliness, keeping to budget, quality control etc).

(c) Ensuring that the different members of staff working on different segments of the project communicate with each other, and with the project manager.

(d) Quality control over work done, perhaps enforced through the use of systems development standards.

(e) Reporting to the steering committee and/or senior management on a regular basis as part of the control procedure, as to how the project is progressing in terms of the four factors mentioned above.

3 NETWORK ANALYSIS

3.1 Network analysis, also known as critical path analysis (CPA), is a useful technique to help with planning and controlling large projects, such as construction projects, research and development projects and the computerisation of systems.

3.2 Network analysis is used where many separate tasks (which collectively make up the whole project) can either happen simultaneously or must follow one after another such that it is difficult to establish the relationships between all the separate tasks. The technique can be applied to any purposeful chain of events involving the use of time, labour and physical resources.

3.3 Its aim is to programme and monitor the progress of a project so that the project is completed in the minimum time and on schedule.

3.4 It pinpoints the parts of the project which are 'critical', ie those parts which, if delayed beyond the allotted time, would delay the completion of the project as a whole.

3.5 The technique can also be used to assist in allocating resources such as labour and equipment.

The technique: drawing a diagram

3.6 Network analysis is quite a simple technique. The events and activities making up the whole project are represented in the form of a diagram.

3.7 Drawing the diagram or chart involves the following steps.

Step 1. Estimating the time needed to complete each individual activity or task that makes up a part of the project.

Step 2. Sorting out what activities must be done one after another, and which can be done at the same time, if required.

Step 3. Representing these in a network diagram.

Step 4. Estimating the critical path, which is the longest sequence of consecutive activities through the network.

3.8 The method of drawing network diagrams explained here closely follows the presentation that you would see if you used the Microsoft Project software package. It is easier and clearer than old-fashioned methods using circles divided into quadrants, dummy activities and so on.

BPP PUBLISHING

3.9   Suppose that a project includes three activities, C, D and E. Neither activity D nor E can start until activity C is completed, but D and E could be done simultaneously if required.

This would be represented as follows.

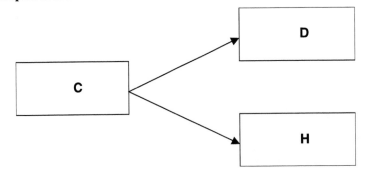

3.10   Note the following.

(a)   An activity within a network is represented by a rectangular box. (Each box is a 'node'.)
(b)   The 'flow' of activities in the diagram should be from left to right.
(c)   The diagram clearly shows that D and E must follow C.

3.11   A second possibility is that an activity cannot start until two or more activities have been completed. If activity H cannot start until activities G and F are both complete, then we would represent the situation like this.

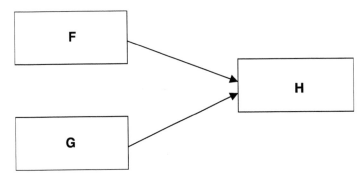

Paths

3.12   Any network can be analysed into a number of different paths or routes. A path is simply a sequence of activities which can take you from the start to the end of the network. In the example above, there are just three routes or paths.

(a)   A C D.
(b)   B D.
(c)   B E.

The critical path

3.13   The time needed to complete each individual activity in a project must be estimated. This duration is shown within the node as follows. The reason for and meaning of the other boxes will be explained in a moment.

Task A	
ID	6 days

3.14   The duration of the whole project will be fixed by the time taken to complete the largest path through the network. This path is called the critical path and activities on it are known as critical activities.

3.15   Activities on the critical path must be started and completed on time, otherwise the total project time will be extended. The method of finding the critical path is illustrated in the example below.

Example: the critical path

3.16

Activity	Immediately preceding activity	Duration (weeks)
A	-	5
B	-	4
C	A	2
D	B	1
E	B	5
F	B	5
G	C, D	4
H	F	3
I	F	2

(a)   What are the paths through the network?
(b)   What is the critical path and its duration?

Solution

3.17   The first step in the solution is to draw the network diagram, with the time for each activity shown.

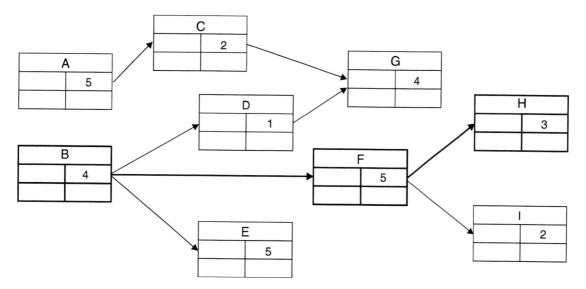

3.18   We could list the paths through the network and their overall completion times as follows.

Path		Duration (weeks)
A C G	(5 + 2 + 4)	11
B D G	(4 + 1 + 4)	9
B E	(4 + 5)	9
B F H	(4 + 5 + 3)	12
B F I	(4 + 5 + 2 + 0)	11

3.19   The critical path is the longest, BFH, with a duration of 12 weeks. This is the minimum time needed to complete the project.

3.20 The critical path is indicated on the diagram by drawing thick (or double-line) arrows, as shown above. In Microsoft Project the arrows and the nodes are highlighted in red.

3.21 Listing paths through the network in this way should be easy enough for small networks, but it becomes a long and tedious task for bigger and more complex networks. This is why software packages are used in real life.

The timing of activities

3.22 Conventionally (at least in professional exams) it is also felt to be useful to calculate the earliest and latest times for activities to start or finish, and show them on the network diagram. This can be done for networks of any size and complexity.

3.23 Project management software packages offer a much larger variety of techniques than can easily be done by hand. Microsoft Project, for instance allows each activity to be assigned to any one of a variety of types: 'start as late as possible', 'start as soon as possible', 'finish no earlier than a particular date', "finish no later than a particular date', and so on. Each different activity may be of a different type and subject to different constraints, just as in real life.

3.24 In real life, too, activity times can be shortened by working weekends and overtime, or they may be constrained by non-availability of essential personnel. In other words with any more than a few activities the possibilities are mind-boggling, which is why software is used.

PERT

3.25 Network problems may be complicated by uncertainty in the expected duration of individual activities. This may be expressed in terms of a most likely, optimistic and pessimistic time for each activity or in terms of a probability distribution of the expected time for each activity.

3.26 Project evaluation and review technique (PERT) introduces a form of time-uncertainty analysis into network analysis. For each activity in the project, optimistic, most likely and pessimistic estimates of times are made, on the basis of past experience, or even guess-work. These estimates are converted into a mean time and also a standard deviation.

3.27 Once the mean time and standard deviation of the time have been calculated for each activity, it should be possible to do the following.
   (a) Estimate the critical path using expected (mean) activity times.
   (b) Estimate the standard deviation of the total project time.

Exam questions

3.28 *Managing Information Systems* questions have never asked candidates to draw a network, but you may be expected to be aware of the technique an to be able to explain its features.

4 GANTT CHARTS

12/95

4.1 Gantt charts may be used to plan the time scale for a project and to estimate the amount of resources required. Gantt charts are popular because they are simple to construct and easy to understand. If you have a Year Planner on your office wall, that is a form of Gantt chart.

4.2 The Gantt chart is used to show the time to be taken for each activity, which commences at the appropriate stage in the project plan. As the activity is achieved the 'bar' is shaded in and it is easy to see if the time scale is being adhered to. Alternatively, an 'actual' and 'estimated' split bar can be used.

4.3 A simple Gantt chart, illustrating some of the hardware-related activities involved in systems development and implementation is shown below.

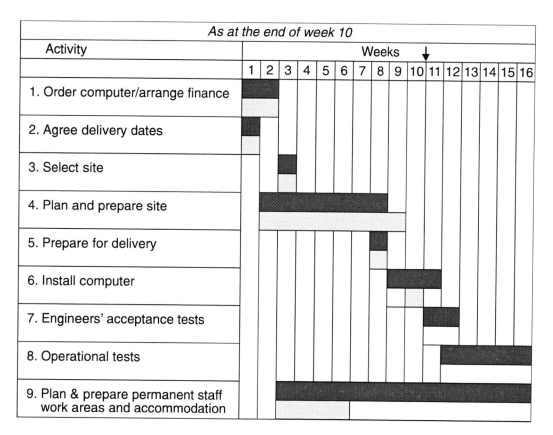

	As at the end of week 10																
Activity	Weeks ↓																
	1	2	3	4	5	6	7	8	9	10	11	12	13	14	15	16	
1. Order computer/arrange finance																	
2. Agree delivery dates																	
3. Select site																	
4. Plan and prepare site																	
5. Prepare for delivery																	
6. Install computer																	
7. Engineers' acceptance tests																	
8. Operational tests																	
9. Plan & prepare permanent staff work areas and accommodation																	

Key

Estimated

Actual

4.4 At the end of the tenth week Activity 9 is running behind schedule and more resources may have to be allocated to this activity if the staff accommodation is to be ready in time for the changeover to the new system.

4.5 Activity 4 had not been completed on time, and this has resulted in some disruption to the computer installation (Activity 6), which may mean further delays in the commencement of Activities 7 and 8.

4.6 One of the main problems with this type of Gantt chart is that it does not clearly reflect the interrelationship between the various activities in the project as does a network diagram. However, a combination of Gantt charts and network analysis might be used for project planning and resource allocation.

Example: Gantt charts and resources

4.7 This example is provided as an illustration of the use of Gantt charts to manage resources (particularly human resources) efficiently, so that you feel happy about describing Gantt charts in exams. It is unlikely that you would actually have to deal with a *numerical* problem.

A company is about to undertake a computer project about which the following data is available.

Activity	Preceded by activity	Duration Days	Workers required
A	–	3	6
B	–	5	3
C	B	2	4
D	A	1	4
E	A	6	5
F	D	3	6
G	C, E	3	3

There is a multi-skilled workforce of nine workers available, each capable of working on any of the activities.

Draw the network to establish the duration of the project and the critical path. Then draw a Gantt chart, using the critical path as a basis, assuming that jobs start at the earliest possible time.

Solution

4.8   Here are the diagrams.

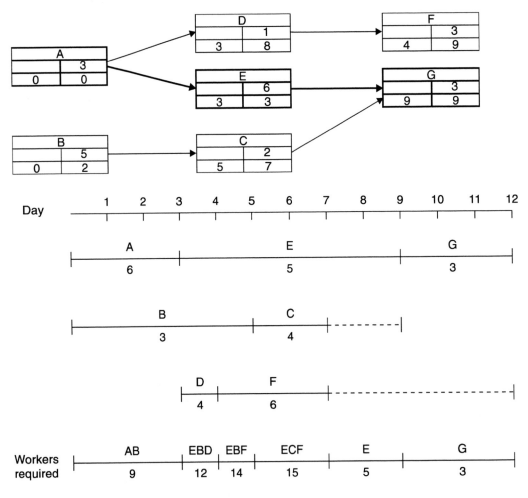

4.9   It can be seen that if all activities start at their earliest times, as many as 15 workers will be required on any one day (days 6-7) whereas on other days there would be idle capacity (days 8-12).

4.10   The problem can be reduced, or removed, by using up spare time on non-critical activities. Suppose we deferred the start of activities D and F until the latest possible days. These would be days 8 and 9, leaving four days to complete the activities by the end of day 12.

4.11 The Gantt chart would be redrawn as follows.

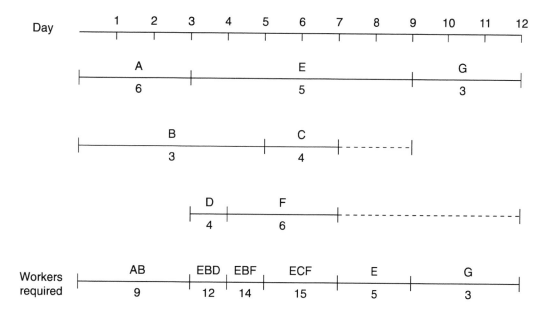

6/99

5 PROJECT MANAGEMENT SOFTWARE

5.1 As we have said repeatedly the project management techniques described above are ideal candidates for computerisation. Project management software packages have been available for a number of years.

5.2 Software might be used for a number of purposes.

(a) *Planning*

Network diagrams (showing the critical path) and Gantt charts (showing resource use) can be produced automatically once the relevant data is entered. Packages also allow a sort of 'what if?' analysis for initial planning, trying out different levels of resources, changing deadlines and so on to find the best combination.

(b) *Estimating*

As a project progresses, actual data will become known and can be entered into the package and collected for future reference. Since many projects involve basically similar tasks (interviewing users and so on), actual data from one project can be used to provide more accurate estimates for the next project. The software also facilitates and encourages the use of more sophisticated estimation techniques than managers might be prepared to use if working manually.

(c) *Monitoring*

Actual data can also be entered and used to facilitate monitoring of progress and automatically updating the plan for the critical path and the use of resources as circumstances dictate.

(d) Reporting

Software packages allow standard and tailored progress reports to be produced, printed out and circulated to participants and senior managers at any time, usually at the touch of a button. This helps with co-ordination of activities and project review.

5.3 Most project management packages feature a process of identifying the main steps in a project, and breaking these down further into specific tasks. For example, one part of a project is a feasibility study. This can be subdivided into a number of tasks. Each of these can be subdivided further, and so forth.

5.4 The package has to deal with the proper allocation of resources (defined as time, money, personnel, even physical objects). Some packages hold resources on a central database. For example Microsoft Project could be linked to an Access or Excel database.

Inputs

5.5 Any project management package requires four inputs.

(a) The length of time required for each activity of the project.
(b) The logical relationships between each activity.
(c) The resources available.
(d) When the resources are available.

5.6 Some software packages will find the optimal solution by presenting all this in the form of a Gantt chart. Others will also undertake more complicated PERT analysis. A modern package is likely to do both, and a lot more besides.

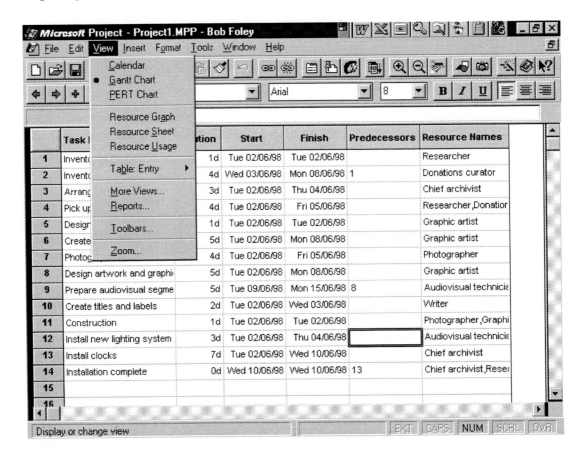

Features

5.7 There are a number of ways of distinguishing between and choosing packages.

(a) Does the package show data related to different aspects of the project on the same screen?

(b) Do projects take their resources from a central pool of resources? Effectively this asks whether the package will support more than one project at a time, so that staff-scheduling decisions on one project can be taken into account in another one.

(c) Is there a facility to record what each individual does? So, if an individual works on several different projects, is it possible to keep a record of what that individual has done, as well as the progress of the projects?

(d) When updating a project, is a record kept as of the original plan, or is it completely overwritten and forgotten?

(e) Does the package deal with non-human resources, such as materials?

(f) Does the package move activities to get the most efficient use of resources, in terms of cost and time?

(g) Is it possible to consolidate different projects into one? Or to create sub-projects from the main project? Microsoft Project, for instance, is able to consolidate up to 80 projects and 249 sub-projects. A project can have up to 9999 tasks and 9999 resources.

(h) Can you build in quality control targets into the project planning.

(i) Is there a feature for exception planning (ie if you overrun cost or time targets)?

6 THE PROJECT TEAM

6/99

6.1 A project team will have an overall project manager, whose role was described in section 2 of this Chapter. It will also have a number of administrative staff such as secretaries.

6.2 Essentially, however, developing a computer system can be divided into two parts.

(a) Designing a program or programs that will do the data processing work that the user department wants, and to the user's specification (for example about response times, accuracy etc).

This involves deciding what hardware there should be, what the input and files should be, how output should be produced, and what programs there should be to do this work.

This is the task of the systems analyst.

(b) Writing the software

Systems analysts

6.3 In general terms, the tasks of the systems analyst are as follows.

Systems analysis

6.4 This involves carrying out a methodical study of a current system (ie some data processing applications) to establish:

(a) what the current system does;

(b) whether it does what it is supposed to do;

(c) what the user department would like it to do, and so what the required objectives of the system are.

6.5 The analysis of the current system might involve a manual data processing system or a system that is already computerised but could possibly be improved or modernised.

Systems design

6.6 Having established what the proposed system objectives are, the next stage is to design a system that will achieve these objectives.

Systems specification

6.7 In designing a new system, it is the task of the systems analyst to specify the system in detail.

6.8 This involves identification of inputs, files, processing, output, hardware, costs, accuracy, response times and controls.

6.9 The system design is spelled out formally in a document or manual called the systems specification (which includes a program specification for each program in the system).

Systems testing

6.10 The analyst will be responsible for systems testing.

Review and maintenance

6.11 Keeping the system under review, and controlling and monitoring system maintenance with the co-operation of user departments.

6.12 The analyst might be responsible for writing and maintaining a user procedures manual - ie a manual for employees in the user department - which would:

(a) explain the computer system in very general terms;
(b) detail the procedures required in the user department to operate the system.

Programmers

6.13 Programmers take over from the systems analysts and have the task of writing the programs. This task involves the following.

(a) Reading the system specification and understanding it.

(b) Recognising what the processing requirements of the program are, in other words, defining the processing problem in detail.

(c) Having defined and analysed the processing problem, writing the program in a programming language.

(d) Arranging for the program to be tested.

(e) Identifying errors in the program and getting rid of these 'bugs' - ie debugging the program.

(f) Preparing full documentation for each program within the system.

Chapter roundup

- Good management of projects is vital. Many systems arrive late, cost more than was budgeted and do not meet user requirements. Project management is concerned with the detailed management of the development of a new system.

- The project manager is responsible for outline and detailed planning, communication, co-ordination and control, problem resolution and quality control.

- There are a number of conflicting pressures in any project. The most significant are usually the requirement for quality, the available resources, time constraints and finance.

- There are tools available to help with project management. The most widely used approaches are critical path analysis and Gantt charts.

- Project management software is available to automate these procedures.

- The project team (besides the overall manager and administrative staff) comprises analysts and programmers.

Test your knowledge

1   What problems might project managers face? (see paras 1.5 - 1.7)

2   What other factors can make projects go wrong? (1.8)

3   What are the phases of project management? (1.20)

4   What factors are in conflict during a project? (2.1 - 2.3)

5   What control activities may be used in project management? (2.8)

6   What is the aim of critical path analysis? (3.3)

7   What is the critical path? (3.14)

8   What are Gantt charts used for? (4.1)

9   What features might be found in a project management software package? (5.7)

10   What does a systems analyst do? (6.3 - 6.12)

Now try illustrative question 28 at the end of the Study Text

BPP PUBLISHING

Chapter 12

SYSTEMS IMPLEMENTATION

This chapter covers the following topics.

1   Installation and implementation

2   Testing

3   Training

4   Documentation

5   File conversion

6   Changeover

Introduction

Even if you have designed the best system in the world things can still go horribly wrong when you actually try to put it in place. Implementation covers a wide range of issues, ranging from simple things like remembering that computers need desks to sit on and cables to link them up, to strategic issues like whether to change systems overnight or take a softly, softly approach.

---

1   INSTALLATION AND IMPLEMENTATION

1.1   The main stages in the implementation of a computer system once it has been designed are as follows.

   (a)   Installation of the hardware and software
   (b)   Testing
   (c)   Staff training and production of documentation
   (d)   Conversion of files and database creation
   (e)   Changeover

1.2   The items in this list do not necessarily happen in a set chronological order, and some can be done at the same time - for example staff training and system testing can be part of the same operation.

1.3   The requirements for implementation vary from system to system as we shall see throughout this chapter.

Installation of equipment

1.4   Installing a mainframe computer or a large network is a major operation that is carried out by the manufacturer/supplier.

1.5   If jut a few PCs are being installed in a small network, the customer may have to install the hardware himself. This should not be difficult, provided that the manufacturer's instruction manuals are read carefully.

Installation of a PC

1.6 The office accommodation for PCs and peripheral equipment will also need a little bit of planning.

    (a) PCs can be used in any office environment, but they generate some heat when they operate (just like any other machine) and so it is inadvisable to put them in small, hot rooms.

    (b) Large desks may be advisable, to accommodate a screen and keyboard and leave some free desk space for the office worker to use.

    (c) There should be plenty of power sockets - enough to meet future needs as the system grows, not just immediate needs.

    (d) If noisy printers are being purchased, it may be advisable to locate these in a separate printer room, to cut down the noise for office workers.

    (e) There should be a telephone close to the computer, for communicating with the dealer or other organisation which provides system support and advice when the user runs into difficulties.

    (f) Cabling for network connections needs to take account of possible future changes in office layout or in system requirements.

Exercise 1

In Europe, Health and Safety legislation governs the siting of PCs. What matters do you think employers have to be careful about?

Solution

Provisions cover the sort of chairs and desks provided, the quality of VDUs and lighting, heat and humidity, the need for regular breaks and the importance of proper training.

1.7 When the hardware has been installed, the software may then need installing too. To install the software, the computer user must follow the instructions in the user's manual. Installing software used to be tedious and lengthy, taking perhaps half an hour for a package, but most new software is provided on CD-ROM and can be installed in minutes.

1.8 PCs almost invariably come with operating software pre-loaded these days, and many suppliers provide other pre-loaded software such as Microsoft Office.

1.9 If possible, back-up copies should be made of all software.

1.10 Whether or not this is done the software should be registered with the manufacturer, either by filling in a registration form and posting it or often, these days, by completing a form on screen and sending it in via telecommunications links.

1.11 Insurance should be arranged against losses due to fire or theft. It is also possible to obtain insurance against accidental loss of data. If all the data on a hard disk were lost, for example, it could be a long job to re-enter all the lost data, but with insurance cover, the cost of the clerk to do the re-inputting would be paid for by the insurance.

Installation of a mainframe computer or minicomputer

1.12 If a mainframe or minicomputer installation is to be successful it must be carefully planned. Many of the issues described above, such as furniture needs, cabling and so on, still apply. The particular problems of planning a large installation include the following.

Site selection

1.13 The site selected for the main computer might be in an existing or a new building. Factors to consider when choosing a site include:

(a) Adequate space for computer and peripherals, including servicing room.

(b) Room for expansion.

(c) Easy access for computer equipment and supplies (it should be unnecessary to knock holes in outside walls, as has happened, in order to gain access for equipment).

(d) Nearness to principal user departments.

(f) Space available for a library, stationery store, and systems maintenance staff.

Site preparation

1.14 The site preparation may involve consideration of certain potential problems.

(a) Air conditioning (temperature, humidity and dust).

(b) Special electricity supplies.

(c) Raised floor (or false ceiling) so that cables may pass from one piece of equipment to another.

(d) Fire protection devices

(e) Furnishings

Standby equipment

1.15 Standby equipment should be arranged, to ensure continuity of processing in the event of power or computer failure. Such equipment may include standby generators and standby computers.

2 TESTING

2.1 Individual programs and collections of programs making up systems must be thoroughly tested *before* implementation, otherwise there is a danger that the new system will go live with faults that might prove costly. The scope of tests and trials will again vary with the size of the system.

2.2 Three types of testing can be identified: program testing, systems testing and acceptance testing.

Program testing

2.3 Program testing, (or 'unit testing' or 'module testing'), entails running the program or a defined part of it with a controlled set of inputs, observing the run-time effect that the inputs have on the program, and examining the outputs to determine whether they are acceptable.

2.4 Much of this testing is done by the programmer informally during the program 'debugging' process, but formal program testing is also necessary. Debugging relies on the program production tools (compilers, debugging packages that examine a program's internal operation), whereas formal program testing may involve other kinds of tools.

Case example

In a modern language such as Visual Basic it is possible to run a program that is being developed to see whether it works, at any time during development, simply at the click of a button. If it does not work, Visual Basic stops at the faulty line of code, highlights it on screen and offers a Help option.

2.5 Formal testing may include manual code inspections, where the programmer reads through every line of code and looks for errors (like proofing a book), or the use of automated tools that analyse software by looking for certain kinds of common errors (those not caught during the normal program production process). This latter is called Computer Aided Software Testing (CAST).

2.6 The input data used to make a program demonstrate its own features are called test data. Test data will be prepared of the type that the program will be required to process. This test data will deliberately include invalid/exceptional items to test whether the program reacts in the right way and generates the required management reports.

2.7 The anticipated results of processing will be worked out in advance and then after processing the test program, there should be an item for item checking against the actual computer output to test whether the program has operated as required.

2.8 Program testing involves performing tests which work through all the logic paths in the code. One methodology for generating this kind of test data is known as 'branch and condition coverage'. Another method is multi-condition coverage, which attempts to generate test data which would exercise all the decision paths in the program code.

2.9 Since program testing is usually performed by programmers themselves, it is highly prone to error. Writers of programs are probably the *worst* people to ask to test their own work, because they will know already what it is supposed to do and that is what they will be inclined to test. Supplementary tests may therefore be performed by peers and management.

Systems testing

2.10 There will then be testing of the 'interface' between individual programs that together make up the system as a whole, in an overall 'systems test'.

2.11 Test data should be constructed to test all conditions. For example, dummy data records and transactions should be input which are designed to test the links between different parts of the system (for instance is data input by one part of the system intelligible as input to another part of the system) and all the data validation routines (for instance is it possible to enter alphabetic characters into a field that is only supposed to have numeric entries, is it possible to omit information in a certain field, and so on).

2.12 Many managers prefer to use historical data in trials, because it is then possible to check the output of the new system against the output that the old system produced. Unusual, but feasible, transactions could also be tested, to see how the system handles them - for example two wage packets in the same week for the same employee.

2.13 Typically a systems test will look at aspects such as the following.

(a) Stress and volume testing, to see whether the system can handle both peaks and steady loads of high volume data.

(b) Usability testing, to evaluate human factors, or usability problems.

(c) Security testing, using test cases that subvert the program's security checks.

(d) Performance testing, to verify that the program meets specific performance objectives.

(e) Compatibility, or conversion testing, to ensure compatibility with external databases.

(f) Regression testing, to see whether any errors have been introduced while fixing another error.

(g) Data integrity testing, to make sure that data is stored in such a manner that it is not compromised when it is updated or retrieved.

Black Box Testing

2.14 System testing checks that the whole system behaves according to the agreed specification and that the criteria for user acceptance (see below) will be met. The purpose of black box testing is to find discrepancies between the external specifications and the program behaviour. A black box tester does not consider the code structure, only the behaviour of the system. Black box tests probe the application not only to determine whether it does what it is supposed to do, but also if it does what it is *not* supposed to do!

Case example: Handling errors

Well-designed systems should *anticipate* the errors that a user is likely to make, such as clicking on a button that would start the next phase of the program before making all the required entries, and they should prevent them from happening if possible or, failing that, generate error messages. We saw an example of error prevention earlier, where a button was only enabled after the user had picked one of two options.

Other common examples include trying to save something to a floppy disk but not putting a floppy disk into the disk drive, or overwriting data without giving users a chance to confirm that this is what they want to do or change their mind.

Acceptance testing

2.15 Acceptance testing is testing of a system by the user department, after the system has passed its systems test. It is sometimes referred to as Beta testing. The purposes of having trials conducted by the user department's managers are to:

(a) find software errors which exist but have not yet been detected;

(b) find out exactly what the demands of the new system are; and

(c) find out whether any major changes in operating procedures will be necessary. (Unanticipated and undesirable changes should certainly *not* be necessary, if the system is to be accepted.)

2.16 Another aspect of the user department trials (or a subsequent stage of trials) might be to train staff in the new system and the new procedures.

2.17 With tailor-made software, acceptance tests should (in theory) overlap with system tests already performed by the system provider, because the provider should already have checked that the system meets agreed acceptance criteria. This will not be the case with packaged software, which may be tested in a 'demo' version or evaluation copy.

2.18 Acceptance testing may be divided into four categories.

(a) *Functionality testing* tests that the requirements that were specified when the system was commissioned have been met. *Usability* tests are the key issue.

(b) *Performance testing* looks at matters such as response time, number of transactions handled per hour, performance when multiple users are using the system, ability to recover in the event of a system crash (eg a power failure) and so on.

(c) *Interface testing* checks that the new system is compatible with existing systems and equipment already in use.

(d) *Environmental testing* considers factors such as noise, heat generation, power consumption and so on.

Exercise 2

Next time you are using a software package such as a word processing package or a spreadsheet package, pretend that it is brand new to you and think about what aspects you would test to see whether you found it acceptable.

Are all the options in all the menus and all the buttons meaningful to you? Do you get the expected results when you click on a button? How easy is it to retrieve data that you have already created? Does it take too long to open, close or save a file? Can you 'turn off' features that you do not want to use? Is the layout and presentation on the screen helpful or unhelpful, and (if the latter) can you change it to suit your own preferences?

You will probably find other tests to perform yourself.

---

3 TRAINING
12/96, 12/98, 12/99

3.1 Staff training in the use of information technology is as important as the technology itself as without effective operation at all levels computer systems can be an expensive waste of resources in any business.

3.2 The issue of training raises the wider matter of how to make personnel at all levels competent and willing to use IT. If organisations wish to encourage end-user computing then a training program can be part of a wider 'propaganda' exercise by information systems professionals.

3.3 Training is not simply an issue that affects operational staff. As PCs are used more and more as management tools, training in information technology affects all levels in an organisation, from senior managers learning how to use an executive information system for example, to accounts clerks learning how to use an accounts management system.

The complete training requirement
12/98, 12/99

3.4 A systematic approach to training can be illustrated in a flowchart as follows.

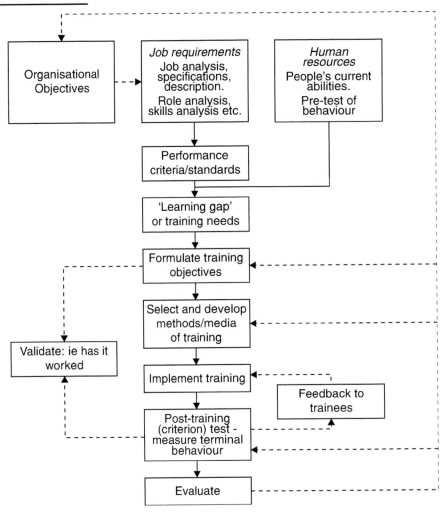

3.5 Note the following points in particular.

(a) Training is provided primarily to help the organisation achieve its objectives, not just for the benefit of staff.

(b) An individual's training need is generally defined as follows.

Required level of competence	X
Current level of competence	(Y)
Training need	Z

(c) Training should be evaluated to make sure that it has worked. If not the method may have been wrong. Whatever the cause, the training need still exists.

Training for managers   12/96, 12/98

3.6 Managers typically have little time for training, so whatever training is provided needs to be very well focused.

(a) Methods will need to be chosen which can achieve maximum benefits in minimum time and with the least disruption of normal working patterns.

(b) An overall plan must me drawn up and agreed with the executives. Some resistance may be expected since the new system may be seen as somewhat threatening to their status and established practices.

(c) The plan may include both formal and informal methods. Formal approaches may be tailored short courses with a carefully selected group; also briefings and demonstrations at management and board meetings. One to one tutorial sessions, use of manuals and disk-based tutorials will also be required. Ongoing support through all stages must be arranged.

(d) In the longer term, encouraging senior executives to participate in development, through, for example, structured walkthroughs. may enhance training. Above all, managers must see the training as non-threatening and potentially rewarding.

Senior management training

3.7 Senior managers are responsible for the overall planning and direction for the organisation. They are not likely to need detailed technical training (what keys to press or buttons to click) but certainly need to know how the system may help strategic decision making. Some elements of the new system may be designed to allow them direct and rapid access to vital information and possibly to generate queries and *ad hoc* reports.

3.8 Senior management can be 'trained' in a number of ways of varying degrees of formality. The completely informal approach might include the provision of information from the following sources.

- Newspapers (most of the quality press run regular articles on IT and computing).
- Subordinates (getting subordinate members of staff to demonstrate a system).
- Individual demonstrations of computer systems for senior executives.

3.9 Semi-formal training is of greater value.

(a) Executive briefings (for example presentation before or after board meetings).
(b) Video demonstrations (for example during lunchtime).
(c) Short seminars, designed around an issue that is narrowly defined.

3.10 Formal sessions such as day courses are necessary if managers are to learn how to use a particular system, for example an EIS or a spreadsheet package.

3.11 Some commentators have argued that senior managers who are knowledgeable about computers and related technologies make wiser decisions in the following areas.

(a) Allocation of resources to information systems (especially if the information system gives an organisation competitive advantage).

(b) Planning for information systems.

(c) Establishing an appropriate corporate culture for technological development.

(d) The establishment of an informed scepticism when dealing with IT professionals means that managers won't be blinded by science, and will be able to communicate their needs more effectively.

(e) Informed managers will have a better understanding of their subordinates' work.

Training middle management

3.12 The type of training middle management receives is likely to be more structured and more tailored to the particular applications within their remit.

3.13 Middle management are responsible for the correct use of systems in an age of distributed processing and end-user computing. Middle management are also responsible for implementing in detail the organisation's computer security policy.

3.14 The accent is also on the business issues. Managers do not necessarily need to know how computers work. They need to know what computing can do for them.

Training users

3.15 Users need a number of different types of computer and systems training.

(a)   Basic literacy in computers such as the concept of a file, updating, maintenance and so forth, might be needed. This might help users relate the workings of a manual system to its computer replacement. Also, some basic ideas as to how to use a computer efficiently can be usefully taught.

(b)   Users also need to get up and running with particular applications quickly, even if they do not go into the finer points of it. If the system is complex, such training gives users an overall view of the system, commands and procedures.

(c)   Users might sometimes need a refresher course, especially if they do not use a particular application regularly.

(d)   Users need training while operating the application (on-the-job training).

3.16   Some of these facilities are provided by the computer system itself. For example, many software packages have a Help facility which enables a user to learn facts about the system while they are using it.

3.17   Computer based training has the advantage of encouraging users to become acquainted with the technology they will be using, and to develop their skills at their own pace. Multimedia training packages exist for many widely-used software packages.

3.18   Training can also be provided by:

•   Reading the user manuals.
•   Attending courses that the dealer or employer provides.
•   Attending courses on a leading software package.

3.19   With large computer systems, extensive training of large numbers of staff will probably be necessary, and so further training measures may include other media.

(a)   Lectures on general or specific aspects of the system - possibly with the use of films, video, tape-recordings, slides, overhead projectors etc.

(b)   Discussion meetings, possibly following on from lectures, which allow the staff to ask questions and sort out problems.

(c)   Internal company magazines, to explain the new system in outline.

(d)   Handbooks, detailing in precise terms the new documentation and procedures. Different handbooks for each function will often be prepared by different persons.

(e)   Using trials/tests on the new system to give staff direct experience before the system goes live.

The benefits of training   12/96

3.20   The benefits may be summarised as follows.

(a)   A better understanding of customer needs and concerns.
(b)   Improved job satisfaction at all levels.
(c)   A management that is seen to take the lead in addressing concerns.
(d)   Greater confidence in planning for the future.
(e)   Better understanding of the relationship between IT and competitive performance.
(f)   Improved communication with IT professionals.
(g)   Development of an IT aware culture throughout the company.
(h)   Understating of the role and problems of subordinates.

4   DOCUMENTATION

4.1   Documentation includes a wide range of technical and non-technical books, manuals, descriptions and diagrams relating to the use and operation of a computer system. Examples include user manuals, hardware and operating software manuals, system specifications and program documentation.

The systems specification

4.2 The systems specification is a complete documentation of the whole system and must always be properly maintained (ie kept up to date) as parts of the system are changed or added to.

4.3 Many of the problems in computer installations arise because of inadequate systems and program documentation and controls must be set up to ensure that updating procedures are always carried out.

Program specifications

4.4 A program specification, or program documentation, is the complete description of a program, usually including notes, flowcharts, a listing of all the codes, and perhaps test data and expected results. There should be a program specification for every individual program in the system.

4.5 Initial specifications are drawn up by the systems analyst and the programmer then uses the specification as the basis of writing and testing the required program.

4.6 When the program has been written and tested, one copy of the final specification will form part of the overall systems specification, and a second copy will be retained by the programmer to form part of the programmer's own documentation for the program.

Computer operations manual

4.7 This manual provides full documentation of the operational procedures necessary for the 'hands-on' running of the system. Amongst the matters to be covered by this documentation would be the following.

(a) Systems set-up procedures. Full details should be given for each application of the necessary file handling and stationery requirements etc.

(b) Security procedures. Particular stress should be placed on the need for checking that proper authorisation has been given for processing operations and the need to restrict use of machine(s) to authorised operators.

(c) Reconstruction control procedures. Precise instructions should be given in relation to matters such as file dumping and also the recovery procedures to be adopted in the event of a systems failure.

(d) System messages. A listing of all messages likely to appear on the operator's screen should be given together with an indication of the responses which they should evoke.

User manual

4.8 At some stage before staff training takes place, the system must be fully documented for the computer user. Matters to be dealt with should include the following.

(a) Input. Responsibilities and procedures for preparation of input including requirements for establishment of batch control totals, authorisation etc.

(b) Error reports. Full explanation of nature and form of error reports (eg exception reports for items rejected by data validation checks) and instructions as to the necessary action to be taken.

(c) File amendment procedures. Full explanation of necessary authorisation and documentation required for file amendment.

(d) Output. What this is, what form it takes, what should be done with it etc.

4.9   The user documentation is used to explain the system to the user and to help to train staff. Additionally, it provides a point of reference should the user have some problems with the system in the future - eg an error condition or a screen message that he or she does not understand.

4.10   When a system is developed in-house, the user documentation might be written by a systems analyst. However, it might be considered preferable for the user documentation to be written by a member of the user's department's staff, possibly a junior manager who has spent some time with the project development team, learning about the system.

System changes manual

4.11   Amendments to the original systems specification will almost inevitably occur, in addition to the computerisation of additional company activities. The objective of the system changes manual is to ensure that such changes are just as strictly controlled as was the case with the original systems development and introduction. Four matters to be covered in this respect would be as follows.

(a) Recording of the request and reason for a change.
(b) Procedures for the authorisation of changes.
(c) Procedures for the documentation of changes.
(d) Procedures for the testing of changes.

5   FILE CONVERSION   6/95

5.1   File conversion, means converting existing files into a format suitable for the new system. File conversion may be a major part of the systems implementation or it may be largely painless, if upgrading say, from version 1 of a standard package to version 2. If it means the conversion of existing manual file records into a medium used by the computer it may be very expensive. It may involve the transcription of records, or parts of them, on to specially designed forms before they are keyed on to the appropriate computer medium.

5.3   Because of the volume of data that must be copied on to the new files, the problem of input errors is a serious one, whatever data validation checks may be operating. (Validation checks are covered in more detail in Chapter 14.)

5.4   Once the file has been created, extensive checking for accuracy is essential, otherwise considerable problems may arise when the system becomes operational.

Existing computer files

5.5   If the system is already computerised on a system that the organisation now wishes to abandon, the difficulties of file conversion will usually (though not always) be reduced. When it comes to the actual transcription from the old files to the new computer files the use of a special conversion program or translation program will speed up the whole process.

5.6   The problem of conversion has reduced significantly as major software manufacturers have realised that it may be a barrier to people using their products. Thus an Excel spreadsheet can be saved in Lotus 1-2-3 format, if this is what the user wants.

Existing manual files

5.7   The stages in file conversion from manual files to computer files, where this is a very complex process, are normally as follows.

(a) Ensuring that the original record files are accurate and up to date.

(b) Recording the old file data on specially designed input documents.

This will usually be done by the user department personnel (with additional temporary staff if required) following detailed instructions laid down by the systems designer or software supplier.

The instructions will include the procedures for allocating new code numbers (a coding system, including check digits if necessary, may have to be designed by this stage) and for checking the accuracy and completeness of the data selected and entered on the input documents (usually verification by another person and the establishment of control totals).

(c) Transcribing the completed input documents on to the computer media.

(d) Data entry programs would include validation checks on the input data. The contents of the file must then be printed out and completely checked back to the data input forms (or even the original file if possible).

(e) Correcting any errors that this checking reveals.

5.8 Other problems of file conversion which must be considered include the following.

(a) The possible provision of additional staff, to cope with the file conversion and prevent bottlenecks.

(b) The establishment of cut-off dates where live files are being converted (should the conversion be during slack times, for example, during holidays, weekends?).

(c) The decision as to whether files should be converted all at once, or whether the conversion should be file by file or record group by record group (with subsequent amalgamation).

Exercise 3

You have been asked to transfer 400 Sales Ledger manual record cards to a PC based system. The program menu has a record create option. Explain how you would set about this process, and the steps you would take to ensure that the task was completed successfully.

Solution

The steps that should be taken are as follows.

(a) Check the manual records, and remove any dead accounts.

(b) Assign account codes to each record, ideally with codes that incorporate a check digit.

(c) If necessary transcribe the data from the card records on to documents which can be used for copying from, for data input.

(d) Add up the number of accounts and the total value of account balances as control totals.

(e) Select the record create option from the program menu and key the standing data and current data on to the new computer file. This should ideally be done at a quiet time, perhaps over a weekend.

(f) Input that is rejected by a data validation check should be re-keyed correctly.

(g) A listing of the records put on to file should be printed out. This listing should be checked for errors, ideally by someone who did not do the keying in. Errors should be reported, and corrections keyed in to amend the data on file.

(h) The program should allow control totals of the number of records put on to the file, and the total value of account balances to be viewed. These control totals should be checked against the manually pre-listed control totals. Discrepancies should be investigated, and any errors or omissions put right.

(i) A back-up copy of the new file should be made.

(j) The data on the new system should then be ready for use.

---

6   CHANGEOVER
6/95

6.1   Once the new system has been fully and satisfactorily tested the changeover can be made. This may be according to one of four approaches.

- Direct changeover
- Parallel running
- Pilot tests
- Phased or 'staged' implementation

Direct changeover

6.2   This is the method of changeover in which the old system is completely replaced by the new system in one move.

6.3   This may be unavoidable where the two systems are substantially different, or where extra staff to oversee parallel running are unobtainable.

6.4   While this method is comparatively cheap it is risky (system or program corrections are difficult while the system has to remain operational): management must have complete confidence that the new system will work.

6.5   The new system should be introduced during slack periods, for example over a bank holiday weekend or during an office closure such as a factory's summer shutdown or in the period between Christmas and the New Year.

Parallel running

6.6   This is a form of changeover whereby the old and new systems are run in parallel for a period of time, both processing current data and enabling cross checking to be made.

6.7   This method provides a degree of safety should there be problems with the new system. However, if there are differences between the two systems cross-checking may be difficult or impossible.

6.8   Furthermore, there is a delay in the actual implementation of the new system, a possible indication of lack of confidence in the new system, and a need for more staff to cope with both systems running in parallel.

6.9   This cautious approach, if adopted, should be properly planned, and the plan should include the following.

(a)   A firm time limit on parallel running.
(b)   Details of which data should be cross-checked - all of it? - some of it on a sample basis?
(c)   Instructions on how errors are to be dealt with - they could be errors in the old system.
(d)   Instructions on how to cope with major problems in the new system.

Pilot operation

6.10   This is cheaper and easier to control than parallel running, and provides a greater degree of safety than does a direct changeover. There are two types of pilot operation.

(a)   Retrospective parallel running

This is an approach in which the new system operates on data already processed by the old system. The existing results are available for cross-checking and the system can be tested without the problems of staffing and disruption caused by parallel running.

(b) Restricted data running

This involves a complete logical part of the whole system being chosen and run as a unit on the new system. If that is shown to be working well the remaining parts are then transferred. Gradually the whole system can be transferred in this piecemeal fashion.

For example, one group of customer accounts from the sales ledger might be run on the new system. Again, the planning should involve the setting of strict time limits for each phase and instructions on how problems are to be dealt with. It must be remembered that two systems have to be controlled and additional staff, as well as a longer period for implementation, may be required.

Phased implementation

6.11 Phased implementation takes two possible forms

(a) It can on the one hand resemble parallel running, the difference being that only a portion of the data is run in parallel, for example for one branch only.

(b) Alternatively, phased implementation may consist of a number of separate direct changeovers, for example where a large system is to be replaced and the criteria for direct changeover apply.

6.12 The use of this method of implementation is best suited to very large projects and/or those where distinct parts of the system are geographically dispersed.

6.13 Where this approach is adopted care must be taken to control any systems amendments incorporated in the later phases in order to ensure that the overall system remains totally compatible.

Chapter roundup

- The main stages in the systems implementation process are installation of hardware and software, staff training, system testing, file creation and changeover.

- Installation of equipment requires careful planning. The user may install a small number of PCs, but larger computers will be installed by the supplier. Considerations include site selection, site preparation and delivery itself.

- Training is a key part of the implementation of a new system. The approach adopted and the medium through which training is given will vary depending on the target audience. Senior management are more likely to be interested in the overall capabilities and limitations of systems, while junior staff need to be taught the functional aspects.

- A system must be thoroughly tested before implementation, otherwise there is a danger that it may not function properly when it goes live. The nature and scope of testing will vary depending on the size of the system. After systems testing is completed, the user department will carry out acceptance testing.

- File creation involves the creation or conversion of files for use with the new system. This is a major part of systems implementation and must be fully controlled to ensure that errors are not allowed to creep into the new files. The process may involve conversion of existing computerised files or may require migration of data from manual records.

- Once the system has been tested and files successfully converted, the system changeover can take place. There are four possible approaches: direct changeover, parallel running, pilot tests and phased implementation. These vary in terms of time required, cost and risk.

Test your knowledge

1   What matters should be considered when installing a PC network? (see paras 1.6, 1.7)

2   Distinguish between three types of testing. (2.3 - 2.15)

3   How are an individual's training needs defined? (3.5)

4   What kind of training do operational users need? (3.15)

5   What might be found in user documentation? (4.8)

6   Why is a system changes manual maintained? (4.11)

7   What are the stages in converting a large manual system into computer files? (5.8)

8   What is parallel running? (6.6)

9   When might phased implementation be appropriate? (6.12)

Now try illustrative questions 17, 18 and 32 at the end of the Study Text

Chapter 13

SYSTEMS MAINTENANCE AND EVALUATION

This chapter covers the following topics.

1   Systems maintenance

2   Evaluation

3   Computer-based monitoring

4   Systems performance

5   Post-implementation review

Introduction

This chapter looks at what happens once a system is up and running.

Throughout its life, a system should operate effectively and efficiently. To do this, the system needs to be maintained and its users need to be supported. The first two sections of this chapter look at how this is done.

The remaining sections look at *evaluation*. This should be an ongoing process to make sure that the system continues to meet requirements. Once it is implemented, a comparison will be made of the objectives and original cost-benefit submissions against actual performance and actual value. The operational characteristics of the system will be reviewed continually.

1   SYSTEMS MAINTENANCE

12/96

Types of maintenance

1.1   There are three types of maintenance activity.

(a)   *Corrective maintenance* is carried out when there is a systems failure of some kind, for example in processing or in an implementation procedure. Its objective is to ensure that systems remain operational.

(b)   *Perfective maintenance* is carried out in order to perfect the software, or to improve software so that the processing inefficiencies are eliminated and performance is enhanced. The replacement of a word processing package written for DOS by a package which offers a Windows environment is an example of perfective maintenance.

(c)   *Adaptive maintenance* is carried out to take account of anticipated changes in the processing environment. For example new taxation legislation might require change to be made to payroll software.

1.2   Corrective maintenance usually consists of action in response to a problem. Much perfective maintenance consists of making enhancements requested by users to improve or extend the facilities available. The user interface may be amended to make software more user friendly.

1.3   The key features of system maintenance ought to be flexibility and adaptability.

(a)   The system, perhaps with minor modifications, should cope with changes in the computer user's procedures or volume of business.

(b) The computer user should benefit from advances in computer hardware technology without having to switch to another system altogether.

The causes of systems maintenance

1.4 Besides environmental changes, three factors contribute to the need for maintenance.

Factor	Comment
Errors	However carefully and diligently the systems development staff carry out systems testing and program testing, it is likely that bugs will exist in a newly implemented system. Most should be identified during the first few runs of a system. The effect of errors can obviously vary enormously.
Changes in requirements	Although users should be consulted at all stages of systems development, problems may arise after a system is implemented because users may have found it difficult to express their requirements, or may have been concerned about the future of their jobs and not participated fully in development.
	Cost constraints may have meant that certain requested features were not incorporated. Time constraints may have meant that requirements suggested during development were ignored in the interest of prompt completion.
Poor documentation	If old systems are accompanied by poor documentation, or even a complete lack of documentation, it may be very difficult to understand their programs. It will be hard to update or maintain such programs. Programmers may opt instead to patch up the system with new applications using newer technology.

The systems maintenance lifecycle

1.5 Corrective and adaptive maintenance should be carried out as and when problems occur, but perfective maintenance may be carried out on a more scheduled system-by-system basis (Sales system in January, Purchases in February, etc).

1.6 Assuming the system is intended to reflect business needs, it ought to be possible to predict with reasonable certainty when business growth will make maintenance necessary. It is possible to contend with increasing volumes and communication needs by enhancing the existing computer system on site, on a modular basis.

(a) Installing disks of greater capacity and higher speed
(b) Installing a more powerful processor
(c) Changing to faster printers
(d) Installing additional terminals or network facilities

1.7 As mentioned, systems analysts will always try to design flexibility into computer systems, so that the system can adapt to change.

1.8 However, there will come a point at which redevelopment is necessary, for example where hardware upgrades or the availability of new software make radical change necessary, or following a company restructuring.

In-house maintenance

1.9 With large computer systems, developed by the organisation itself, in-house systems analysts and programmers might be given the responsibility for software maintenance.

1.10 To ensure that maintenance is carried out efficiently, the principles of good programming practice should be applied.

(a) Any change must be properly authorised by a manager in the user department (or someone even more senior, if necessary).

(b) The new program requirements must be specified in full and in writing. These specifications will be prepared by a systems analyst. A programmer should use these specifications to produce an amended version of the program.

(c) In developing a new program version, a programmer should keep working papers. He or she can refer back to these papers later to check in the event that there is an error in the new program or the user of the program asks for a further change in the program.

(d) The new program version should be tested when it has been written. A programmer should prepare test data and establish whether the program will process the data according to the specifications given by the systems analyst.

(e) Provisions should be made for further program amendments in the future. One way of doing this is to leave space in the program instruction numbering sequence for new instructions to be inserted later. For example, instructions might be numbered 10,20,30,40 etc instead of 1,2,3,4.

(f) A record should be kept of all program errors that are found during 'live' processing and of the corrections that are made to the program.

(g) Each version of a program (versions that are produced with processing modifications or corrections to errors) should be separately identified, to avoid a mix-up about what version of a program should be used for 'live' operating.

Software maintenance

1.11 With purchased software (whether off the shelf or bespoke), the software house or supplier is likely to provide details of any new versions of the software as they are produced, simply for marketing purposes.

Maintenance contracts

1.12 There is also likely to be an agreement between the supplier of software and the customer for the provision of a software support service. A maintenance contract typically includes the following services.

(a) *Help*

When a customer runs into difficulties operating the system help will initially be given by a telephone 'hot line'. If a telephone call does not resolve the problem, the software expert may arrange to visit the customer's premises (within a period of time agreed in the contract), although this would be rare for standard packages.

(b) *Information*

Extra information about using the package may be provided through factsheets or a magazine sent free to subscribers. This may include case studies showing how other users have benefited from using the package in a particular way and technical tips for common user problems

(c) *Updates*

Free updates are provided to correct errors in part of a package, or if there is something inevitable that will mean that some aspect of a package has to be changed.

For example payroll software has to reflect the latest Finance Act, and users of version 4 of Sage Sterling's payroll package who took out a SageCover contract could expect to receive version 4.0 initially , and then versions 4.1, 4.2 etc as tax legislation changed.

(d) *Upgrades*

When the whole package is revised the contract often provides for subscribers to get the new version at a heavily discounted price. Upgrades usually include new features not found in the previous versions or updates.

(e) *Legal conditions*

We saw an example of some of these in the licence agreement in Chapter 8. There will be provisions about the duration of the contract and in what circumstances it terminates, about the customer's obligations to use the software in the way it was intended to be used, on the right sort of hardware, and not to make illegal copies. The liability of the supplier will also be set out, especially regarding consequential loss.

Hardware maintenance

1.13 Computer hardware should be kept serviced and maintained too. Maintenance services are provided:

(a) by the computer manufacturers themselves; or
(b) by third-party maintenance companies.

1.14 Maintenance of hardware can be obtained in two ways.

(a) On a contract basis. PC maintenance contracts are usually negotiated annually.
(b) On an *ad hoc* basis - ie calling in a maintenance company whenever a fault occurs.

Exercise 1

Draft a set of procedures to guide systems staff in the maintenance of a new system.

Solution

Guidelines for the Management of the New System

Maintenance is required in order to correct system errors and to ensure that the system is updated and modified to meet users' requirements.

The following guidelines should be observed:

(a) Responsibility for maintenance lies with the Head of Systems to whom all maintenance reports should be addressed.

(b) Planned/preventive maintenance procedures should be preferred to re-active procedures that respond only to faults. However, corrective maintenance will be required if the system fails.

(c) Adaptive maintenance may be required to anticipate and respond to changes required by the users; for example the introduction of new product ranges may require software modification or upgraded storage space.

(d) Systems documentation must be maintained at a high standard, regularly reviewed and modified as required. Users must be encouraged to report immediately any MIS understandings or concerns . All changes/modifications must be fully documented.

Agreed quality standards must be published and regular testing and error reporting established. Benchmarking may be used. Feedback from users and in particular customers must be sought.

(f) Hardware maintenance is the responsibility of the supplier who is obliged to provide same day service by agreement in response to requests.

(g) The Head of Systems and in-house staff will maintain software. Telephone support from suppliers is also available.

(h) Requests for requirements changes should be recorded in detail and referred to the Head of Systems for attention.

(i) Head of System is responsible for maintaining systems compliance with legislation for example the Data Protection Act.

(j) Only approved software may be used and no unauthorised copies taken. Measures to protect the system from viruses must be rigorously maintained.

2 EVALUATION

12/96, 6/97, 12/99

2.1 In most systems there is a constant need to maintain and improve applications and to keep up to date with technological advances and changing user requirements. A system should therefore be reviewed after implementation, and periodically, so that any unforeseen problems may be solved and to confirm that it is achieving and will continue to achieve the desired results.

2.2 The system should have been designed with clear, specified objectives, and justification in terms of cost-benefit analysis or other performance criteria.

2.3 Just as the feasibility of a project is assessed by reference to technical, operational, social and economic factors, so the same criteria can be used for evaluation. We need not repeat material that you have covered earlier, but here are a few pointers.

Cost-benefit review

2.4 A cost-benefit review is similar to a cost-benefit analysis, except that actual data can be used.

2.5 For instance when a large project is completed, techniques such as DCF appraisal can be performed again, with *actual* figures being available for much of the expenditure.

Exercise 2

A cost-benefit review might categorise items under the five headings of direct benefits, indirect benefits, development costs, implementation costs and running costs.

Give two examples of items which could fall to be evaluated under each heading.

Solution

Direct benefits might include reduced operating costs, for example lower overtime payments, and higher turnover resulting from increased order processing capacity from a new system.

Indirect benefits might include better decision-making and the freeing of human 'brainpower' from routine tasks so that it can be used for more creative work.

Development costs include systems analysts' costs and the cost of time spent by users in assisting with fact-finding.

Implementation costs would include costs of site preparation and costs of training.

Running costs include maintenance costs and software leasing costs.

Efficiency and effectiveness

2.6 In any evaluation of a system, two terms recur. Two key reasons for the introduction of information systems into an organisation are to improve the efficiency or the effectiveness of the organisation.

Efficiency

2.7 Efficiency can be measured by considering the resource inputs into and the outputs from a process or an activity.

2.8 An activity uses resources such as men, money and materials. If the same activity can be performed using fewer resources, for example fewer men or less money, or if it can be completed more quickly, the efficiency of the activity is improved. An improvement in efficiency represents an improvement in productivity.

BPP
PUBLISHING

2.9 Automation of an organisation's activities is usually expected to lead to greater efficiency in a number of areas.

(a) The cost of a computer system is lower than that of the manual system it replaces, principally because jobs previously performed by human operators are now carried out by computer.

(b) The accuracy of data information and processing is improved, because a computer does not make mistakes.

(c) The speed of processing is improved. Response times, for example in satisfying customer orders, are improved.

Effectiveness

2.10 Effectiveness is a measurement of how well the organisation is achieving its objectives.

2.11 Effectiveness is a more subjective concept than efficiency, as it is concerned with factors which are less easy to measure. It focuses primarily on the relationship of the organisation with its environment. For example, automation might be pursued because it is expected that the company will be more effective at increasing market share or at satisfying customer needs.

2.12 Computing was originally concerned with the automation of 'back office' functions, usually aspects of data processing. Development was concerned with improving efficiency.

2.13 Recent trends are more towards the development of 'front office' systems, for example to improve an organisation's decision-making capability or to seek competitive advantage. This approach seeks to improve the effectiveness of the organisation.

3 COMPUTER-BASED MONITORING   *12/99*

3.1 Computers themselves can be used in systems evaluation. Three methods used are hardware monitors, software monitors and systems logs.

Hardware monitors

3.2 Hardware monitors (not visual display units) are devices which measure the presence or absence of electrical signals in selected circuits in the computer hardware.

3.3 They might measure idle time or levels of activity in the CPU, or peripheral activity. Data is sent from the sensors to counters, which periodically write it to disk or tape.

3.4 A program will then analyse the data and produce an analysis of findings as output. It might identify for example inefficient co-ordination of processors and peripherals, or excessive delays in writing data to backing storage.

Software monitors

3.5 Software monitors are computer programs which interrupt the application in use and record data about it. They might identify, for example, excessive waiting time during program execution. Unlike hardware monitors, they may slow down the operation of the program being monitored.

Systems logs

3.6 Many computer systems provide automatic log details, for example job start and finish times or which employee has used which program and for how long. The systems log can therefore provide useful data for analysis.

(a) Unexplained variations in job running times might be recorded.
(b) Excessive machine down-time is sometimes a problem.
(c) Mixed workloads of large and small jobs might be scheduled inefficiently.

4 SYSTEMS PERFORMANCE

12/99

4.1 In general terms the performance of a system may be evaluated on the basis of whether it meets the basic needs to provide information of the required quality (timely, accurate, relevant to business needs, clear etc).

4.2 A simple test is whether the information that the system is capable of providing is actually being used: in other words, do users have *confidence* in it.

4.3 However, it is not possible to identify and isolate every consequence of a project and the impact of each on organisational effectiveness. To achieve some approximation to a complete evaluation, therefore, certain indirect measures must be used.

(a) Significant task relevance attempts to observe the results of system use.

For example, document turnround times might have improved following the acquisition of a document image processing system, or minutes of meetings might be made available and distributed faster following the addition of a company secretarial function to a local area network.

(b) The willingness to pay of users might give an indication of value.

Users can be asked how much they (their department) would be prepared to pay in order to gain the benefit of a certain upgrade, for example the availability of a particular report. Inter-departmental pricing will be a critical factor in the success of this approach.

(c) Systems logs may give an indication of the value of the system if it is a 'voluntary use' system, such as an external database.

(d) User information satisfaction is a concept which attempts to find out, by asking users, how they rate their satisfaction with a system. They may be asked for their views on timeliness, quality of output, response times, processing and their overall confidence in the system.

(e) The adequacy of system documentation may be measurable in terms of how often manuals are actually used and the number of errors found or amendments made. However, low usage of a user manual, for instance, may mean either that the manual is useless or that the system is so good that it is self-explanatory.

Exercise 3

Operational evaluation should consider, among other issues, whether input data is properly provided and output is useful. Output documents are often considered by users to be of marginal value, perhaps of use for background information only. In spite of this there is a tendency to continue producing existing reports.

How might you identify whether a report is being used?

Solution

The method chosen depends on how imaginative you are.

You could simply cease production of the report and see if anyone asks for it when it fails to appear. (If they ask for it simply in order to add it to a file, you can draw your own conclusions.)

A study could be carried out to see what each recipient of the report does with it and assess its importance.

A report pricing structure could be implemented - this would be a strong incentive to functional management to cancel requests for unnecessary output.

4.4 Performance reviews will vary in content from organisation to organisation, but the matters which will probably be looked at are as follows.

(a) The growth rates in file sizes and the number of transactions processed by the system. Trends should be analysed and projected to assess whether there are likely to be problems with lengthy processing time or an inefficient file structure due to the volume of processing.

(b) The clerical manpower needs for the system, and deciding whether they are more or less than estimated.

(c) The identification of any delays in processing and an assessment of the consequences of any such delays.

(d) An assessment of the efficiency of security procedures, in terms of number of breaches, number of viruses encountered.

(e) A check of the error rates for input data. High error rates may indicate inefficient preparation of input documents, an inappropriate method of data capture or poor design of input media.

(f) An examination of whether output from the computer is being used to good purpose. (Is it used? Is it timely? Does it go to the right people?)

(g) Operational running costs, examined to discover any inefficient programs or processes. This examination may reveal excessive costs for certain items although in total, costs may be acceptable.

Improving performance

4.5 Computer systems efficiency audits are concerned with improving outputs from the system and their use, or reducing the costs of system inputs. With falling costs of computer hardware and software, and continual technological advances there should often be scope for improvements in computer systems, which an audit ought to be able to identify.

Outputs from a computer system

4.6 With regard to outputs, the efficiency of a computer system would be enhanced in any of the following ways.

(a) More outputs of some value could be produced by the same input resources.

For example:

(i) If the system could process more transactions.

(ii) If the system could produce more management information (eg sensitivity analysis).

(iii) If the system could make information available to more people who might need it.

(b) Outputs of little value could be eliminated from the system, thus making savings in the cost of inputs.

For example:

(i) If reports are produced too frequently, should they be produced less often?

(ii) If reports are distributed too widely, should the distribution list be shortened?

(iii) If reports are too bulky, can they be reduced in size?

(c) The timing of outputs could be better.

Information should be available in good time for the information-user to be able to make good use of it. Reports that are issued late might lose their value. Computer systems could give managers immediate access to the information they require, by means of file enquiry or special software (such as databases or spreadsheet modelling packages).

(d) It might be found that outputs are not as satisfactory as they should be, perhaps because:

  (i) Access to information from the system is limited, and could be improved by the use of a database and a network system.

  (ii) Available outputs are is restricted because of the method of data processing used (eg batch processing instead of real-time processing) or the type of equipment used (eg stand-alone PCs compared with client/server systems).

Exercise 4

What elements of hardware and software might restrict the capabilities of a system?

Solution

A system's capabilities might be limited by the following restrictions.

(a) The size of the computer's memory.
(b) The power of the processor.
(c) The capacity of the computer's backing storage.
(d) The number of printers linked to the computer.
(e) The number of terminals.
(f) The software's capabilities.

Inputs to a computer system

4.7 The efficiency of a computer system could be improved if the same volume (and frequency) of output could be achieved with fewer input resources, and at less cost.

4.8 Some of the ways in which this could be done have already been mentioned.

(a) Multi-user or network systems might be more efficient than stand-alone systems.

Multi-user systems allow several input operators to work on the same files at the same time, so that if one person has a heavy workload and another is currently short of work, the person who has some free time can help his or her busy colleague - thus improving operator efficiency.

(b) Real-time systems might be more efficient than batch processing.

(c) Using computers and external storage media with bigger storage capacity.

A frequent complaint is that 'waiting time' for the operator can be very long and tedious. Computer systems with better backing storage facilities can reduce this operator waiting time, and so be more efficient.

(d) Using more up to date software.

4.9 Management might also wish to consider whether time spent checking and correcting input data can be eliminated. An alternative method of input might be chosen. For example bar codes and scanners should eliminate the need to check for input errors.

BPP PUBLISHING

Exercise 5

Draw up a brief set of procedures for reviewing the performance of a MIS.

Solution

Procedure for reviewing the performance of the existing MIS:

(a) Check the performance of the MIS against the business objectives - ensure that the information systems strategy fully supports the corporate plan.

(b) Measure the capacity of the system to handle the forecast growth rate in transactions.

(c) Ensure that there is sufficient hardware capacity for the continued efficient service and anticipated demand for increased storage.

(d) Check performance of peripherals, for example. print servers and printers.

(e) Analyse errors and report areas of concern.

(f) Review system reliability, noting matters such as frequency of breakdowns and particularly security.

(g) Check the operating system, particularly for security.

(h) Carry out a full cost benefit analysis.

(i) Invite user feedback:

    (i) Management and staff should be consulted to ensure reliability and that outputs meet requirements.

    (ii) Customers should be consulted to ensure the system supports satisfaction.

(j) Review staff expertise: check on recruitment and training schemes and the level of staff resources.

Some elements of the performance testing should be regularly conducted to ensure standards are maintained. Benchmarking may be used to monitor such matters as the processor speed and test data may be used for audit and security. Regular reports should be made to senior management with clear recommendations.

5 POST-IMPLEMENTATION REVIEW

5.1 Post-implementation review should establish whether the objectives and targeted performance criteria have been met, and if not, why not, and what should be done about it.

5.2 In appraising the operation of the new system immediately after the changeover, comparison should be made between actual and predicted performance. This will include (amongst other items):

(a) consideration of throughput speed (time between input and output);
(b) use of computer storage (both internal and external)
(c) the number and type of errors/queries;
(d) the cost of processing (data capture, preparation, storage and output media, etc).

5.3 A special steering committee may be set up to ensure that post-implementation reviews are carried out, although the internal audit department may be required to do the work of carrying out the reviews.

5.4 The post-implementation measurements should not be made too soon after the system goes live, or else results will be abnormally affected by 'teething' problems, lack of user familiarity and resistance to change.

The post-implementation review report

5.5 The findings of a post-implementation review team should be formalised in a report.

(a) A summary of their findings should be provided, emphasising any areas where the system has been found to be unsatisfactory.

(b) A review of system performance should be provided. This will address the matters outlined above, such as run times and error rates.

(c) A cost-benefit review should be included, comparing the forecast costs and benefits identified at the time of the feasibility study with actual costs and benefits.

(d) Recommendations should be made as to any further action or steps which should be taken to improve performance.

Chapter roundup

- There are three types of systems maintenance. Corrective maintenance is carried out following a systems failure, perfective maintenance aims to make enhancements to systems and adaptive maintenance takes account of anticipated changes in the processing environment.

- The criteria for systems evaluation mirror those used in the feasibility study. A system can be evaluated by reference to technical, operational, social and economic factors. Similarly, the techniques used are similar to those already employed. A cost-benefit review can be performed and compared with the original cost-benefit analysis, and investment appraisal techniques are still applicable.

- Efficiency is a measure of how well resources have been utilised irrespective of the purpose for which they are employed. Effectiveness is a measure of whether the organisation has achieved its objectives.

- Systems evaluation may use computer-based monitoring. Methods include the use of hardware monitors, software monitors and systems logs.

- Performance reviews can be carried out to look at a wide range of systems functions and characteristics. Technological change often gives scope to improve the quality of outputs or reduce the extent or cost of inputs.

- During the post-implementation review, an evaluation of the system is carried out to see whether the targeted performance criteria have been met and to carry out a review of costs and benefits. The review should culminate in the production of a report and recommendations.

Quick quiz

1 What factors contribute to the need for maintenance? (see para 1.4)
2 What are the principles of good programming practice? (1.10)
3 What provisions might you find in a software maintenance contract? (1.12)
4 What criteria are used for systems evaluation? (2.2, 2.3)
5 What is a hardware monitor? (3.2 - 3.4)
6 What matters might a performance review consider? (4.4)
7 How can outputs be improved? (4.6)
8 What would you expect to see in a post-implementation review report? (5.5)

Now try illustrative questions 20 and 33 at the end of the Study Text

Chapter 14

AUDIT AND SECURITY

This chapter covers the following topics.

1   Risk management

2   Back-up procedures

3   Controls over data integrity

4   Computer audit

5   Passwords and logical access systems

6   Personnel security planning

7   Hackers and viruses

8   Privacy and data protection

Introduction

In this final chapter we look at some of the more practical aspects of the management of information systems: how to make sure that you keep the information you have, how to make control the quality of the information you have and how to protect it from those who may wish to steal it, misuse it, or damage it in some way.

---

1   RISK MANAGEMEMT

Risk and risk management

1.1   With so much more data being held in computerised form, and much higher investment in IT, all organisations should attempt to identify threats to its information systems, ie potential dangers which, if realised, would destroy or alter the working of an information system and the vulnerability in the information system (ie its weak points).

1.2   The best way of dealing with such risks is to avoid them completely, in other words to modify the system so that it is not vulnerable to risk. Failing this, risk must be managed.

1.3   Organisations and their environment change constantly and so risk management is an ongoing process, not a one-off exercise. A regularly reviewed security policy is needed, not simply a collection of measures adopted ad hoc.

1.4   Risk management involves three stages.

(a)   Risk assessment

    (i)   Identification of risks

    (ii)   Quantification of risks

    (iii)   Placing risks in order of potential loss

    The importance of some attempt to quantify potential loss in financial terms is that this is a measure against which the cost of safeguards can be assessed.

(b) Risk minimisation

    (i) Identification of counter-measures

    (ii) Costing of counter-measures

    (iii) Selection of counter-measures. Insignificant risks may not justify the cost of setting up and operating controls.

    (iv) Implementation of counter-measures

    (v) Draw up contingency plans in case all counter-measures are ineffective

Scenario analysis is a technique whereby descriptions of a number of possible loss-causing events are circulated to the relevant functional managers who assess which are the most probable. Security measures are taken against any events which are thought likely to result in loss.

(c) Risk transfer (insurance)

It is impossible to eliminate all risk. Risks that cannot be covered by security measures should be insured against, so that at least the financial consequences are not too severe.

Contingency planning
12/97, 6/98

1.5 A contingency is an unscheduled interruption of computing services that requires measures outside the day-to-day routine operating procedures. The preparation of a contingency plan is one of the stages in the development of an organisation-wide security policy. A contingency plan is necessary in case of some terrible disaster occurring to the system, or if some of the security measures discussed elsewhere fail.

1.6 A disaster occurs where the system for some reason breaks down, leading to potential losses of equipment, data or funds. The victim, however, cannot simply wait before continuing operations. The system must recover as soon as possible so that further losses are not incurred, and current losses can be rectified.

Exercise 1

What actions or events might lead to a systems breakdown?

Solution

System breakdowns can occur in a variety of circumstances, for example:

(a) fire destroying data files and equipment;
(b) flooding (so it is best not to site the computer room in a basement);
(c) a computer virus completely destroying a data or program file;
(d) a technical fault in the equipment;
(e) accidental destruction of telecommunications links (eg builders severing a cable);
(f) terrorist attack;
(g) system failure caused by software bugs which were not discovered at the design stage;
(h) internal sabotage (eg logic bombs built into the software);
(i) accidental errors by employees;
(j) failure to take back-ups.

1.7 Any contingency plan must therefore provide for:

(a) standby procedures so that some operations can be performed while normal services are disrupted;

(b) recovery procedures once the cause of the breakdown has been discovered or corrected;

(c) the personnel management policies to ensure that (a) and (b) above are implemented properly.

Contents of a contingency plan

1.8   The contents of a contingency plan will include the following.

Section	Comment
Definition of responsibilities	It is important that somebody (a manager or co-ordinator) is designated to take control in a crisis. This individual can then delegate specific tasks or responsibilities to other designated personnel.
Priorities	Limited resources may be available for processing. Some tasks are more important than others. These must be established in advance. Similarly, the recovery program may indicate that certain areas must be tackled first.
Backup and standby arrangements	These may be with other installations, with a company (eg a computer bureau) that provides such services; or manual procedures.
Communication with staff	The problems of a disaster can be confounded by poor communication between members of staff.
Public relations	If the disaster has a public impact, the recovery team may come under pressure from the public or from the media.
Risk assessment	Some way must be found of assessing the requirements of the problem, if it is contained, with the continued operation of the organisation as a whole.

Standby facilities

1.9   Standby facilities which can be used for disaster recovery include the following.

   (a)   Computer bureaux can agree to make their own systems available in the event of an emergency. Such an arrangement has to be specified in advance, as there might be other demands on a bureau's resources.

   (b)   Co-operating with other organisations in the locality, through a mutual aid agreement, may be a way of pooling resources. However, these other organisations themselves might not, in the event, be able to spare the computer time.

   (c)   Disaster standby companies offer office premises with desks, telephones and storage space which are equipped with hardware and possibly software of the same type as that used by their customers.

   (d)   Hardware duplication. The provision of back-up computers is obviously costly if these systems have no other function. However, many organisations use several smaller computer systems rather than a single, large one, and find that a significant level of protection against system faults can be provided by shifting operations to one of the systems still functioning.

2   BACK-UP PROCEDURES   *6/98*

2.1   Back-up means to make a copy in anticipation of future failure or corruption. A back-up copy of a file is a duplicate copy kept separately from the main system and only used if the original fails.

Re-creating file data when a file is lost or corrupted

2.2   It is possible for computer files to become corrupted when being written to becoming damaged and possibly unreadable. Files may also be deleted in error.

2.3 The purpose of backing up data is to ensure that the most recent usable copy of the data can be recovered and restored in the event of loss or corruption on the system.

2.4 A related concept is that of archiving. Archiving data is the process of moving (by copying) data from primary storage, such as a hard disk, to tape or other portable media for long-term storage.

2.5 Archiving provides a legally acceptable business history, while freeing up hard disk space.

2.6 In a well-planned data back-up scheme, a copy of backed up data is delivered (preferably daily) to a secure off-site storage facility.

2.7 A tape rotation scheme can provide a restorable history from one day to several years, depending on the needs of the business.

2.8 A well-planned back-up and archive strategy should include:

(a) A plan and schedule for the regular back-up of critical data.
(b) Archive plans.
(c) A disaster recovery plan that includes off-site storage.

2.9 Regular tests should be undertaken to verify that data backed up can be successfully restored.

2.10 The intervals at which back-ups are performed must be decided. Most organisations back up their data daily.

2.11 A rotation scheme that provides an appropriate data history must be selected. The Grandfather, Father, Son scheme uses twelve tapes - allowing recovery of three months data.

Grandfather, Father, Son back-up rotation scheme

Tape No.	Tape name	When written to	Overwritten
Tape 1	Son 1	Every Monday	Weekly
Tape 2	Son 2	Every Tuesday	Weekly
Tape 3	Son 3	Every Wednesday	Weekly
Tape 4	Son 4	Every Thursday	Weekly
Tape 5	**Father** week 1	**First** Friday	**Monthly**
Tape 6	Father week 2	Second Friday	Monthly
Tape 7	Father week 3	Third Friday	Monthly
Tape 8	Father week 4	Fourth Friday	Monthly
Tape 9	Father week 5 (if needed)	Fifth Friday	Monthly
Tape 10	**Grandfather** month 1	**Last business day** month 1	**Quarterly**
Tape 11	Grandfather month 2	Last business day month 2	Quarterly
Tape 12	Grandfather month 3	Last business day month 3	Quarterly

2.12 Even with a well planned back-up strategy some re-inputting may be required. For example, if after three hours work on a Wednesday a file becomes corrupt, the Tuesday version can be restored – but Wednesday's work will need to be re-input.

3   CONTROLS OVER DATA INTEGRITY

Data integrity and controls

3.1   Data will maintain its integrity if it is complete and not corrupted. This means that:

(a)   the original capture of the data must be controlled in such a way as to ensure that the results are complete and correct;

(b)   any processing and storage of data must maintain the completeness and correctness of the data captured;

(c)   that reports or other output should be set up so that they, too, are complete and correct.

3.2   Controls must therefore be put in place to ensure that:

(a)   problems are identified and put right when they occur;

(b)   errors are recognised and eliminated;

(c)   there is a record of all processing that occurs;

(d)   all the data that *should* be processed *is* processed, at the correct time and in the correct order;

(e)   the system is capable of recovery following a breakdown.

Some of these controls may be simple manual clerical checks. Others can be performed by the software.

Controls over input

3.3   Human error is the greatest data security weakness in computer systems, and controls ought to be applied to reduce the likelihood of errors, or to identify errors and the loss of data when these occur.

3.4   The extent of the input controls will depend on the method of processing input data (eg keyboard input, OCR document input etc) and the cost of making an input error. If the consequences of input errors would be costly, the system should include more extensive input controls than it would need if the cost of making input errors were insignificant.

Controls over data capture

3.5   Errors in data capture are difficult to spot once they have been made, because they are often errors on the 'source' document.

(a)   They can be reduced by double-checking. One person's work might provide a cross-check on the accuracy of another's. For example, errors in recording suppliers' invoices in the purchase day book could be double-checked by getting another person to add up the total amount of invoices received that day, from the invoices themselves.

(b)   The system can be designed to reduce the likelihood of errors arising in the first place, by including as much pre-printed information on the data recording document as possible, and by giving clear instructions about how data documents should be filled in.

(c)   The use of turnround documents and OCR, MICR, bar coding, or in some applications, plastic cards with magnetic strips containing some of the input data, could be used to reduce the need for manually-prepared input data, and so limit the frequency of data capture errors.

Controls over transcribing data

3.6   If input data must be prepared manually, controls can be applied to minimise the number of errors.

258

(a) Staff who prepare data for input should be well-trained and properly supervised.

(b) Data input documents should be designed in a format to help the person preparing the data to fill them in properly.

(c) As we have see, when data is input by keyboard, the screen should be designed to help the keyboard operator to input the correct data.

Controls over processing

File identification checks

3.7 A program can check that the correct file has been loaded for processing before it will begin its processing operations. It can do this by checking the 'label or 'header' properties of the file, and comparing this data with the equivalent data for the file that it has been instructed to process. In other words, if the computer has been instructed to process file A, it will first of all check that file A has indeed been loaded for processing, and that it is the correct version of the file.

Checkpoints and recovery procedures

3.8 A checkpoint or *restart program* is a utility that intervenes at intervals (checkpoints) during the running of a program, and dumps the work done so far on to a back-up file.

3.9 Should anything turn out to be 'wrong' with the running of the program or if the system suddenly crashes, the checkpoint/restart program can be used to get the program back to a checkpoint/restart position before the error occurred, and restart the program with conditions exactly as they were before - for example copying back the contents of the dump file into the memory.

Exercise 2

Give a modern example of a checkpoint program.

Solution

In Microsoft Office applications there is an Autosave utility, which the user can set to save work automatically every, say, 15 minutes.

Control totals

3.10 A control total is the sum of specified fields. It might be any of the following.

(a) The number of records on a file.

(b) The total of the values of a particular field in all the records on a file - eg the total of debts outstanding in all the customer records on a sales ledger file.

(c) The number of records in a batch (batch control total).

(d) A hash total, which is a control total that has no meaning, except as a control check; for example, the total of supplier code numbers on a purchase ledger file.

3.11 Control total reconciliation checks are often written into programs to ensure that no records have been lost or duplicated, input files have been read fully and all output records have been written to the output files.

Verification and validation

3.12 Verification is the process of ensuring that the data that has been input is the same as the data on the source document.

3.13   Validation is the process of ensuring that the data that has been input has a value that is possible for that kind of data, for example that a number is not more than a certain amount.

3.14   Data should be subjected to both types of control if possible because it may be in a valid form (for example, four digits) but be totally inaccurate.

Data verification

3.15   One method of data verification if data must be converted from one form to another for input (for example from a paper document on to disk) is to input the data twice and then get the software to perform a like-for-like comparison.

3.16   The most common method of verification, however is encouraging staff to look for errors. If input is done by keyboard, the input data will be shown on screen, and a visual check on the data can be made. For instance if a customer code is keyed in, the screen might display the name and address of the customer automatically and this will alert the user if he has entered the wrong code.

Validation checks

3.17   Many checks on the validity of input data can be written into the system's programs.

3.18   When a validation check identifies an error, the record concerned will probably be rejected and processed no further without correction. Rejection reports will be printed out or messages displayed on a VDU screen.

3.19   Some data validation checks are outlined below. You ought to be aware what they are and when each type of check would be suitable. Obviously each application will have validation checks which are relevant to its particular processing requirements: not all of these checks are necessary in all circumstances.

Range checks

3.20   These are designed to ensure that the data in a certain record field lies within predetermined limits. For example in a wages application, the program may contain instructions to reject any clock card with 'hours worked' outside the range 10-80 hours, and to print out a special report (for checking) for any clock card with hours worked outside the range 35-60.

Limit checks

3.21   Sometimes called credibility or reasonableness checks, these are very similar to range checks, but check that data is not below a certain value, or above a certain value. In the previous example, the check on 'hours worked' might be that the value in the record field should not exceed 80 (or, in other words, is in the range 0-80).

(a)   With a range check, there is an upper and lower bound

(b)   With a limit check, there is either an upper or lower bound, but not both.

Existence checks

3.22   These are checks to ensure that the data is valid within a particular system. For example if the user inputs a stock code a program would check that the stock code exists by looking up the stock code number of the record against a reference file.

Format checks

3.23 Format checks help to ensure that the format (and size) of the data in a field is correct, for example:

(a) check that the format is all numeric 1234 (here, four figures)

(b) check that the format is all alphabetic ABCDE (here, five letters)

(c) check that the format is alphanumeric A123 (here, one letter followed by three figures)

Consistency checks

3.24 These involve checking that data in one field is consistent with data in another field. For example, in a payroll system, there might be a check that if the employee is a Grade C worker, he or she must belong to Department 5,6 or 9.

3.25 A consistency check is also called a cross field validation check.

Completeness checks

3.26 A check can be made to ensure that all records have been processed. For example, if a weekly processing run must include one record for each of the 5 working days of the week, a completeness check can ensure that there are 5 input records, one for each day.

3.27 Completeness checks on individual fields would be checks that an item of data has not been omitted from an input record.

Check digits

3.28 Computer records make extensive use of codes but it is very difficult for the human eye to detect an error in a code on a casual inspection.

3.29 By splitting codes into several groups of three or four digits, divided by a space or stroke (eg credit card numbers), it makes it easier for the data preparation staff to write codes without making errors. However, coding errors, especially transposition errors, may well escape detection before input to a computer system.

3.30 To avoid the situation where the computer treats an incorrect code number as the correct one, systems of self-checking numbers are used. The most common have check digits. These are digits that are added to the end of the code and give the whole new number some special mathematical property.

3.31 Check digits are commonly used in computer systems for key field identification codes (eg customer number, employee number, student number) but may not be considered necessary where the volume is low and/or the code number is less than five digits, because the likelihood of data collection errors or data preparation errors will be much smaller.

Exercise 3

The effectiveness of controls over input is not always as great as a computer user might like. Evaluate the effectiveness of the following five typical checks on input to a purchase ledger system.

(a) Input transaction displayed on VDU screen with keyboard input, for a visual check by the input clerk.

(b) Check digit in the supplier account code number.

(c)   Batching records with a batch header control slip.

(d)   Display of supplier account details on screen when the account code is keyed in.

(e)   Double keying-in of all input transactions by different staff.

Solution

(a)   This depends on how good the input clerk is at his or her job. The risk of keying-in errors will be high. Also there is a possibility of a deliberate keying-in error by a dishonest clerk.

(b)   This reduces the risk of error in the input of the account code number. But it is a check on just one field of data, and so is limited in the number of errors it can find.

(c)   Batching is a time-consuming operation, but it should identify the loss of data, or the failure to input data records.

(d)   This should prevent errors where the wrong supplier account is updated. However, the error depends on the input clerk checking the screen and looking at the account details displayed. Experience shows that clerks will often not bother to do this when they have a lot of input records to key in.

(e)   This should identify most keying-in errors, and also prevent dishonesty or fraud by an input clerk. It is particularly useful where only range and format checks are possible, since these do not necessarily prevent transcription errors. However, double keying-in takes twice the effort and cost of once-only keying-in.

Output controls

3.32   A system should be designed to include certain controls over output from computer processing.

(a)   In a batch processing system, where data is sent off to a computer centre, there should be a check to make sure that all batches have been processed and returned.

(b)   All input records that have been rejected by data validation checks and master file update checks must be looked at to find out the cause of the error.

Corrected data should then be prepared for re-input. Some errors might need immediate correction, such as rejected input records in a payroll program for preparing the monthly salary payments to staff.

(c)   Output should be correctly distributed, and a record kept of the distributions that have been made. Careful controls are needed over confidential outputs, to make sure that they do not get into the wrong hands.

(d)   Output on to tapes, files and CDs should be properly labelled and stored.

Exercise 4

Drawing on the whole of the knowledge you have acquired from this Study Text, explain *briefly* how would you ensure that a computerised database provided reliable and up to date information.

Solution

Here are some possible measures. You may have had further ideas.

(a)   Ensuring the highest quality data enters the system. In this connection using appropriate verification and validation checks.

(b)   Training of staff to meet the required performance standards (regularly reviewing effectiveness and assessing further training needs).

(c)   Close liaison with systems developers to ensure that the database structure meets my current and future needs.

(d)   Ensuring the procedures are in place for a proper maintenance contract and appropriate back-up and emergency procedures.

(e)   Carrying out suitable systems audits to check for data integrity and guard against fraud.

(f)   Installing security measures; physical security of the environment and levels of passwords to restrict access.

(g) Review the legal obligations to ensure system complies with such legislation as the Data Protection Act and relevant property legislation.

(h) Regular checks on the output, its accuracy, relevance, format, presentation etc.

(i) Obtaining feedback from other system users to ensure that the service provided by the system gives them confidence and satisfaction. In this connection the views of shareholders, stockbrokers, insurers, property tenants and others will be valuable.

4 COMPUTER AUDIT

Audit of computer systems

4.1 The obvious problem with auditing a computer system is that processing operations cannot be seen, and the results of processing might be stored on disk.

Audit trails

4.2 The original concept of an audit trail was to print out data at all stages of processing so that a manager or auditor could follow transactions stage-by-stage through a system to ensure that they had been processed correctly.

4.3 Modern computer methods have now cut out much of this laborious, time-consuming stage-by-stage working but there should still be some means of identifying individual records and the input and output documents associated with the processing of any individual transaction.

4.4 An audit trail should be provided so that every transaction on a file contains a unique reference back to the original source of the input (eg a sales system transaction record should hold a reference to the customer order, delivery note and invoice). Where file records are updated several times, or from several sources, the provision of a satisfactory management and audit trail is more difficult but some attempt should nevertheless be made to provide one.

Round the computer and through the computer audits

4.5 Some years ago, it was widely considered that it was possible to audit a computer based system without having any detailed knowledge of computers.

4.6 The auditor would audit 'round the computer' by ignoring the procedures which take place within the computer programs and concentrating solely on the input and corresponding output. Audit procedures would include checking authorisation, coding and control totals of input and checking the output with source documents and clerical control tests.

4.7 This view is now frowned upon and it is recognised that one of the principal problems facing the auditor is that of acquiring an understanding of the workings of the computer system itself.

4.8 It is now customary for auditors to audit 'through the computer'. This involves an examination of the detailed processing routines of the computer to determine whether the controls in the system are adequate to ensure complete and correct processing of all data.

4.9 One of the major reasons why the 'round the computer' audit approach is no longer considered adequate is that as the complexity of computer systems has increased there has been a corresponding loss of audit trail. One way the auditor can try to overcome the difficulties of lost audit trails is by employing computer aided audit techniques (CAATs).

Computer assisted auditing techniques (CAATs)

4.10 There is no mystique about using a computer to help with auditing. You may well use common computer assisted audit techniques all the time in your daily work without realising that this is what you are doing.

    (a) Most modern systems allow data to be manipulated in various ways and extracted into an ad hoc report. For instance a complete list of debtor balances could be filtered so that only a list of those over their credit limits was printed out.

    (b) Even if reporting capabilities are limited, the data can often be exported directly into a spreadsheet package (sometimes using simple Windows-type cut and paste facilities in very modern systems) and then analysed, say, by sorting in order of highest balances, or recalculating totals using the SUM function.

    (c) Most systems have searching facilities that are much quicker to use than searching through print-outs by hand. This offsets the so-called 'loss of audit trail' to a significant extent. The trail is still there, even though it may have to be followed through in electronic form.

4.11 There are a variety of packages specially designed either to ease the auditing task itself (for example selecting records to investigate, based on various statistical sampling techniques or calculating audit risk), or to carry out audit interrogations of computerised data automatically. There are also a variety of ways of testing the processing that is carried out.

Using the right files

4.12 Before any audit software is run, the auditors should check the identity and version of the data files and programs used, whether they are taken from the company's records and systems or supplied by themselves. This will normally involve checking with external evidence, such as control totals, and looking at file lengths, dates, times or other file properties.

Audit interrogation software

4.13 Interrogation software performs the sort of checks on data that auditors might otherwise have to perform by hand.

    (a) Programs may have to be written specially, in which case the internal auditor must take care not to rely to too great an extent on the IT staff whose systems and processing are being examined.

    (b) Packages are available commercially from a variety of software suppliers and also from firms of external auditors.

4.14 Here are some of the uses of audit packages.

    (a) Identify trends, pinpoint exceptions and potential areas of concern

    (b) Locate errors and potential fraud by comparing and analysing files according to end user criteria

    (c) Recalculate and verify balances

    (d) Identify control issues and ensure compliance with standards

    (e) Age and analyse accounts receivable, payables or any other time-sensitive transactions

    (f) Recover expenses or lost revenues by testing for duplicate payments, gaps in invoice numbers or unbilled services

    (g) Test for unauthorised employee/supplier relationships

    (h) Automate repetitive tasks by creating custom applications or batches

4.15 Audit interrogation software is particularly appropriate during substantive testing of transactions and especially balances. By using audit software, the auditors may scrutinise large volumes of data and concentrate skilled manual resources on the investigation of results, rather than on the extraction of information.

Test data

4.16 An obvious way of seeing whether a system is processing data in the way that it should be is to input some test data and see what happens. The expected results can be calculated in advance and then compared with the results that actually arise.

4.17 The problem with test data is that any resulting corruption of the data files has to be corrected. This is difficult with modern real-time systems, which often have built in (and highly desirable) controls to ensure that data entered *cannot* easily be removed without leaving a mark. Consequently test data is used less and less as a CAAT.

Advanced audit facilities

4.18 The results of using test data would, in any case, be completely distorted if the programs used to process it were not the ones normally used for processing. For example a fraudulent member of the IT department might substitute a version of the program that gave the correct results, purely for the duration of the test, and then replace it with a version that siphoned off the company's funds into his own bank account.

4.19 To allow a continuous review of the data recorded and the manner in which it is treated by the system, it may be possible to use CAATs referred to as 'embedded audit facilities'.

4.20 An embedded facility consists of audit modules that are incorporated into the computer element of the enterprise's accounting system. Two frequently encountered examples are Integrated Test Facility (ITF) and Systems Control and Review File (SCARF).

Integrated test facility

4.21 Integrated Test Facility involves the creation of a fictitious entity (for example a department or a customer) within the framework of the regular application. Transactions are then posted to the fictitious entity along with the regular transactions. The results produced by the normal processing cycle are compared with what should have been produced, which is predetermined by other means.

Systems Control and Review File (SCARF)

4.22 To operate *SCARF* each account record in a system is given two 'auditor's' fields: a Yes/No field indicating whether or not SCARF applies to this account; and a monetary value which is a threshold amount set by the auditors.

4.23 Subsequently all transactions posted to a SCARF account which had a value in excess of the threshold amount would also be written to a separate 'SCARF' file. This technique thus enables the auditors to monitor material transactions or sensitive accounts with ease and provides an assurance that all such transactions are under scrutiny.

Other techniques

Simulation

4.24 Simulation (or 'parallel simulation)' entails the preparation of a separate program that simulates the processing of the organisation's real system. Real data can then be passed not only through the system proper but also through the simulated program. For example the simulation program may be used to re-perform controls such as those used to identify any missing items from a sequence.

Program logic and coding

4.25 Two further types of CAATs worth mentioning are:

(a) logical path analysis, which will draw flowcharts of the program logic; and

(b) code comparison programs, which compare the original specified program to the current program to detect unauthorised amendments.

Knowledge-based systems

4.26 Decision support systems' and expert systems can be used to assist with the auditors' own judgement and decisions. This is likely to save time and money as such methods increase the efficiency of the audit procedures used, and the maintenance of audit records. Other cost savings include the reduction in the number of staff required, and the fact that routine tasks can be assigned to technicians, who are helped by the expert system.

Internal audit

4.27 Internal auditors are full-time staff whose function is to monitor and report on the running of the company's operations. The management of an organisation will wish to establish systems to ensure that business activities are carried out efficiently. They will institute clerical, administrative and financial controls. The task of internal audit is to ensure that these systems and controls are operating as they should be, and to suggest improvements if not.

4.28 The Auditing Practices Board defines internal audit as:

'An appraisal or monitoring activity established by management and directors for the review of the accounting and internal control systems as a service to the entity. It functions by, amongst other things, examining, evaluating and reporting to management and the directors on the adequacy and effectiveness of components of the accounting and internal control systems.'

4.29 Internal audit was originally concerned entirely with the financial records, checking for weaknesses in the accounting systems and errors in the accounts. The function of internal audit has now been extended to the monitoring of all aspects of an organisation's activities.

Maintaining efficiency

4.30 Internal audit work in this area can be divided into a number of activities.

(a) *Review of the accounting and internal control systems*: the establishment of adequate accounting and internal control systems is a responsibility of management and the directors which demands proper attention on a continuous basis. Often, internal audit is assigned specific responsibility for reviewing the design of the systems, monitoring their operation and recommending improvements thereto.

(b) *Examination of financial and operating information*: this may include review of the means used to identify, measure, classify and report such information and specific enquiry into individual items including detailed testing of transactions, balances and procedures.

(c) *Review of the economy, efficiency and effectiveness* of operations including non-financial controls of an organisation. Operational audit will look at *ways* of working, for instance how information is exchanged between different departments. This may simply be a review of office layout or it may be the type of work that is now more commonly known as Business Process Re-engineering.

(d) *Review of compliance* with laws, regulations and other external requirements and with internal policies and directives and other requirements including appropriate authorisation of transactions.

Identifying fraud

4.31 Internal audit also often involves *special investigations* into particular areas, for example suspected fraud. The detailed analysis of transactions that the internal auditor carries out is the most likely control to reveal inconsistencies in data that may suggest that fraudulent activity is taking place, and internal audit skills in auditing transactions and systems and setting up controls are an effective means of determining the extent of a fraud, how a fraud was perpetrated, how it can be avoided in future.

4.32 The more common types of fraud are as follows.

- Ghost employees
- Miscasting of the payroll
- Stealing unclaimed wages
- Collusion with external parties
- Teeming and lading
- Altering cheques and inflating expense claims
- Stealing assets
- Issuing false credit notes
- Failing to record all sales

4.33 Almost all of these deceptions are easier to perpetrate in organisations that have computerised information systems, because the data is stored electronically: it cannot physically be seen by humans unless it is converted into another format. Moreover, factors such as increased computer literacy and emphasis in systems on accessibility of data has increased opportunities to commit fraud.

4.34 This means, on the one hand, that internal auditors now have to be expert in computer systems, but on the other, that they have available to them sophisticated Computer Assisted Audit Techniques, as described above.

4.35 The role of the internal auditor has thus changed in recent years from that of number cruncher to that of detective and highly skilled systems expert.

5 PASSWORDS AND LOGICAL ACCESS SYSTEMS

5.1 Passwords are a set of characters which may be allocated to a person, a terminal or a facility which are required to be keyed into the system before further access is permitted. Passwords can be applied to data files, program files and to parts of a program.

(a) One password may be required to read a file, but another to write new data to it.

(b) The terminal user can be restricted to the use of certain files and programs (eg in a banking system, junior grades of staff are only allowed to access certain routine programs).

5.2 In order to access a system the user needs first to enter a string of characters. If what is entered matches a password issued to an authorised user or valid for that particular terminal the system permits access. Otherwise the system shuts down and may record the attempted unauthorised access.

5.3 Keeping track of these attempts can alert managers to repeated efforts to break into the system; in these cases the culprits might be caught, particularly if there is an apparent pattern to their efforts.

5.4 The restriction of access to a system with passwords is effective and widely used but the widespread and growing use of PCs and networks is making physical isolation virtually impossible. The wider use of information systems requires that access to the system becomes equally widespread and easy. Requirements for system security must be balanced by the operational requirements for access: a rigidly enforced isolation of the system may significantly reduce the value of the system.

5.5 Passwords ought to be effective in keeping out unauthorised users, but they are by no means foolproof.

(a) By experimenting with possible passwords, an unauthorised person can gain access to a program or file by guessing the correct password. This is not as difficult as it may seem when too many computer users specify 'obvious' passwords for their files or programs. In addition computer programs are available that run through millions of possible combinations at lightning speed until the correct one is found.

(b) Someone who is authorised to access a data or program file may tell an unauthorised person what the password is, perhaps through carelessness.

(c) Many password systems come with standard passwords as part of the system, such as LETMEIN. It is essential for these to be removed if the system is to be at all secure. Such common passwords become widely known to people in the industry using similar packages.

(d) Password systems they rely upon users to use them conscientiously. Users can be extremely sloppy with their security control. Passwords are often left in plain view or 'hidden' beneath keyboards or inside desk drawers where virtually anyone could readily find them. A password system requires both a software system and strong organisational policies if it is to be effective.

BPP - Best Password Practice

Here is a checklist of points to be observed by computer users to whom passwords have been allocated.

- Keep your password secret. Do not reveal it to anyone else.

- Do not write it down. The second easiest way of revealing a password is to write it on an adhesive label and stick this to the VDU, the desk beneath the keyboard, the inside of a desk drawer or the underside of an overhead filing cabinet.

- Change your password regularly.

- Change and use your password discreetly. Even though a password does not show up on screen, it is easy for onlookers to see which keys are being used. (FRED is a popular password for this reason; the relevant keys are close together on a QWERTY keyboard.)

- Do not use an obvious password. (FRED is an obvious password. Your name or nickname is another)

- Change your password if you suspect that anyone else knows it.

Logical access systems

5.6 Whereas physical access control (doors, locks etc) is concerned with the prevention of unauthorised persons gaining access to the hardware, logical access control is concerned with preventing those who already have access to a terminal or a computer from gaining access to data or software.

5.7 In a logical access system, data and software, or individual computer systems, will be classified according to the sensitivity and confidentiality of data.

(a) Thus payroll data or details of the draft corporate budget for the coming year may be perceived as highly sensitive and made available to identified individuals only.

(b) Other financial information may be made available to certain groups of staff only, for example members of the finance function or a certain grade of management.

(c) Other data may be unrestricted.

5.8 A logical access system performs three operations when access is requested.

(a) Identification of the user.
(b) Authentication of user identity.
(c) Check on user authority.

Database controls

5.9 Databases present a particular problem for computer security. In theory, the database can be accessed by large numbers of people, and so the possibility of alteration, unauthorised disclosure or fraud is so much greater than with application-specific files.

5.10 It is possible to construct complicated password systems, and the DBMS can be programmed to give a limited view of its contents to particular users or restrict the disclosure of certain types of information to particular times of day. It is possible to build a set of privileges into the system, so allowing authorised users with a particular password to access more information.

5.11 However, there are problems ensuring that individuals do not circumvent the database by means of inference. If you ask enough questions, you should be able to infer from the replies the information you are really seeking.

5.12 For example, the database forbids you to ask if John is employee Category A. However, if you know there are only three employee categories, A, B, and C, and there is no prohibition on asking about categories B and C, you can work out the members of category A by process of elimination (ie neither B, or C, therefore A).

5.13 So-called 'inference controls' exist to make this difficult by limiting the number of queries, or by controlling the overlap between questions.

6   PERSONNEL SECURITY PLANNING   *6/98, 12/99*

6.1 Certain employees will always be placed in a position of trust, for example senior systems analysts, the database administrator and the computer security officer. With the growth of networks, almost all employees may be n a position to do damage to a computer system.

6.2 Although most employees are honest and well-intentioned, if they wish to do so, it may be relatively easy for individuals to compromise the security of an organisation.

6.3 The types of measure which can be used to control personnel people as follows.

(a) Careful recruitment
(b) Job rotation
(c) Supervision and observation by a superior
(d) Review of computer usage (for example via systems logs)
(e) Enforced vacations

6.4 The key is that security should depend on the minimum possible number of personnel; although this is a weakness, it is also a strength.

Job sensitivity analysis

6.5 Job sensitivity analysis is a system of review by the security and personnel functions, which seeks to identify risks by performing an analysis of each job and the potential for fraudulent behaviour inherent in the design of that job.

6.6 Every individual in an organisation has some opportunity to commit fraud. The potential which they will have to do so depends on a number of factors.

(a) Ability to gain access to critical resources
(b) Time available to plan and carry out fraudulent activities
(c) Skill
(d) Motivation

6.7 Job security analysis involves identification of valuable assets, for example portable computers, payments made to customers or postings to suspense accounts, and considers all those staff who might have an opportunity to cause loss.

6.8 There are a number of indications, or warning signs, which may suggest that an employee's behaviour should be investigated more closely. Many can be contained under the heading of evidence of unduly lavish lifestyles.

(a) Unexplained wealth, enabling for example purchase of a new car or house.

(b) Higher than usual spending patterns, on holiday entertainment, gambling etc.

(c) Liaisons with staff from rival businesses.

(d) Lack of respect for the organisation, for example poor timekeeping, expressions of disaffection or insubordination.

(e) Regular working 'after hours' even when this does not seem necessary.

6.9 There may of course be perfectly rational explanations for any of these indicators. The key is that any suspicions should be handled with utmost sensitivity. Unfounded accusations of dishonesty can at best ruin the individual's career, and a loss of staff morale is also likely.

6.10 At the same time, a 'softly softly' approach may warn the fraudster that he or she has been placed under suspicion. Absolute secrecy should be maintained while investigators set to work.

Computer fraud   *12/99*

6.11 Computer fraud usually involves the theft of funds by dishonest use of a computer system.

6.12 The type of computer fraud depends on the point in the system at which the fraud is perpetrated.

(a) *Input fraud.*

Data input is falsified; good examples are putting a non-existent employee on the salary file or a non-existent supplier to the purchases file.

(b) *Processing fraud.*

A programmer or someone who has broken into part of the system may alter a program. For example, in a large organisation, a 'patch' might be used to change a program so that 10 pence was deducted from every employee's pay cheque and sent to a fictitious account to which the perpetrator had access. A 'patch' is a change to a program which is characterised by its speed and ease of implementation.

(c) *Output fraud.*

Output documents may be stolen or tampered with and control totals may be altered. Cheques are the most likely document to be stolen, but other documents may be stolen to hide a fraud.

(d) *Fraudulent use of the computer system.*

Employees may feel that they can use the computer system for their own purposes and this may take up valuable processing time. This is probably quite rare, but there was a case of a newspaper publisher's computer system being used by an employee to produce another publication!

Recent developments increasing the risk of fraud

6.13 Over the last few years there have been rapid developments in all aspects of computer technology and these have increased the opportunities that are available to commit a fraud. The most important of the recent developments are as follows.

(a) *Computer literacy.*

The proportion of the population which is computer literate is growing all the time. Once people know how to use a computer, the dishonest ones among them may attempt computer fraud. It is much easier to 'hide' an electronic transaction: it is not 'visible', or not in the same sense as a paper-based one, in any case.

(b) *Communications.*

The use of telephone links and other public communication systems has increased the ability of people outside the company breaking into the computer system. These 'hackers' could not have operated when access was only possible on site.

(c) *Reduction in internal checks.*

The more computers are used, the fewer the tasks left to personnel to carry out. A consequence of this is often a reduction in the number of internal checks carried out for any transaction.

(d) *Software controls.*

Improvements in the *quality of software* and the controls available has not kept pace with the improvements in hardware. Distributed systems and networked PCs have become very common but this has caused the control over central databases and programs to be relaxed.

Discovery and counteracting computer fraud   *12/99*

6.14 The management of every company must be conscious of the possibility and costs of computer fraud and everything must be done to avoid it. Employees (including directors) are the most likely perpetrators of fraud. A dishonest employee will be rare, but temptation should be avoided by giving no opportunity or motive to staff.

(a) All staff should be properly trained and should fully appreciate their role in the computer function. They should also be aware of the consequences of any fraud they might perpetrate.

(b) Management policy on fraud should be clear and firm. Management should have a positive approach to both the possibility and prevention of computer fraud.

(c) Risk analysis should be carried out to examine where the company is exposed to possible fraud.

(d) In the computer area itself controls in the system and training will both be important.

(e) Other areas should also be examined, such as recruitment and personnel policies.

(f) Particular care should be taken when there are changes in programs or when new software and hardware are acquired.

7   HACKERS AND VIRUSES   6/98

Telecommunications dangers

7.1   When data is transmitted over a network or telecommunications link (especially the Internet) there are numerous security dangers.

(a)   Corruptions such as viruses on a single computer can spread through the network to all of the organisation's computers. (Viruses are described at greater length later in this chapter.)

(b)   Disaffected employees have much greater potential to do deliberate damage to valuable corporate data or systems because the network could give them access to parts of the system that they are not really authorised to use.

(c)   If the organisation is linked to an external network, persons outside the company (hackers) may be able to get into the company's internal network, either to steal data or to damage the system.

Systems can have firewalls (which disable part of the telecoms technology) to prevent unwelcome intrusions into company systems, but a determined hacker may well be able to bypass even these. (There is more on hackers below.)

(d)   Employees may download inaccurate information or imperfect or virus-ridden software from an external network. For example 'beta' (free trial) versions of forthcoming new editions of many major packages are often available on the Internet, but the whole point about a beta version is that it is not fully tested and may contain bugs that could disrupt an entire system.

(e)   Information transmitted from one part of an organisation to another may be intercepted. Data can be 'encrypted' (scrambled) in an attempt to make it unintelligible to eavesdroppers, but there is not yet any entirely satisfactory method of doing this. (See below. The problem is being worked upon by those with a vested interest, such as credit card companies, and will no doubt be resolved in time.)

(f)   The communications link itself may break down or distort data. The worldwide telecommunications infrastructure is improving thanks to the use of new technologies, and there are communications 'protocols' governing the format of data and signals transferred (see below). At present, however, transmitted data is only as secure as the medium through which it is transmitted, no matter what controls are operated at either end.

Encryption and other safety measures

7.2   Encryption involves the translation of data into code. To read an encrypted file, you must have access to a 'key' that enables you to decrypt it. Unencrypted data is called plain text; encrypted data is referred to as cipher text.

7.3   There are two main types of encryption: asymmetric encryption (also called public-key encryption) and symmetric encryption. An encryption scheme produces encrypted output, which requires a unique 'key' to decrypt.

7.4   This can either be a 'symmetrical' key (both encrypt and decrypt use the same key) or 'asymmetrical' (encrypt and decrypt keys are different). A widely used public-key Data Encryption Standard is the RSA standard. RSA stands for Rivest, Shamir, and Adelman, the inventors of the technique.

7.5   The RSA algorithm is based on the fact that there is no efficient way to factor very large numbers. Deducing an RSA key would require an extraordinary amount of computer processing power and time. It is therefore seen as a very secure system.

7.6   The RSA algorithm has become the de facto standard for industrial-strength encryption, especially for data sent over the Internet. It is built into many software products, including Netscape Navigator and Microsoft Internet Explorer.

7.7   RSA encryption uses an 'asymmetrical' key. The encryption key, the 'public key', is significantly different from the decryption key, the 'private key'.

Case example: encryption

Suppose you want to encrypt text from a web page. You decide on a key of 12345.

Using your public key, you RSA-encrypt the 12345, and put that at the front of the data stream (possibly followed by a marker or preceded by a data length to distinguish it from the rest of the data).

Then follow the 'encrypted key' data with the encrypted web page text, encrypted using the key '12345'. Upon receipt, the decrypt program looks for (and finds) the encrypted key, uses the 'private key' to decrypt it, and gets back the '12345'.

It then locates the beginning of the encrypted data stream, and applies the key '12345' to decrypt the data. The result: a very well protected data stream that is reliably and efficiently encrypted, transmitted, and decrypted.

7.8   Encryption is the only secure way to prevent eavesdropping (since eavesdroppers can get round password controls, by tapping the line or by experimenting with various likely passwords).

7.9   Encryption involves scrambling the data at one end of the line, transmitting the scrambled data, and unscrambling it at the receiver's end of the line.

7.10   Authentication is a technique of making sure that a message has come from an authorised sender. Authentication involves adding an extra field to a record, with the contents of this field derived from the remainder of the record by applying an algorithm that has previously been agreed between the senders and recipients of data.

7.11   Dial-back security operates by requiring the person wanting access to a network to dial into it and identify themselves first. The system then dials the person back on their authorised number before allowing them access.

Hacking

7.12   A hacker is a person who attempts to invade the privacy of a system.

7.13   Hackers require only limited programming knowledge to cause large amounts of damage. The fact that billions of bits of information can be transmitted in bulk over the public telephone network has made it hard to trace individual hackers, who can therefore make repeated attempts to invade systems. Hackers, in the past, have mainly been concerned to copy information, but a recent trend has been their desire to corrupt it.

7.14   Phone numbers and passwords can be guessed by hackers using electronic phone directories or number generators and by software which enables rapid guessing using hundreds of permutations per minute.

7.15   Default passwords are also available on some electronic bulletin boards and sophisticated hackers could even try to 'tap' messages being transmitted along phone wires (the number actually dialled will not be scrambled).

Viruses

7.16 A virus is a piece of software which infects programs and data and possibly damages them, and which replicates itself.

7.17 Viruses need an opportunity to spread. The programmers of viruses therefore place viruses in the kind of software which is most likely to be copied. This includes:

(a) Free software (for example from the Internet).
(b) Pirated software (cheaper than original versions).
(c) Games software (wide appeal).
(d) E-mail attachments (often with instructions to send the message on to others).

7.18 The problem has been exacerbated by the portability of computers and disks and the increased availability and use of e-mail.

7.19 It is consequently very difficult to keep control over what disks are inserted into an organisation's computers and similarly what files are received via e-mail.

7.20 The two most destructive viruses of recent times are:

- Melissa - which corrupts Microsoft Office documents
- Love bug – which attacks the operating system

7.21 Viruses can spread via floppy disk, but the most destructive viruses utilise e-mail links – travelling as attachments to e-mail messages. When the file attachment is opened or executed, the virus infects that system. Recent viruses have been programmed to send themselves to all addresses in the users electronic address book.

Type of virus	Explanation/Example
File viruses	File viruses infect program files. When you run an infected program the virus runs first, then passes control to the original program. While it has control, the virus code copies itself to another file or to another disk, replicating itself.
Boot sector viruses	The boot sector is the part of every hard disk and diskette which is read by the computer when it starts up. If the boot sector is infected, the virus runs when boot the machine.
Overwriting viruses	An overwriting virus overwrites each file it infects with itself, so the program no longer functions. Since this is very easy to spot these viruses do not spread very well.
Worms	A worm is a program which spreads (usually) over network connections. It does not attach itself to a host program.
Dropper	A dropper is a program, not a virus itself, that installs a virus on the PC while performing another function.
Macro viruses	A macro virus is a piece of self-replicating code written in an application's 'macro' language. Many applications have macro capabilities including all the programs in Microsoft Office. The distinguishing factor which makes it possible to create a virus with a macro is the existence of auto-execute events. Auto-execute events are opening a file, closing a file, and starting an application. Once a macro is running, it can copy itself to other documents, delete files, and create general havoc in a person's system. These things occur without the user explicitly running the macro. Melissa was a macro virus.

Case example

Love bug virus creates worldwide chaos

A computer virus which exploits office workers' yearnings for love shut down computer systems from Hong Kong to the United Kingdom yesterday and caused untold millions of pounds worth of delays and damage to stored files across the world.

The virus, nicknamed 'the love bug' is carried in an email with the heading 'ILOVEYOU'.

The text of the message reads: 'Kindly check the attached love letter from me!' A click on the attached file launches the virus, which promptly spreads by sending itself to everyone in the recipient's email address book, overloading email systems.

Once embedded in a host computer, the virus can download more dangerous software from a remote website, rename files and redirect Internet browsers. 'It's a very effective virus. It's one of the most aggressive and nastiest I've ever seen,' said Kieran Fitzsimmons of MessageLabs, which screens millions of company emails for viruses. 'It manifests itself almost everywhere in the computer.'

One tenth of the world's mail servers were down as a result of the love bug, he said. Estimates suggested that between 10% and 30% of UK businesses were hit.

At the UK arm of Reed International, publisher of trade magazines, IT engineers alerted staff with Tannoy announcements after the bug had already crippled their computer system. 'It completely wipes out your network,' said Sarah Perkins of PC Pro magazine. 'Ours is down and we're going to lose a day's business.'

The virus spread west from Asia as offices opened and workers checked their emails. The only clue to its origins lies in the first few lines of the code which makes it work. They are headed: 'I hate go to school.' The next line identifies the author as 'spyder' and the next refers to 'Manila, Philippines'.

IT specialists described the love bug as **'a visual basic worm'** far **more dangerous** and fast-spreading than the similar **Melissa virus, which also replicated itself by email**. Melissa infected about a million computers and caused £50m of damage.

ILOVEYOU is eight times bigger, sends itself to everyone in a recipient's address book instead of just the first 50 (and then deletes the address book), and, unlike Melissa, **tampers with operating systems**.

By yesterday afternoon MessageLabs had picked up 10,000 infected emails. The highest number in one day until now has been 700. Last night another virus tracker, TrendMicro, was reporting more than 800,000 infected files around the world, the bulk of them in the US. One expert said the love bug spread 'like wild fire' in Britain after 11.30am. 'It's taking out computers right, left and centre,' he said.

Adapted from The Guardian May 5, 2000

Jokes and hoaxes

7.22 Some programs claim to be doing something destructive to your computer, but are actually 'harmless' jokes. For example, a message may appear suggesting that your hard disk is about to be reformatted. Unfortunately, it is **easy to over-react** to the joke and cause more damage by trying to eradicate something that is not a virus.

7.23 There are a number of common hoaxes, which are widely believed. The most common of these is **Good Times**. This hoax has been around for a couple of years, and usually takes the form of a virus warning about viruses contained in e-mail. People pass along the warning because they are trying to be helpful, but they are wasting the time of all concerned.

Identification of a virus

7.24 There are two ways of identifying a virus. The first is to identify it before it does any damage. The second is to identify it when it is activated.

7.25 It is difficult for the typical user to identify the presence of a virus. There are sometimes tell-tale signs, such as slight changes in file lengths as displayed in the directory, or additional disk activity before a program is run, but more sophisticated controls than this are needed.

(a) Anti-virus software such as Dr Solomon's is capable of detecting and eradicating a vast number of viruses before they do any damage. Upgrades are released regularly to deal with new viruses. The software will run whenever a computer is turned on and will continue to monitor in the background until it is turned off again.

(b) Organisations must have procedures to guard against the introduction of unauthorised software to their systems. Many viruses and trojans have been spread on pirated versions of popular computer games.

(c) Organisations, as a matter of routine, should ensure that any disk or e-mail attachment received from outside is virus-free before the data is downloaded.

(d) Any flaws in a widely used program should be rectified as soon as they come to light.

8 PRIVACY AND DATA PROTECTION

Why is privacy an important issue?

8.1 In recent years concerns have been raised regarding the potential to misuse the large volume of information about individuals held on computer files.

8.2 In particular, it was felt that an individual could be harmed by the existence of data which was inaccurate or misleading and which could be transferred to unauthorised third parties at high speed and little cost.

8.3 In the UK the relevant legislation is the Data Protection Act 1998. This Act replaced the earlier Data Protection Act 1984. (The Data Protection Act is not mentioned in the Managing Information Systems syllabus. However, the Act is relevant to a number of management control issues that are referred to in the syllabus eg control, risk, and security.)

The Data Protection Act 1998

8.4 The Data Protection Act 1998 is an attempt to protect the individual.

Definitions of terms used in the Act

8.5 In order to understand the Act it is necessary to know some of the technical terms used in it.

(a) *Personal data* is information about a living individual, including expressions of opinion about him or her. Data about other organisations (eg supplier or customer companies) is not personal data, unless it contains data about individuals who belong to those other organisations.

(b) *Data users* are organisations or individuals who control the contents of files of personal data and the use of personal data which is processed (or intended to be processed) automatically - ie who use personal data which is covered by the terms of the Act.

(c) A *data subject* is an individual who is the subject of personal data.

The data protection principles

8.6 Data users must comply with the Data Protection Principles contained in the Act. These are shown in the following table.

DATA PROTECTION PRINCIPLES

1   Personal data shall be processed fairly and lawfully and, in particular, shall not be processed unless:

(a)   At least one of the conditions in Schedule 2 is met. *(See paragraph 8.9(c) of this Chapter.)*

(b)   In the case of sensitive personal data, at least one of the conditions in Schedule 3 is also met. *(See paragraph 9.11(d) of this Chapter.)*

2   Personal data shall be obtained only for one or more specified and lawful purposes, and shall not be further processed in any manner incompatible with that purpose or those purposes.

3   Personal data shall be adequate, relevant and not excessive in relation to the purpose or purposes for which they are processed.

4   Personal data shall be accurate and, where necessary, kept up to date.

5   Personal data processed for any purpose or purposes shall not be kept for longer than is necessary for that purpose or those purposes.

6   Personal data shall be processed in accordance with the rights of data subjects under this Act.

7   Appropriate technical and organisational measures shall be taken against unauthorised or unlawful processing of personal data and against accidental loss or destruction of, or damage to, personal data.

8   Personal data shall not be transferred to a country or territory outside the European Economic Area unless that country or territory ensures an adequate level of protection for the rights and freedoms of data subjects in relation to the processing of personal data.

The coverage of the Act

8.7   Key points of the Act can be summarised as follows.

(a)   With certain exceptions, all data users have to register with the Data Protection Registrar.

(b)   Individuals (data subjects) are awarded certain legal rights.

(c)   Data holders must adhere to the data protection principles.

Registration under the Act

8.8   A data user must apply to be registered on the Data Protection Registrar. Each entry in the Register relates to a data user. Unless a data user has an entry in the Register, personal data must not be held. Registered data users must only hold and use data for the purpose(s) registered.

8.9   Features of the 1998 legislation are:

(a)   Individuals have the right to go to court to seek redress for any breach of data protection law, rather than just for certain aspects of it.

(b)   All filing systems that are structured so as to facilitate access to information about a particular person now fall within the legislation. This includes systems that are paper-based or on microfilm or microfiche. Personnel records meet this classification.

(c)   Processing of personal data is forbidden except in the following circumstances.

(i)   With the consent of the subject (person).
(ii)   As a result of a contractual arrangement.
(iii)   Because of a legal obligation.
(iv)   To protect the vital interests of the subject.
(v)   Where processing is in the public interest.
(vi)   Where processing is required to exercise official authority.

(d) The processing of 'sensitive data' is forbidden, unless express consent has been obtained or there are conflicting obligations under employment law. Sensitive data includes data relating to racial origin, political opinions, religious beliefs, physical or mental health, sexual proclivities and trade union membership.

(e) Data subjects have the right to a copy of data held about them and also the right to know why the data are being processed.

Chapter roundup

- Risks should be assessed, and minimised or transferred if possible. Organisations should develop contingency plans to be activated in the event of major or long-term systems problems. Standby facilities include computer bureaux and co-operation with other organisations.

- Back-up procedures are essential to guard against deliberate or accidental damage to data. Methods include the grandfather-father-son approach and dumping.

- Back-ups should be stored off-site.

- Controls should be built in to a system and cover inputs, processes and outputs.

- Verification ensures that the data input is the same as the data in the source document.

- A wide variety of validation checks can be built into programs and data, including range checks, limit checks, consistency checks and check digits.

- Computer audit is a necessary element of the review of many computer systems. Auditors should audit through the computer. Computer assisted audit techniques can be used to read files, extract information and carry out audit work. CAATs include audit interrogation software and test data.

- Certain personnel will always be placed in a position of trust. This means that systematic controls over their roles cannot be maintained, however a number of measures are possible. Job sensitivity analysis seeks to identify the opportunity to commit fraud which is inherent in each post in the organisation.

- A logical access system is concerned with preventing those persons who have gained physical access from gaining unauthorised access to data or software.

- Passwords can be applied to data files. A password is a set of characters which are required to be keyed into a system before further access is permitted. Although password systems can be extremely sophisticated, they all depend on user discipline.

- A hacker is a person who attempts to invade the privacy of a system by circumventing logical access controls. The Computer Misuse Act 1990 was an attempt to address this growing problem.

- A virus is a piece of software which corrupts the operations of programs and, given the opportunity, replicates itself throughout a system. Macro viruses are currently the cause of much concern.

- When data is transmitted over telecommunications links, there are a number of security risks. One method of preventing eavesdropping is encryption. Authentication ensures that a message has come from an authorised user.

Quick quiz

1 What are the three stages of risk management? (see para 1.4)

2 What should a contingency plan contain? (1.8)

3 What is the purpose of a back-up? (2.4)

4 What controls can be exercised over processing? (3.7 - 3.11)

5 What is a range check? (3.20)

6 What is a format check? (3.23)

7 What is the purpose of an audit trail? (4.2 - 4.4)

8 What uses might an audit interrogation package have? (4.14)

9 Write out a checklist of best password practice? (5.5)

10 What types of computer fraud are there? (6.12)

11 What controls can be used to prevent fraud? (6.13)

12 What warning signs might suggest that an employee is perpetrating a fraud? (6.14)

13 What security dangers arise due to telecommunications links? (7.1)

14 What is encryption? (7.2)

15 What controls are needed to avoid viruses? (7.25)

16 Why is privacy an important issue? (8.1 - 8.2)

Now try illustrative question 19 at the end of the Study Text

BPP
PUBLISHING

Illustrative questions and suggested answers

1   **SYSTEMS THEORY**

(a) Define the key concepts of systems theory.

(b) Explain the relevance of those concepts to the design of administrative systems within an organisation.

2   **CLASSIFICATION OF SYSTEMS**

Define two main classifications of system and give a commercial example of each.

3   **INFORMATION LEVELS**

Typically, information within an organisation can be classified into three levels.

Using a typical manufacturing company as background, define the three levels and give examples of the information which would be provided at each level. In what way does the destination level influence the presentation of information?

4   **MIS AND DECISION MAKING**

To what extent do management information systems have an impact on organisations in terms of structure and the decision making process?

5   **COMPUTER BASED FINANCIAL MODELS**

Computer based financial models can be developed using either modelling systems or spreadsheet packages (eg Lotus 123, Microsoft Excel). Examine their relative features and the type of application for which each would be most suitable.

6   **MANAGEMENT OF CHANGE**

A feature of the work of the systems analyst could be described as the management of change. Outline ways in which a systems development group could minimise the negative aspects and maximise the positive aspects of organisational change.

7   **EXTERNAL INFORMATION**

Describe how an organisation could structure and implement formal methods and procedures for gathering information to monitor its external environment.

8   **DISTRIBUTED DATA PROCESSING**

Examine the reasons behind the trend towards distributed data processing and consider the issues this raises for the management of computer operations.

9   **FEASIBILITY REPORT**

(a) Outline the main sections of a feasibility report and briefly explain the purpose of the typical contents of each section.

(b) An important part of any feasibility report is a section giving a financial justification for the proposed system. Describe in detail the matters dealt with in this section.

10 **FACT FINDING**

An important aspect of systems analysis is the 'fact finding' stage of a systems investigation. Depending on the circumstances and the system being studied, several different methods of fact finding may be used.

BPP PUBLISHING

You are required to:

(a)   State three methods of fact finding.

(b)   Give their advantages and disadvantages and the circumstances in which each might be used.

11   STRUCTURED METHODS

Approaches to systems analysis have changed in recent years to include 'structured methods' (or 'methodologies').

(a)   What does the term 'structured method' mean?

(b)   List and briefly describe three advantages of using such an approach for the development of business systems.

12   LOGICAL AND PHYSICAL DESIGN

In relation to systems development processes explain what is meant by the terms logical and physical design.

13   CHARTING TECHNIQUES

Examine how dataflow diagrams are used in the development of systems.

14   DECISION TABLES

Explain how *decision tables* are used in the development of systems.

15   DATABASE

Some computer installations, particularly the larger, more sophisticated ones, are using databases in which to store the organisation's data.

You are required to:

(a)   Define a database.

(b)   List and explain briefly five of the advantages claimed for a well-designed database.

(c)   Explain briefly three of the major problems associated with the implementation and operation of a comprehensive database.

(d)   Distinguish between the logical and physical structure of data.

16   DATABASE ARCHITECTURE

(a)   Draw a diagram to show the principal levels of architecture of a database system and the place of the Database Management System (DBMS) within it.

(b)   Contrast the terms *security* and *integrity* as they apply to databases.

17   FILE CONVERSION

File conversion (or file creation) is always a major practical problem when a new computer-based system is being implemented.

Assume that a new computer-based accounting system is to be implemented and source data are at present held in various types of clerical files in several locations.

You are required to describe:

(a)   The objectives of file conversion.
(b)   The typical problems that would be encountered in the situation outlined.
(c)   The way the file conversion process should be planned and controlled.

18 RECRUITMENT AND TRAINING

During the course of systems development new staff may have to be recruited and existing staff may have to be retrained in preparation for the changeover to the new system.

How should management and the systems analyst(s) deal with the problems of staffing, and what methods of training and communication should be adopted?

19 SECURITY OF INFORMATION SYSTEMS

Examine the factors management must consider when evaluating the security of information systems. Your answer should cover both physical security and security from unauthorised human intervention.

20 MAINTENANCE OF SOFTWARE

Describe 'maintenance' in the software context, giving reasons why the need for it arises.

MID-SANSHIRE HEALTH AUTHORITY (21-24) *Pilot paper*

Mid-Sanshire Health Authority (MSHA) employs about 100 staff in five departments; administration, services development, finance, medical services and information technology. They are responsible for the provision of health services for a population of 600,000 residents in Mid-Sanshire and have an annual turnover of £2.2m. Principal duties of the MSHA are as follows:

(a) Maintaining lists of medical practitioners.
(b) Paying practitioners and managing their contracts.
(c) Maintaining an up-to-date patient register.
(d) Dealing with complaints.

However, recent government legislation has extended the MSHA role to include a role in the provision of primary health care, a more direct approach to health promotion and providing more information to the public.

In response to the new legislation the services development section have formed a committee to formulate a new management strategy for the provision of information. They intend to develop an entirely new system using the top-down approach.

21 Formulate the problem definition emphasising the user viewpoint using appropriate soft systems tools.

22 Advise the new committee on how the new information system should support the planning and setting of objectives at all levels of the organisation.

23 Make recommendations for the terms of reference, membership and roles of persons appointed to the committee.

24 Explain how the organisational style and culture may influence the development of the new system.

ROBINSON-HEATH FINANCIAL SERVICES (25-28) *Pilot paper*

You are called to the office of the managing director of Robinson-Heath Financial Services, a large company employing 1,200 staff based in your own country. As a new trainee, you are presently assigned to the computer services section for one month as part of your induction programme. The managing director asks you to look into ways to reduce the time spent on systems development, 'we have highly trained staff with excellent technical skills but we still get behind schedule with our projects', she tells you. Further discussion reveals that they still use a traditional systems development cycle and there is minimal user involvement until the implementation stage. An early version of SSADM is used for all projects.

25 List the basic features of SSADM and consider the extent to which they encourage user involvement.

26 Evaluate the use of the structured systems methodology in conjunction with the traditional systems development cycle and consider why the projects may be unduly time consuming.

27 In the form of a memorandum to the managing director, suggest ways to reduce the time spent, increase user participation and develop quality systems.

28 Set out the main principles of project management and explain how you would review the effectiveness of the project management techniques used.

TONE ZONE LEISURE CENTRE (29-32)

The Tone Zone Leisure Centre is due to open six months from now. Located in a busy city centre the new venture is expected to be successful and will offer a wide range of sports and leisure facilities. They will be offering a subscription membership scheme and expect their main income to be from swimming, hire of health facilities, hire of main hall, squash court and gymnasium bookings.

The number of individual activities available for booking is expected to be about 120 at the start.

The management of the Centre is anxious that the administration should help them to be cost effective by maximising utilisation and revenue.

29   Identify the principal information needs of the management and show how they relate to the Centre objectives.

30   Discuss the effects upon the system of changes in the wider social environment.

31   Evaluate the database approach to supporting decision making in the Centre.

32   Draft a programme for training the Centre staff in using and maintaining the system.

NORMAN (33-36)

You are asked to review the effectiveness of a new product delivery computer system which has been in live operation for just three weeks. The system is a new addition to a larger order processing system and its main function is to prepare instructions for scheduling delivery of products from stock. Output, in the form of despatch notes, is printed in the transport office.

Whilst reviewing the operations you meet Norman, who is the stock controller responsible for the despatch notes. Norman does not appear to know what is happening and does not even know what he is supposed to do. The stationery on the printer runs out and Norman does not even know how to change it.

33   List the steps you would take to review the performance of the product delivery computer system.

34   Draw a dataflow diagram to show a typical order processing system and decompose the product delivery processes to the next level of detail.

35   Explain why Norman was not suitably prepared for his part in the new system.

36   Write a memorandum to the Head of Systems Development explaining the difficulties experienced by Norman the stock controller and recommending suitable remedial action.

1 SYSTEMS THEORY

(a) Systems theory began to develop in the 1940's among a number of writers from widely ranging professional 'disciplines'. General systems theory attempts to give a general definition to the concept of an 'organised system', to classify different types of systems, and where possible to build mathematical models which describe them. Whether the systems are biological, psychological, sociological, organisational, financial etc, certain concepts and principles will have a common or similar application. In this way systems theory enables experts from various disciplines to draw on a single set of principles to apply in their own particular area of specialisation.

Any system can be viewed as being composed of subsystems, each of which is composed of sub-subsystems and so on in a *system hierarchy*. The features of a systems hierarchy can be described according to the following propositions developed by J van Gigch.

(i) A system is composed of subsystems.

(ii) Given any system, it is always possible to find another system of which that system is a part (except for the final 'Universal' system).

(iii) Given two systems, the one system comprising the other can be called the high-level system in relation to the system it comprises, which is called the low-level system.

(iv) A hierarchy of systems exists whereby low-level systems are comprised into high-level systems.

(v) Low-level systems are in turn made up of other systems, for which they can be considered as high-level systems.

(b) An understanding of the concepts of systems theory is relevant to the design of administrative systems, as the experience of experts and researchers in other fields could, when relevant, be applied in this sphere of activity. The application of systems theory may achieve the following.

(i) Highlight the dynamic aspects of the business organisation, and the factors which influence the growth and development of all its subsystems.

(ii) Create an awareness of subsystems, each with potentially conflicting goals which must be brought into line with each other. This is particularly important in respect of the setting of budgets or standards.

(iii) Help in the design and development of information systems to help decision makers ensure that decisions are made for the benefit of the organisation as a whole.

(iv) Help identify the effect of the environment on systems. The external factors that affect an organisation may be wide ranging. The government (in all its forms), competitors, trade unions, creditors, shareholders, etc all have an interactive link with an organisation, and the administrator's role within that organisation.

2 CLASSIFICATION OF SYSTEMS

There are no two classifications of system that could be described as 'the main two'; rather, there are a number of alternative ways of classifying systems (eg open and closed systems, natural systems and contrived systems, static and dynamic systems etc). Given the requirement in the question to give commercial examples of the two classifications, it might be appropriate to discuss deterministic and self-organising systems, although to do so would omit a third category, probabilistic or stochastic systems.

A deterministic system is one in which various states or activities follow on from each other in a completely predictable way; ie given that A will happen, B must happen, then C etc.

A self-organising system is one which adapts and reacts to a stimulus, but in a way that is uncertain, so that the same input (stimulus) to the system will not always produce the same output (response).

There are few, if any, commercial examples of a truly deterministic system, because sales and purchases, which are at the centre of commercial operations, are not deterministic events themselves. However, mathematical models of some commercial operations are built as though they are deterministic in nature. Examples of deterministic models are the economic batch quantity model for inventory control, which assumes that stock demand and supply lead times etc are fully predictable events. A critical path network model similarly assumes that all the activities in a project can be foreseen with certainty, and their exact durations specified.

BPP PUBLISHING

Some simple computer processing of bulk data might also be described as a deterministic system (eg payroll programs) because the input, processing and output are all required to conform to a fixed, and predetermined pattern.

An example of a self-organising system is a commercial organisation itself. Any system which involves human relations and human judgements must make some allowance for the unpredictability of both stimuli and responses. Management-trade union relationships provide a particular example of a system where events conform to a general pattern of rules and procedures, but variations from the 'rules' are quite normal and even necessary. Another example is provided by competition in a market system, and the response of competitors to marketing initiatives taken by one company in the market. (Attempts to express 'game theory' as a stochastic system have so far had only limited success).

3   INFORMATION LEVELS

Information within an organisation (as distinct from information provided by an organisation to external users, such as shareholders, the general public, pressure groups, competitors, suppliers, customers etc) can be analysed into three levels. These levels of information are referred to as strategic, tactical and operational.

(a)   *Strategic information*

Is used to plan the objectives of their organisation and to assess whether the objectives are being met in practice. In a manufacturing company such information includes overall profitability, the profitability of different segments of the business, future market prospects, the availability and cost of raising new funds, total cash needs, total manning levels and capital equipment needs etc. Much of this information must come from environmental sources, although internally generated information will also be used. Strategic information will be used for management decision making in strategic planning.

(b)   *Tactical information*

Is used to ensure that the resources of the business are employed (and the efficiency and effectiveness of their use monitored) to achieve the strategic objectives of the organisation. Such information includes productivity measurements (output per man or per machine hour) budgetary control or variance analysis reports, cash flow forecasts, manning levels and profit results within a particular department of the organisation, labour turnover statistics within a department, short-term purchasing requirements etc. A large proportion of this information will be generated from within the organisation (ie as feedback) and is likely to have an accounting emphasis. Tactical information is usually prepared regularly - perhaps weekly or monthly, whereas strategic information is communicated irregularly and is used for the decision making process usually referred to as management control.

(c)   *Operational information*

Is used to ensure that specific tasks are planned and carried out properly within a factory or office. In the payroll office, for example, operational information relating to day rate labour will include hours worked each week by each employee, his rate of pay per hour, details of his deductions, and, for the purpose of wages analysis, details of the time each man spent on individual jobs during the week. In this example the information is required weekly, but more urgent information, such as the amount of raw materials being put to a production process, may be required daily, hourly or, in the case of automated production, second by second. Operational information relates to the level of decision making usually referred to as operational control.

Historical information might be used immediately (for operational control) but less frequently for management control and only occasionally for strategic planning. Information can be collected and stored for future use, although presumably there will be a limit to its useful life. Strategic planning may use information gathered several years ago and associate it with current information both internal and external, so as to analyse past trends and predict the future. Management control may also use information several years old (to compare past and current performance) but historical information is more likely to have a limited useful life. Operational control information has a short life span.

Any information must be relevant to the purpose for which a manager wants to use it. The destination level of the information is very important as the information must be material to the user but without going into unnecessary and time consuming detail (for a particular user) in order to achieve pointless accuracy. For example:

(a) Operational control may need information to be accurate to the nearest penny, minute or kilogram (eg for job costing);

(b) Management control may be satisfied with costs rounded to the nearest £100 or £1,000. Greater detail would serve no purpose;

(c) Strategic planning may be satisfied with figures to the nearest ten thousand, hundred thousand or even million pounds. Estimates to the nearest penny at this level of decision-making would be so inappropriate as to remove confidence in the information from the managers using it - ie to have a counter productive effect.

In all cases, the information and reports must be relevant to the particular user. In practice far too many reports fail to keep to the point and contain purposeless, irritating paragraphs which only serve to vex the managers reading them.

4   MIS AND DECISION MAKING

Management Information Systems provide information which allows management to do their job properly. MIS exist in all organisations and the impact they have on management and decision making depends on the quality of the system and the information provided. The information systems in an organisation, formal or informal, should suit the management structure and aid the decision making process.

An MIS should provide information to facilitate planning and control decisions which are made in all activities and at all levels of management. The well established model set out by Robert N Anthony provides for three levels of management: operational, tactical and strategic. By implication therefore a good system will provide useful information to the right management level. Each level of management requires different types of information.

At the *operational* level managers are concerned with the practical concerns of carrying out day to day activities. Decisions will be concerned with for example achieving a production deadline or making payments to suppliers.

Tactical management is responsible for controlling resources effectively and efficiently to achieve the organisation's objectives. This may involve planning for the medium to long term, such as pricing a new product or budgeting for the new financial year. The data used may be the same as that at operational level but use will be made of exception reporting and summaries.

Strategic management is responsible for setting the strategy and objectives of the organisation. This involves long term planning and will require internal and external information to be considered. Examples are the decision to move to new premises, acquire a business or diversify. The information required at this level is often unstructured and unpredictable and as such more difficult to incorporate in formal MIS.

In order for MIS to present relevant information to the right people it is important to define the management structure and individual responsibilities. Management information systems are more effective given a formal structure to work to.

The effectiveness of information flows is crucial and may highlight deficiencies in the management structure. Information flows run both upwards through the different levels of management and sideways between various activities. Defining the direction and details of these flows is an important factor when assessing the effectiveness of MIS. Designing a formal and well planned management information system may lead to a redefinition of management responsibilities and the information flows between activities. This should improve the standard of information provided to management.

Information must be generated and presented to allow decisions to be made at any level of management. Management information systems can have a significant impact on the decision making process by providing high quality, timely and relevant information. However not all MIS are of a high quality and the impact can be a negative one. Unplanned systems which have evolved over a period of time may not respond to change quickly enough. Formal systems should be designed to be flexible.

Although decisions vary at each level of management, the decision-making process does not. Decision are triggered by the recognition of a problem. Information gathering enables alternative courses of action to be identified and a final choice to be made. It is the job of a management information system to provide information to enable planning and control decisions to be made.

BPP PUBLISHING

The information and systems required depends on the type of decisions to be made; different decisions follow directly the three tiered structure of management described by Anthony. MIS at *operational* level will probably consist of the processing systems which carry out day to day tasks; these provide the information required to make routine decisions. Computerised information systems often make operational decisions.

Tactical management identifies problems from regular exception reporting and analysis and the systems used interact closely with those at operational level. The solution to unstructured problems may require the provision of decision support systems. Often computerised, these aim to provide enough information, from internal and external sources, to allow a judgement to be made.

It is often difficult to formalise systems to provide *strategic* information as it is often unpredictable and largely generated from external sources. However, an MIS can still be used for gathering and analysing information.

Information systems can be used not only to solve a problem, but also to evaluate the success of a solution at a later stage. This is a most important aspect of decision making as it adds to the control an organisation has over its operations.

5 COMPUTER BASED FINANCIAL MODELS

Modelling systems

Modelling systems for financial models are often developed in-house by large organisations or research companies.

Modelling packages were initially developed for larger computers (mainframes and minis) but are now available for microcomputers too.

(a) They are powerful programming languages.
(b) They are capable of carrying out complex processing routines.
(c) They can be used in a multi-user, or even a network system.
(d) They can be used with a powerful (relational) database, or very large data files.

They should be used in preference to spreadsheets for complex applications (eg involving a large number of inter-related variables), and multi-user applications.

Spreadsheet packages

The facilities and capabilities of spreadsheet packages are continually improving, with the development of new and better packages or add-ons to existing packages. Essentially, however, the features of spreadsheets are as follows.

(a) They are used with microcomputers, either on stand-alone machines or on a network.

(b) Although spreadsheets might seem large, the maximum size of a spreadsheet model is much less than the potential size of a financial model built with a modelling package.

(c) Spreadsheet models are built with fairly simple programming languages, and are not capable of carrying out many of the complex routines that financial models can.

(d) Although spreadsheets can be linked to a database or a large data file, their capabilities for handling large files are much less than those of financial models.

Summary

Spreadsheets are more appropriate for smaller and simpler modelling applications. Where larger and more complex models are required, a financial modelling package would be more appropriate.

6 MANAGEMENT OF CHANGE

In systems development changes are introduced in organisations which may cause significant problems. These problems may be anticipated or forestalled and so the maximum benefit is delivered from the system. Some activities which may be employed to minimise problems and maximise benefits are as follows.

(a) Users should be involved in a significant manner in the design and development of the system. There will be two main benefits from such an approach: first, users will influence the system design so that it reflects their needs more closely; and second, this involvement will cause some users to identify more closely with the system and act as change agents themselves. A further benefit will be that the system is no longer an unknown and unfamiliar entity which may be threatening; involved users will better understand its effect upon the organisation and their place in it.

(b)   New work practices should be introduced after consulting with the employees involved and with a due consideration for the impact which these practices may have upon earnings, job satisfaction, etc. If possible, any new procedures or forms should be introduced well in advance of the system introduction so that users have time to familiarise themselves with them. In many cases the improvements due to computerisation are only partly due to the capabilities provided by the computer. Manual systems may often be significantly improved simply by applying rigorous systems analysis and design principles to understanding their operation. In doing this, careful attention needs to be given to the information handling, communication and processing as with computerised systems.

No systems analysis is complete without also considering the environment in which the system will function, it should be adapted to the environment and require organisational changes only where essential. The implementation of a system should not be seen as a disruptive intrusion in what would otherwise be a happy, well run organisation.

(c)   Training should be planned for during the period leading up to systems introduction and schedules should be arranged so that all involved personnel receive adequate and timely instruction in how to use the system. Employees benefit from receiving their training in small groups having immediate access to the system or a prototype, and training is generally most effective if it is delivered in easily comprehensible blocks. Too much information at one time can overwhelm the user.

The objectives of a systems analyst in introducing change is to maximise system benefits while simultaneously minimising the disruption to the organisation and its employees. In doing so three broad principles should be observed:

(i)   Introduce changes gradually and in 'digestible' stages.

(ii)   Establish good working relationships with the users and understand their needs for the system and criticisms of it.

(iii) Develop a positive relationship with management so that system developments are sympathetically supported.

7   **EXTERNAL INFORMATION**

Some aspects of an organisation's external environment will be more important for the organisation than others. Just what the most important aspects are will vary from organisation to organisation. The first step that should therefore be taken is for an individual or a committee to be appointed to establish (and subsequently review) what aspects of the external environment should be monitored by formal methods and procedures.

(a)   The aspects of the environment that might be monitored include the following.

(i)   *Competitors.* Information should be gathered about what competitors are doing, how successful they are and how much of a threat they are.

(ii)   *Suppliers.* Information should be gathered about suppliers and potential suppliers, their prices, product or service quality and delivery dates etc.

(iii) *Customers.* An organisation should always try to be aware of the needs of its customers, to identify changes in these needs, to recognise potential market segments, and to assess the size of a potential market. Customer awareness is vital for new product development and successful selling.

(iv) *Legal changes.* Changes in the law might affect how an organisation operates, and any such changes should be monitored.

(v)   *Political changes.* Some organisations are affected by national or local politics. The defence equipment industry is just one such example. If politics can be important, the organisation should try to monitor political decisions at both national and local level.

(vi) *Financial and economic conditions.* Most organisations have to monitor developments in financial and economic conditions. As just one example, a large company's treasury department must be aware of current money market interest rates and foreign exchange

BPP PUBLISHING

rates. As another example, the general rate of inflation is significant for decisions about wage increases for employees.

(b) Once the main sources of environmental information have been identified, an organisation should then establish:

    (i) The most appropriate *sources* for obtaining this information. This will vary according to the nature of the information.

    (ii) The individuals or departments whose *task* it should be to gather the information, and where appropriate, disseminate it through the organisation to other people who might need it.

    (iii) The *form* in which the information should be disseminated through the organisation.

(c) Sources of information include:

    (i) Suppliers' price lists and brochures.

    (ii) Published reports and accounts (of competitors, suppliers and business customers).

    (iii) Government reports (often, reports on specific topics. Economic and trade reports, for example, are frequently produced by central government).

    (iv) Government statistics.

    (v) External databases provided by specialist organisations, probably via the Internet.

    (vi) Newspaper and magazine reports.

(d) Individuals or departments should be made responsible for obtaining information about certain aspects of the environment. In some cases, the individual department will collect information that it wishes to use itself. In other cases, there will be a need to distribute information throughout the rest of the organisation, and procedures should be established for doing this. Methods of distributing information would include:

    (i) Routine reports or in-house circulars.
    (ii) The company magazine.
    (iii) A company database, to which various offices can have access via computer terminals.

8 DISTRIBUTED DATA PROCESSING

There are various reasons for the trend towards distributed data processing.

(a) An important factor has been the development of networking technology over the past decade. Hardware are software developments mean reliable efficient networks are now the norm. Microsoft Windows NT and Novel Netware are the most widely used network operating systems.

(b) User needs have also changed. Mainframe computers, for users who can afford one, provide a centralised form of processing, whereas in many organisations, there is a preference for independent data processing (ie decentralised processing) at a local level. Decentralised processing can be carried out by stand-alone micros (eg PCs and PC-compatibles).

However, distributed data processing offers the advantages of a mixture of decentralised processing ('local' computers) and the advantages of common, centralised processing facilities, such as a single database or a shared program library.

(c) Distributed data processing systems - ie networks - can be provided to suit a user's specific needs, with the required number of microcomputers, mainframes, and database files etc. Access to certain files or programs can be restricted to specified users, and so on. The flexibility in system design has contributed towards the growth in the use of networks.

(d) Networks are available at a cost that many users, including medium-sized and even small firms, can afford.

The issues that the trend towards distributed data processing raise are as follows.

(a) Management can set up an organisational structure, and then devise a DP system that fits in with this structure, and is best suited to its needs, instead of having to accept a certain DP system (eg stand-alone micros, or a single centralised mainframe) and then building an organisational structure around the DP system.

(b) If an organisation already has separated local processing, management might be able to consider ways of linking existing equipment into a network, so as to improve the DP system. The technology of 'connectivity' is improving.

(c) When new data processing systems are being planned, management should consider the advantages and disadvantages of adding the new system into its existing DP network.

(d) With networks, local computer users can obtain access to a common database, and to the processing facilities of a larger computer in the network. The full potential of networking can only be exploited if user-friendly software is available which allows non-technical computer users to interrogate files and produce reports etc. Management should therefore become more aware of the availability of software utilities such as report writers, query languages and fourth generation languages (for writing or 'generating' new user programs).

(e) The implications for staff *training* and *office routines* should be considered. Local area network systems allow greater flexibility in office routines and job responsibilities, and each office should try to develop a local 'expert' with reasonable knowledge of the workings of the network as a whole.

9   FEASIBILITY REPORT

(a)   The main sections of a feasibility report are as follows.

(i)   *Introduction.* Description of the purpose of the report, why it was commissioned and what it proposes to recommend.

Terms of reference. This specifies the limits or constraints on the report, and so identifies the boundaries of the investigation.

Method of carrying out the feasibility study. A brief description of how the study was carried out should be given. If the method seems worthy of a fuller description, this should be given in an appendix to the report.

(ii)   *Problem definition.* The purpose of the study will be to resolve a problem of organisation or procedural systems, or to introduce a new system to replace an existing one, or to introduce a new system where one does not exist already.

The feasibility report should specify clearly what the study group identifies as the purpose of the system to be proposed, in terms of what the organisation is trying to achieve.

The results of preliminary investigations are described here.

If the report is proposing a new system, it should explain how the new system will integrate with existing systems.

(iii)   *Outline of project specifications.* This contains a description of the alternative systems considered, and how far each of these would satisfy the objectives. Alternatives which fail to satisfy those objectives should be explained, and then discarded from further consideration in the report.

(iv)   *Reasons for selection of preferred profit option.* The preferred system should be identified, and described further in subsequent sections of the report. (If more than one viable option remains, all of them should be explained in some detail.)

The effect of introducing the system on current operations, output levels, efficiency, staffing, equipment used, organisation etc.

Financial justification. The costs of the system, and the benefits envisaged.

A consideration of how successfully the option might achieve the objectives of the organisation, in commissioning a new system.

A comparison of the options, and an indication of preference.

A *recommendation* as to which option, if any, should be selected and developed into a new system. (A recommendation might be to continue with the existing system, or to defer a change until new system capabilities and more advanced equipment are available on the market.)

(v)   *Specification of selected profit option.* The proposed system should be described below. Although systems design work should not proceed too far, in case the recommendations of the report are turned down, the report should contain adequate information about the type of system, equipment needed, input, output, files, procedures and programs, speed of

BPP
PUBLISHING

processing, staffing, changeover procedures from the old to the new system, possible deficiencies in the system, costs, benefits etc. This information can be used to weigh up the report, and subsequently to monitor progress in the development of the actual system (on the assumption that during design work, some of the items envisaged in the feasibility study turn out to be impractical, inefficient or insufficient).

(b) The section of the report on financial justification should include the following.

(i) *Operating costs.* The incremental (or 'relevant') costs of the system should be identified, including:

- Staff costs (clerical, computer operations etc)
- The cost of stationery and other supplies
- The cost of external services (eg bureaux)
- The cost of system maintenance
- Accommodation costs (if incremental to existing costs)
- Any other additional costs.

(ii) *Operating costs saved*

- Staff costs
- Stationery and other supplies
- Accommodation
- Other

(iii) Net increase or reduction in operating costs.

(iv) Any incremental revenue benefits (eg higher sales volumes) from the proposed system.

(v) *Development costs*

- Systems design, development and testing
- Staff costs (or bureau costs etc) of file conversion
- Equipment costs
- Installation costs for new equipment
- Staff training costs
- Sale price of any existing equipment or accommodation no longer required

(vi) Consideration of intangible or qualitative benefits.

(vii) A summary of costs and benefits, probably presented as a discounted cash flow analysis.

10   FACT FINDING

(a) Three methods of fact finding are:

- Interviews
- Questionnaires
- Observation

Interviews involve face-to-face discussions between the analyst and individuals with knowledge of the system. The analyst asks questions and obtains answers, comments and suggestions.

Questionnaires are written lists of questions. These can be used by a systems analyst in an interview, or given to respondents, who will be asked to write answers in their own time and return the completed questionnaire.

Observation involves the analyst in watching the system in operation as an observer.

(*Note.* A fourth method of fact finding that could also be discussed is the study of historic records and documents. This is a form of observation).

(b) The advantages and disadvantages of these three methods are as follows.

(i) *Interviews.* As a fact finding technique, interviewing will to some degree be appropriate in almost all situations. It may be particularly useful where the proposed system will involve a number of related areas in the existing system. This is because it is usually the case that only by talking to all parties involved will the analyst gain a total view and proper understanding of the interaction of the various parts of the system.

Interviewers need background information on those interviewed and many find this valuable later on during implementation. It gives an opportunity to discuss in-depth opinion as well as fact and he may learn of suggestions that are worth looking into further.

294

However, interviewing is an acquired skill and depends upon the co-operation of those being interviewed. It can be costly in time and effort and the rewards are unpredictable.

(ii) *Questionnaires.* In many ways, the ideal solution to the problem of fact finding will involve a certain amount of direct contact between the analyst and those members of staff concerned with the day to day running of the system. However, it may sometimes be physically impossible, or at least highly impractical, for the analyst to personally talk with all staff members. This may either be because of the sheer numbers of staff involved and/or the decentralised nature of the business organisation. It is in such situations that the use of questionnaires may have to be considered.

Questionnaires can sample a wide range of opinion and collect useful statistics in a short space of time, particularly if those questioned cover a large geographical area. There are potentially many problems with a questionnaire. The response rate may be poor, analysis of a lengthy questionnaire can be costly and design of a good questionnaire is not easy, particularly if consistency of answer is needed to be checked by cross referencing answers.

Where questionnaires are to be distributed for completion by staff members, it is essential that the questions themselves have been designed in such a way that ambiguities are avoided. There is also a danger with questionnaires that staff may give the reply which they feel is expected of them, rather than perhaps what they see as the answer in 'real life'. For these reasons, questionnaires should only be used where the system details which the analyst is enquiring about are comparatively simple.

A questionnaire might be used to survey a new product when the potential customer base numbers many thousands.

(iii) *Observation.* Studying by observation requires a base level of knowledge about a system and should provide experience of the details of the system which is needed if changes are to be introduced. It can be a cheap means of gaining knowledge of a system and has the advantage of showing what actually happens, not what you expect or believe to be happening. On the other hand, direct observation is time consuming and may provoke a reaction in those observed which makes it difficult to allow normal working practice to go ahead as normal. It is for this reason that it would perhaps be necessary to make a number of separate observations, at random intervals, rather than forming an opinion based upon a single visit.

Observation is a useful 'follow-up' procedure, used to gain confirmation that a system is outlined 'in theory', perhaps in an interview does actually work 'in practice'.

It might be used for example whenever the flow of documents through a system needs to be assessed for efficiency.

11 STRUCTURED METHODS

(a) The term 'structured method' relates to the techniques which are now used by systems analysts to achieve a formal methodology in their approach to the tasks for which they are responsible. One such method is a step-by-step top down approach which begins with the logical design of a system and progresses in stages to physical design, implementation and maintenance. Each stage must be completed before the next one begins. Specific documents must be produced at each stage as evidence that the stage of systems development has been completed, and the documentation is also used:

(i) For communication of information about the system and its design and development.
(ii) As a memory aid to the system analyst.

The output from one stage is used as input to the next stage.

The most noteworthy aspect of this approach is its formal methodology. If systems analysts use structured methods, they will be unable to take short cuts, or use their own individual approach to designing and documenting a system and thus greater overall control of the project is more readily achieved.

(b) Some of the advantages of structured analysis techniques have been touched on in the answer to (a) above. Notwithstanding this, three advantages of an analyst using structured methods may be seen as:

(i) With the improved understanding of the stages in systems development which results from the greater effort put into recognising the various activities which have to be undertaken and the link between them, it becomes much simpler to evaluate the overall project in terms of both time and costs.

(ii) The proper use of structured methods should enable there to be greater confidence that the end result will be a system of higher quality. This is because the approach involves the strict application of proven methods whereby later stages have been satisfactorily completed. In addition, it is likely that the subsequent work will act as a further check on the 'accuracy' of that already completed.

(iii) The use of standards and the modular approach adopted should mean that any future maintenance/amendments required for the system will be more readily achieved. The discipline of requiring full documentation for all work done which is a feature of this approach should also mean that the company will not be adversely affected by changes in personnel on the development side.

12 LOGICAL AND PHYSICAL DESIGN

It is possible to describe a system in a number of ways. A system can be analysed in terms of its components (ie a collection of hardware and software items). Alternatively, a system can be examined in terms of what it does (eg the detail of the processing operations it performs). Finally a system can be viewed abstractly, in terms of its *logical design*.

The logical design of a system is the design of the system in concept, what the system is meant to achieve, rather than detailed implementation. The *physical design* of the system not only specifies hardware, but also the exact design as to how a particular procedure will be implemented in software. Theoretically, it is not impossible for one logical design to be implemented in more than one physical way (eg use different hardware, different programming languages).

The distinction between logical and physical design is at the heart of a commonly used design methodology, structured analysis.

Structured analysis is a formal methodology which begins with the logical design of the system and progresses, step by step towards physical implementation, with each stage completed before the next is commenced. The final output from each stage is used as the starting point for the next stage.

In the design of a computer system, seven stages can be outlined.

(a) Problem definition. In this stage, the problem is outlined, and ends with a statement of the scope and objectives of the proposed system, although it might only go as far as to recommend a feasibility study.

(b) A feasibility study is carried out, to see if there is a feasible solution to the problem outlined.

(c) After this stage, a rough outline of a proposed system will prepared. This wili contain no details of physical implementation, and may for example simply consist of a number of data flow diagrams. Were implementation issues to be discussed at this stage, the valuable contribution that users can make to systems design would be made less effective, as they would be unable to suggest amendments to a design which is too technical.

A stable logical model of the system is prepared.

(d) Once the logical model has been agreed, a number of outline designs will be made, with perhaps a cost/benefit analysis for each.

(e) The system is now designed in detail. Typical documents produced at this stage are the systems specification, program specifications etc.

(f) The system is now designed, tested and implemented. Programs may be designed using struct-ured narratives (eg structured English that follows certain prescribed logical rules).

(g) Maintenance involves the regular review and updating of the computer system.

13 CHARTING TECHNIQUES

A dataflow diagram illustrates the ways in which the data is handled by the program. It focuses on the functions which are performed rather than upon the detailed logic or programming instructions necessary for performing the functions. It typically uses few blocks to describe a program's operations but the objective is to describe what data is used, where it is used, modified or manipulated, where it is stored and what reports use it. The data flow diagram reveals:

Sources of data: where data is originated, by whom, what data is originated and how much, where and who it comes from.

Data stores. The data which is stored in the system, where it is stored (on-line, manually, etc) and information about how it should be stored.

Processing needed: the various computations or data manipulations (sorting, aggregation, summarisation, etc) performed.

Destinations of data: these may be storage devices or reports which use the data, or some information derived from the data.

The data flow diagram permits a specification to be drawn up which recognises more fully the types and volumes of data handled and is more able to describe how it is used by the organisation. This too is a base since new systems will often seek to extend or enhance existing system capabilities. One advantage of a data flow diagram is that it aids in determining the appropriate volume of data that a system should be designed to handle. In addition the specification may specify more clearly than the diagram the data which is to be used and how it should be handled, processed, stored and reported.

14 DECISION TABLES

Decision tables are used as a method for defining the processing operations required to perform some programme function. The basic format consists of a table with four quadrants and types of entries. The top half of the table shows the various conditions which are possible and the various combinations of them which may occur. The bottom half of the table shows the responses or options which may be undertaken and an indication whether the option would be selected under each possible combination of conditions. A simple example is shown below:

Condition	Occurrence							
Key customer?	Y	Y	Y	Y	N	N	N	N
Order over £1,000?	Y	Y	N	N	Y	Y	N	N
Credit good?	Y	N	Y	N	Y	N	Y	N
Give 5% discount	X		X					
Give 2% discount		X			X	X		
Give no discount				X			X	X
'Hold' order						X		X

This approach aids programming since it provides a logical framework to describe decisions. By listing the various conditions which the system must confront the options to be selected for each combination the programmer is better able to design and implement programmes. The table may be reviewed more readily by both programmers and operations personnel so that any oversights may be more quickly detected. A more important aspect is that it reveals combinations of conditions which might not other-wise be considered or which would be thought trivial. Decision tables provide an explicit mechanism for programming conditional decisions.

15 DATABASE

(a) A database could be defined as a collection of any type of data with a structure that removes the need for the duplication of files and meets the information needs of a large section of an organisation. It is defined in the CIMA's *Computing terminology* as: 'in its strict sense...a file of data structured in such a way that it may serve a number of applications without its structure being dictated by any one of those applications, the concept being that programs are written around the database rather than files being structured to meet the needs of specific programs'.

(b) Five advantages of a well designed database are:

(i) If duplication of information is removed, then updating information is made easier with fewer errors.

(ii) The amount of file storage space for data is reduced.

(iii) The time taken to access different parts of the same database should be less than accessing separate files.

BPP
PUBLISHING

(iv) The database can be extended to bring in new data in a structure that is well understood by those who need to use it. (A well-designed database should be flexible so that it can be extended without affecting existing applications that already use this database.)

(v) Time is saved if data are entered into a system only once.

(c) Three major problems associated with the implementation and operation of a database are:

(i) The start-up costs can be prohibitive if the gains are not well understood or defined.

(ii) The software to maintain and access a database can be complex, and also rigid and expensive. Once locked into a structure imposed by the software, then changing to use another software package is very difficult and expensive.

(iii) All users accessing the data must agree on certain protocols. Its effectiveness is diminished if this control cannot be maintained.

Note. You could also make the points that:

(iv) It is difficult to make a database fully comprehensive without incurring system design and development costs that are not justified by the benefits obtained.

(v) There might be security problems, with the danger of unauthorised access to the database file from any of the terminals linked to the system.

(d) The physical structure of data is the way data is stored for access by a particular program. The logical structure of data is the way that the data appears to a user, usually through the software (eg a hierarchical or tree structure, a plex structure, or a relational structure).

16 DATABASE ARCHITECTURE

(a) Diagram showing principal levels of architecture in a database system and place of database management system within it.

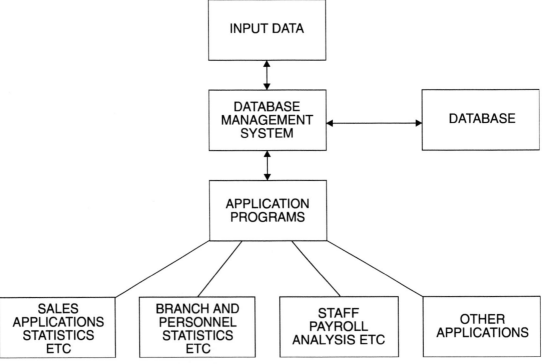

The database contains the data needed by all the applications relevant to it. However, it need not necessarily be accessed by an application program as such. Many database systems enable users to access specified items of information by means of a query language (if a relational language) or a data manipulation language. An alternative diagram of database architecture is given below.

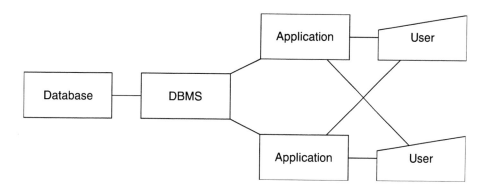

(b) *Security* and *integrity*

'Security' is a concept that applies to all computer systems and computer files, not only databases. Ultimately, any threat to a computer system is a threat to the data it processes and the information it stores. Some definitions of security are stricter than others: one defines security as 'protection against unauthorised alteration of stored data' (Sphere Dictionary of Computing). Others are broader: 'security implies protection from a risk' (Penguin Dictionary of Computing).

As far as databases are concerned there are some aspects of security which are relevant to all computer systems. The hardware has to protected against theft or damage; backup copies of files should be made in case data is lost, corrupted or destroyed. As well as physical threats, security should be maintained so that theft or unauthorised access and copying (eg industrial espionage, hacking) does not occur. Passwords are one way of restricting access. Controls and checks are also needed during system development: these include full testing, checking of program documentation.

Security relating to a database system will include the general measures outlined above. As well as security measures over hardware and system access, care must be taken to ensure that individual database files are not accessed by those who are unauthorised to see them. Not all data is required by each application, and so an application view may be made. For individual users, a password system may ensure data security, as each password may only give access to specific items of data. So, the security problem with a database is that all the data is in one, easily accessible location. In the circumstances, the damage done by viruses could be considerable.

Integrity on the other hand is a concept relating not so much to external sources of damage, but is more to do with the internal consistency of the data itself. One definition of integrity is that data is resistant 'to alteration by system errors' meaning that the contents of files will not be altered by errors in system software. An alternative definition defines integrity as 'an attribute of a set of data signifying that the data is self-consistent (eg a hash total check has proved valid) and consistent with the information system the data is representing (eg a validity check has proved valid). In a database system the concept of integrity carries the connotation that only one update to a data item need to be made, when a fact about it changes. The possibility of the same data item appearing differently on different files is therefore eliminated.

In short, security refers to the prevention of damage to data, and unauthorised access and use of it. Security refers to measures which ensure data integrity. Data integrity refers to those qualities of data which make it valid.

17   FILE CONVERSION

(a) The objectives of file conversion are to produce a file on a specified medium which is capable of being read or written by the computer software involved and which is free from errors. Until master file conversion has taken place, a computer system (eg a sales ledger system or payroll system) cannot become operational.

(b) Some typical problems encountered in file conversion are:

(i) Are source documents accurate and complete?

(ii) Are the source documents up to date?

(iii) Are the source documents in a form amenable to data input?

(iv) Do different departments in the organisation maintain compatible codes or descriptions for the same information?

(v)   If different sections have conflicting data then who is correct?

(vi)   What measures can be taken to ensure, as far as possible, that the converted file is free from input errors (eg keying-in errors)?

(c)   Planning a file conversion and controlling the work should proceed according to the following guidelines.

     (i)   Set a timetable for conversion, if possible try to do the conversion in a period when the volume of transactions is low.

     (ii)   If possible, do a dummy run to see if all the information needed is available, and that the input programs and the data validation routines are all working as planned.

     (iii)   Decide upon a date after which no further information is to be held by the old methods, making sure that all subsequent data are held in a form able to be transcribed into the new system until the system is proved.

     (iv)   Make sure that all relevant staff have been allocated enough time for training in the new system.

     (v)   As well as running the data validation programs, make continuous appraisal by means of output listings for the scrutiny of senior staff.

     (vi)   Try to plan for the quickest possible changeover to the new system, giving the least disruption to users. Make sure all the key staff are available during the exercise and that disruption due to hardware failure has been properly assessed and covered.

     (vii)   Authorise whatever overtime is necessary to ensure that file conversion takes place according to the scheduled timetable.

18   RECRUITMENT AND TRAINING

During the planning of the systems implementation the systems analyst must estimate staffing requirements for the different activities involved in the implementation procedures. These are likely to vary between the development period and the commencement and running of operations. Some of the existing staff may have to be retrained to use the computer, other user department staff may have to alter their manual procedures to accommodate the use of the computer, and computer experienced staff may have to be brought in to cope with technical aspects of the system. When recruiting staff it is advisable, where possible, to recruit as many as is feasible from within the organisation. This policy will help to maintain good staff relations and reduce suspicion in the 'new methods'. It is usually helpful however, if some of the staff have had computer experience in other installations (eg systems analysts, programmers and operators), particularly if the new system is a large one.

The systems analyst must ensure that all the staff involved in the new system will understand their job and will work willingly to achieve successful conversion and operation. He must achieve confidence in the new system and deal objectively with any problems which may arise. Very often he may work with the steering committee to plan and organise the whole programme of recruitment and training. Depending on the particular requirement of the system, various methods of communication and training may be necessary.

These methods include:

(a)   Lectures on general, or specific aspects of the system - possibly with the use of films, video, tape-recordings, slides, overhead projectors etc.

(b)   Discussion meetings, possibly following on from lectures, enabling the staff to ask questions and sort out problems.

(c)   Structural courses on the use of data processing equipment (these may be provided by the manufacturer).

(d)   Visits to other organisations/manufacturers computer departments to see how such systems work and, hopefully, arouse interest and keen anticipation.

(e)   Internal company magazines, to explain the new system in outline.

(f)   Handbooks, probably derived from the systems specification, detailing in precise terms the new documentation and procedures. Different handbooks for each function will often be prepared by different persons. For example:

(i)   Systems specifications - prepared by systems analysts.

(ii)   Software manuals - prepared by manufacturers/software houses.

(iii)   Program specifications - prepared by senior programmers.

(iv)   Computer operating instructions - prepared by programmers.

(v)   Data preparation instructions - prepared by systems analysts and the operations manager.

(vi)   Data control/library procedures - prepared by the systems analysts and the operations manager (with possible internal/external involvement).

(vii)   Clerical procedure manuals - prepared by user department representatives.

The persons responsible for the communication and training must take care over the preparation of the courses and material used. It is essential that interest is aroused and maintained, and so both courses and material must be well written, well presented and make an impact on the staff members. Illustrating narrative or lectures with pictures, graphs, histograms, Gantt charts, networks etc will help to create an appealing training package.

Naturally, the number of staff involved in a computer application will vary with the size of the installation. With many mini-computer and micro-computer systems a very small number of people (eg 1 or 2) may be involved, the various data processing responsibilities and functions being combined (with obvious internal control problems). In larger organisations where a medium/large computer installation is being developed or used there should be a clear division of responsibilities within the data processing department. In particular, the two main functions of systems development (analysis and programming) and computer operations (processing and controlling data) should be kept separate. Although it is impossible to be categorical, the personnel to be recruited might include:

(a)   The management services director (he may already exist in a large organisation).
(b)   The Information Systems/Information Technology manager.
(c)   Systems analysts.
(d)   Programmers.
(e)   Database administrator.
(f)   Operations manager.
(g)   Operations staff.

19   SECURITY OF INFORMATION SYSTEMS

There are several factors which management must consider in evaluating an information system's security.

Physical security relates to the ability to protect the hardware and media which hold programs and data from destruction, loss or damage. In most cases this protection may be provided by a specialised environment, particularly for mainframes. A computer room typically has special environmental controls for temperature and humidity. In addition, access may be strictly controlled both to the room and to programs or data. A data library may be used to store costly programs or sensitive data and careful records kept on which employees have had access to them. This reduces the potential that information or programs will be stolen or damaged. The physical environment can be controlled, and insurance can be taken in case of physical damage. A similar concern is often found with the power supplies used. In any installation the equipment is highly sensitive to minor fluctuations in voltage. Special power supplies are often used for mainframes and smaller computers may be similarly protected through comparable smaller power supplies or power line filters. Data, on the other hand, cannot be so readily protected from misappropriation. A data library may be used to control particularly sensitive data but copies might still be made. The major method of providing physically secure data is to use backup procedures so that an archived copy of the data is always kept.

Operations security has two main purposes: to prevent unauthorised users to access or use data, and to prevent authorised users from mis-using the data or damaging it through ignorance. Unauthorised users may be excluded from the system (particularly programs or sensitive data) by a variety of mechanisms. A password system which issues each authorised user with a personal code. This code must then be used whenever the user wishes to access a program or data. The system will then confirm that the user is, in fact, qualified or permitted to do so. If not, the system will then either shut down or warn the user that they are attempting something which they are not allowed to do. In addition some better systems also record the unauthorised attempts at access and provide reports to management. These may then be reviewed to see if some users may be trying to break the system's security. If consistent patterns are seen, some corrective or disciplinary action may be necessary.

BPP
PUBLISHING

No system may be made entirely secure from unauthorised human attempts to use, or mis-use it. The objective of a security system is to make the likelihood of detection and the costs of the effort outweigh the potential benefits. System security is largely dependent upon the people and policies which the organisation has in place. If the employees have poor attitudes towards computer security they can undermine even the most powerful techniques. On the other hand, if employees are conscientious about security they may themselves provide a significant barrier to unauthorised users. Both technology and motivation are needed if a security program is to succeed.

20   MAINTENANCE OF SOFTWARE

Maintenance in the software context is the amendment of computer programs where they have been found to contain errors or where the computer user has decided that they ought to be capable of doing additional processing routines or should process some data in a different way. Programs might also require adaptation to meet new external requirements eg new legislation, or because of changes in the general hardware and software of the system of which they are a part.

(a)   *Error correction*

Although all programs should be thoroughly tested before they are used for 'live' processing, it is sometimes the case that 'bugs' in the system are only revealed once live processing has been implemented. In this situation, it is essential that the errors are corrected as soon as possible, with every effort being made to ensure that all data records, reports etc affected by the errors are also corrected as part of the process of program maintenance.

(b)   *Changes in user requirements*

Most businesses will experience the need to change their systems in some way as they adapt to changed circumstances or simply because they have learned from experience that existing procedures could be achieved in a more effective way. Given such genuine reasons for change, it is essential that software maintenance is readily available to ensure that user needs are met.

(c)   *External factors requiring change*

Maintenance of software may be required as a result of such external factors as industry practice (eg metrication) or new legislation either fiscal (eg new tax rates) or general (eg The Data Protection Act). All businesses may have a need to respond to such external forces in the adaptation of their software.

(d)   *Changes in general hardware and software*

As more aspects of a company's activities are computerised, new user requirements are introduced etc, there may well be a need for additions to and/or replacement of existing hardware and software configurations. Such changes may well require the amendment of existing programs in order to cope with the new environment.

MID-SANSHIRE HEALTH AUTHORITY (21-24)

21   A widely used soft systems tool is Checkland's *Soft Systems Methodology*. This is a methodology which aims to bring about improvement by activating in the people involved in the situation a learning cycle which is ideally never-ending. An iterative process is followed, using systems concepts to debate perceptions of the real world and then taking action in the real world. This leads to changes in the real world.

The users of SSM are 'would-be improvers' of the problem situation, here the services development section. The situation which they are seeking to improve is the formulation of a new management strategy for the provision of information. Under SSM, there are two interacting streams of structured enquiry which together lead to the implementation of changes to improve the situation.

Logic-driven stream of enquiry

Under this stream of enquiry, models of human activity systems are named, modelled and used to illuminate the problem situation.

The *relevant system* has already been selected. It is a system for the provision of information. Because this is a notional human activity system whose boundaries do not coincide with the real-world manifestation, it is not a primary task system but an issue-based relevant system. This is a system which is relevant to mental processes not (currently) embodied in formalised real-world arrangements.

Next the system must be named, or given a *root definition*. The root definition expresses the core purpose of a purposeful activity system. This is expressed as a transformation process, from input to output. It requires a consideration of CATWOE: possibilities are given below.

(a) *Customers*: the staff of the MSHA.

(b) *Actors*: the services development section.

(c) *Transformation process*: the conversion of data to management information.

(d) *Weltanschauung*: that the population requires the provision of health services.

(e) *Owners*: the board of MSHA.

(f) *Environmental constraints*: legislation.

A root definition might be 'a system to provide information to management by converting data to management information in order to support the provision of health services'.

A *conceptual model* is then created, usually in diagrammatic form, and this is used to structure enquiry into the problem situation.

Cultural stream of enquiry

This consists of three examinations of the problem situation. The first examines the intervention itself, the second examines the system as social system and the third examines it as a political system.

Once the two systems of enquiry have been followed, it is necessary to define the changes which would improve the problem situation. SSM then addresses implementation of the changes, which may be categorised as culturally feasible or systemically desirable.

22 To: Services development section strategy committee
     From: Administrator
     Date: 8 June 20X1
     Subject: Information system

This memorandum describes how the new information system should support the planning and setting of objectives at all levels of the organisation.

It is common to divide management functions into three layers: senior; middle; and operational. These layers of management perform different functions, and in order to do so their information needs also differ. This both affects the content of the information they need, and the means of its presentation.

Senior management

Senior management exercise control over the long-term strategic direction of an enterprise. If MSHA seeks to enter into a joint venture agreement with, say, a neighbouring authority, this will be a decision for senior management. Senior management are therefore responsible for the overall performance of the enterprise in its environment. Many senior management decisions are one-off and relatively unstructured.

As senior management decisions are of a strategic nature, the information they need will not necessarily be provided from within MSHA. Strategic information generated internally is likely to be summary in nature. They will need to know key facts as to how MSHA is performing (eg percentage of population reached in health awareness campaigns, profitability). These can be provided as a matter of routine, but much of the information provided at this level might be ad hoc (eg looking into particular areas of operations).

Information traditionally at this level has been provided in the form of hard-copy reports, whether on a regular basis or as a result of the ad hoc exercises they sponsor. However, the growth of decision support systems (eg with a spreadsheet base) and executive information systems (which allows the user to drill down into more detailed layers of information, or to rove at will through the organisation's databases) are giving senior management the benefits of computer processing power.

As senior managers are infrequent or ad hoc users of computers, user-friendliness is of primary importance so that expensive managerial time is not wasted in learning arcane computer languages or procedures. Graphics is likely to be popular in illustrating data.

Middle management

The role of middle management is more circumscribed. They are responsible for controlling and monitoring the organisation. They take decisions of a tactical nature, which are more short term than those taken by senior management.

The sort of information needed are more detailed summaries of the operation of the organisation, including waiting lists, demand for beds, same day treatments, cash flow forecasts, variance analysis, and accounting ratios.

Much of this information is control information and will be provided as a matter of routine on a regular basis. The exception reporting principle may be introduced here, so that middle management attention can be directed to where it is needed. Middle management has also been the link between the broad strategic outlook of senior managers and the detailed running of the operation, so that senior management actions are channelled through them. Middle managers set short term plans for their area of control.

Information can be presented to middle managers on-screen or in hard copy printed reports, regularly produced. Their knowledge of the systems must be quite detailed, so that they have a detailed understanding of system output, and can draw conclusions from it.

Operational management and staff

At this level, the very detail of MSHA's operations and processing is performed. Here, control is maintained over input, and these users are likely to have the most extensive contact with a computer system. It is also easier for them to learn its procedures as they are regular and frequent users. At this level, users are rarely concerned with aggregates, but wish to ensure that the detail of transactions are processed correctly.

The information needed is routine and fairly structured. In some circumstances it might be simply confirmation that something has been processed. The feedback needs to be immediate.

23   The committee co-ordinating the development of computer based systems will normally include representatives of top management from each department affected by the project. The function of such a committee is to set up and control the feasibility study group and to act as the 'intermediary' between the study group and the board of directors of MSHA. Obviously, the precise composition and terms of reference of such a committee will depend considerably upon the particular organisation. However, the terms of reference are likely to include the following.

   (a)   The *determination of overall objectives and policies* for the organisation's information systems activities. For example, management may wish to reduce staffing and administrative costs, to improve management forecasting, to provide a better service for patients etc.

   (b)   The *establishment of guidelines* for the development of computer based processing and management information systems.

   (c)   The setting up of a *study group* (or groups) to investigate and report on existing information systems with recommendations as to their improvement or development. The steering committee would be responsible for the composition and the appointment of the members of each study group, which should include representatives of user departments as well as 'technical' experts such as systems analysts.

   (d)   The *co-ordination and control* of the work of the study group, in respect of time, cost and technical quality of the investigations.

   (e)   The *evaluation of the results* of the studies made, and the presentation of those results, in the form of a final report and recommendations to the management board.

   (f)   *Monitoring and controlling* individual development projects, eg monitoring progress, and actual costs compared with budget etc.

   (g)   Ensuring that projects are worth their *cost*, ie that their benefits (financial or otherwise) outweigh their costs.

   (h)   Possibly, giving *approval* to new projects, at the feasibility study and system specification stages. Alternatively, to make recommendations for acceptance to the authority's management board.

   (i)   Possibly, to *authorise capital expenditure* on new hardware or software packages and to liaise with suppliers.

   (j)   To monitor and *review each new system after implementation* to check whether the system has met its objectives. If it has not, to investigate the reasons for the system's failure, and take any suitable control or remedial measures.

Membership may include the following.

(a) The information director or a senior IS staff member to ensure that the management board is committed to the project and to ensure technical feasibility.

(b) The financial controller or a senior accountant for technical financial advice relating to costs and benefits.

(c) Senior user management, perhaps including a senior medical consultant, a senior staff nurse and an administrator.

24 Most management information systems are not designed, but grow up informally, with each manager (depending on his or her drive and initiative) making sure that he or she gets all the information needed to do the job. It is virtually taken for granted that the necessary information flows to the job, and to a certain extent this is so. Much accounting information, for example, is easily obtained, and managers can often get along with frequent face-to-face contact and co-operation with each other. Such an informal system works best in small companies, but is inadequate in a large organisation, especially one which spreads over a large region, like a health authority.

The consequences of a poor MIS might be dissatisfaction amongst staff who believe they should be told more, a lack of understanding about what the targets for achievement are and a lack of information about how well the work is being done. Some information systems are designed or planned, often because the introduction of computers has forced management to consider its information needs in detail. This is especially the case in large organisations, and MSHA has been forced to reconsider its strategy because of the introduction of the new legislation.

Management should try to design the management information system for their enterprise with care. If they allow the MIS to develop without formal planning, the MIS will almost certainly be inefficient because data will be obtained and processed in a random and disorganised way and the communication of information will also be random and hit-and-miss. For example, without formal planning and design of the MIS, the following situations are likely.

(a) Some managers will prefer to keep data in their heads and will not commit information to paper. When the manager is absent from work, or is moved to another job, his stand-in or successor will not know as much as he could and should about the work because there would be no information to help him.

(b) Not all data is collected and processed that ought to be, and so valuable information that ought to be available to management would be missing from neglect.

(c) Information is available but not communicated to the managers who are in a position of authority and so ought to be given it. The information would go to waste because it would not be used. In other words, the wrong people would have the information.

(d) Information is communicated late because the need to communicate it earlier is not understood and appreciated by the data processors.

These are the types of problems which a lack of user involvement in development could give rise to. The key to success is for MSHA to encourage users to become involved in the process. A number of formal systems methodologies, for example Mumford's participative approach, recognise the importance of people and the way they behave. This can broadly be termed the socio-technical approach, which views the organisation from the individual and the overall organisational perspective. The approach is based on the principles of participation. The goal is not simply the production of a technically efficient system, but also the creation of conditions supporting a high level of job satisfaction. If MSHA has a culture of participation, this may lead to the development of a system which encourages productivity, quality, co-ordination and control.

ROBINSON-HEATH FINANCIAL SERVICES (25-28)

25 The key features of SSADM are set out below. Most of these could equally well be attributed to any structured systems methodology.

Project management

The structured framework of a methodology helps with planning. It defines the tasks to be performed and sets out when they should be done. Each step has an identifiable end product. This allows control by reference to actual achievements rather than to estimates of progress. Users are able to see progress as clearly as systems professionals can.

BPP PUBLISHING

Techniques

Three techniques are used in SSADM: dataflow diagrams, logical data structures and entity life histories. These allow information to be cross-checked between diagrams and ensure that the delivered system is close to the final system, in other words that the necessity for later enhancements is minimised. For example, an event in an entity life history will match data flows which trigger processes on the dataflow diagrams. These techniques and others are available in different methodologies.

The specification

A logical design is produced that is independent of hardware and software. This logical design can then be given a physical design using whatever computer equipment and implementation language is required.

Users

Users are involved with development work from an early stage. Their involvement is a critical factor in the success of any development. SSADM encourages better communication between users and developers.

Documentation

Documentation is produced throughout the project. This gives a comprehensive and detailed picture of the system and helps understanding of the system. This makes the consequences of proposed changes clear and encourages user feedback.

Contractors

SSADM and other commercial methodologies are used widely enough to be known to many systems professionals. This is obviously an advantage, as it reduced dependence on individual suppliers or contractors.

Methodology

A methodology provides a set of development standards to which all parties can adhere.

Emphasis on graphical techniques

The emphasis on diagramming makes it easier for relevant parties, including users, to understand the system than if narrative descriptions were used. Some narrative can be used; however if this is excessive, the advantage of the diagramming techniques is lost.

26   The traditional systems development cycle was developed in the 1960s by the National Computing Centre to provide a disciplined approach to systems development which could be applied almost anywhere. It is a model of the development life cycle and contains six stages.

The systems development lifecycle approach to systems development was adopted by many organisations. It provided a model of how systems should be developed. The *success* of the cycle can be attributed to a number of factors. It imposed a disciplined approach to the development process, it encourages communication between systems professionals and 'ordinary' users and it recognises the importance of analysis and design, previously much neglected. While it has some advantages, it had a number of drawbacks, some of which, although not in direct conflict with SSADM, do not embrace the same philosophy.

Ignoring management

While it is efficient at automating operational areas within easily defined processing requirements, such as payroll, the information needs of middle and senior management can be ignored. Computerisation is seen as a means of speeding up high-volume routine transaction processing, not providing information for decision making. Computerisation is seen as a means to save money which would otherwise be spent on an army of clerks. SSADM encourages user involvement and invites management at all levels to specify their requirements. Of course, unrealistic requirements may not be met.

No radical rethink of current operations

When computer systems were first introduced, they were modelled after the manual systems they were replacing. All that happened was that clerical procedures carried out by people were computerised. Where computerisation is more ambitious, it can lead to a potentially beneficial rethink of the way the organisation carries out its activities. SSADM produces a logical design independent of hardware and software requirements, encouraging a less constrained approach to developments.

User requirements poorly defined

Much systems design is based around what the user, at an early stage in the development of a system, has specified as to what output is required. This ultimately determines what is input to the system, the file structures introduced and so forth. However, output requirements can be altered, even during systems development, and this can result in substantial design modifications. It has been estimated that a simple change in user requirements costs over 20 times as much to rectify after acceptance testing than after the design phase. Software maintenance consumes about 70% of the cost of developing a system. In SSADM, the user is involved throughout the process and so the risk of divergence between requirements and actual development is reduced.

Documentation

Much system documentation was written for programmers and specialists. It was highly technical, more of a technical manual than a guide for the user. Problems could also occur, if inadequately documented modifications led to 'bugs' elsewhere in the system. With SSADM, documentation is rigorously demanded and documentation standards are high.

Systems not complete

Many routine transaction processing systems could not cope with unusual situations, and so some complicated processing was still performed manually. In short, the system had been inadequately designed. SSADM's emphasis on logical design reduces the problem.

Applications backlog

Time overruns mean that systems take a long time to develop. The applications backlog is the systems in the pipeline whose development has been delayed. One of the causes is the time spent to maintain old systems. In some times over 60% of time spent by the programming section of a DP department will be spent on maintenance. SSADM, by encouraging standardisation on a single method, ensures that development is done in the same way each time and thus provides a basis for estimation, management, control and subsequent maintenance.

27 To: Managing Director
    From: Computer services section
    Date: 14 September 20X1
    Subject: Systems development

This memorandum suggests ways of reducing the time spent on systems development, increasing user participation and developing quality systems.

Traditional systems development cycle

I do not consider the use of the traditional systems development cycle to be viable in conjunction with SSADM (refer part (b) above). I recommend that we switch entirely to SSADM. Features of SSADM are described in Appendix A (refer part (a) above).

Prototyping

In the traditional systems development process the user is isolated from any close contact with the system during its development. Typically the user is intensively involved during the design stage during which the system functions and requirements are defined so that a system specification is produced. This specification then serves as a design document during the system design and implementation phase so that the system analysts and programmers know what to produce. The weaknesses of this approach are manifold but two major ones are described here.

(a) Many users have little real idea of what computer systems are or how they operate. This ignorance is a very poor foundation for building a systems specification. This type of user typically does not know what information is important for designing the system with the natural consequence that these systems are often incomplete or fail to achieve the required level of functionality. In these instances the user faces major communication problems with the systems professionals: he may or may not know the application to be implemented but is unaware of the aspects which are important for the successful implementation and operation of the system.

(b) A second drawback to traditional methods arises with even experienced users. Users often have incorrect or unrealistic ideas about what systems can do or how various functions might operate. In the traditional approach these ideas would not be corrected until the system itself was delivered. In these instances users would feel let down and often regard the systems as failures. An additional problem arises because applications tend to evolve over time so that system specifications become less appropriate. If, as with many mainframe systems, the development effort takes a relatively long time the delivered system may no longer effectively perform the application it was intended to perform.

Systems prototyping can significantly reduce these problems by allowing the user to participate actively in the systems design and development process. Rather than producing a detailed specification the prototyping approach aims at producing a simplified version of the system, a prototype, which the user may then try out. Typically, the user might be able to try out data input screens or perform file enquiries. The advantage of this approach is that the user actually sees a system in operation and can judge its usefulness and operation. This is extremely useful for users who are unfamiliar with information systems since they often revise their specifications as they become more familiar with the system's workings. The great advantage of this approach is the reduction in system modifications or enhancements - users can notice deficiencies before systems are delivered so that specifications may more fully address user needs.

CASE tools

Structured methods are reasonably widely used in a number of organisations. They are mandatory in many government IT functions. Their use, although standardising many results, does impose quite an overhead in terms of increased demands for correct form filling at stages of the software production process, as well as a requirement for larger amounts of other paperwork particularly in relation to updates and standards. CASE tools can reduce the effort required to perform some of the stages of the structured methodology by automatically producing the required stages. Many CASE tools go some way towards producing working programs.

The CASE tool should provide the following facilities.

(i)   Support for the methodology used by the IT function.

(ii)   Ability to interface directly to the central data dictionary.

(iii)   Access and version control, to prevent unauthorised use and to ensure the right 'master' is being worked on.

(iv)   Graphical prototyping facilities to assist in the production of reports, screens etc.

(v)   Ability to assess the impact of changes and also to validate design work.

(vi)   Facilities called code-generators to produce program output in a variety of programming languages.

(vii)   Ability to function on a reasonable-specification PC while maintaining control for a multi-member team.

Conclusion

We should give serious consideration to the use of prototyping and CASE tools to speed up our systems development. Prototyping in particular will increase user participation, as will greater emphasis on SSADM. These measures should contribute significantly to the development of quality systems.

28   The introduction of a new computer system can have a number of effects on the organisation.

(a)   It can be costly in terms of personnel (team of system analysts or programmers if developed in-house, consultancy fees if developed by outsiders).

(b)   Even if an application package is purchased, this can still be an expensive item.

(c)   The right hardware must be purchased

(d)   It is costly in terms of management time and attention. Managers from user departments inevitably get involved in systems development projects. Also different managers can have different ideas as to what is desirable.

(e)   It is disruptive (staff have to take time off work to be trained).

A project involves the management of a number of disparate, yet interdependent activities, within a timetable and a budget set in advance. A particular project is unique, in that by its nature it is not a repetitive activity.

Efficient management of the resources and process of the project is therefore important for the organisation and the achievement of the project's objectives.

A basic approach to project management would be as follows.

(a)   *Delegation of overall responsibilities.* A steering committee comprising senior user department personnel, a member of the finance department and various systems professionals is appointed to oversee the project. If the organisation has an Information Director, this individual is likely to have a key role on the steering committee.

(b)   *Appointment of a project manager.* This individual plans manages and executes the project and is responsible for its successful completion. The project manager presents the timetable and budget to the steering committee for their approval and authorisation.

(c)   *Project planning.* The goals of the project identified, and the activities needed to achieve them are outlined. These are then matched to the manpower resources available, so that a project timetable can be outlined and agreed. The timetable will indicate when each activity has to be completed, and in which order. Each stage of the project is then planned in its own right. The stages of the project may be determined by the systems development methodology adopted: SSADM lays down a sequence of six stages, excluding the feasibility study.

(d)   *Controlling the project.* Actual outcomes are compared to the plan and any difficulties dealt with as soon as they become apparent. Regular progress meetings should be held by the project manager with members of the project team to monitor performance. Specified documentation is produced at the end of each stage for review and approval, in accordance with quality control criteria established for projects of this nature. At the end of each stage, progress will be reported to the steering committee. Users should be consulted, as their approval is necessary to demonstrate that the project is meeting its objectives.

(e)   *Output of the project.* This must meet any technical criteria of the organisation. This means that all the relevant documentation must be completed to an adequate standard, project files must be cross referenced, and there should be a clear relationship evidenced between the work done in the various successive stages of the project.

In summary, therefore, the project is controlled in two ways. Firstly the technical quality of the output is reviewed. Secondly, the efficiency with which the project tasks are carried out is also subject to management review and control.

The effectiveness of project management techniques used can be assessed during the life of the project and when it is completed. Participants should be asked for feedback, but, more formally, the project manager should estimate the causes for each departure from standard, and take corrective measures. This will require the establishment of a suitable management information system, so that the project manager can obtain feedback on the timetable for and success of stages of the development as each is undertaken. The monitoring process should take into account four criteria.

(a)   Time, by reference to PERT or Gantt charts.
(b)   Resources, by measuring available resources and percentage utilisation.
(c)   Costs, by reference to the MIS and budgets.
(d)   Quality, as appropriate.

TONE ZONE LEISURE CENTRE (29-30)

29   Organisations are structured in a number of different ways. In larger organisations executive power is held by senior management, who are not involved in the day to day operations of the organisation. The decisions which senior management are required to make will be of a different kind from those made by staff in ensuring the smooth running of departments and processes. In a smaller organisation the same people may be called on to make different types of decision. What is clear is that when a problem arises in any organisation, a decision will have to be reached as to how to resolve that problem.

In order to reach a decision in response to a problem, a decision maker usually goes through a process of defining the problem, identifying alternative courses of action, evaluating these and then making the decision. To do this he requires information at several stages, for example to understand why the problem has arisen, and what the effect of different courses of action will be. The type of information required depends on the type of decision being taken.

Robert N Anthony identified three distinct areas of decision-making. Senior management, in setting an organisation's policies and objectives, are involved in *strategic planning*. They delegate to middle management the job of obtaining and using efficiently resources to meet those objectives within the parameters laid down. Middle management therefore exercise *management control*. Individual tasks are performed to meet the plans of middle management and these are subject to *operational control*, usually requiring programmed decisions.

As noted above, a decision can only be reached once information pertaining to that decision has been obtained. The information required for each level of decision-making may also be seen as a hierarchy of *strategic* information, *tactical* information and *operational* information.

BPP PUBLISHING

(a) *Strategic* information is used by senior management to set the organisation's objectives and to assess whether those objectives are being met. Strategic information is derived from internal and external sources. Internally to TZLC, senior management must have information on, for example, profitability and market share of the business and business segments, on cash requirements and on staffing and asset levels. Externally, they require information on competitors, interest rates, consumer attitudes to health and fitness, environmental concerns and legislation.

(b) *Tactical* information is used by middle management in applying the resources of the business and in monitoring how those resources are employed. Much of this is internal, including variance analyses and departmental profitability (by activity). Some external information may also be required, for example the state of the sector's labour market and typical price movements.

(c) *Operational* information is used to ensure that a specific individual task is planned and performed properly. This type of information is almost entirely internally generated, for example overtime levels, facility usage information and accident/safety reports.

30 The Tone Zone Leisure Centre exists in the wider social environment, but is distinct from it. However, many organisational objectives are pursued in relation to the organisation's environment.

As well as receiving inputs from the environment for the express purpose of producing outputs, the organisation is affected by the environment in a number of different ways. This is because an organisation's environment is itself diverse. The environment is in a state of change. Change occurs at different rates.

(a) Some change is long-term and slow (for example population growth, change in the age distribution of the population).

(b) Some changes are dramatic, but infrequent (for example findings on safety of sunbeds).

(c) Other changes are immediate (for example a competitor starts a discount battle).

The elements which make up the organisation's environment can be categorised as follows. The effects of changes are also shown.

(a) The *marketplace* consists of customers and trends in design and consumer tastes. Changes in attitudes to 'the body beautiful' will affect usage as would, for example, British gold medallists in gymnastics events at the Olympics.

(b) The *competition* includes both existing competitors and new competitors. A second health centre opening in the vicinity would affect business.

(c) *Government* determines financial and political policies and has an effect on the macro-economic environment within which the organisation operates. Increases in interest rates might decrease disposable income and cause usage to fall.

(d) The *general public* reflects changes in the behaviour and expectations of society as a whole. The growth of 'ethical' investment funds reflects a new pressure on corporate activity. Society's attitudes towards competitive sport are changing.

(e) *Ecology*, or the natural environment, is affected by the organisation's activities. Does the centre have any 'green' initiatives which it can publicise?

(f) *Technology* may affect not only individual processes within the organisation, but also the approach the organisation adopts towards the environment. Availability of advanced electronic monitors attached to machines in the gym might increase their popularity.

31 The flexibility and accuracy provided by database packages is ideally suited to MIS because it allows a wide range of data to be input only once to update more than one application and to be presented to management for a number of different uses.

An advantage of database systems is the consistency of data across an organisation because the data is only input once. A common problem in many organisations is that individual departments may use different systems to hold the same information, leading to potential discrepancies and conflicts. The knowledge that a single information package is being used company-wide will increase management confidence in the decision making process.

Databases also fulfil other requirements of Management Information Systems, namely ease of use and a broad availability to many users. In business today information is always required 'now' and delays which may occur in order to piece information together from various sources are often not acceptable.

Databases can cross the boundaries of individual activities. For example, health facility and gymnasium information may be combined for marketing purposes, or finance and administration may both require costing information. This capability clearly justifies the use of databases where information from different activities is required to be brought together.

Predominantly, though, information from a database flows vertically up and down an organisation hierarchy. It may therefore feed systems which can be used by the bookings receptionist or the MD from the same base of information. All levels of management can work from the same information and a database is especially useful to strategic management who can, if necessary, search down to enquire on the more detailed operational data.

It is worth noting that the advantages of databases do not negate the existence of file management systems. Not all organisations have the expertise to use databases and indeed, powerful application packages will still be required in many organisations. They may lack flexibility but they do the job for which they are designed. However, many companies are increasingly looking to databases to provide most of their information requirements.

The application specific approach would result in separate data files for each activity, for example separate records for use of health facilities, main hall, squash courts and the gymnasium. If research indicates that squash players who use the pool are also likely to use a solarium, then a new solarium can be marketed to those members specifically. Using application specific files, a search of both the swimming records *and* the squash records would be necessary.

What is needed is a means of getting at this information and building up a rounded picture of each customer with details of *all* the services provided. Good marketing information would enable far more accurately targeted marketing campaigns to be performed and eliminate much wasted activity in inappropriate marketing, perhaps because a customer already used a facility or is not the type of person likely to require a particular service.

32 It is assumed that a one day course is to be run. Longer courses could obviously cover these and other topics in more detail.

9.00 - 9.15   Registration and coffee

9.15 - 9.30   Introduction from managing director of the Centre

9.30 - 10.30   Computer literacy and familiarisation (I)

Obviously, there must be a familiarisation process, and an attempt to explain to the staff how the new system will affect them in their jobs. This process must discuss why the new system is necessary and what it means for the staff. It will be important to explain how they will be retrained to do jobs in the new system, how they will not be left behind by the technological process, and how the new equipment will not disrupt the social fabric of their working relationship with colleagues. The aim of this familiarisation process could begin to persuade staff that there is a need for the system, and to give them confidence that they can handle the change from methods used in previous jobs.

10.30 - 10.50   Break

10.50 - 12.00   Computer literacy and familiarisation (II)

There must be an introduction to computers, which explains in broad outline what a computer does, and how it affects office working. A training film might be available for show. The aim should be to give staff a basic grounding in computer knowledge.

12.00 - 12.30   Discussion and questions

12.30 - 1.30   Lunch

1.30 - 3.00   Hands-on session

Staff should be introduced to the physical hardware that they will have to use. Terminal keyboards should be available to give staff some direct experience of what they are like. If possible, they should be given a few minutes' practice each, perhaps with the aid of an instruction program on the use of terminals. This will be part of the familiarisation process.

3.00 - 3.20   Break

3.20 - 4.45   Detailed operation

BPP PUBLISHING

There must be a session on how the new system will work in some detail, in particular in the ways it will affect the staff directly. The explanation of the new system will undoubtedly give rise to numerous queries. These should be discussed at some length, to reassure staff that all eventualities have been foreseen.

4.45 - 5.15   Discussion and questions

5.15 - 5.30   Final speech from MD

Since there is a limit to the information that trainees can absorb in one day, they should be provided with ample documentation and notes to take away with them.

NORMAN (33-36)

33 The systems development lifecycle includes as part of its last stage a requirement that a new system be subject to *review*. This is usually referred to as a post-implementation review. In certain methodologies, the review stage is not included. This does not mean that it should not be performed, it simply means that the particular methodology does not address the later stages of development, being more concerned with analysis and design.

The review should *evaluate* the success of the project. To do this, a comparison will be made of the objectives and original cost-benefit submissions against actual performance and actual value. The operational characteristics of the system will also be reviewed.

The system should have been designed with clear, specified *objectives*, and justified in terms of *cost-benefit analysis* or other *performance criteria*. Post-implementation review should establish whether the objectives and targeted performance criteria have been met, and if not, why not, and what should be done about it.

Planning the review

Such an evaluation must be planned, so that suitable measurements can be made on the basis of the *old* system. The post-implementation measurement should not be made too soon after the system goes live, or else results will be abnormally affected by 'teething' problems, lack of user familiarity and resistance to change.

Performing the review

In appraising the operation of the new system immediately after the changeover, comparison should be made between actual and predicted performance. This will include (amongst other items) consideration of throughput speed (time between input and output), use of computer storage (both internal and external), the number and type of errors/queries and the cost of processing (data capture, preparation, storage and output media, etc).

It should be the steering committee's responsibility to ensure that post-implementation reviews are carried out, although the internal audit department may be required to do the work of carrying out the reviews.

Just as during the feasibility study the feasibility of a project is assessed by reference to technical, operational, social and economic factors, so the same criteria can be used for evaluation. For example, a *technical* evaluation might ask the following questions.

(i)   Is the *throughput rate* from data capture to receipt of output acceptable?

(ii)   Is there sufficient *secondary storage* to keep the necessary data, including back-ups and archive data?

(iii)   Are *response times* acceptable for given processing volumes?

Reporting on the review

The findings of a post-implementation review team should be formalised in a report.

(a)   A *summary* of their findings should be provided, emphasising any areas where the system has been found to be unsatisfactory. The report should recommend what action(s) should be taken.

(b)   A review of system *performance* should be provided. This will address the matters outlined above, such as run times and error rates.

(c)   A *cost-benefit review* should be included, comparing the forecast costs and benefits identified at the time of the feasibility study with actual costs and benefits.

(d)   *Recommendations* should be made as to any further action or steps which should be taken to improve performance.

34

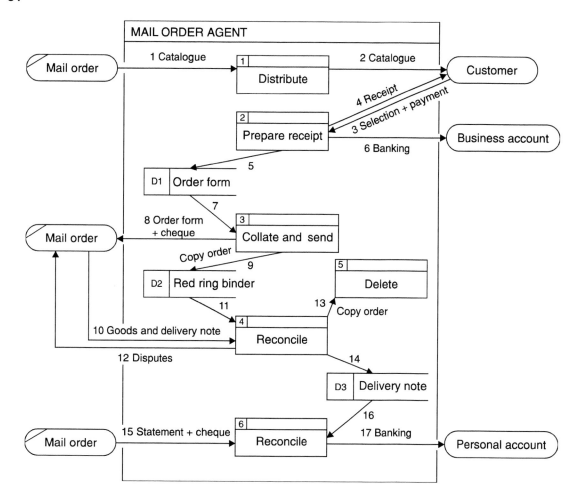

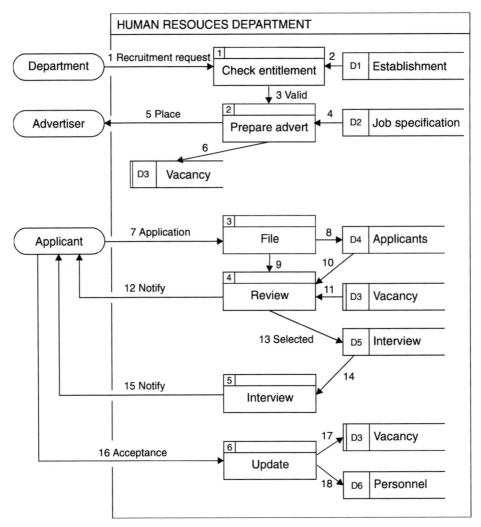

HUMAN RESOUCES DEPARTMENT

Department → 1 Recruitment request → [1] Check entitlement → 2 → D1 Establishment

Check entitlement → 3 Valid → [2] Prepare advert

Prepare advert → 5 Place → Advertiser

Prepare advert → 4 → D2 Job specification

Prepare advert → 6 → D3 Vacancy

Applicant → 7 Application → [3] File → 8 → D4 Applicants

File → 9 → [4] Review

Review → 10 → D4 Applicants

Review → 11 → D3 Vacancy

Review → 12 Notify → Applicant

Review → 13 Selected → D5 Interview

D5 Interview → 14 → [5] Interview

Interview → 15 Notify → Applicant

Interview → 16 Acceptance → [6] Update

Update → 17 → D3 Vacancy

Update → 18 → D6 Personnel

35 The situation described is a rather extreme example of the types of problem which may occur when a new computer system is installed. There are two types of issue to consider here. Firstly it is not clear how well staff have been prepared for the idea of computerisation in general terms: for example, its likely effect on their working practices and the benefits it can bring. Secondly, it is clear that Norman has not been trained in what he is supposed to do.

Effect of computerisation

Any systems development brings a great deal of change to users - the familiar, however unsatisfactory it may be, is replaced by the unknown, so that a user's working practices and environment may change beyond all recognition. Users may not therefore embrace the systems development process wholeheartedly. Many people are averse to change. Change brings disruption to working practices and effort is required on the part of the user to understand and adopt a new system.

Users may be reluctant to become involved through fear of loss of their job; computers are seen as replacing people as tasks become automated. Even if the individual does not fear redundancy, it is unlikely that a whole department will continue to operate without some kind of re-definition of roles of redeployment of resource. Established teams may become broken up. Norman may have a number of concerns.

Analysts must use appropriate skills to involve users. A belief that analysts are 'techies', ruthless in their approach and themselves having all the characteristics of a computer and none of a human being, may discourage users from involvement. Analysts require an understanding of user concerns and tenets, so that these can be understood and overcome.

Training

It appears that Norman has not been adequately trained. First of all, some basic computer literacy training would have been of benefit; this could have dealt with such matters as dealing with printers. Benefits of proper training include the following.

(a) *Best practice.* Formal training ensures that users follow good working practices. This is particularly important in the area of general policy and procedure, eg computer security, back-up routines etc.

(b) *Software capabilities.* Since the organisation is likely to have spent considerable amounts on software, it is worth making users aware of the software's capabilities on more than some kind of assumed 'need to know' basis. This will encourage users to make best use of systems and operate them in the most efficient and effective way.

(c) *Confidence.* Users will be given confidence in their ability to use the system - without formal training they may be reduced to flicking through manuals and left with a feeling of uncertainty as to what they are doing.

(d) *Assistance.* Formal training is important if only to point out the user-friendly features of a system and the existence of 'help' screens. The user will be given some indication of where to turn for assistance.

(e) *Feedback.* It is easier to monitor the success of formal training than informal training. Follow-up procedures will identify the aptitude of trained staff for the tasks they do, and changes can then be made where necessary.

(f) *Surroundings.* Users can be given an awareness of how their jobs fits into the whole system entity. An understanding of how tasks are related may lead to suggestions for improvement.

36 To: Head of Systems Development
From: Product delivery system review team
Date: 30 August 20X1
Subject: New product delivery system

This memorandum explains the difficulties experienced by Norman, the stock controller, following introduction of the new product delivery computer system. It also suggests possible remedial action.

Situation

The product delivery system has now been live for three weeks. Norman is not at all well-acquainted with his revised role following introduction of the new system. No computerised despatch notes have been issued for three weeks. All deliveries are still being accompanied by manual tickets.

Recommendations

The recommendations to remedy this situation are as follows.

(a) Explain to Norman the purpose of the computer system
(b) Give Norman and his staff a basic computer literacy session (2 hours duration)
(c) Give Norman on-the-job training in his new role (estimated 7 hours over next 4 days)
(d) Implement formal training procedures for all future developments

Purpose of system

This should include a description of the benefits of computerisation.

(a) The *accuracy* of information is improved.
(b) The *volume* of information which can be processed is increased.
(c) The *speed* at which information becomes available is higher.
(d) The *workforce* is freed up for more skilful and judgmental work.
(e) There is greater *access* to information available to more people.

Computer literacy

For raw beginners, computer literacy should include such areas as the following.

(a) Switching hardware on and off.

(b) Basic printer troubleshooting, giving an awareness of the difficulties of actually connecting an 'intelligent' printer and convincing it to stay on line.

(c) How menu systems work.

(d) Password discipline.

(e) Back-up procedures.

(f) Office regulations.

(g) Health matters, such as maintaining a good posture.

(h) Safety, such as risk of electrocution.

(i) Basic keyboard skills.

Training

If the company is going to get as much out of technology as it can, familiarity with IT must be spread throughout all levels of the organisation. Just as computerisation will be impeded if systems are not user-friendly, so the successful adoption of IT will not occur if the organisational culture is not computer-friendly.

It should seem obvious that training for an individual system installation is necessary. However, the issue of training does raise the wider matter of how to make personnel at all levels competent and willing to use IT. If management wishes to encourage end-user computing then a training programme can be part of a wider 'propaganda' exercise by information systems professionals.

Future procedures

From the above, it should be clear that users need a number of different types of computer and systems training.

(a) Basic *literacy* in IT such as the concept of a file, updating, maintenance and so forth, is needed. This might help users relate the workings of a manual system to its computer replacement. Also, some basic ideas as to how to use a computer efficiently can be usefully taught.

(b) Users also need to learn how to use a *particular application* quickly, even if they do not go into the finer points of it. If the system is complex, such training gives users an overall view of the system, commands and procedures.

(c) Users might sometimes need a *refresher course*, especially if they do not use a particular application regularly.

(d) Users need training while operating the application (*on-the-job training*).

It can become a major exercise, once a system is in the process of implementation, to undertake staff training for possibly dozens of employees. Here are some of the ways to meet these requirements.

(a) Traditional 'class room' lectures given at training centres.
(b) Computer based training (CBT) involves on screen practice on the system itself.
(c) In-house video production, involving interactive videos.
(d) Clear and comprehensive documentation and manuals for the system.

Glossary
and Index

ADSL Asymmetric Digital Subscriber Line. A data transmission system that offers data transfer rates of up to 8 Mbps, considerably faster than ISDN. ADSL allows information to be sent out over ordinary copper wires and simultaneous use of the line by numerous data flows.

Advanced Manufacturing Technology (AMT) An approach to manufacturing which encompasses automated production technology, computer assisted design and manufacturing, flexible manufacturing systems and robotics and a wide array of innovative computer equipment.

AI *see* Artificial intelligence.

ALU *see* Arithmetic and Logic Unit.

Analogue signal A signal that varies smoothly and continuously in amplitude and time. (Compare *digital signal*.)

Apple Macintosh A microcomputer that was the standard for graphics-based applications in the early 1980s and is still highly popular amongst certain users.

Application packages Ready-made programs written to perform a particular job (as opposed to operating systems programs which control the workings of the computer, and as opposed to general purpose packages that can be used for a range of jobs).

Arithmetic and logic unit (ALU) The part of the CPU where the arithmetic and logic operations are carried out. These include arithmetic (for example adding and multiplying) and logical functions such as comparison, branch operations (a branch instruction changes the order of program instructions) and movement of data. In a PC, the control unit and the ALU are built on a single microchip.

Artificial intelligence (AI) A discipline concerned with using computers to perform operations which require intelligence when carried out by humans, for example learning and decision making.

Assembler A program that translates programs written in assembly language into machine code.

Assembly language A low-level language enabling a program in machine code to be readable by humans. Symbols are used to represent elements of the machine code. The programmer is able to use easily learned and understood operation mnemonics (for example, ADD, SUB and MULT).

Asynchronous data transmission Transmission of data in a continuous stream, each operation ending with a signal to indicate that it is complete (compare synchronous data transmission).

ATM Automated Teller Machine, in other words a 'hole in the wall' cash machine.

Back-up An extra copy of data made as a security measure in case the original version is damaged.

Backing store Where information is held for reference purposes when it is not being worked on directly. This usually means either a disk or the next device down in the memory 'hierarchy'.

Bandwidth is one of the things that determines the amount of data that can be sent down a telecommunications line. It is the range of frequencies that the channel can carry. Frequencies are measured in cycles per second, or in Hertz. The wider the bandwidth, the greater the number of messages that a channel can carry at any particular time.

Bar code Groups of marks which, by their spacing and thickness, indicate specific codes or values. A typical bar code has 13 digits, each being represented by two bars, whose thickness and spacing determines the digit in question.

BASIC Beginners All-purpose Symbolic Instruction Code. A high-level programming language which is used in non-specialist applications. BASIC is designed for beginners, particularly on PCs.

Batch A group of related items input to a computer over a period of time not requiring immediate processing.

Baud rate Speed of data transmission. Measured in baud, usually equal to bits per second.

Bit Either of the digits 0 and 1. *Bit* stands for BInary digiT. A bit is the smallest unit of information in any computer system. Each individual storage element in a computer's memory consists of a simple circuit which can be switched ON or OFF. These two states can be conveniently expressed by the numbers 1 and 0 respectively. Also see *byte*.

Bureaucracy An organisation culture typical of large organisations where there is a formal structure and where activities are carried out according to well-established rules and procedures.

Bus Data is transferred within the CPU or between CPU and peripherals by means of 'bus circuitry'. A bus carries a number of bits (depending on its size) along a number of tracks.

Business process re-engineering (BPR) Re-organising a business according to the processes it performs rather than the functions it performs (for example a sale is a process that is traditionally handled not only by what are called 'sales' people, but also by accounts people, warehousing people and so on).

Byte A group of eight bits. A byte may be used to represent a character, for example a letter, a number or another symbol. Since a byte has 8 bits, there are 256 (2^8) different combinations of 1s and 0s. This is sufficient to cover numeric digits, upper and lower case alphabets, punctuation marks and other symbols.

C and C++ A programming language originally developed for use with Unix. It combines features of high-level and low-level languages and is particularly popular with professional programmers.

CAAT *see* Computer Assisted Audit Technique.

Cache Additional memory which may be inserted between the CPU and the memory proper. Cache memory facilitates access to the main memory.

CAD *see* Computer Aided Design.

Card reading devices Devices that are capable of understanding information held on the magnetic strip of a typical credit card or in the microprocessor chip embedded in a Smart card.

CASE *see* Computer Aided Software Engineering.

CD-ROM Compact Disk Read Only Memory. The most common kind of optical disk. They use similar technology to the laser based compact disc audio system. They can hold far more data than conventional ('floppy') removable disks.

Central processing unit (CPU) The 'brain' of the computer. It is a collection of electronic circuitry and registers that carries out the processing. The CPU is divided into three areas, the control unit, the arithmetic and logic unit (ALU), and the main store, or memory. The set of operations that the CPU performs is known as the *instruction set*, or repertoire, and this determines in part the *speed* at which processing can be performed.

Character The smallest working unit of information in most computer applications.

CIM *see* Computer Integrated Manufacturing.

Closed system A system which is isolated and shut off from its external environment, and independent of it, so that no environmental influences affect the behaviour of the system nor does the system exert any influence on its environment.

Coaxial cable like the cable used to link a TV aerial to a television set, consists of a central copper wire which is insulated and surrounded by a further conducting wire. This allows data to be transferred hundreds of times faster than copper wire.

COBOL Common Business Oriented Language. A high-level programming language used in business applications.

COM *see* Computer Output on Microform.

Compiler A program that translates high-level language program (source code) into object code (normally machine code), prior to execution of that program. (Compare *interpreter*.)

Computer 'A machine that, under the control of a stored program, automatically accepts and processes data, and supplies the results of that processing' (British Computer Society).

Computer Aided Design (CAD) Use of computer technology to assist in the design of a product, particularly in engineering and architecture.

Computer Aided Software Engineering (CASE) A package that provides a set of software tools to support a programming method.

Computer Assisted Audit Technique (CAAT) A means of checking the operation of a computer system. Test data is data prepared by the auditor for processing by the computer system to see if it produces the correct results (which are already known). Audit software is used to generate test data, check calculations, extract information for additional analysis and so on.

Computer Integrated Manufacturing (CIM) The use of computers to control and co-ordinate manufacturing and materials handling equipment.

Computer Output on Microform (COM) Output transferred directly to microfilm or microfiche, usually for archive purposes.

Configuration The way in which the computers in a system are connected to one another. Computer-to-computer links might be via internal cable (and so 'local') or via a data transmission link, so that geographically distant computers can be made to communicate directly with each other. A computer configuration might consist of a stand-alone computer with its peripheral equipment and one user, a computer whose peripheral equipment includes several terminals for several different users, or networks of inter-communicating computers with shared files.

Control unit Part of the CPU. The control unit receives program instructions, one at a time, from the main store and decodes them. It then sends out control signals to the peripheral devices, co-ordinated by a clock. The number of pulses (cycles) produced per second is usually measured in megahertz (MHz) and is an indication of processing speed.

CPU *see* Central Processing Unit.

Critical path In *network analysis*, the longest sequence of consecutive activities through the network.

Critical success factors Matters all of which are critical to the furtherance of the company's aims.

Cybernetics The study of the evolution, adaptation and control of systems. A general cybernetic control model has five stages: identification of system objectives, measuring achievements/outputs of the system, comparing achievements with objectives, identifying what corrective action might be necessary, and implementing corrective action.

Data capture Where data is recorded for subsequent use in processing, ideally in such a way as to be directly convertible into a machine-sensible form. Data capture may

occur far away from the main computer, or the equipment may be on-line. For example, a sales transaction in a supermarket also captures useful information abut stock movements.

Data Flow Diagram (DFD) A diagram that shows sources of data, processes, and data stores and the flow of data between them.

Data Unprocessed information , the raw material for data processing.

Database Management System (DBMS) Software that builds, manages and provides access to a database, allowing a systematic approach to the storage and retrieval of data.

Decision support systems Computer systems used by management to aid in making decisions on issues which are unstructured. Decision support systems combine conventional data access with a wide range of information gathering and analytical tools.

Desktop publishing (DTP) software includes facilities for page layout and design and the inclusion of pictures and diagrams.

Deterministic system A system in which the values of each 'input variable', and the way in which the variables interact, are known with certainty.

Digital means 'of digits or numbers'. A computer uses information including letters and other non-numeric symbols, in a coded (binary) form.

Digital signal A signal whose voltage at any particular time is at one of two discrete levels (on/off, true/false). (Compare analogue signal.)

Digital Versatile Disc (DVD) Disk format for storing digital information. Pre-recorded DVDs have a storage capacity of 4.7 gigabytes (14 times the capacity of CDs). Data is read optically using a laser as the disk rotates. Popular for multimedia applications, particularly feature films.

Direct access Access to storage such that each item of data is read or retrieved in a constant time irrespective of the location in store of the previous item accessed.

Direct data entry Feeding input directly into a computer using a keyboard. As input is at normal typing speed this is normally restricted to low volume applications, file enquiries, updates in real-time systems, and the control of computer operations.

321

Disk drive The mechanism that causes a disk to rotate.

Disk storage The most commonly used backing storage medium. Data is held on a number of circular, concentric tracks on the surfaces of the disk, and is read or written by rotating the disk past read/write heads. The data on a disk is located by its sector, as each track and sector has a unique identification number. See also optical storage.

Distributed processing a system in which there are several autonomous but interacting processors and/or data stores at different geographical locations linked over a communications network. In other words, distributed processing links several computers together.

Document reader An input device which reads marks or characters made in predetermined positions on special forms.

Document reading methods reduce human 'intrusion' into data capture and cut out the need to transcribe manually-prepared data on to a computer-sensible input medium. Document reading methods of data collection involve the use of a source document that both humans and computers can read. The data on the source document might be pre-printed, or added later by manual processing, but in either case the source document itself is fed in to the computer.

Dot matrix printer A dot matrix printer has a head containing a series of steel pins or 'needles'. Characters are constructed by pressing a combination of these pins against the print ribbon, and so on paper each character appears as a matrix of small dots.

DTP *see* Desktop Publishing.

Dumb terminals Computer terminals (keyboard and VDU) which do not include a CPU and so cannot do independent data processing. A dumb terminal relies on the central computer for its data processing power.

Duplex Simultaneous two-way transmission of data (also referred to as full duplex).

DVD *see* Digital Versatile Disc.

Dynamic problem A problem in which the variables change and the relationships between them change and interact. The problem 'How much profit will be made' is a dynamic one in the real world. A dynamic model, therefore, will be continuously changing, either because new data is input to keep its parameters up to date or because new specifications are made to alter the model design.

Electronic Funds Transfer at Point of Sale (EFTPOS) Systems by which customers in shops and at petrol stations can use a plastic card to purchase goods or services. The card is swiped through a terminal and the customer's card account or bank current account is debited automatically.

Electronic point of sale (EPOS) devices use bar coding and scanners and act both as cash registers and as terminals connected to a main computer. This enables the computer to produce useful management information such as sales details and analysis and stock control information very quickly.

Encryption The process of scrambling data, transmitting the scrambled data and then unscrambling it.

Entity A source or destination of data.

Exchangeable disk pack A pack, or cartridge, of hard magnetic disks used with larger computers.

Executive information system An information system which gives the executive a straightforward means of access to key internal and external data.

Expert systems Computer programs that allow users to benefit from expert knowledge and information.

Extranet An intranet that is accessible to authorised outsiders.

Feedback Information about actual achievements that is returned (fed back) to its source.

Feedforward control A control system in which deviations in the system are anticipated, so that 'corrective action' can be taken in advance of them actually happening.

Fibre-optic cable is made out of thin glass strands, through which pulses of light (as opposed to electricity) are passed in *digital* form.

Field A group of characters which together represent a single data item, eg employee name or book value of asset. A group of related fields forms a record.

File access File access means locating individual records in a file. The way in which a file can be accessed will depend on how the file is organised, but access might be serial, sequential or direct.

File organisation File organisation refers to the way in which records are held on a file, with a view to the retrieval of data/information. For this purpose it is necessary to give each record in the file a key field by which it can be identified. File organisation might be unordered, sequential or random.

Fixed length records all contain the same number of characters.

Floppy disks An exchangeable circular, flexible disk (typically 3½ or 5¼ inches in diameter) which is held permanently in a square paper sleeve or a rigid plastic case.

FORTRAN FORmula TRANslation. A high-level programming language used in scientific and mathematical applications.

Fourth generation languages (4GLs) An ill-defined term that refers to software intended to help computer users or computer programmers to develop their own application programs more quickly and cheaply. A 4GL, by using a menu system for example, allows users to specify what they require, rather than describe the procedures by which these requirements are met. The detail is done by the 4GL software.

Front end processors A multi-user system might use a front-end processor positioned between the terminals and the 'host' computer. The front-end processor handles data communications, for example the organisation of incoming messages from terminals and the despatch of outgoing messages. Thus it might be responsible for assembling messages into packets, parity checks, message labelling and the removal or insertion of stop or start bits in asynchronous mode.

Full duplex is data transmission in both directions simultaneously.

General purpose packages An off-the-shelf program that can be used for processing of a general type, but the computer user can apply the package to a variety of specific uses of his own choice. Spreadsheet packages, word processing packages and desktop publishing packages are examples.

Gigabyte (Gb) 2^{30} (1,073,741,824) bytes. The term is widely used to mean 1 billion bytes or 1,000 megabytes.

Graphical User Interface (GUI) Now the main means by which humans communicate (or 'interface') with machines. A GUI uses pictorial symbols that help to make computer operations intuitive for human users, such as a button with a magnifying glass that is clicked to make the image on a VDU bigger. Microsoft Windows is the best-known GUI.

Half-duplex A system of data transmission in either direction but not simultaneously.

Hard disks A type of magnetic disk for data storage. A modern business PC invariably has an internal hard disk incorporated inside the microcomputer itself. The hard disk has much larger storage capacity than the floppy disk or CD-ROM and is used to store the operating software and main applications software as well as data files.

Hardware The machines comprising the physical components of a computer system, such as processor, screen, keyboard and printer.

High-level languages were developed to overcome the low-level language difficulty of machine dependency. Such programming languages have an extensive vocabulary of words and symbols and they improve the productivity of programmers. There is no clear visible relationship between a high-level language program and the machine code language that it eventually becomes. High-level language source programs are shorter than lower level language source programs, and program writing time is quicker. They speed up testing and error correction. The program is easier to understand (and easier to learn). Examples are FORTRAN, COBOL and BASIC. They are also know as third-generation languages.

IBM compatible A microcomputer like those launched in the early 1980s by IBM. Most modern PCs are 'clones' of this type of microcomputer.

Indexed sequential access is a term used to describe direct access to records that are held in a key field order in file - ie are filed sequentially - using an index to locate individual records directly.

Information *Output* from a system which has been processed to give it meaning. (Compare *data*.)

Inkjet printers, as their name suggests, work by sending a jet of ink on to the paper to produce the required characters. They are quiet and produce reasonable quality output, but are slower than laser printers.

Input device A unit which accepts *input* for processing by a computer, for example a keyboard, a bar code reader or a VDU.

Integrated software Integrated software refers to programs, or packages of programs, that perform a variety of different processing operations, using data which is compatible with whatever operation is being carried out.

Integrated Systems Digital Network (ISDN) A telecommunications network that carries information in digital form as opposed to the analogue form of older networks. ISDN makes it possible to send voice, data and fax from a single desktop computer system over telecommunications links without a modem.

Interface Either the point at which two pieces of application software are linked in a computer system (eg where sales ledger information is read by the nominal ledger and used to update the latter) or the circuitry which enables the CPU to communicate with its peripherals or the computer to communicate with its user. (See also parallel interface, serial interface, and Graphical User Interface.)

Internet A global network that enables millions of computers and other devices to communicate with each other.

Interpreter An interpreter takes a program written in a high level program language and executes it, statement by statement (ie instruction by instruction) directly during the running of the program. With an interpreter, there is no need for a compiler to produce machine code language in advance. (Compare *compiler*.)

Intranet An internal network that utilises internet protocols – used to share information.

ISDN *see* Integrated Systems Digital Network.

Java A programming system that can be used to build applications that run on all types of computer.

Just-in-Time A technique of organising work flows, to allow rapid, high quality, flexible production whilst minimising waste and stock levels. JIT includes *Just-in-Time production*, whereby items are only produced when needed for the next stage of production, and *Just-in-Time purchasing*, which tries to ensure that stocks of raw materials arrive only just before the time when they are needed.

Kb Kilobyte. Strictly 1,024 (2^{10}) bytes, but widely used to denote 1,000 bytes.

Key field A field in a record which is used to locate or identify that record, eg customer account codes in a sales ledger master file.

Keyboard A typical computer keyboard has 102 or more keys and is a development of the QWERTY typewriter keyboard.

Kilobyte (Kb) 2^{10} (1,024) bytes. The term is widely used to mean 1,000 bytes.

LAN Local Area Network. Network of linked computers in a single geographical location (ie one site or building). (Compare WAN.)

Laptop A type of portable personal computer.

Laser printers A type of printer that works by means of a laser beam shining on to a photoconductive drum. They print a whole page at a time. The resolution of printed characters and diagrams with laser printers is very high.

Leased line A special, private, telecommunications link provided at a fixed charge per annum. Many organisations will lease a number of lines to construct their own private 'networks'. If an organisation requires frequent or constant communications links, it will be more likely to lease private lines.

Line printers A line printer prints a complete line in a single operation, usually printing between 600 and 1,000 lines per minute.

Local area network (LAN) A system of interconnecting PCs and other devices over a small area, typically within a few hundred metres. A LAN will usually be located on a single site, and does not need modems. This characteristic distinguishes LANs from wide area networks (WANs).

Logical data structure A model (also known as an entity relationship model) showing the logical data requirements of a system independently of the system's (physical) organisation and processes.

Low-level language A programming language structured to match the operation of a computer, eg assembly language or machine code. (Compare high-level language.)

Machine code A computer can only deal with instructions which are in binary form (the 1 and 0 corresponding to on and off). Every program must be in a computer's machine code before the computer will do anything with it.

Macros A facility that allows the user to automate a sequence of commands.

Magnetic ink character recognition (MICR) The recognition by a machine of special formatted characters printed in magnetic ink.

Magnetic stripe cards A plastic containing machine-sensible data on a magnetic stripe, which is a thin strip of magnetic recording tape, about 1.2 cm wide, stuck to the back of the card. The magnetic card reader converts this information into directly computer-sensible form.

Magnetic tape Plastic tape coated with a magnetic material deposited in grains, each of which may be magnetised in one of two possible directions. To each of the directions, the significance 0 or 1 is attached which means that data can be written, stored, and read from tape. As with domestic audio tape, a recording can be erased and the tape used for a completely different purpose.

Magnetic tape cartridge and cassette A backing storage medium. They are similar to but larger in size than a normal audio cassette (being ¼" wide) and are 300-600 feet long. They have a capacity of up to 60 megabytes, depending on size and format. Cartridges are being used increasingly in 'streaming mode' to provide a back-up file copy for data held on hard disks. Fast tapes which can be used to create a back-up file very quickly are known as tape streamers.

Mainframe A large computer in terms of price, power and speed. Mainframes are typically used for centralised processing applications in large commercial organisations such as banks.

Management control 'The process by which managers assure that resources are obtained and used effectively and efficiently in the accomplishment of the organisation's objectives' (Anthony).

Management information system (MIS) A system that presents information to management.

Master file A file containing reference data, which is normally altered (updated) infrequently and also cumulative transactions data which is built up over time.

Materials requirements planning (MRP) A stock control method in which a master production schedule (MPS) is drawn up based on firm orders and forecast sales for a given period into the future. The production quantities and timings shown in the MPS are translated into materials needs.

Mb Megabyte. Strictly 1,048,576 bytes (2^{20}), but widely used to denote one million bytes.

Mechanistic system See *deterministic system*.

Megabyte (Mb) 2^{20} (1,048,576) bytes. The term is widely used to mean 1 million bytes or 1,000 kilobytes.

MegaHertz (MHz) An indication of processing speed. One MHz is one million pulses (cycles) per second.

Memory (also known as main store, internal store or immediate access storage). This is circuitry which is used to store data temporarily within the CPU whilst the computer is operating. A distinction can be made between two main types of memory, random access memory (RAM) and read-only memory (ROM).

MHz *see* MegaHertz.

MICR *see* Magnetic Ink Character Recognition.

Microcomputers A computer less powerful than a minicomputer. See Personal computer.

Minicomputer A computer whose size, speed and capabilities lie somewhere between those of a mainframe and a PC.

MIS *see* Management Information System.

Modem MOdulator-DEModulator. Computer equipment stores and uses data by means of electrical pulses, in discrete digital (or 'bit') form, but much of the telephone network still handles data in analogue form. Therefore there has to be a device – a modem – at each end of the telephone line that can convert (MOdulate) the data from digital form to analogue form, and (DEModulate) from analogue form to digital form.

Mouse A device used in on-screen graphics and as an alternative or a supplement to using the keyboard to input instructions.

MS-DOS An operating system (developed by Microsoft) widely used in microcomputers pre-Windows.

Multi-user system A computer configuration in which several users, each with their own VDU and keyboard are be connected to the same computer, with the ability for all the users to carry out processing work simultaneously.

Multiplexor A device used where it is necessary to send data from several sources down a single line at the same time, preventing data from one source being mixed up with data from another.

Multitasking Performing several tasks at once.

Negative feedback Information which indicates that a system is deviating from its planned or prescribed course, and that some re-adjustment is necessary to bring it back on to course.

Network analysis A method of controlling operations which aims to programme and monitor the progress of a project so that the project is completed in the minimum time.

Network Computer A computer without a hard drive that downloads its applications from a network.

Networks An interconnected collection of autonomous computers. Several sorts of networks exist (see LANs, WANs), giving a variety of speed/cost/capacity trade-offs.

Noise Interference caused by any fault in the communication process.

Non-programmed decision One which is subject to uncertainty about its outcome.

Notebook A type of portable personal computer.

Object code A program in *machine code* capable of being understood and executed by the computer. It is produced by translating a program from *source code* using a *compiler*.

Object program A program translated from programming language into its machine code (or machine language) version (1s and 0s).

OCR see Optical Character Recognition.

Off-the-shelf packages A software package that is ready made rather than a one-off creation tailored to the requirements of a specific user.

Open system A system connected to and interacting with its environment. It takes in influences from its external environment, which it also influences by its behaviour.

Operating system (OS) A program which provides the 'bridge' between applications software and the hardware.

Operational control 'The process of assuring that specific tasks are carried out effectively and efficiently' (Anthony).

Optical character recognition (OCR) A method of input involving a machine that is able to read ordinary characters by optical detection of the shape of those characters.

Optical mark reading (OMR) is an automated data input technique. Values are denoted by a line or cross in an appropriate box, whose position represents a value, on a preprinted source document. The document is read by a device which senses the mark in each box using an electric current and translates it into machine code.

Optical storage Storage of data on optical disks. The capacity of optical disks is very high compared with magnetic media. CD ROMs and DVDs are optical disks.

Output devices accept output from a processing device and convert it into a form which is usable by the computer's human operators. The most common output devices are printers and screens.

Packet switching A data message is divided up into 'packets' of data of a fixed length, usually 128 bytes, and transmitted through the network in these separate packets. Each packet contains control data, which identifies the sender of the message and the address of the recipient. At the receiving end the packets of data are re-assembled into their full message, which is transmitted to the recipient.

Page printers A printer that prints a whole page at a time, for example a laser printer.

Parallel interface A connection between devices by which data is transmitted along a number of wires each carrying one bit at the same time, for example, eight bits may be transmitted simultaneously as a byte along eight separate wires. (Compare serial interface and USB.)

Parallel transmission In a bit parallel transmission, eight lines are required as each bit in a byte is transmitted at the same time over its own channel. High speed connections between computers usually use parallel transmission. Compare serial transmission.

Pascal A high-level programming language derived from ALGOL. Pascal is well-suited to programming with structured programming techniques.

Pen-based computer A type of portable personal computer that allows input by writing on the screen.

Pentium A microprocessor manufactured by Intel, the current standard CPU for new PCs.

Peripheral A term used to denote any input, output or auxiliary storage device, ie a unit requiring connection to the CPU.

Personal computer (PC) The term personal computer was originally applied to small, low-cost microcomputers manufactured for home rather than business use, with early machines being developed by companies like Commodore. Now it generally means the type of computer widely used in most small to medium sized businesses.

Pixel (Derived from Picture Element.) The smallest individual element of a graphics image. In computer displays a pixel is a 'dot' on the screen. The fewer the pixels on screen, the larger they will be: the resolution of any picture will be low. More and smaller pixels enable detailed high-resolution display.

Pocket computer A type of portable personal computer.

Portable computers A type of personal computer, compatible with desktop machines, that can be easily carried about and used outside the office. A typical portable computer is about the size of a telephone directory.

Positive feedback Information resulting in control action which causes actual results to maintain (or increase) their path of deviation from planned results.

Probabilistic system See *stochastic system*.

Program A set of instructions which. It is usually held in the computer's internal store or 'memory' whilst the instructions are being carried out. Programs are needed to make the computer's machinery process data. The general term used to describe programs is software.

Programmed decision One whose outcome can be predicted, and relied upon to turn out as expected.

Programming languages Computers can only accept instructions consisting of patterns of 1s and 0s, but it is neither practical nor efficient to write programs constructed in this way. Programming languages are easier for programmers to 'code' in. A programming language is neither the 'normal' written language of humans, nor is it the strings of 1s and 0s (machine code) used by processors. Translation software is used to convert code written in a programming language into the form understood by the computer.

Public transmission links If an organisation only requires occasional communication links, it will probably use public lines, with links being set up to transmit a message and closed when the transmission is competed.

Qualitative information Information that cannot be expressed in numbers.

Quantitative information Information that can be expressed in *numbers*.

Random access refers to the retrieval of data from a randomly-organised file. The method of random access will depend on the method used to put records on to the file in the first place, either by calculating a key value from data on the record or by reference to an index.

Random access memory (RAM) is memory that is directly available to the CPU. It holds the data and programs in current use. Data can be written on to or read from random access memory. RAM is 'volatile' which means that the contents of the memory are erased when the computer's power is switched off.

Random file organisation With random organisation, records are put on file in one of two ways: either in some way that corresponds to a key value, which is calculated from data on the record when it is filed, or by means of an index. When a record is put on file, its key field is listed sequentially in an index, which shows the address location on file where the record is to be placed.

Read-only memory (ROM) is a memory chip into which fixed data is written permanently at the time of its manufacture. ROM is 'non-volatile' memory, which means that its contents do not disappear when the computer's power source is switched off.

Real-time system A system in which processing is almost simultaneous with input.

Record A group of related fields. For example, a customer record on the sales ledger file will include fields for name, address, customer reference number, balance owing, and credit limit.

Reference file A file containing reference data, which is normally altered (updated) infrequently. Examples of a reference file are a price list and manuals of company regulations and procedures. Reference files are often classified as a type of master file because they contain 'standing' reference data.

Remote access describes access to a central computer installation from a terminal which is physically 'distant'.

Remote job entry A method of processing in which the computer user inputs data, from a remote terminal.

Resolution The amount of information that can be shown on a visual display. Resolution is measured in lines or pixels.

Resources, sometimes referred to as the '4 Ms', are men, materials, machines and money. However, time, space (land and buildings) and information are also very important resources.

Risk involves situations or events which may or may not occur, but whose probability of occurrence can be calculated statistically and the frequency of their occurrence predicted from past records.

ROM *see* Read Only Memory.

Sensitivity analysis A term used to describe any technique whereby decision options are tested for their vulnerability to changes in any 'variable' such as expected sales volume, sales price per unit, material costs, or labour costs.

Sequential access is the access of records on a sequentially organised file, without using an index. Sequential access is faster than serial access. Since records on a sequentially organised file are in key field order, once the

particular record has been located, there is no need to check through the rest of the file.

Sequential file organisation A file's organisation is sequential if the records on the file are in a logical sequence according to their key field, for example in alphabetical order, or in numerical order. Sequential files must be maintained in sequence.

Serial access The only way of retrieving records from an unordered file is to start at the first record on the file, then go on to the next record, and the next, and so on through to the end of the file. This is known as serial access, which is the access of data by reading all records physically preceding the required record until the required record is found.

Serial file organisation A file has a serial, organisation if the records are in no particular order or sequence on the file. (Transaction files may have an unordered organisation.) This is not the same as random organisation.

Serial interface A connection between devices by which *data* is transmitted one bit at a time along the same wire. (Compare *parallel interface* and *USB*.)

Serial transmission In bit serial transmission, each bit making up a character is sent one after the other down the line. Bit serial transmission is the most common method and is used for voice transmission over the public telephone network. Compare parallel transmission.

Simplex transmission is transmission in one direction only. For example, a computer can be used to send out messages to a terminal (a remote printer or screen) but the terminal cannot send data back.

Simulation The imitation of real-world conditions. In business use, a simulation model could refer to any mathematical model which reflects the relationships between certain variables in real-world conditions.

Smart cards A plastic card in which is embedded a microprocessor chip. A smart card would typically contain a memory and a processing capability. The smart card is used in a similar way to magnetic stripe cards, but are much harder to duplicate, and so are more secure. On the other hand, the technology is more expensive to produce.

Software A program or set of programs that tell the computer what to do.

Source code A program in a human-readable form (usually in a high-level language).

Source program A program written in a programming language is called the source program.

Spreadsheet A type of *general purpose* software package with many business applications. The term 'spreadsheet' is 'the term commonly used to describe many of the modelling packages derived from the likeness to a "spreadsheet of paper" divided into rows and columns' (CIMA, *Computing Terminology*).

Stand-alone computers A computer that is not connected to any other computers.

Stochastic system A system in which some variables may have any value from a range of possible outcomes, in other words where little is certain, although probabilities can be assigned to the different outcomes.

Storage devices hold data or information on file until it is needed for processing. Processed data may also be put on to an external storage file. Hard or floppy disk drives and disks, and CD-ROM drives and discs are the most common forms.

Storage Internal storage *(memory)* within the *CPU* or backing storage (eg disk or tape).

Strategic planning 'The process of deciding on objectives of the organisation, on changes in these objectives, on the resources used to attain these objectives, and on the policies that are to govern the acquisition, use and disposition of these resources' (Anthony)

Strategy The sum of an organisation's *long-term* objectives, affecting its position in its *environment*.

Streamers Fast tapes which can be used to create a back-up file very quickly.

Structured decisions See *programmed decisions*.

Sub-systems A sub-set of a larger system. For example the management accounting section and the financial accounting section are sub-systems of the accounting department, which itself is a subsystem of the organisation as a whole.

Supercomputer A computer used to process very large amounts of data very quickly, for example in meteorological or astronomical applications. Manufacturers of super-computers include Cray and Fujitsu.

SVGA See *Visual display unit*.

Synchronous transmission With synchronous transmission, data is transmitted between the sending and receiving machines at a constant rate, and so there is no need for start signals and stop signals between each character that is transmitted. The rate of transmission is controlled by a clock, which is usually the computer's internal clock.

System software Another term for operating system software.

Tape storage Storage of data on magnetic tape.

Third-generation languages *see* High-level languages.

Total quality management (TQM) applies a belief in quality to the management of *all* resources and relationships within the firm as a means of developing and sustaining a culture of continuous improvement which focuses on meeting customers' expectations. One of the basic principles of TQM is that the cost of preventing mistakes is less than the cost of correcting them.

Transaction file A transaction file contains records that relate to individual transactions that occur from day to day.

Transcription The process of inputting data by keyboard so that it can be converted into the electronic pulses on which the computer circuitry operates.

Translation software is used to convert code written in a programming language into the form understood by the computer.

Transmission media There are a variety of physical media over which data can be sent, including copper wire, coaxial cable, fibre-optic cable and microwave radio. The choice affects speed, reliability and volume of messages to be transmitted.

Turnaround document A document that is initially produced by computer, then used to collect more data, and then re-input to the computer, probably using MICR or OCR, for processing. A common example is the payment counterfoils sent out by large organisations with their computer-produced bill, which is returned with payment and then used for inputting payment data to a computer.

Unix An *operating system* developed for general use with a wide range of mainframes and minicomputers.

Unordered file organisation A file has an unordered, or serial, organisation if the records are in no particular order or sequence on the file. (Transaction files may have an unordered organisation.) This is not the same as random organisation.

USB Universal Serial Bus. An external bus standard that supports data transfer rates of 12 Mbps. A USB port can be used to connect peripheral devices, such as mice, modems, and keyboards. USB is expected to completely replace serial and parallel ports.

Utilities A utility program is a program which performs a function that may be required by a number of other programs or in a number of circumstances.

Variable length records In a file with variable length records, each record may contain a different number of fields and corresponding fields may have a different number of characters.

VDU *see Visual display unit.*

VGA *see Visual display unit.*

Visual display unit (VDU) The VDU (or screen or monitor) displays input or output items as text, letters and numbers or in graphical form. It may display in colour, or black and white (monochrome). VDUs may be based on cathode ray tubes, liquid crystal displays or gas plasma display. Most screens are 14 or 15 inch. The screen's resolution is the number of pixels that are lit up. IBM's VGA standard offers a resolution of 640 × 48; Super VGA, or SVGA, offers resolutions up to 1,024 × 768. Higher resolution requires more processing power.

WAN *see* Wide Area Network.

Website A location on the Internet that provides information in text and graphic form.

What if analysis A form of sensitivity analysis.

Wide Area Network (WAN) A network of computers linked over long distances by a telecommunications network. (Compare *LAN.*)

WIMP Windows, Icons, Mouse, Pull-down menu.

Winchester disk A number of flat hard disks sealed into an airtight pack. They have a very high recording density.

WYSIWYG What You See Is What You Get. Describes any screen display which mirrors with reasonable accuracy the eventual printed output.

Validation checks, 238, 260
Variance trend, 31
Verification, 259
Videoconferencing, 76
Videodisks, 52
Viewdata, 87
Virtual reality, 77
Viruses, 272, 274
    identification of, 275
Visual Basic, 207
Voice mail, 75
Voice messaging, 75
Volume, 7

Wal-Mart, 199
Watson, 41
Websites, 79
What if? analysis, 33
What if?' questions, 36
Wide area networks (WANs), 101
WIMP, 68
Windows, 68
Windows 2000, 106
Windows 95, 106
Windows 98, 77, 106
Windows CE, 107
Windows ME, 106
Windows NT, 106
Wireless Application Protocol (WAP), 73
Wizards, 85
Word processing, 66
Work patterns, 60
Work-centred analysis (WCA), 135
Workflow, 113
World Wide Web (www), 78, 83
Worms, 274
www, 83

X25, 108

Yahoo!, 80

Zero base budgeting, 50